E
78
S7F6

—REGULATIONS—
FINES ARE CHARGED FOR OVERDUE AND/OR
LOST LIBRARY MATERIALS; AND, IN ACCOR-
DANCE WITH BOARD POLICY 8741, "GRADES
TRANSCRIPTS, DEGREES, AND REGISTRATION
PRIVILEGES SHALL BE WITHHELD UNTIL ALL
LIBRARY BOOKS OR OTHER LIBRARY MATERIALS
ARE RETURNED (TO THE LIBRARY CIRCULATION
DESK)."

Contra Costa College Library
2600 Mission Bell Drive
San Pablo, California 94806

Apache
Navaho
and Spaniard

by JACK D. FORBES

CONTRA COSTA COUNTY LIBRARY
DISCARD
SAN PABLO, CALIFORNIA

UNIVERSITY OF OKLAHOMA PRESS : NORMAN

SEP 16 1976

E
78
S7F6
J

By Jack D. Forbes

Apache, Navaho, and Spaniard (Norman, 1960)
*Warriors of the Colorado: The Yumas of the Quechan Nation
and Their Neighbors* (Norman, 1965)

The original publication of this work was aided by a grant from the Ford Foundation.

Library of Congress Catalog Card Number: 60–13480

Copyright 1960 by the University of Oklahoma Press, Publishing Division of the University. Manufactured in the U.S.A. First edition, 1960; second printing, 1963; third printing, 1971.

Apache, Navaho, and Spaniard is Volume 115 in *The Civilization of the American Indian Series*.

To Professor Donald C. Cutter,
scholar, teacher,
and friend

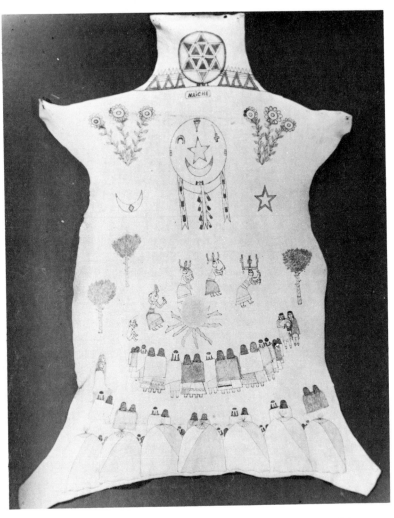

An Apache decorated deerskin. This one was made by Naiche, a Chiricahua Apache.

Courtesy Southwest Museum

Preface

卐

The purpose of this book is to trace in the greatest possible detail the history of the Southern Athapascans and their relations with other Indians and with the Spanish Empire from the first written records until 1698. This terminal date has been chosen because it is the most appropriate point of division between *c.*1535 and 1821—the extremes of the period of Hispano-Athapascan relations. The year 1698 marks the end of one stage and the beginning of another within this period.

The author anticipates that this detailed work will serve as a guide to the events of Southern Athapascan history from 1540 to 1698—a guide to be used by archaeologists, anthropologists, ethnohistorians, and other persons interested in southwestern Indian history. Obviously, general information would be of little or no use to these readers. There is already an abundance of generalized information on the Southwest and a serious lack of detailed, year-by-year historical documentation. Because of the lack of fundamental historical research, many of the generalizations current in contemporary secondary sources are inaccurate. This account is an attempt to remedy this situation.

Many persons aided the author in his project of tracing the early history of the Southern Athapascans. In particular, Professor Donald C. Cutter of the University of Southern California was instrumental in interesting the author in the problem, and his aid and encouragement have been greatly appreciated. Professor Frank D. Reeve of the University of New Mexico deserves thanks for his interest and help in the Coronado Library, and Mrs. Ella L. Robinson of the Southwest Museum Library has earned a debt of gratitude for her forbearance in filling the author's many requests for materials. Professors Donald Rowland, Russell Caldwell, Frances Bowman, and William Wallace of the University of Southern California are to be thanked for their encouragement and editorial criticism. My wife, Barbara Ann Forbes, deserves to be regarded as coauthor of this book, for she aided in the research, served as a traveling secretary throughout the Southwest and in Spain, and read and criticized every page of the manuscript. Finally, I wish to thank the Social Science Research Council for providing financial assistance, in the form of a Research Training Fellowship, without which this book could not have been written.

Jack D. Forbes

Simi, California

Contents

◖◗

Illustrations

Maps

Introduction

⚜

The Southern Athapascans,[1] as the name implies, are those Indians speaking a language of the Athapascan linguistic family and residing in the southern portion of that family's distribution area. The Southern Athapascans have a number of things in common, aside from their geographical location. Similarities in languages make all of the known Athapascan languages or dialects mutually intelligible to some degree; and all of the groups belonging to the Southern Athapascans were at some time referred to as Apaches. Prior to about 1850, the Navahos were usually called Navaho Apaches, but in the last one hundred years they have been considered as a group distinct from the Apaches. Thus one could conceivably dispense with the cumbersome term "Southern Athapascans" and speak of "Apaches" or "Apacheans." However, certain factors make this simplification undesirable. Some Southern Athapascans were treated by the Europeans as being non-Apache as often as, or more often than, they were treated as Apaches. Furthermore, at least one anthropologist, John P. Harrington, has attempted to distinguish the eastern components of the Southern Athapascans from their western fellows by limiting the use of the term "Apache" to the latter group. This procedure is historically unacceptable because the easterners have been called Apaches since the 1590's. Never-

[1] Sometimes spelled "Athapaskan" or "Athabascan."

theless, it would seem the wiser course to use a universally acceptable term for the entire group.[2]

The Athapascan language family can be divided geographically into three major divisions: the southern, the northern (or Canadian-Alaskan), and the Pacific Coast. The northern has long been regarded as the largest and most important division, whereas the other two branches have been classified as subsidiary and formed by recent migrations. In all probability, however, the southern division was as large as the northern in pre-European contact times and cannot be considered as an offshoot of the northerners. Unfortunately, adequate population statistics for the pre-1600 era are lacking. However, the southern division was probably at least three times larger at that time than during the post-1850 period, for which statistics are available. By 1850, many Southern Athapascan groups had disappeared, and others were greatly reduced in number. Allowing for the decrease in population which occurred in the southern area between 1600 and 1850, it is possible that this group was formerly as large as the northern group. Future studies may, in fact, indicate that the southern division was the largest of the three.[3]

The traditional view of Athapascan history considers members of this family as relative newcomers to America and Southern Athapascans as recent migrants into the Southwest from Canada. In fact, anthropologists such as Frederick Webb Hodge and Albert H. Schroeder assert that the Apaches were still in the process of migrating south and southwest after 1600. Other scholars have examined Apache and Navaho cultures in order to find proof of a recent northern origin, and even the languages

2 See John P. Harrington, "Southern Peripheral Athapaskawan Origins, Divisions and Migrations," *Smithsonian Miscellaneous Collections.* Vol. C (1940). The findings of most anthropologists who have studied the culture of the Southern Athapascans in detail are in opposition to Harrington's views. See, for example, Grenville Goodwin, "The Southern Athapaskans," *Kiva,* Vol. IV, No. 2(1938); Charles S. Brant, "Kiowa Apache Culture History: Some Further Observations," *Southwestern Journal of Anthropology,* Vol. IX, No. 2(1953); Andrée F. Sjoberg, "Lipan Apache Culture in Historical Perspective," *Southwestern Journal of Anthropology,* Vol. IX, No. 1(1953).

3 Grenville Goodwin also expressed the opinion that the Southern Athapascans probably equaled the northerners in number in aboriginal times. See his "The Southern Athapaskans," *Kiva,* Vol. IV, No. 2(1938), 5.

Modern names for geographical features supplied.

Athapascan Distribution
    c. 1600 for Southern Athapascans
    c. 1850 for Other Tribes

and mythology of these Indians have been dissected for the purpose of obtaining such evidence. Interestingly enough, these "migrationists" ignore to a great extent the possibility of cultural diffusion from north to south as an explanation of northern traits in the Southwest.

Certain factors have come to light which call for a re-examination of the traditional assumptions of a recent movement of Apaches and Navahos to the Southwest, of a recent migration of Athapascans to the Pacific Coast, and of the picture of the Canadians as possessors of the true and original Athapascan culture. For example, archaeology now reveals that ancestors of the Navahos were living in New Mexico as early as the 1400's and perhaps as early as the 900's. At Promontory Point, Utah, Athapascan-like remains show considerable antiquity and are similar to Dismal River (Plains Apache) sites of a later date. However, Athapascan-like remains do not prove that the people who lived in that region spoke an Athapascan language. A language group does not often possess a single culture of its own, and even a superficial glance at cultural distribution reveals little correlation with linguistic distributions. Nevertheless, the Southern Athapascans seem to have considerable time depth in New Mexico, at least.[4]

Cultural studies also reveal that theories of recent migration should be reviewed, for the southern and Pacific Coast Athapascan cultures, although perhaps containing certain northern and "Athapascan" traits, were well integrated into the larger culture areas where they existed. That is, these Athapascans were not possessors of a radically intrusive or foreign way of life but were in general related culturally to their neighbors. For example, on the Pacific Coast the Hupas were thoroughgoing members of the way of life in northwestern California, and their material culture can scarcely be distinguished from that of their Algonkian and Hokan neighbors. Racially, they form one stock with

[4] See Edward Twitchell Hall, Jr., "Recent Clues to Athapascan Prehistory in the Southwest," *American Anthropologist*, Vol. XLVI, No. 1(1944); Carling Malouf, "Thoughts on Utah Archaeology," *American Antiquity*, Vol. IX, No. 3(1944); and James H. Gunnerson, "Plains-Promontory Relationships," *American Antiquity*, Vol. XXII, No. 1(1956).

these same neighbors, and the only major elements which they have in common with other Athapascans are their language and, to some degree, their kinship systems. Certainly this integration must have required a great deal of time. In the Southwest those Athapascans living near the Pueblo Indians show Pueblo Indian influences, those in Texas show Texas traits, and those near La Junta (the junction of the Río Grande and the Conchos rivers) show La Juntan influences. The Southern Athapascans, although possessing a basic culture of their own, show precisely those variations which would be due to the influence of their Southwestern neighbors. For example, it is the Mescalero, Lipan, Jicarilla, and Kiowa Apache groups (using modern terminology) which show Plains influences upon the basic Southern Athapascan substratum. This is to be expected, for these peoples lived at least in part on the plains in post-1800 times and farther out on the plains in the pre-1800 period. On the other hand, if a recent migration of the Western and Chiricahua Apaches from the southern plains had occurred (as many have asserted) one would also expect them to show Plains traits to some degree, but, on the contrary, their orientation is more in the direction of the Navaho and Pueblo tribes (this is not true to any great extent with the Chiricahua). Furthermore, historical evidence places the Western Apaches in their historical region as early as the 1580's. Culturally, the Western Apaches and the Navahos appear to have long been in association, although the former are much closer linguistically to the Chiricahuas and Mescaleros. Thus once again it can be seen that the historical geographical positions of the Southern Athapascans correspond, in general, with cultural positions and give no indication of widespread migration or intrusion. On the contrary, they give evidence of a long period of contact in the same general geographical position as in the recent historical era.

Another argument against a recent northern origin for the Southern Athapascans is to be seen in the fact that all of the surviving groups from the Kiowa Apache to the Lipan reveal, according to certain anthropologists, a basic "Apache" culture belonging not to Canada but to the Southwestern culture area.

Charles S. Brant has compared the culture of the Kiowa Apaches, who lived in the Black Hills area prior to 1800, with that of the Kiowas, the Apaches of the Southwest, and the Sarsis—the southernmost Canadian group. Mr. Brant concludes:

> The older view [of Kiowa Apache culture] based on nothing more than assumption and declaration that the Kiowa Apache are a "typical Plains tribe" or that their origin lies with the northern Athabascan peoples not only cannot be substantiated, but the evidence cited definitely controverts it. We have shown . . . that Kiowa Apache culture is historically derived from that of the Apache of the southwest. More specifically it is a species of the easternmost variety of Apache culture, very closely related to that of the Jicarilla and Lipan tribes. We have shown further that the Plains traits in Kiowa Apache culture were superficial and probably recent accretions to the basic Apache substratum.[5]

Similarly, Andrée F. Sjoberg places the culture of the Lipan Apaches with that of the other Southern Athapascans, in spite of certain "Plains-like" characteristics.[6] Harry Hoijer indicates that all of the known Southern Athapascan tongues were derived from a common linguistic ancestor,[7] and from the evidence of Brant, Sjoberg, and others, it appears that their basic culture also stems from a common source. Thus the surviving Southern Athapascans, from the Kiowa Apaches to the Chiricahuas, should be treated as a cultural-linguistic unit, and any migration theory must account for the differentiation which has taken place between the various groups—a differentiation which would appear to have been well established by 1600. Likewise, any migration theory must take into consideration the fact that there does not appear to be a gradual cultural progression from the Sarsis to the Chiricahuas. Thus, as far as migration is concerned, the southern division should be treated as a unit which was separated from

5 Brant, "Kiowa Apache Culture History," *Southwestern Journal of Anthropology*, Vol. IX, No. 2(1953), 199–200. This basic Apache culture is to be distinguished from a sometimes proposed basic Athapascan culture.

6 Sjoberg, "Lipan Apache Culture in Historical Perspective," *Southwestern Journal of Anthropology*, Vol. IX, No. 1(1953), 98.

7 Harry Hoijer, "The Southern Athapaskan Languages," *American Anthropologist*, Vol. XL, No. 1(1938).

the Canadians for a considerable period of time before internal differentiation occurred.

There are a number of other facts which challenge any theory proposing a recent migration from the north. Three of them stand out in importance: First of all, the southern distribution of the Athapascans does not correspond to the southern distribution of northern and Plains objects such as skin clothing, the sinew-backed bow, the skin tipi, and the travois. For example, the sinew-backed bow was possessed by the Julimes of La Junta, apparently a non-Athapascan group, but it was not used by the Chiricahuas. Similarly, skin clothing was used by non-Athapascans such as the Tonkawas, Yavapais, and Utes but not by the Sumas and Mansos, who were apparently Athapascan. The tipi was not used by the Suma, Manso, Jano, Jocome, Cholome, Western Apache, and Navaho (Athapascan) groups but was used by many non-Athapascan peoples. The travois was absent from the cultures of the Western Apaches and other groups. If the Southern Athapascans were recent migrants from the north, one would expect a more general distribution of these northern objects among them. The southernmost Athapascans—the Sumas, Mansos, Janos, Jocomes, and Cholomes—were apparently living in their historically established geographical locations as early as 1530–80, and by that time they were well integrated into the culture pattern of the northern Chihuahua–Río Grande Valley area—another fact that argues against a recent migration from the north.[8]

Secondly, the Pimas of the 1690's had a tradition to the effect that the Apaches were among the tribes which forced the abandonment of Casa Grande, Arizona. This indicates that the Athapascans could not have been newcomers to southern Arizona in the 1600's and that they were probably in the area in the 1400's, when the abandonment of Casa Grande is said to have occurred.[9]

Furthermore, both the White Mountain and the San Carlos

8 For a general discussion of the cultures of the surviving groups see Goodwin, "The Southern Athapaskans," *Kiva*, Vol. IV, No. 2(1938).

9 Juan Mateo Manje, *"Breve Noticia . . . de la Pimeria,"* 1697, manuscript in Book 970 of BMH (Biblioteca del Ministerio de Hacienda, Madrid, Spain). Hereinafter cited as Manje, *"Breve Noticia,"* BMH 970.

branches of the Western Apaches have cycles of tales relating to contacts with the peoples of prehistoric villages located at Dewey Flat on the Gila River and at the confluence of Gilson Wash and the San Carlos River in Arizona. These prehistoric peoples, called *Indà* ("enemies") and *Bàtcì,* were hostile and raided the Apaches who—according to the tales—were living in the mountains to the north. Later, the enemies abandoned their towns and moved to the south. Another Western Apache tale refers to a time when these Athapascans were living in the Cibecue region and cliff dwellers were living to the west of them in the Tonto Basin. The cliff dwellers allegedly took some Apache property; hostilities developed; and the cliff dwellers were forced to move south to the Salt River Valley, where they became known as the Pimas. Western Apaches refer to both the cliff dwellers and the Pimas as *Sáikìné* ("Sand House People"). The Dewey Flat ruin was abandoned about 1400, as were the other prehistoric villages. Thus it seems logical to assume that the ancestors of the Western Apaches were in Arizona by 1400, probably living in the Mogollon Rim—Little Colorado River area.[10]

On the basis of the above evidence, supplemented by the archaeology of northwestern New Mexico, it seems highly probable that Athapascans were living in the area from northwestern New Mexico to Arizona in the 1400's. Some historical evidence indicates an even greater antiquity for the Apaches in the New Mexico region. Two independent sources inform us that the Apaches who surrounded New Mexico in the 1600's thought of themselves and were thought of as the "original" people of the area occupied by the Puebloans at that time. Fray Alonso de Benavides, living in New Mexico from 1626 to 1630, wrote:

> All these nations [of Pueblo Indians] settled in this most northerly region [New Mexico] in order to escape the intolerable cold and to find there a milder climate, but they met with opposition and resistance from the native inhabitants of this whole land, that is, from the huge Apache nation.[11]

10 Grenville Goodwin, *The Social Organization of the Western Apache,* 63, 64, 68, 69.

11 Alonso de Benavides, *Fray Alonso de Bernavides' Revised Memorial of 1634*

In other words, Fray Benavides is saying that the central Río Grande Valley of New Mexico was at one time inhabited by the Apaches and that the Pueblo Indians, coming from a colder region (from the northwest, as archaeology would to some extent indicate), drove the Apaches from this area. This thesis is reinforced by a statement of Juan de Villagutierre y Sotomayor, writing in the 1690's. Villagutierre declared that

> the Apaches have burned some of their [the Pueblo Indians'] pueblos many times, because they [the Apaches] always say that they are the natives of that settled land, or at least that they went to it first before those others [the Pueblo tribes] populated it, and as a result they always go about in pretension of throwing them out of it.[12]

There are thus good reasons for holding that the Athapascans were in central New Mexico in the 1200's or 1300's and were later driven out by Pueblo Indians coming from the Four Corners–Canyon de Chelly region. This thesis is partially borne out by archaeological evidence that before about 1300 many of the Pueblo Indians of central New Mexico lived to the northwest and west. It naturally follows that some other group or groups of Indians were living in central New Mexico prior to the migrations of the 1300's, and the testimony of Benavides and Villagutierre indicates that the Athapascans were included.

Prior to 1400, the area of southwestern New Mexico was occupied by the developers of the Mogollon-Mimbres culture. For some unknown reason these Indians apparently abandoned their old area of occupation and, at least in part, migrated south to Chihuahua between 1200 and 1300. During the same era, the Salado people of southeastern Arizona migrated southwest and joined the Hohokams in south central Arizona. The vacated areas of the Mogollon-Mimbres and Salado peoples were apparently occupied by Athapascans. Thus there appears to have been

(trans. and ed. by Frederick Webb Hodge, George P. Hammond, and Agapito Rey), 81, hereinafter cited as Benavides, *1634*.

[12] Juan de Villagutierre y Sotomayor, "*Historia de la Conquista, Perdida, y Restaurazión de el Reino y Provincias de la Nueva México en la América Septentrional*," c. 1698, manuscript in BN (Biblioteca Nacional de Madrid, Madrid, Spain). Hereinafter cited as Villagutierre y Sotomayor, BN 2822.

a general southward migration trend among these several groups of peoples—as well as among the Puebloan peoples—between 1200 and 1400. This evidence agrees with and reinforces the testimony of Benavides and Villagutierre and allows one to postulate the theory that Athapascans were occupying at least a part of the region from central to west central New Mexico in the pre-1300 period and that they were displaced by southward moving Puebloans about 1300. Because of pressure from the Puebloans, the Athapascans in turn displaced the Saladoans and the Mogollon-Mimbres peoples in southwestern New Mexico and southeastern Arizona. Needless to say, this theory is tentative, and future archaeological and historical research will have to be brought to bear on the problem.

It should be obvious from the above discussion that any thesis of a recent Athapascan movement from Canada to the Southwest must be examined critically. Likewise the assumption that the "original" area of Athapascan occupation in America was in northern Canada and Alaska must be re-examined. From a strictly theoretical point of view, it would seem that when a group of people becomes divided into three or more widely separated divisions, two of which are nearly equal in size, one would be more logical in postulating several outward migrations from a central source, rather than in proposing that one branch remained stationary and the others moved away from it. For example, there is certainly no a priori reason for assuming that the Athapascans could not have been united in the area which lies between the historical locations of the southern and northern groups and near the area of the Promontory Point archaeological sites. This area, from Montana to Alberta, Canada, embraces some of the coldest regions of inhabited North America and certainly would have provided the climate necessary for the acceptance of "northern" traits.

There is evidence which tends to indicate that the Athapascans of Canada and Alaska have indeed moved northward, although it cannot be shown that they ever resided in the United States. For example, there is historical evidence to support a northward or northwestward movement of the Sarsi-Chipewyan groups of northern Athapascans. It is a well-known fact that the Algonkians of Canada, particularly the Crees and the Ojibwas, began pushing west in the 1600's as a result of several factors— including the acquisition of French arms, the need to exploit new fur-producing regions, and the displacement of their eastern neighbors by the Iroquois. This westward movement in turn displaced such groups as the Blackfeet, Atsinas, Piegans, Kutenais, and Siouans and led to occupation of the Alberta-Montana plains by the first three of these groups. In theory, at least, it is possible to postulate that the Sarsis were as far south as Montana prior to the beginning of this phenomenon. In any case it is known that some of the Sarsi-Chipewyan groups were displaced by the better-armed Crees.

At the very least, the above analysis should indicate that a re-examination of the traditional assumptions regarding Athapascan prehistory is necessary. The old tendency to consider all American Indian migrations from north to south, because of a supposed recent Asiatic origin for all or part of the Indians, must apparently be discarded.[13]

In the account which follows a number of little-known southwestern and north Mexican tribes will be treated as Athapascans, although they have not been generally regarded as such. These include the Janos, Jocomes, Sumas, Mansos, Cholomes, Jumanos of southwestern Texas, Sibolos, Pelones of Texas, and Padoucas. The evidence relating to a linguistic identification of these groups, except for the Padoucas, will be found in an article

13 Interestingly, Harry Hoijer compares the historical use of kinship terms by the various Athapascans with a theoretical "Proto-Athapascan" system and discovers that the Lipan and Kiowa Apaches have been the most conservative of the southerners in that they have preserved 67 per cent of the Proto-Athapascan usage. The Jicarillas have kept 50 per cent, the Chiricahuas-Mescaleros 33 per cent, the Navahos 17 per cent, and the San Carlos (Western) none. On the whole, the northerners have been more conservative, although the Sarsis have preservd only 50 per cent. The combination of survivals kept by the Sarsis differs from those of the Lipan, Kiowa, and Jicarilla Apaches. On the basis of his theoretical reconstruction, Hoijer proposes that the Southern Athapascans migrated from the north in two waves, principally because of the preservation of more traits by the Kiowa, Lipan, and Jicarilla Apaches, as well as because of the linguistic relatedness of these groups. Hoijer, "Athapaskan Kinship Systems," *American Anthropologist*, Vol. LVIII, No. 2 (1956).

published separately.[14] The Padoucas will not be dealt with at any great length because they are primarily significant in post-1700 times and because their identity as Plains Apaches has been well demonstrated by George Bird Grinnell (1920), Frank Secoy (1951), and George E. Hyde (1959), as well as by the archaeology of Dismal River sites. Historical evidence on the problem is conclusive, for an examination of the documentary sources shows that the Plains Apaches were called Padoucas by their eastern neighbors and by the French until the mid-1700's, and after that date the term continues in use as the name applied to the Kiowa Apaches—the only Athapascan group left on the high plains after the mid-1700's. Throughout the period from 1740 to 1800, the Comanches dominated the high plains, and they were usually called Ietanes or Laitanes by the eastern Plains tribes. The term "Padouca" was reserved for the Kiowa Apaches' ancestors living in the area of the Black Hills and the upper Platte River. After 1800, some Anglo-Americans confused the Comanches and other tribes with the Padoucas.[15]

Naturally enough, the history of the Southern Athapascans from 1540 to 1698 must be viewed for the most part through Spanish eyes. Thus it must always be borne in mind that the description of any event will be a description from the Spanish point of view and may not, therefore, be objectively true. Certainly the Indian viewpoint is seldom revealed in Spanish sources, and the historian who wishes to present the truth as far as possible must always attempt to see through the biases and preconceptions of the Spanish writers.

Any study of the Southern Athapascans during the era of Spanish intrusion into the Southwest must take into considera-

[14] See Jack D. Forbes, "Unknown Athapascans: The Identification of the Jano, Jocome, Suma, Manso and other Indian Tribes of the Southwest," *Ethnohistory*, Vol. VI, No. 2(1959).

[15] Frank R. Secoy, "The Identity of the Padouca: An Ethnohistorical Analysis," *American Anthropologist*, Vol. LIII, No. 4(1951), Pt. 1; George Bird Grinnell, "Who Were the Padouca?" *American Anthropologist*, Vol. XXII, No. 4(1920); Alfred Barnaby Thomas, *After Coronado: Spanish Exploration Northeast of New Mexico, 1696–1727;* Pierre Margry, *Découvertes et Établissements des Français dans l'Ouest et dans le Sud de l'Amérique Septentrionale (1614–1754),* VI; and A. P. Nasatir, *Before Lewis and Clark.*

tion the development of the Spanish establishment on the northern frontier of New Spain, and, needless to say, Hispano-Athapascan relations will occupy a good portion of any such study. In attempting to reconstruct Athapascan history in the Southwest before 1700, it will be necessary to study the advance of the Spanish Empire insofar as it has significance for the main purpose of the subject.

ABBREVIATIONS USED IN THIS WORK

AGI   Archivo General de Indias, Seville, Spain.

AGN   Archivo General y Público de la Nación, Mexico, D. F., Mexico.

BLT   Bancroft Library, University of California, Berkeley, California. Transcripts.

BMAE   Biblioteca del Ministerio de Asuntos Exteriores, Madrid, Spain.

BMH   Biblioteca del Ministerio de Hacienda, Madrid, Spain.

BN   Biblioteca Nacional de Madrid, Madrid, Spain.

MN   Museo Naval, Madrid, Spain.

NMA   New Mexico Archives, Coronado Library, University of New Mexico, Albuquerque, New Mexico.

UTA   University of Texas Archives, Austin, Texas.

Apache
Navaho
and Spaniard

A Navaho man, dressed for the Mountain Way Chant.

Courtesy Southwest Museum
G. Wharton James Collection

CHAPTER I

The Athapascans
Meet the Spaniards

ⵀ

The Spanish conquest of the valley of Mexico was an event of great significance for the Indians of the American Southwest. Spanish armies, aided by Mexican Indian allies and slaves, turned to new fields of endeavor, some of them looking to the north. Rapidly, tribe after tribe was subdued, and seemingly nothing was to stop or slow down the Spanish juggernaut until, early in the 1530's, the cruel and ruthless conquistador Nuño de Guzmán was halted by the fierce resistance of the Cahita Indians in southern Sonora. The Spanish army then retreated to Culiacán in present-day Sinaloa.

The northward advance of the Spanish Empire in America might not have reached the area of the Apache Indians in the sixteenth century if tales of northern wealth and rich cities had not been circulated by Alvar Núñez Cabeza de Vaca and his companions after their journey across the continent, from Texas to Sonora and Sinaloa. The gold-hungry Spaniards of New Spain took over these rumors and twisted them to suit their dreams and hopes, and the legend of another Mexico to be conquered was born.

Cabeza de Vaca began his adventure as a member of the ill-fated expedition of Pánfilo Narváez to Florida. After being shipwrecked on the coast of Texas, Cabeza de Vaca's small group of Spaniards and one Negro slave, Esteban, began making their

3

way towards the Spanish settlement of Pánuco on the Gulf of Mexico coast. However, before beginning their journey, they had to serve as slaves of the Texas coastal Indians, and when they began their trek, they had little property to set them off from Indians. The extent of their cultural impact upon the American Indian was probably negligible.[1]

There has been a great deal of disagreement among scholars about the route taken by Cabeza de Vaca's party after they abandoned their idea of going to Pánuco and turned to the west. Some have proposed that they traveled across the plains of Texas and crossed southern New Mexico.[2] It seems more likely, however, that they wandered across northern Mexico, south of the Río Grande, until reaching the area of the junction of the Río Grande and the Río Conchos of Chihuahua (hereafter referred to as the La Junta region). Here the Cabeza de Vaca party, probably in 1535, made contact for the first time during the journey with agricultural people, living in permanent houses and cultivating beans and pumpkins.[3]

After taking leave of the agricultural people, who were, it seems, the ancestors of the Julime Indians of the same La Junta region, the Cabeza de Vaca group traveled north and west along the Texas bank of the Río Grande, among poor peoples who had no maize. Thus they traveled until reaching the crossing of the river, perhaps as far north as the present El Paso region. Then they turned toward the west and continued for twenty

[1] When the Spaniards reached Sinaola, they were no different from Indians in their dress and looks. They also spoke bad Castilian. See Andrés Pérez de Ribas, *Historia de los Triumphos de Nuestra Santa Fee entre Gentes las más Bárbaras y Fieras del Nuevo Orbe*, 24.

[2] Cleve Hallenbeck, *Alvar Núñez Cabeza de Vaca.*

[3] The identification of the La Junta region as the first agricultural area reached by Cabeza de Vaca not only agrees with the geography in the narrative of the journey but also with the known facts regarding La Junta. In 1581, 1582, and subsequently, the region was inhabited by agricultural peoples, with permanent houses; and, in 1581, they remembered Cabeza de Vaca. See George P. Hammond and Agapito Rey (eds. and trans.), *Obregón's History of 16th Century Explorations in Western America*, hereinafter cited as *Obregón's History*; Harbert Davenport (ed.), "The Expedition of Pánfilo de Narváez," *Southwestern Historical Quarterly*, Vol. XXVII, Nos. 2–4 (1923–24), Vol. XXVIII, No. 1 (1924), 302; and Fanny Bandelier (trans.), *The Journey of Alvar Núñez Cabeza de Vaca and His Companions from Florida to the Pacific, 1528–1536*, 150–52.

days, still among non-agricultural groups, until reaching the maize country of Sonora. From Sonora to Culiacán—a Spanish settlement—the journey was much easier, as they were among people with more food.[4]

In all probability, Cabeza de Vaca failed to contact the Apaches, since he did not enter the area later occupied by those Indians, but some individual Apaches may have seen the wanderers at La Junta. From later documentary evidence, it is known that the Apaches continually traded and were in contact with the La Junta Indians after 1582,[5] and an old "Teyas" Indian (the Teyas seem to have been Plains Apaches) met by Coronado in 1541 remembered having seen Spaniards.[6] In all likelihood, however, the Spaniards did contact the Mansos, a group of Indians related to the Apaches who lived in the region of El Paso, and the Sumas, another Athapascan group. In 1565 the Indians of the Casas Grandes region of Chihuahua, who were probably Sumas, remembered having met Cabeza de Vaca.[7]

The influence of this small group of Europeans upon the Indians was probably not as great as it was upon the conquest-hungry Spaniards in Mexico. These Spaniards listened eagerly to the tales of rich cities to the north, and even the viceroy, Antonio de Mendoza, became interested in the possibility of a new empire to be conquered. By 1538 this interest had taken the form of sending a Franciscan priest, Fray Marcos de Niza, to the north in order to verify the rumors about great cities. He was to be guided by the Negro Esteban, who had been purchased for the purpose. However, Fray Marcos was not only to be an explorer, but he was also to inform the Indians about their new masters, or as Viceroy Mendoza said:

[4] Davenport, "The Expedition of Pánfilo de Narváez," *Southwestern Historical Quarterly*, Vol. XXVII, Nos. 2–4 (1923–24), Vol. XXVIII, No. 1 (1924), 57–65.

[5] From 1582 to about 1700, the "Jumanes" were friendly with the La Junta natives, while the rest of the Apaches were usually hostile. After 1700 the Apaches as a whole became allies and friends of the Julimes. See Forbes, "Unknown Athapaskans," *Ethnohistory*, Vol. VI, No. 2 (1959).

[6] George P. Hammond and Agapito Rey (eds. and trans.), *Narratives of the Coronado Expedition, 1540–1542*, 301, hereinafter cited as *Coronado Narratives*.

[7] *Obregón's History*, 201–202. For a discussion of the problems involved in the identification of the Sumas and Mansos see Forbes, "Unknown Athapaskans," *Ethnohistory*, Vol. VI, No. 2 (1959).

You must explain to the natives of the land that there is only one God in heaven, and the emperor on earth to rule and govern it, whose subjects they must all become and whom they must serve.[8]

On March 7, 1539, Fray Marcos set out for the north, passing among a variety of peoples. Everywhere he went he gathered new rumors on the "seven cities" from the Indians. Esteban, meanwhile, had been sent ahead, and he gathered an entourage of Indian women. His methods were not well received, and he was killed by the people of Cibola, that is, by the Zuñis. They killed him because, among other things, the Indians of Chichil-ticale—probably Apaches—had told them that Esteban was a bad man because he had assaulted their women.[9] Fray Marcos blissfully followed the Negro until he reached the area of Chichilticale, in southern Arizona, where he learned that Esteban had been killed.[10]

There is some doubt about what Fray Marcos did after learning of Esteban's fate. Possibly, as he claims, he went on to a spot where he obtained a view of Cibola. However, there are very sound reasons for doubting the reliability of his testimony, and from the internal features of the narrative, as well as from Fray Marcos' character, it is to be questioned that he ever went any farther north than southern Arizona.[11] Certainly many of the Spaniards who went with him to Cibola in 1540 doubted that he had been there before![12] At any rate, it is well known that Fray Marcos de Niza returned to Mexico and spread glowing accounts

[8] Instructions of Antonio de Mendoza, November, 1538, in *Coronado Narratives*, 60.

[9] Letter of Francisco Vásquez de Coronado, August 3, 1540, in *Coronado Narratives*, 177. See also Castañeda's History, in *Coronado Narratives*, 198, for information on Esteban and his women.

[10] *"Relación"* of Fray Marcos de Niza, in Joaquín F. Pacheco and Francisco de Cárdenas (eds.), *Colección de Documentos Inéditos*, III, 328–50, hereinafter cited as *Colección de Documentos Inéditos*.

[11] See Carl O. Sauer, "The Discovery of New Mexico Re-considered," *New Mexico Historical Review*, Vol. XII, No. 3 (1937), 270–87, and "The Credibility of the Fray Marcos Account," *New Mexico Historical Review*, Vol. XVI, No. 3 (1941), 233–43. For another approach see Lansing B. Bloom, "Who Discovered New Mexico?" *New Mexico Historical Review*, Vol. XV, No. 2 (1940).

[12] Castañeda's History, in *Coronado Narratives*, 198.

of a fantastic new kingdom, richer and greater than Mexico. These stories helped to stimulate interest in northern conquest and to recruit soldiers for the mammoth expedition now planned under the leadership of Francisco Vásquez de Coronado.

As a preliminary to the Coronado invasion of the north, Captain Melchior Díaz was sent out from Culiacán on November 17, 1539. He was to reconnoiter the proposed route—an easy task for him, as he had been on the Sinaloa frontier for a number of years, having been there to welcome Cabeza de Vaca in 1537. He went 100 or 150 leagues to the north, reaching the southern edge of the so-called *despoblado*—the mountains of southern, eastern, and central Arizona—"between here [Culiacán] and Cibola."[13] Somewhere in this area of northern Sonora or southern Arizona, Díaz met people who had lived at Cibola for fifteen or twenty years, and consequently he learned a great deal about the Zuñis. However, he also reported that the people had received him coldly and with mean faces because the Cibolans had told them that the Spaniards were mortal and should be killed.[14]

Thus a basic antagonism against the Spaniards had already developed in the area from Sonora to New Mexico by 1539, and this hostility cannot be entirely explained by the activities of Esteban alone. In all probability the Indians of this area knew well enough the character of their would-be conquerors, because of reports from the south, for Spanish slavers had been raiding north from Culiacán for years. In his narrative, for example, Cabeza de Vaca states that all of the people within thirty or forty leagues of Culiacán were being raided by Spanish slave hunters and were living in great alarm and fear.[15] Likewise, Fray Marcos noted in 1539 that Spaniards were raiding for slaves as far north as the Río Sinaloa.[16] Certainly the Indians of Sonora had received many reports of such outrages, and these accounts coupled with the memory of Nuño de Guzmán's bloody entrance

13 Letter of Antonio de Mendoza, April 17, 1540, in *Coronado Narratives*, 157.
14 *Ibid.*, 157.
15 Davenport, "The Expedition of Pánfilo de Narváez," *Southwestern Historical Quarterly*, Vol. XXVII, Nos. 2–4 (1923–24), Vol. XXVIII, No. 1 (1924), 63.
16 Report of Fray Marcos de Niza, in *Coronado Narratives*, 64.

into southern Sonora in 1531, were probably enough to prejudice the natives against the Europeans. This prejudice may well have extended to New Mexico.

On April 22, 1540, the mammoth expedition of Francisco Vásquez de Coronado departed from its organization point, Culiacán. The expedition was much too large to go in one unit, and the largest section of the army with the bulk of the livestock was always behind an advance guard of approximately seventy-five mounted soldiers and thirty servants led by Coronado himself.[17] From the Río Sinaloa, the Conqueror of the North ordered ten soldiers on horseback to go ahead and explore the dangerous Sonora portion of the route. They went north to the valley of Los Corazones, named by Cabeza de Vaca, and found nothing but poor Indians who fought them with poisoned arrows.[18] When Coronado advanced, the Sonora natives evidently made a point of avoiding the Spaniards, for it was reported that on the entire trip "no kind of food" was found, and consequently one Spaniard and several Negroes and Indians had died of hunger and thirst.[19]

After entering the present area of Arizona, the Spaniards came to a "pass" called Chichilticale where a change in the culture and the language of the Indians was noted.[20] Castañeda, a chronicler of the expedition, says of the Indians of the valley of Suya encountered before Chichilticale, "They have the same dress, language, ceremonies, and customs and all else found up to the despoblado [wilderness] of Chichilticale."[21] Unlike the previously encountered Sonorans, the new people "live by hunting and in rancherias, without permanent settlements. Most of the region [the area from Chichilticale to Zuñi] is uninhabited. There are large pine forests and pine nuts in abundance."[22]

[17] *"Traslado de las nuevas y noticias . . . ,"* in *Colección de Documentos Inéditos,* XIX, 529.

[18] Villagutierre y Sotomayor, BN 2822.

[19] *"Traslado de las nuevas y noticias,"* in *Colección de Documentos Inéditos,* XIX, 529–30.

[20] Juan de Jaramillo says: "We named this pass Chichilte-calli, for we heard from some Indians whom we met farther back that it was called by this name." Narrative of Juan de Jaramillo, in *Coronado Narratives,* 296. Also found in *Colección de Documentos Inéditos.*

[21] Castañeda's History, in *Coronado Narratives,* 250.

There has been a great deal of speculation concerning just who these non-agricultural and nomadic peoples were. The consensus of opinion, however, has been that they were Apaches, and it is quite likely that they were members of the Jocome group.[23] There has also been considerable disagreement about the precise route taken by the Coronado expedition, and it seems that this problem cannot be easily resolved, as the accounts of the journey are rather indefinite on the matter.[24]

It is known, nevertheless, that the nomadic people avoided the Spaniards after this initial contact, for the region between Chichilticale and Zuñi was apparently thought by the explorers to be uninhabited—a *despoblado*. It is easy to assume that the natives, inspired by rumors from the south, merely remained hidden,[25] and quite possibly some of them went ahead to warn Zuñi of the Spaniards' coming. At any rate, when García López de Cárdenas was sent ahead to explore the mountainous area with fifteen horsemen, he met four Indians; and although signs of peace were at first made, a skirmish followed. These Indians were probably Cibolans, although Apaches could have been among them;[26] but, whoever they were, they served to forewarn the Zuñis that enemies were coming. When, on July 7, 1540, the

22 *Ibid.,* 252.
23 There are really only three possibilities involved: One is that the people in question were Apaches, another is that they were Jocomes, and a third that they were Yavapais. These tribes were the only seminomadic groups in the area in later times. The Yavapais are eliminated, however, because they were apparently late-comers to the area.
24 It has usually been accepted that Coronado went up the valley of Sonora, in Sonora, and then followed the Río San Pedro Valley in Arizona, to a point where he angled off for Zuñi, that is, to the northeast. One scholar has, however, proposed that the expedition went farther to the west, to Casa Grande, Arizona, before turning east. This, however, seems very unlikely.
25 See Harrington, "Southern Peripheral Athapaskawan Origins, Divisions and Migrations," *Smithsonian Miscellaneous Collections,* Vol. C (1940), 522. The term *despoblado* is ambiguous. For example, in 1680, Fray Francisco de Ayeta describes the area from El Paso north to New Mexico as a *despoblado* inhabited by Apaches. See Memorial of Fray Francisco de Ayeta, *Guadalajara* 139, in AGI (Archivo General de Indias, Seville, Spain).
26 It is certainly possible that the Zuñis and the Apaches were on friendly terms in 1540, as there was, apparently, trade and contact between Zuñi and Sonora, by way of *Apachería;* and, likewise, in 1692 we read of Salinero Apaches who were allies of the Zuñis. See Letter of Francisco Vásquez de Coronado, August 3, 1540, in *Coronado Narratives,* 171.

army reached Hawikuh—the first Zuñi pueblo—the Indians had already removed all of their women, children, and old people in preparation for the expected contest. It seems very possible, also, that the Zuñis had taken the precaution of calling upon aid from neighboring peoples, including the Apaches, for López de Cárdenas says that the Spaniards "found all the Indians of Cibola and the people of other places who had gathered to meet them with force."[27]

The Zuñis and their allies were not strong enough to withstand the determined attack of Coronado's small, but well-armed and hungry, army. The Spaniards succeeded in occupying and despoiling the first of many New Mexican pueblos which were fated for such an end. Their success was not a satisfying one, however, for no riches in gold and silver were found, and Fray Marcos de Niza had to flee back to Mexico with the soldiers' curses following him.

Coronado did not give up hope of finding a rich kingdom to conquer, and rumors of the provinces of Tusayan (the Hopi), Tiguex (the Río Grande Valley), and Quivira were to keep his soldiers moving from place to place for several years. Soon after the subjugation of the Zuñis,[28] Coronado dispatched Pedro de Tovar, Fray Juan de Padilla, and about twenty soldiers to Tusayan. The Hopis were afraid—being well aware of the nature of these newcomers—and a battle resulted in which a pueblo was sacked and destroyed by the Christians. The Spaniards were able, subsequently, to obtain information on the Colorado River which led Coronado to send López de Cárdenas to its banks, thus discovering the Grand Canyon.[29]

[27] Testimony of García López de Cárdenas, in *Coronado Narratives*, 344, and Letter of Francisco Vásquez de Coronado, August 3, 1540, in *Coronado Narratives*, 171.
[28] The other Cibolans fled from their pueblos and were unable to offer serious resistance after the first battle. *Ibid.*, 174.
[29] Castañeda's History, in *Coronado Narratives*, 214–15. The Espejo expedition of 1582–83 saw the ruined Hopi pueblo. See George P. Hammond and Agapito Rey (eds. and trans.), *Expedition into New Mexico Made by Antonio de Espejo, 1582–1583, as Revealed in the Journal of Diego Pérez de Luxán*, 96, hereinafter cited as the *Relation of Pérez de Luxán.*

The Spaniards also turned their attention to the east, and, prompted by a visit paid them by Bigotes, a Cicuyé (Pecos) chief, Hernando de Alvarado, Fray Juan de Padilla, and soldiers were sent to explore the Río Grande Valley area. They made contact with the hostile people of Acuco pueblo (Acoma) and continued on to Tiguex and Pecos.[30] At Pecos, Alvarado purchased the Turk, a slave who was a native of the interior—probably having been sold to the Puebloans by the Plains Apaches.[31] The Turk was to play a very important part in the eventual failure of the Coronado adventure.

While Alvarado was at Pecos, López de Cárdenas and another party of soldiers went to the Tiguex area and set up permanent headquarters for the Spanish Army of Occupation. In doing so, they forced the Indians to abandon a pueblo, and the Indians lost all of their belongings in the process.[32] This incident caused, quite naturally, a great deal of animosity toward the Spaniards, but Coronado's large army—the main army had now reached Cibola, and the combined forces moved subsequently to Tiguex —had to be housed and fed. As conquerors, the Spaniards considered that they had every right to take what they pleased, and, in fact, Coronado "was empowered to allot the pueblos and *repartimientos* (allotments of Indians for tribute-paying purposes) among the conquerors who went with him."[33]

Unfortunately, during this period when all of the pueblo Indians of New Mexico were surely animated with fear and excitement, almost nothing is known about the Athapascans of the area. The narratives of the Coronado expedition fail to reveal anything about them, with the exception of those living between Sonora and Zuñi—the Chichilticale nomads—and the Apaches of the plains to the east of Pecos. However, archaeological investigations in the region of Governador, New Mexico—west of the Río Grande Valley, in the northern part of the state—reveal that the hogan-building Navaho Apaches—now known simply

30 *Ibid.*, 217–18.
31 The Plains Apaches maintained a lively traffic in slaves of other Plains tribes —notably of the Quivira—with the Pecos in later times.
32 Castañeda's History, in *Coronado Narratives*, 219–20.
33 *Obregón's History*, 13.

as the Navahos—were in that area as early as 1500.[34] Thus they were certainly aware of the Spanish invasion of New Mexico, and the Indians' ideas of the Spaniards were being formed. Therefore, one must understand the character of the Spanish occupation of the Pueblo region to understand the subsequent Apache animosity toward the sons of Cortés.

Assuredly, ideas acquired about the Spaniards were not favorable to the formation of a high opinion of their morality or justice. From the very first, the forces of Coronado revealed themselves as wealth-hungry bandits and not as conquerors who had come to establish a permanent kingdom. For instance, when the Turk informed Coronado that the Pecos Indians had some gold bracelets which had formerly belonged to him, Alvarado was sent to Cicuyé to get the gold—by fair means or foul. The chief Bigotes was enticed into Alvarado's tent, placed in chains, and held as a prisoner for more than six months. The Pecos were made hostile by this highhanded act, and their animosity was to cause the conquerors considerable difficulty at a later date.[35]

Furthermore, difficulties ensued almost immediately between the invaders and the Indians of Tiguex, the latter certainly resenting the occupation of their pueblos by the intolerant, brazen, and womanless Spaniards. By the time that the main army reached Tiguex, in December, 1540, Coronado had already burned a pueblo.[36] A full-scale war soon broke out as a result of a number of factors. First, the natives were alarmed by the seizure of the Pecos chief Bigotes. Also, Coronado asked for three hundred or more pieces of clothing, his method being to send soldiers unexpectedly to visit the twelve Tiguex pueblos, and "there was nothing the natives could do except take off their own cloaks and hand them over."[37] An incident occurred which precipitated the war when a Spaniard went to a pueblo and had an Indian hold his horse. While the latter was holding the

[34] Hall, "Recent Clues to Athapascan Prehistory in the Southwest," *American Anthropologist*, Vol. XLVI, No. 1 (1944), 100. The tree-ring dates range from 1491 + x to 1541 ± 20, as well as from 1656 to later times.

[35] Castañeda's History, in *Coronado Narratives*, 221.

[36] *Ibid.*, 222–23.

[37] *Ibid.*, 224.

animal, the Spaniard "ravished or had attempted to ravish his [the Indian's] wife."[38]

The Tiguex people, justifiably outraged at such immorality and injustice, revolted, capturing a large number of Spanish horses and killing them in a palisaded area. A fierce battle ensued as the Spaniards under López de Cárdenas attempted to storm the pueblo several times. Finally, after smudge pots had been set aflame in the buildings, approximately two hundred Indians offered to surrender to Pablo de Melgosa and Diego López. Their offer was accepted, and they were ushered into the tent of López Cárdenas, who later affirmed that he hadn't known of the peace agreement—although that seems unlikely. Coronado had given orders that no one was to be taken alive, and López de Cárdenas ordered "that 200 stakes be driven into the ground to burn them alive." After the burning had started, one hundred Indians who were still in a tent grabbed weapons which were at hand and began to fight, but "none escaped alive except a few who had remained concealed in the pueblo."[39] Thus hundreds of American Indians died because they objected to oppression and the raping of a woman, but Spanish authority had been questioned, and the Indians had to pay for that crime.

The Pueblo Indians were not defeated in one battle, and the war continued. Several months of snow halted combat for a time, and the Spaniards entertained ideas of making peace with one of the rebel pueblos. López de Cárdenas was sent to Tiguex, but three Indians attempted to kill him, and he was saved only by the proximity of his thirty soldiers. The possibility of an easy pacification then failed as the people of several pueblos fled to the mountains. At Tiguex, López de Cárdenas succeeded in drawing out some of the people and cut a few down, but he failed to defeat them. In fact, a siege began which lasted for almost two months and as a result of which four or five Spaniards died and one hundred were wounded. Most or all of the Indians were killed in the defense of their pueblo.[40]

[38] *Ibid.*, 224–25.
[39] *Ibid.*, 225.
[40] *Ibid.*, 227–29.

The Spaniards continued their offensive against several other pueblos, including one called Arenal, and the Indians continued to flee to the country. The invaders "pursued and killed many of them."[41] By the early spring of 1541, much of the major warfare was completed, and some of the Keres pueblos—such as Chia (Zia)—were forced to submit. "However, the twelve pueblos of Tiguex were never resettled as long as the army remained in that region no matter what assurances were given them."[42] In spite of months of warfare, the powerful and large Spanish army had failed to conquer the Pueblo Indians of the Río Grande Valley. The Pueblos had simply taken up residence in the mountainous areas, as they did in subsequent years when under Spanish attack. This warfare undoubtedly had a tremendous impact upon the Pueblos' neighbors, the Apaches, with refugees probably coming to live with the Athapascans—especially with the Navahos.[43]

In the meantime, Coronado had been listening to the tales of rich kingdoms to the east from Indians who were seemingly anxious to entice the Spaniards into leaving Tiguex. He learned, among other things, of the provinces of Axa and Quivira (Quibira) and of a king named Tatarrax.[44] Anxious to set out for these provinces, Coronado and a large part of his army left Tiguex on April 23, 1541, just as soon as the Indians of that area had been rendered relatively impotent as enemies.[45] He took the Pecos chief Bigotes with him to Cicuyé, where he acquired a native of Quivira, Xabe, as a slave. Xabe, the Turk, another Quiviran named Sopete, and other Indians were to serve as guides for the expedition to the plains.[46]

For over two months the Army of Coronado wandered across the plains of eastern New Mexico, the Texas Panhandle, Oklahoma, and—according to some authorities—Kansas. During

[41] *Ibid.*, 229.

[42] *Ibid.*, 230–34.

[43] There is evidence of refugee Pueblo influence upon the Navaho Apaches.

[44] Villagutierre y Sotomayor, BN 2822.

[45] Letter of Francisco Vásquez de Coronado, October 20, 1541, in *Coronado Narratives*, 186.

[46] Castañeda's History, in *Coronado Narratives*, 235, 237.

this time they experienced the difficulty of traveling in a land with few outstanding landmarks, and they were almost completely dependent upon their guides—at least one of whom was trying to lead the Spaniards astray. After traveling about seventeen days—one source indicates fourteen days and another fewer still—the adventurers came upon a rancheria of Querechos, Apache Indians who followed the buffalo.[47] Coronado was impressed by the skin tipis of the plainsmen and also remarked that "these people have the best physique of any I have seen in the Indies."[48]

> Their tents are in the shape of pavilions. They set them up by means of poles which they carry for the purpose. After driving them in the ground they tie them together at the top. When they move from place to place they carry them by means of dogs, of which they have many. They load the dogs with their tents, poles, and other things.[49]

Thus in 1541 Europeans met more or less typical Plains Indians for the first time.

For several days the army remained in the land of the Querechos, and then, after two to five days more, they came upon a group of Indians hunting buffalo.[50] These Indians were spoken of as the Teyas and, according to the Spanish testimony, were enemies of the Querechos. Nevertheless, because of their geographical location and way of life they seem also to have been Apaches. In fact, they probably were either the Lipan or Jumano Apaches of later times or a group closely related to them.[51] The Lipans' or Jumanos' mode of living was similar to that of the

[47] See *ibid.*, 235; Letter of Coronado, October 20, 1541, in *Coronado Narratives*, 186; and Narrative of Jaramillo, in *Coronado Narratives*, 300.

[48] Letter of Coronado, October 20, 1541, in *Coronado Narratives*, 186.

[49] *Relación del Suceso*, in *Coronado Narratives*, 293. The *Relación del Suceso* is also printed in *Colección de Documentos Inéditos*, XIV.

[50] Jaramillo disagrees and indicates that it was twenty or thirty days from the Querechos to the Teyas. See Narrative of Jaramillo, in *Coronado Narratives*, 301.

[51] There is evidence that the Lipan Apaches, or a branch of them called the Pelones, were hostile to the other Plains Apaches prior to 1700. John P. Harrington asserts that "Teya" was a Pecos name for the eastern Apaches. See Harrington, "Southern Peripheral Athapaskawan Origins, Divisions and Migrations," *Smithsonian Miscellaneous Collections*, Vol. C (1940), 512.

Teyas, and the latter group, like the Querechos, painted their bodies and faces.[52] An old, blind Teyas remembered having seen four other Spaniards closer to New Spain—to the south—and the Coronado party inferred that this was a reference to Cabeza de Vaca's journey.[53] The Teyas had a large pile of buffalo hides near their rancheria which was appropriated by the Spaniards, in spite of the natives' protests.[54] Probably because of the large numbers of the invaders, the Teyas refrained from open hostility.

This rancheria of Plains Indians was located one day west of "an arroyo flowing between some barrancas [cliffs] in which there were good meadows."[55] Coronado led his army to this gorge or ravine, and a large rancheria of Teyas was found in the bottom of it. The availability of water and feed for the livestock and other pressing needs led the Conqueror of the Plains to camp there with his army for several days in the latter part of May, 1541.

Many persons, hoping to be able to trace the route taken by the Coronado Army, have attempted to locate this canyon of the plains, and it has usually been identified as the now-famous Palo Duro Canyon of the Red River, located near Amarillo in the Texas Panhandle. However, there are several other arroyos "flowing between some barrancas" in that area, and Palo Duro Canyon is only one of the more likely possible locations where Coronado had to make decisions on the future course of his expedition.[56] Such decisions had to be made because troubles had arisen, for the army was short on supplies, and no maize had been acquired since leaving Pecos—all sources agree that neither the Querechos nor the Teyas grew maize.

The major problem faced by the army, however, was how to find Quivira, because the guides could not be relied upon. Juan de Jaramillo asserted, for example, that the Turk "had guided

[52] Letter of Coronado, October 20, 1541, in *Coronado Narratives*, 186, and *Relación del Suceso*, in *Coronado Narratives*, 292.

[53] Narrative of Jaramillo, in *Coronado Narratives*, 301.

[54] Castañeda's History, in *Coronado Narratives*, 237.

[55] Narrative of Jaramillo, in *Coronado Narratives*, 302.

[56] Although the Palo Duro Canyon guides show you the exact spot where Coronado first came upon the gorge, and a Coronado Lodge is now located near by.

us away from the route we were to follow, and had led us over the plains as he did in order that we would exhaust our food."[57] Also, the Teyas "did not corroborate the information that the Spaniards had heard before, to the effect that Quivira was to the north," and they said that a good route could not be found.[58] Thus the Spaniards were placed in a serious dilemma, and it was apparently decided to depend upon Sopete and some Teyas Indians as guides.

A junta was held to discuss the problem, and it was decided that Coronado should choose thirty men and proceed on to Quivira, while the balance of the army returned to New Mexico. However, the location of this separation has not been clearly established. One source—Jaramillo—indicates that they parted at the barranca referred to above.[59] On the other hand, Castañeda says that Coronado sent out exploring parties from that place, and, four days away, they discovered other rancherias. He says further:

> This was densely populated country. It produced abundant frijoles, plums like those of Castile, and wild grapes. These pueblos of rancherias extended for a three days' journey. It was called Cona. From this place a few Teyas, for so these people were called, accompanied the army. They traveled with their packs of dogs, their women and children, to the last of the rancherias, where they furnished guides to proceed beyond.[60]

Thus, continues Castañeda, the army reached "the last barranca," which was one league from bank to bank with a small river at the bottom. Here the army rested before separating, and the Spaniards had an excellent opportunity to observe the Plains Apaches closely:

> These natives are intelligent people. The women are well treated, and through modesty they cover their whole body. They wear shoes and buckskins of dressed skins. The women wear blankets over their short underskirts, all of skins, with sleeves

57 Narrative of Jaramillo, in *Coronado Narratives*, 301.
58 Castañeda's History, in *Coronado Narratives*, 239.
59 Narrative of Jaramillo, in *Coronado Narratives*, 302.
60 Castañeda's History, in *Coronado Narratives*, 238–39.

tied at the shoulders. They wear a sort of short tunic over their underskirts, with small fringes reaching to the middle of the thigh.[61]

From this barranca Coronado led his thirty men on to the north or to the east, depending upon which source one utilizes. The journey began inauspiciously as the Teyas guides ran away, and the country wore an unwelcome aspect. Coronado himself records that they met with few arroyos or rivers, lacked wood and had to burn cow (buffalo) dung, had to go without water often, and for forty-two days they lived on nothing but buffalo steaks.[62] Jaramillo contradicts part of the above by asserting that they were never lacking water and positively states that they went always to the north, until reaching the River of Saints Peter and Paul about thirty days from the barranca of the Teyas.[63] This river has been identified by many scholars as the Arkansas River of modern times, this supposition being generally supported by the other sources which tend to place Quivira to the north of New Mexico by several degrees. Those scholars who have attempted to restrict Coronado's activity to the state of Texas seem to do so with little foundation.[64]

The guide Sopete recognized the River of Saints Peter and Paul as being that of Quivira and said the villages were downstream. The army then crossed the river and followed its north bank, turning their route to the northeast. After traveling for three days down the river, Coronado encountered a group of warriors who were hunting buffalo to supply their village, which was about three or four days farther downstream.[65] The Indians started to flee, but they were quieted as Sopete called to them in their own language. At this point Coronado dispatched a letter to the province of Arahei or Harahey, which was said to be farther off, probably to the north. He hoped to locate sur-

61 *Ibid.*, 239.
62 Letter of Coronado, October 20, 1541, in *Coronado Narratives*, 187.
63 Narrative of Jaramillo, in *Coronado Narratives*, 302–303.
64 For the opposite point of view see David Donoghue, "The Route of the Coronado Expedition in Texas," *New Mexico Historical Review*, Vol. IV, No. 1 (1929), and "The Route of the Coronado Expedition in Texas," *Southwestern Historical Quarterly*, Vol. XXXII, No. 3 (1929).
65 Narrative of Jaramillo, in *Coronado Narratives*, 303.

vivors of the Narváez expedition or other Christians; however, the letter was returned unanswered.[66]

The adventurers then visited the first six or seven villages of Quivira, located on small arroyos which flowed into the River of Saints Peter and Paul. There were evidently two such arroyos with an uninhabited area between them. The Spaniards spent several days traveling this area, going eventually to the remotest part of Quivira, which was expressed to them by the word "teucarea."[67] The *Relación del Suceso* says, on the other hand, that "Taraque" was another pueblo which the Spaniards apparently did not reach.[68]

The wealth which the army had expected to find did not materialize, of course, and Coronado's followers were very angry with the Turk, who had deceived them. As a result, this brave Indian, for whom the present-day Pueblo Indians should probably erect a statue, was garroted. He was said to have confessed that the Pecos Indians had persuaded him to lead the Spaniards astray. Furthermore, he was accused of persuading the Quivira natives to withhold maize from the troops, of planning a revolt, and of trying to get the Quivirans to attack the army.[69]

The province of Quivira, governed by Chief Tatarrax, whom Coronado met, has often been located in the neighborhood of Wichita, Kansas. This is probably another attempt at too precise an identification, considering the vagueness of the documentary evidence. The Quivira Indians have been equated with

[66] Villagutierre y Sotomayor, BN 2822.

[67] Narrative of Jaramillo, in *Coronado Narratives*, 304. This remotest part of Quivira, called "teucarea," seems to be identical with the nation of the "Touacara" found on the lower Canadian River by La Harpe in 1719. These Touacaras were associated with the Toayas (Tawehash) and Iscanis and were apparently the Tawakonis. This, of course, is good evidence to support the thesis that the Quivirans were Caddoan-speaking people of the Wichita-Tawehash division. On the other hand, it presents a problem in that if Coronado met the Teucareas in Kansas, on the Arkansas River, then they must have migrated southward into central Oklahoma between 1542 and 1719. This is possible, since it is known that the Osages were always pressing upon the Caddoans from the east. See Herbert Eugene Bolton (ed. and trans.), *Athanase de Mézières and the Louisiana-Texas Frontier, 1768–80*, I, 46.

[68] *Relación del Suceso*, in *Coronado Narratives*, 292.

[69] Testimony of Coronado, September 3, 1544, in *Coronado Narratives*, 236; Castañeda's History, in *Coronado Narrative*, 241; and Narrative of Jaramillo, in *Coronado Narratives*, 304.

the Wichita tribe primarily on the basis of a cultural resemblance between the maize-growing, straw house-using Quivirans of Coronado and the later Wichitas. However, this again seems to be an oversimplification, and it is more likely that the province of Quivira included much more than one tribe, for, as Coronado says, there were twenty-five villages—each with its own language.[70] On the basis of all the evidence at hand, Quivira, should be equated with the whole group of Caddoan-speaking natives located to the north of the Caddos and to the south of the Pawnees and including the Tawehash, Tawakonis, Iscanis, Kichais, and several other groups as well as the Wichitas.[71]

After Coronado and his men had departed for Quivira, the remainder of the army had returned to New Mexico, guided by some Teyas Indians who were familiar with the country. The result was that, whereas it had taken them thirty-seven days to reach the barrancas, the return journey lasted only twenty-five, because they were using a more direct route.[72] They reached the Pecos River about thirty leagues below their former crossing place. This fact may indicate that the barrancas and the lands of the Teyas were farther south than has heretofore been thought, for if it was quicker to go from the barrancas to Pecos Pueblo by way of a point thirty leagues—some seventy-five miles—farther south on the Pecos River, then it follows that the lands of the Teyas lay south or southeast of Pecos. Palo Duro Canyon, on the other hand, lies to the east of that pueblo. It seems quite likely, for this reason, that the barrancas of Coronado were actually the canyons of the Brazos River near present-day Lubbock, Texas.

The Teyas guides informed the Spaniards that the Pecos River flowed for a distance of twenty days of travel to a spot where it joined the Tiguex (Río Grande), then the combined streams flowed toward the east again.[73] This, of course, indicates considerable knowledge of southern regions by the Teyas as does

[70] Letter of Coronado, October 20, 1541, in *Coronado Narratives*, 188.

[71] There is some doubt that the Wichitas existed as a tribe at an early date. They may be only the "modern" version of the Tawehash and others.

[72] Castañeda's History, in *Coronado Narratives*, 242.

[73] *Ibid.*, 243.

also the fact that the old Indian among them had seen what was probably the Cabeza de Vaca party a few years before.

Meanwhile, the corps of soldiers led by Coronado had seen enough of Quivira and early in August, 1541, determined to return to New Mexico. Five or six Quivirans guided them

> back over the same route we had come as far as the point where I have said we came upon the Saints Peter and Paul River. Here they abandoned our previous route and, taking off to the right [that is, in a more or less westerly direction], they led us by watering places and among the cattle [buffalo] and over good road.... Finally we came to the region, and recognized it, where, as I said at the beginning, we had found the rancheria [of the Querechos] where the Turk took us away from the route we should have followed.[74]

This more direct route was said to have been only two hundred leagues instead of the three hundred and fifty leagues traveled on the way to Quivira.[75]

The returning Army of Coronado, fatigued by this tremendous journey, probably hoped to be able to relax upon reaching New Mexico, but, on the contrary, they found the natives still hostile and war continuing. At Pecos they were met by Tristan de Luna y Arellano, who could report that since July of that year he had forced the people of Yuque-Yuque to abandon two pueblos, that the Americans' provisions had been acquired, and that the people of Pecos were hostile. In fact, he had fought a four-day battle with the Pecos Indians, killing two prominent natives on the first day.[76]

While Coronado had been on the buffalo plains, in July and August, 1541, a party of Spaniards had left Tiguex and marched about eighty leagues down the Río Grande, visiting what were probably the Piro pueblos. Then they traveled until they found that the river disappeared underground and learned from the natives that it reappeared as a large stream later on.[77] These Spaniards were probably near the region of El Paso in Athapas-

74 Narrative of Jaramillo, in *Coronado Narratives*, 305–306.
75 *Relación del Suceso*, in *Coronado Narratives*, 292.
76 Castañeda's History, in *Coronado Narratives*, 244–45.
77 *Ibid.*, 245.

can (Apache or Manso) territory. In later years, it was noted that the Río Grande flowed underground above El Paso.[78]

The beginning of the year 1542 found the army of Coronado still in the north, without having located any gold and silver. The Indians of Tiguex and Pecos were still hostile, as undoubtedly were all the rest, and the Spaniards were unable to reduce them to submission. If, from the first, all of the resources of the expedition had been applied to the end of establishing a firm hold in New Mexico, that area would probably have been tied securely to the Spanish Empire. However, the strength of the enterprise had been dissipated in idle marches, and the cruel, highhanded policy of banditry had alienated the American Indians. This, coupled with the infirmity of Coronado, was enough to condemn the expedition to failure and to lead to the decision of returning to New Spain.

By April, 1542, the army was ready to abandon New Mexico. Nevertheless, not all of those who had come with Coronado were willing to leave. The documents indicate that a number of Mexican and Tarascan Indians—probably along with some from Sinaloa—and several Negroes remained among the Pueblo Indians. These American Indians and Africans, wise to the ways of the Spaniards, undoubtedly helped the New Mexicans catch up on Mexican history from Cortés to Guzmán. It also appears that a Tarascan named Andrés remained among the Quivira.[79] Several priests also decided to remain in the new lands, although probably for different motives than the Indians. Fray Luís went to the pueblo of Pecos, taking with him a slave named Cristóbal. Fray Juan de Padilla and Fray Juan de la Cruz, accompanied by the Quivira guides, a Portuguese named Andrés del Campo, a mestizo, and a Negro, returned to Quivira. According to the known evidence, Fray Juan de Padilla and Fray Juan de la Cruz were killed, en route or in Quivira, but del Campo and some

[78] In 1752 the Río Grande dried up thirty leagues above El Paso and re-emerged twenty leagues below that settlement. The intervening fifty leagues were dry. See Eleanor B. Adams (ed.), "Bishop Tamarón's Visitation of New Mexico, 1760," *New Mexico Historical Review,* Vol. XXVIII, No. 3 (1953), 195.

[79] Narrative of Jaramillo, in *Coronado Narratives,* 306.

of the others escaped and reached Pánuco after what must have been a very difficult journey. The fate of Fray Luís is not known; however, it is to be assumed that he was killed by the justifiably anti-Spanish Pecos Indians.[80]

The exit of the Coronado Army from New Mexico, Arizona, and Sonora was an inglorious one for the retreating Spaniards. The march from Tiguex is not described, but the march from Cibola is: "For two or three days the natives [the Zuñis apparently] never ceased to follow the rear guard of the army to pick up any baggage or Indian servants . . . they rejoiced at keeping some of our people."[81] The *despoblado* between Cibola and Chichilticale was otherwise passed without incident, but at the latter place the retreating conquerors were met by Juan Gallego who had new troops and supplies. He had bad news, however, to the effect that the natives of Sonora—probably the Ópatas—had revolted and destroyed the Spanish supply station and settlement of San Gerónimo de Corazones. There had been dissension among the Spaniards there, and after the commander, Melchior Díaz, had left to explore the Colorado River area, a group of soldiers deserted to Culiacán. The remainder dishonored the Indian women—a frequent Spanish crime—imposed an excessive tribute, and were otherwise cruel, with the result that the already hostile Indians killed the soldiers and left nothing to be found by later expeditions except several mestizo children.[82]

Juan Gallego had found the Sonorans still in revolt and had had daily skirmishes with the Indians, perhaps as far north as Chichilticale—thus Apaches or Jocomes may have been involved. This Spanish officer had apparently led ruthless reprisals against the rebels, destroying several villages without warning and engendering so much hate that Coronado's retreating army had to fight its way to the valley of Corazones. From there the con-

---

[80] *Ibid.*, 307; Gerónimo de Zarate Salmerón, *"Relaciones de todas las cosas, que en el nuevo México se han visto . . . ," "Virreinato de Méjico,"* tomo I, MN (Museo Naval, Madrid, Spain) 567, hereinafter cited as Zarate Salmerón, *"Virreinato de Méjico,"* tomo I, MN 567; and Castañeda's History, in *Coronado Narratives*, 262, 270.

[81] *Ibid.*, 272.

[82] *Obregón's History*, 162–63, 168.

querors of the North continued their retreat to New Spain and reached Culiacán by June, 1542.[83]

The Coronado expedition was, from Spain's point of view, a definite failure. The stubborn defense of the independence-loving Pueblo Indians, the revolt of the oppressed Sonorans, and the vast distances involved had combined to defeat the purposes of the Spaniards. This defeat, coupled with the Mixton War in New Spain, made 1542 a year of setbacks for the Spanish Empire. For the American Indians to the north, however, it was, undoubtedly, a year of rejoicing. They were now free—but for how long? The Pueblo Indians must have wondered if the Spaniards would someday return, and very likely some preparations were made for future defense. Certainly, the minds of the Indians were steeled against the Europeans both from the memory of the Spanish invasion and from stories probably circulated by the Mexicans, Tarascans, and Negroes who remained among them.

The Athapascans must have been almost as affected by anti-Spanish feeling as were the Pueblo tribes, for without a doubt there was a great deal of contact between the two peoples. The documents connected with the Coronado expedition, while saying little or nothing about the Western and Navaho Apaches, give us a considerable amount of information on the plains groups, the Querechos, and the Teyas and on their relations with non-Athapascans.

It has often been assumed that the Apaches were basically predatory Indians prone to raid their neighbors and, in general, a bad group of tribesmen. In particular, students of Pueblo Indian history, noting the almost continuous warfare between the Apaches and the settled people of New Mexico after 1700, have assumed a prehistoric origin for Apache raiding. In part, at least, the Coronado documents—and later ones—do reveal warfare between Pueblo peoples and Athapascans prior to 1598—the date of the first successful Spanish entrance into New Mexico. However, they also reveal that there was considerable commerce and friendly contacts between the two peoples. As a matter of fact, there is no evidence that any Athapascans were at

[83] Castañeda's History, in *Coronado Narratives*, 272–75, 277–78.

war with any Pueblo groups in 1540–42. For example, Castañeda says,

> The Teyas whom the army met, although they were brave, were
> known by the people of the towns as their friends. The Teyas
> often go to the latter's pueblos to spend the winter, finding shel-
> ter under the eaves, as the inhabitants do not dare to allow
> them inside. Evidently they do not trust them, although they
> accept them as friends and have dealings with them.[84]

Both the Querechos and the Teyas carried on a lively trade
with the Pueblo Indians—the trade being mostly in buffalo and
deerskins, meat (pemmican), maize, and blankets. "The cattle
and deerskins that they do not need, and the meat dried in the
sun, they trade for maize and blankets to the natives at the river
[of Tiguex]."[85] These Apaches impressed the Spaniards very
favorably. Castañeda says, "They are gentle people . . . and
are faithful in their friendship."

There is some evidence that the peaceful relations existing
between the Teyas and the Pueblo Indians were a fairly recent
development in 1540, for a report says in reference to Tiguex:

> There are in this province seven other pueblos, uninhabited
> and in ruins, belonging to the Indians who daub their eyes,
> and about whom the guides told your lordship. They say that
> they border on the cattle, and that they have maize and straw
> houses.[86]

The Indians "who daub their eyes" seem to be the Teyas, for
it was said that "they decorate their eyes."[87] On the other hand,
the report is based on secondhand information and may, therefore, be considered inaccurate in part. When traveling between
Pecos and Quirix (the province of the Keres Indians near the
Río Grande), the Spaniards came upon a pueblo which was almost deserted and which seemed to have been destroyed recently.
Farther on was another large pueblo, completely destroyed.

[84] *Ibid.*, 258.

[85] *Relación del Suceso,* in *Coronado Narratives,* 293.

[86] Report on Journey of Hernando de Alvarado, 1541, in *Coronado Narratives,*
183.

[87] Castañeda's History, in *Coronado Narratives,* 238.

> All that we could find out about it was that some sixteen years before [i.e., in the 1520's] some people called Teyas had come in large numbers to that land and had destroyed their pueblos. They besieged Cicuye [Pecos] but could not take it because it was strong. Before leaving the land they made friends with all.[88]

Thus it seems that the Teyas had, at the very least, a war with some of the Pueblos, and then—perhaps still in the 1520's— peace was made.

It is both surprising and interesting that the Spanish accounts record more contacts between the Teyas and Pueblo people than between the Querechos and Puebloans, especially since the Querechos' lands lay between Pecos and the Teyas' barrancas. Furthermore, the Querechos and the Teyas were described as hostile to each other, and this situation, of course, would have impeded the Teyas' passage to New Mexico for trade and for war. However, it may be that the lands of the Teyas lay not to the east of the Querechos but to the south or southeast and could have therefore spread in an arc with the western end nearer the pueblos.[89]

The relations between the Athapascans and the Caddoans of Quivira seem to have been the same as they usually were in later centuries—hostile. Coronado says that the people of Quivira, the Teyas, and the Querechos "all are enemies of one another."[90] There is little doubt that the Plains Apaches sold captive Quivirans to the Pecos and other Pueblo Indians, for the Spaniards of Coronado were able to acquire a number of Quivira slaves in New Mexico. Likewise, Apache slaves taken in battle by the Caddoans were probably sold to the east, as they were in later times.

The relations between the Athapascans of Chichilticale—Gila Apaches or Jocomes—and other peoples is never expressed explicitly in the Spanish documents. However, they were seemingly at peace with both the Zuñis and the natives of Sonora, for both Fray Marcos de Niza and Captain Melchior Díaz found, in

[88] *Ibid.,* 257.

[89] This is another reason for holding that the barrancas of the Teyas were much farther south, in relation to Pecos, than Palo Duro Canyon.

[90] Letter of Coronado, October 20, 1541, in *Coronado Narratives,* 188.

1539, evidence of contact between Sonora and Cibola. No such evidence would have existed, of course, if the Indians in that area had been hostile.[91] This is not to say, however, that relations in the area of Arizona had always been peaceful, for in 1697 the Pimas of the Gila River cherished a tradition to the effect that the Apaches had been among the tribes responsible for the abandonment of Casa Grande—a ruin near Coolidge. Archaeologists estimate that the destruction of Casa Grande occurred about the year 1400, which perhaps suggests an improvement in the intertribal relations of the area by 1539.[92]

There is considerable evidence that the seminomadic Apaches cannot be branded as the initiators of all the wars of New Mexico or as the only warlike people in that area. For example, the warriors of Acoma (a Keres pueblo) were described as "robbers who were feared throughout the land."[93] The people of Pecos were also to be feared, for they "pride themselves because no one has been able to subjugate them, while they dominate the pueblos they wish."[94] Thus the idea that every abandoned pueblo, or every shift of population in New Mexico, was due to the Apaches may be looked upon with doubt. The *Relación del Suceso* says,

> The reason that these pueblos [of the Pueblo Indians] are settled as they are [with an eye for defense] is believed to be due . . . in part . . . to the war they wage against each other.[95]

The failure of the well-armed and experienced Spanish Army of Coronado to defeat the Pueblo Indians and the long periods of time necessary to capture besieged pueblos—in spite of the horses which the invaders possessed, the Spaniards' knowledge of European methods of attacking a fortification, and their not

[91] There is very good evidence to indicate that the Pimas—both Gilas and Sobaipuris—were friendly with the Apaches prior to 1693, when the Spainards separated them.

[92] Manje, *"Breve Noticia,"* BMH 970.

[93] Castañeda's History, in *Coronado Narratives,* 218.

[94] *Ibid.,* 256–57.

[95] *Relación del Suceso,* in *Coronado Narratives,* 294. See Ralph Linton, "Nomad Raids and Fortified Pueblos," *American Antiquity,* Vol. X, No. 1 (1944), for a discussion of Athapascan-Pueblo relations and relative effectiveness in war.

having the burden of women and children to protect—certainly demonstrate the fighting ability of the Pueblo Indians. Thus one may doubt that the Apaches, with only bows and arrows, could have done what Spaniards with steel weapons and gunpowder had great difficulty in accomplishing. It is actually rather difficult to accept the thesis that a band of Indians on foot, always faced with the obligation of protecting their own women, children, and possessions, could have taken the time—or had the strength—to besiege a well-defended pueblo. Certainly, they would have had no means of quick retreat, without horses, and any loss of the initiative would have been fatal.

Thus the idea of the Apaches as an essentially predatory race of Indians is probably best treated as a figment of the imagination. Nevertheless, the Spaniards were to know them as relentless and fierce enemies for hundreds of years.

CHAPTER II

Mines,
Missionaries
and Mounted Indians

The year 1542 was a tremendously crucial one for both the Spanish Empire and the Indians of New Spain. The failure of the Coronado expedition and the savage Mixtón War were full of discouragement for the sons of Cortés and, at least in part, encouragement for the race of Moctezuma. However, the Indians of Mexico were divided in the revolution of Jalisco. Many aided the Spaniards, and their aid, in the end, determined the failure of the war for the rebels.

The Mixtón War was not a total defeat for the native race, for the Spaniards were forced to allow their Indian allies to use horses, and thus the mounted Indian appeared. At first he served as an ally of the European, but soon he was to become a deadly enemy. Furthermore, a leader of the rebels, Tenamaxtle, escaped, and his raids troubled the Spaniards of Guadalajara well into the 1550's. Other refugees also continued the war, carrying hatred of the invaders to the north and helping to build a bridge of historical causation between the Mixtón War and the subsequent Chichimeca War.[1]

The Spanish Empire in New Spain might have retreated in 1542, or, at best, its further advance might have been seriously retarded except for another event which took place in the same year—an event with great consequences for both Spaniards and

[1] See Philip Wayne Powell, *Soldiers, Indians and Silver*, 29–30, 159.

Indians. Rich mines were discovered in Zacatecas, the home of the seminomadic Zacateco Indians, and Europeans began to stream towards the north to reap the rewards of gold and silver. This new "mining frontier" was to bring the Spanish empire, within eighteen years, to the vicinity of the Athapascans and, within fifty-six years, to the occupation of New Mexico.

The northward movement of the Spanish Empire in Mexico was a very important chapter in the history of the Apache Indians, for Hispano-Apache relations were largely to dominate Southern Athapascan affairs from 1600 to 1821; and the techniques of Indian relations established by the empire from 1542 to 1600 were to determine in large part the Spanish methods used with the Apaches in subsequent years.

The advance of the mining frontier into Zacatecas was not received with joy by the Chichimecas, the seminomadic and freedom-loving tribes of the central Mexican plateau. By 1550–51 the Zacatecos, Guachichiles, Guamares, and Pames were at war with the invaders, and this bitter war was to continue in the same area until about 1600. The Indians proved themselves to be far from helpless and soon became accustomed to fighting Europeans. For example, in 1551 the Guamares raided an *estancia* ("ranch"), stealing livestock, and in 1554 Indians attacked a wagon train of sixty wagons, carrying off 30,000 pesos worth of goods and mules to haul away the booty.[2] Thus by the early 1550's these Indians were making use of European livestock and probably were already riding horses.

Significantly, the Chichimeca War was constantly extended to the north, for other Indians kept joining the contest, and, in spite of the risk involved, the Spaniards continuously extended their mining activity northward. By 1554 mines had apparently been discovered at Mazapil, near soon-to-be-founded Saltillo, and thus the Spaniards had crossed the Chichimeca lands, for Saltillo was at the northern limits of the Guachichile area.[3]

[2] *Ibid.*, 29, 33, 61.

[3] Charles Wilson Hackett (ed. and trans.), *Historical Documents Relating to New Mexico, Nueva Vizcaya and Approaches Thereto, to 1773*, I, 16–17, hereinafter cited as Hackett, *Historical Documents*, and Joseph Arleguí, *Chrónica de la*

Apache tribes are shown within shaded area. Modern names of rivers are supplied.

The Northern Frontier, 1542–1600

In the same year of 1554 Francisco de Ibarra, financed by the wealth of Zacatecas, entered Durango and discovered many very rich mines, such as Sombrerete and San Martín. By 1560 he, or his followers, had penetrated into Chihuahua and the mines of Santa Bárbara, Indehe, and San Juan del Río were producing revenue for the Crown of Spain. In 1563 Ibarra became governor of the new province of Nueva Vizcaya. The northward advance of the mining frontier was halted at Santa Bárbara (near present-day Parral, Chihuahua); but Ibarra did not cease his activity, for by-passed areas were explored, and the new provinces of Topia and Sinaloa were invaded. Thus in less than twenty years Spanish soldier-miners crossed many leagues of territory occupied by Indians who were hostile or who later became hostile. Virtually unknown geographically, this country was now *una tierra de guerra*—"a land of war."[4]

Wherever Francisco de Ibarra's miners went, bloodshed soon followed. In fact, from 1560 to 1600 Nueva Vizcaya was in an almost continual state of war, as one tribe after another responded to the naked thrust of Spanish imperialism. Significantly for the Apaches, some of the Indians involved were not far from Athapascan boundaries. For example, the area of Saltillo was aflame as the Guachichiles revolted time after time, and the Coahuilas to the north soon joined the war. The new colony of León and the mines of New Almaden (present day Monclova) were at first to the north of this area of war, but not for long, as the Coahuilas' northern neighbors—some of whom may have been Athapascans—became involved.[5]

On the frontier of Durango, Indehe, and Santa Bárbara, the powerful Tepehuanes leagued themselves with an anti-Spanish conspiracy, and the northern Zacatecos spread sedition and car-

---

Provincia de N.S.P.S. Francisco de Zacatecas, 225. Hackett's dates may be about ten years too early. See Powell, *Soldiers, Indians and Silver*, 101.

[4] For accounts of the advance of the frontier see *Relación de Ibarra*, in *Colección de Documentos Inéditos*, XIV, 463–82; *Obregón's History*; Pérez de Ribas, *Historia de los Triunphos de Nuestra Santa Fee*; Villagutierre y Sotomayor, BN 2822; and John Lloyd Mecham, *Francisco de Ibarra and Nueva Vizcaya*.

[5] See Arleguí, *Chrónica de la Provincia de Zacatecas*, 17; Report of Francisco de Urdiñola, March 4, 1587, *Guadalajara* 28, in AGI; and Service of Francisco de Urdiñola, December 16, 1591, *Guadalajara* 28, in AGI.

ried on open war. To the north of the Río Nazas and Santa
Bárbara other wild, warlike, and fiercely independent peoples
took up the song of war as the Spanish mines of Indehe and,
perhaps, of Santa Bárbara were established within their territory.
These tribes were, from south to north, the Cabezas and Salineros, the Tobosos, Cocoyomes and Acoclames, and the Chisos.
The Chisos ranged into the Big Bend country of Texas and were,
undoubtedly, in contact with the Apaches—in particular, with
the Jumano Apaches (often called Jumanos, Xumanes, and
"Apaches Jumanes" by the Spaniards) who adjoined them on
the north. It is impossible to say exactly when the Chisos became involved in the Nueva Vizcaya War, but their southern
friends were in it by 1560, and it is known that some Chisos
were at war with the Europeans by 1600.[6]

To the west of the above-mentioned tribes lay another tier
of Indian nations, including, from south to north, the Conchos,
Cholomes, and Julimes—referred to as Patarabueys in early accounts. These North American Indians had hostilities with Spanish slave-raiders quite early, and warlike relations continued
until at least 1598.[7] This fact is particularly important because
the Julimes lived partly in Texas and were close friends and
neighbors of the Jumano Apaches—so close that they were considered to be the same nation in 1582.[8] Furthermore, there is a
very real possibility that the Jumanos were actually involved in
some skirmishes that occurred in the 1580's.

The impact of the Spanish frontier upon the Indian was not
confined to warfare, however, for several important cultural
changes took place among the natives of Nueva Galicia—which
included most of the old Chichimeca territory—and Nueva Vizcaya. The Spaniards needed laborers to work in the mines and

6 See Hackett, *Historical Documents*, II, 141–43; *Relación de Ibarra*, in *Colección de Documentos Inéditos*, XIV, 463–78; and "*Relación Hecha por Joan de
Miranda . . . ,*" in *Colección de Documentos Inéditos*, XVI, 563–67.

7 See *Obregón's History*, 273–317; George P. Hammond and Agapito Rey (eds.
and trans.), *The Gallegos Relation of the Rodríguez Expedition to New Mexico*,
253, hereinafter cited as the *Gallegos Relation;* Herbert Eugene Bolton, *Spanish
Exploration in the Southwest, 1542–1706*, 172–73, hereinafter cited as Bolton,
Spanish Explorations; and Hackett, *Historical Documents*, I, 397.

8 See Forbes, "Unknown Athapaskans," *Ethnohistory*, Vol. VI, No. 2 (1959).

the *estancias de labor* ("farms and ranches") which developed to supply the miners with food. Mexicans, Tlaxcalans, and other conquered Indians came north in large numbers, but local labor was also needed. Since at first the seminomadic northerners were not inclined to such work and were hostile anyway, the slave-raiding system developed. It has been noted that slave raids extended as far north as Texas (La Junta) to supply the mines of Santa Bárbara, and in other areas slave labor was in equal demand. The system seems to have reached a peak from 1575 to 1585, and all its evils were in force. For example, by the 1580's it was such an important business that the soldiers started wars in order to get slaves. The latter were treated cruelly, and for punishment their hands and feet might be cut off.[9]

The slave-labor system seems to have been partially replaced by a more or less voluntary labor system, whereby natives were recruited to work in the *estancias* and were remunerated for their services. In this way Indians from as far away as southern Texas came to work in the area of Santa Bárbara and Parral in Chihuahua. These northerners, many of whom were Athapascan Jumanos in later times, were, of course, subject to all the cultural influences of Spanish frontier society, most of which were probably evil. Nevertheless, some useful things were undoubtedly learned, such as horseback riding (if not already known) and various Hispanic crafts. Items of European manufacture could be acquired and traded as far away as coastal Texas.[10]

The period of the Chichimeca War, the first Nueva Vizcaya War, and the mining frontier—1550 to 1600—is particularly important for the appearance of the mounted Indian as a barrier to Spanish imperialism. The spread of horses and mules northward was extremely rapid during this period, and tribe after tribe acquired the use of them. It has been noted that in 1554 the Chichimecas raided a wagon train and used the captured

[9] Powell, *Soldiers, Indians and Silver*, 109–10, 184–86.

[10] An important trade route was established from Parral up the Río Conchos to the Julimes, and then across Texas to the coast. Trade was carried on by the Jumano Apaches. For a secondary discussion of this trade see J. Charles Kelley, "Juan Sabeata and Diffusion in Texas," *American Anthropologist*, Vol. LVII, No. 5 (1955).

mules to carry away the booty.[11] In the early 1580's and 1590's the Tepehuanes and Zacatecos were causing a great deal of damage in Nueva Vizcaya (present-day Durango) by stealing mules and horses.[12] By 1580 most of the inhabitants of Nueva Galicia must have had horses, for it was reported of Captain Gabriel Ortiz Fuenmayor that "since 1580 he has been working at this type of pacification, giving freely of his goods (great quantities of food, clothing, horses, colts, and many other things)" to the Guachichiles.[13] The Spaniards would never have *given* horses to the Indians unless the latter had already acquired the use of them and had the possibility of getting them from a different source.

Further evidence of the rapid spread of horses is to be seen in the fact that a 1582 report states that the Chichimecas had more horses than their "proper owners" and that the Guichichiles were trading this stolen livestock for women and weapons in the *tierra adentro* (i.e., to the north). In the southern range of Chichimeca territory there was a center for handling this livestock. "They have corrals and ride herd on thousands of cattle they have stolen. From here they herd cattle to the tierra adentro and trade them to other rancherias for women and arms."[14] In 1585 it was said that "they [the Chichimecas] are no longer content to attack the highways on foot, but they have taken to stealing horses and fast mares and learning to ride horseback."[15] However, it was not completely necessary for the Indians to take their mounts in war, for Juan Suárez de Peralta reported in 1579 that in New Spain "there are today a very large number of horses and mares, so many that they go wild in the country, without owner, which ones are called *cimarrones*." In fact, there were wild horses who lived for twenty years without having an owner.[16]

Needless to say, the horse was a very marketable commodity

[11] *"Descripción de la Villa de Nombre de Dios,"* May, 1608, BN 3064, p. 28.
[12] *Ibid.*
[13] See Powell, *Soldiers, Indians and Silver,* 205, 210.
[14] *Ibid.,* 50, 175.
[15] *Ibid.,* 50.
[16] Juan Suárez de Peralta, *"Noticia Inédita sobre los Caballos en Nueva España,"* *Revista de Indias,* Año V, No. 15 (Enero–Marzo, 1944), 324.

among the Indians, and the Chichimecas were soon trading them to the north. The northern Mexican tribes were active in acquiring animals on their own, however, for in the 1580's the Indians of the Saltillo area revolted, killed a Spaniard, and stole many mules and horses.[17] The northernmost theft of horses occurred in July, 1590. Gaspar Castaño de Sosa had abandoned New Almaden (Monclova, Coahuila) in order to take the settlers from that place and conquer New Mexico. On the Río de Nadadores they camped for a few days among Indians who proceeded to carry off their horses.[18] This fact is not surprising, for these Indians had been in contact with the Spaniards for a number of years. On the other hand, the theft is important because the Coahuila tribes were in contact with the Jumano Apaches and other Texas Indians. It seems almost certain that some horses did reach southeastern Texas during the 1590's, for in neighboring Nuevo León the Indians revolted, stealing goats and horses and forcing the Spaniards to retire to Saltillo.[19]

As has been noted previously, the Indians to the north of Nueva Vizcaya—the Tobosos and their allies—were at war with the Spaniards as early as 1560. It is not known when they began to capture livestock or learn to ride horses, but by 1576 they had become so powerful that the rich mines of Indehe and San Buenaventura were abandoned, and Santa Bárbara could not be worked.[20] Certainly Indians who were able to carry on such warfare had captured livestock and were mounted. In the 1590's campaigns were undertaken against the Tobosos because of their taking livestock. This, of course, is extremely significant for a study of the Southern Athapascans, for their close proximity to the Tobosos would have soon acquainted them with the horse. In 1574 a Spanish soldier of the Nueva Vizcaya frontier reported, after participating in a number of campaigns:

> and by information [gotten] from some of them [the Chichimecas, perhaps Tobosos] whom at times I have captured, I have

[17] Service of Francisco de Urdiñola, December 16, 1591, *Guadalajara* 28, in AGI.
[18] Memoria of Gaspar Castaño de Sosa, in *Colección de Documentos Inéditos*, IV, 284.
[19] Alonso de León, *Historia de Nuevo León*, 95–98.
[20] Powell, *Soldiers, Indians and Silver*, 114.

received reliable [news] that, a hundred leagues inland to the north, there is a great population of natives who treat and trade with the said Chichimecas and encourage them and give them aid and assistance in order to commit the said injuries [on the Spaniards]. They barter profitably with hides and metals rich in silver (this is what the said Chichimecas use to decorate and paint their bodies) for the mules, horses, Christian Indians and slaves which they [the Chichimecas] steal in this way. It will be of much benefit to your royal service for that people to to be discovered, conquered and brought under your royal service. They have the name Quibira.[21]

This document would seem to indicate that the Indians of Texas were getting horses and mules as early as the 1570's, for, although these Quivirans were probably not as far north as the Quiviras of Coronado, they were certainly in—or bordering upon—Texas. The distance from Santa Bárbara to La Junta was considered to be about eighty leagues, and thus it is quite possible that the Julimes were the Indians who were buying goods from the Chichimecas. From the 1680's to the 1760's, there is a wealth of evidence showing that the Julimes and Jumano Apaches were intensive traders and that the Jumanos carried goods from La Junta to east Texas and the area immediately south of Quivira.[22] There is no known reason to suppose that this interest in trade was a late development.

It is certain that by 1600 all of the Indians of Nueva Galicia and Nueva Vizcaya were acquainted with, and the owners of, horses—the numbers possessed by different groups varying. In fact, as early as 1608, it was said that none of the Indians of Durango—Tepehuanes, for the most part—traveled on foot, as all possessed horses.[23] Between the years of 1595 and 1600, the original Chichimeca War was brought to a close, and from 1600 to 1604, a lull resulted in the Nueva Vizcaya fighting. Thus the northward spread of the horse into the area of the United States may have slowed down. However, it seems very likely that by 1600 there were a number of horses as far north as southern

21 Second Petition of Melchior de Alva, 1574, *Indiferente* 1384, in AGI.
22 *"Descripción de la Villa de Nombre de Dios,"* May, 1608, BN 3064, p. 47.
23 *Ibid.*

Texas. Undoubtedly this number was to be augmented in subsequent years by peaceful trading, for the Spaniards then had no particular reason for trying to halt the spread of the horse—already a phenomenon beyond their control. By the 1620's there were herds of wild horses roaming northern Mexico.[24]

The fifty years preceding 1600 were significant ones for the Spaniard as well as for the Indian. The wars with the seminomadic tribes of the Mexican Plateau had forced the invaders to develop a new system of dealing with such peoples, and the experience gained was to be applied in relations with the Apaches after 1600. The first policy of the Spanish frontier was to subdue the natives by killing them, if necessary, or enslaving them, when possible. However, the continued resistance of the Indians and their increased effectiveness when mounted caused the Europeans to develop a more effective system. This approach first took only a military form, as groups of soldiers were stationed in particularly important places—the presidio system—and campaigns were then made from these bases. The soldiers, however, were apparently of a low caliber, and warfare was stimulated rather than eliminated.[25]

Finally, by the 1580's, the Spaniards realized that military action was not enough. The Indians had to be pacified; they had to be brought to a genuine peace—not just defeated in a campaign. For this purpose the policy of bribing the natives to settle down was adopted, and this technique was continued by the Spaniards throughout the balance of their years in America. Once the Indians had been brought to peace, however, there was still a problem: How was it possible to keep them congregated and make them into *ladinos*—that is, to make Hispanicized Indians, laborers, and taxpayers of them? For this purpose, as well as for genuine missionary zeal, the mission system was adopted on the northern frontier.

[24] In 1628 a Spanish party reached the area of Santa Bárbara, Chihuahua, and "thirty mules ran away after the herds of wild mares, and, for all their careful searching, fifteen of them could not be found again." "True Report" of Fray Estevan de Perea, 1632, in Benavides, *1634*, 210–11. In 1621 the road from Saltillo to Zacatecas was so full of wild mares that they could not be counted. Domingo Lázaro de Arregui, *Descripción de la Nueva Galicia*, 129.

[25] Powell, *Soldiers, Indians and Silver*, 184, 186.

The primary objective of the missions was to gather the semi-nomadic Indians into a "reduction"—a village or mission community—where the natives would be "reduced" to the Roman Catholic religion, taught how to build houses, taught agriculture, and forced to adopt the Spaniards' mode of dress. They would learn the Spanish (or Mexican) language, and their tribal heritage would be destroyed. After a period of such "brain washing," they were expected to emerge as useful subjects of the King of Spain, although, of course, still Indians, and still inferior to Spaniards. Thus the primary purpose of the missions was a secular one, with the religious aspect probably secondary —except, perhaps, to the priest involved. Since the Pope had given the King of Spain almost complete control over the Catholic Church in the Americas and all tithes were collected and all expenses met by the Crown, the missions were definitely a royal institution.

There were priests on the northern frontier very early, but apparently they were there primarily to serve the Spanish-speaking communities.[26] In 1584 the Bishop of Guadalajara, claiming that the costs of the Indian wars were too great, proposed a new method for peace. The wars not only cost money but

> furthermore, for each nation thus conquered, others nearby, seeing what Spaniards do and thus fearing them, become hostile and fight, and the process is endless.

Instead, he favored the mission system and proposed several settlements along the northern frontier, including one at Indehe. Each congregation was to have two or three Franciscan priests, up to eight soldiers (to keep the Indians from running away or revolting), and Christianized Mexicans or Tlaxcalans to aid in the converting and teaching.[27] Actually, the Jesuits seem to have been the first order to begin work in the north, establishing missions in the 1590's among the Tepehuanes and Laguneros of Parras. However, Franciscans were starting *conver-*

26 As early as 1581, Fray Agustín Rodríguez was preaching to the Toboso and Concho Indians near Santa Bárbara. See Benavides, *1634*, 51.

27 Powell, *Soldiers, Indians and Silver*, 182.

siones of Conchos and Tobosos by 1604.[28] By this date the mission system had spread to New Mexico as well, and plans had already been made to "reduce" the Apaches.

By 1598, when Juan de Oñate was marching north to invade the lands of the Pueblo and Apache Indians, the northern frontier of New Spain was some forty years old, and the course of Southern Athapascan history from that time forward was in good part already determined by the events of the preceding years. The trend of Spanish-Indian relations in northern New Spain had been established; the mounted Indian had appeared; and the knowledge of the Spaniard as a cruel and dangerous enemy had spread throughout the region.[29]

[28] See *Annual de 1598*, BMH 971, and Arleguí, *Chrónica de la Provincia de Zacatecas*, 84.

[29] For a more detailed discussion of the northward spread of the horse see Jack D. Forbes, "The Appearance of the Mounted Indian in Northern Mexico and the Southwest, to 1680," *Southwestern Journal of Anthropology*, Vol. XV, No. 2 (1959).

CHAPTER III

Slaves,
Silver,
and Souls

Although the northern limits of the Spanish Empire in Mexico remained approximately the same from 1560 to 1598, a number of expeditions penetrated the regions farther inland, making contact with Apaches and their neighbors. The Europeans were attracted to those little-known regions for a number of reasons. Two stand out in importance: the search for wealth and a desire for converts to the Roman Catholic faith. The Spaniards were not satisfied with the mines that they had already discovered in Mexico, and they were constantly on the lookout for signs of mineral wealth beyond. Any rumors of rich ores were greeted with interest, and every unknown area was thought to have rich resources. Legends of wealthy kingdoms to the north constantly circulated, and fabulous Quivira was always to be a lure for credulous Spaniards.

There was another type of wealth to be secured in the north however, perhaps not as valuable as gold and silver but easier to find, for there were many Indians to be conquered. The practice of Indian slavery seems to have been very common on the northern frontier, although it was supposed to apply only to enemies captured in war; but then, after all, it was easy to begin a war, and who could tell whether an expedition was a campaign or a raid for slaves? In form and results they differed but little from each other. On the other hand, it was not necessary to take slaves in order to profit from Indian conquests. One might be granted a village or pueblo of natives as a *repartimiento* or encomienda and live an easy life on the tribute of the conquered.

One of the greatest of the Indian conquerors of New Spain was Francisco de Ibarra, the first governor of Nueva Vizcaya. In 1565 he determined upon a journey into the unknown northern regions, apparently with the view of discovering the area of New Mexico.[1] The expedition was organized in the newly subdued province of Sinaloa. It was to consist of sixty soldiers, three hundred pack and saddle horses, twelve or thirteen male and female Indian servants, and two very important interpreters. The first of the latter was Diego de Soberanes, Ibarra's page, who could speak the dialect of Sinaloa—Cahita, the language of the Yaqui, Mayo, and Sinaloa peoples.[2] The other interpreter was an Indian woman, Luisa, of the Sinaloa village of Ocoroni. She knew the Mexican language (Náhuatl) "and three other languages of those provinces" to which they were going. Apparently, Luisa had escaped from or had been left behind in Sonora by the Coronado expedition, and she was said to be a native of Culiacán. Her linguistic knowledge included the ability to speak in all the languages from Ocoroni to the valleys of Señora and Corazones in Sonora, thus encompassing the Cahita, Pima, and Ópata-Jova languages.[3]

The Spanish members of the expedition included Francisco de Caravajal, who had been in New Mexico with Coronado, and Baltasar de Obregón, the chronicler of the enterprise.[4]

The adventurers traveled north along the valley of the Río Yaqui, passing through the lands of the Yaquis and the Pimas, or as Obregón calls them, the Caytas or Caitas and the Pima Aytos or Pimahitos.[5] The natives were supposedly very astonished at the sight of horses and Negroes, having not seen such

[1] The date is not established absolutely. See Mecham, *Francisco de Ibarra and Nueva Vizcaya*, 162–80, for a general discussion of the journey.

[2] *Obregón's History*, 86, 152.

[3] *Ibid.*, 79, 83.

[4] *Ibid.*, 213, and *Coronado Narratives*, 96. Caravajal had been wounded in New Mexico.

[5] *Obregón's History*, 164, 194.

things, apparently, for more than twenty years.[6] The Indians of the Corazones Valley still cherished the memory of their victory over the Spaniards in 1542, and they were generally hostile in 1565. The towns of Guaraspi and Cumupa were passed, and the little army reached Sahuaripa, an important Ópata pueblo in eastern Sonora.[7] Here the Indians planned formal resistance to the invasion, but Ibarra's interpreters offered peace rather than war. This gesture was not accepted by the warlike Ópata, and a battle ensued in which the Spaniards were placed on the defensive. Ibarra had to order

> every soldier to keep two horses tied at night to prevent the enemy from shooting them, as they were stealing the horses and killing them with arrows.[8]

This would seem to indicate that the Spaniards had about 120 horses left, out of the original 300. Some had probably perished during the hard journey, but the natives of Guaraspi had already stolen a number, and now the Ópatas were capturing and killing more.[9] Thus the Indians of Sonora were capable of acquiring horses in 1565, whether they had the knowledge to mount them or not.

In the sixteenth century Sahuaripa was, as it is today, near the eastern frontier of Sonora. As Obregón says:

> This valley and town of Caguaripa is on the frontier of the Indians of the plains. These people [the Ópatas of Sahuaripa] are very skilful, warlike and better versed in the use and practice of war than all other people in the provinces as far as the vaqueros [people of the plains], called Querechos.[10]

Thus the Ópatas' eastern neighbors in 1565 are said to be the Querechos, who are also their betters in war.

---

6 *Ibid.*, 156, 161.

7 Sahuaripa was near the territory of the Jovas, a group related to the Ópatas. However, the pueblo belonged to the Ópatas. See *"Descripción del Obispado de Durango," "Virreinato de Méjico,"* tomo I, MN 567, and *"Relación de las Misiones que la Compañia de Jesús tienne en el Reyno de Nueva Vizcaya,"* BMH 971.

8 *Obregón's History*, 178, 180, 186.

9 *Ibid.*, 174.

10 *Ibid.*, 178.

43

Obregón, in his account, repeatedly asserts that the Querechos were to be found near Sonora. He says that the people of Guaraspi are skillful in the art of war, "due to the fact that they are neighbors of the most valiant and daring people in those provinces. These are the Querechos, who follow the cattle [buffalo]." The same information is repeated for the people of Cumupa and, as has been seen, for the Ópatas of Sahuaripa: both are said to be skillful in war because of being neighbors of the Querechos.[11]

It seems that Baltasar de Obregón places "Querechos," the buffalo-hunting Apaches of Coronado, in the neighborhood of southern Sonora because both Ibarra and Obregón assumed that they were much nearer to New Mexico than they really were. Consequently, they gave the name "Querechos," to the semi-nomadic peoples they were to meet to the east of Sonora, in the present-day Casas Grandes Valley of Chihuahua. Another possibility is, however, that Caravajal, who had probably seen Coronado's Querechos in 1541–42, saw some cultural or racial similarities between the natives of northwestern Chihuahua and the Plains Apaches.

After leaving Sahuaripa, Ibarra and his now somewhat discouraged group of explorers marched for two days to the last pueblo of the Ópatas, which consisted of two hundred terraced houses. An interpreter reassured the Indians, but, nevertheless, they were more hostile than friendly. This was the last pueblo of the settled people of Sonora, and "the confederation [against the Spaniards] came to an end in this town. . . . Here they came to the limits of the lands of their [the Ópatas' of Sahuaripa] friends."[12] Before leaving the village Ibarra prudently acquired "two Indian slaves who were from the plains" to use as guides for the next phase of the journey, which was the difficult task of crossing the rugged mountains separating eastern Sonora from the valley of the Río Casas Grandes in Chihuahua.[13]

After spending many days in mountainous country, the Spaniards finally reached the sought-for valley and found "abandoned

11 *Ibid.*, 174–75.
12 *Ibid.*, 193.
13 *Ibid.*, 195, 197.

houses of two and three stories," thus reaching, apparently, the famous ruins left by the Casas Grandes people when they deserted the area in 1400–50.[14] After reaching these "better lands," they met "the first Indian of the plains," who was very frightened and had to be run down by two horsemen. After being captured, he was presented with gifts and sent to reassure his people. The two slaves acquired from the Ópatas had previously run away, and thus the Spaniards had to use sign language to communicate with him, as they had no interpreter "who could understand the natives of the plains and of the region toward the north."[15] Thus the Spaniards had apparently reached a people who spoke a language not related to either the Pima-Tepehuan, Cahita-Ópata-Taraumara, or Náhuatl branches of the Uto-Aztecan language family.[16]

The region of Casas Grandes was inhabited eighty-five years later (when our knowledge of the area is first complete) by the Suma Indians, apparently an Athapascan group. Near by—to the south and southeast—were the Conchos, a group classified as belonging to the Cahita-Ópata-Taraumara branch of the Uto-Aztecan family.[17] The people contacted by Ibarra in 1565 must have been either Sumas or Conchos, because of their way of life, as well as their location. The Conchos, however, are disqualified by their apparent use of a Uto-Aztecan tongue. As a result, the natives encounted by the Spaniards of Ibarra were in all probability Sumas.

As the explorers traveled down the Casas Grandes Valley to the north, they met three hundred "Querechos" with their women and children, along with the Indian they had captured and regaled previously. These Indians had seen Cabeza de Vaca —or other Spaniards—in the 1540's and regarded them as children of the sun. The natives were described as sun worshipers,

14 Paul S. Martin, George I. Quimby, and Donald Collier, *Indians Before Columbus*, 214–16.

15 *Obregón's History*, 198.

16 The expedition's interpreters could understand and speak all of these languages.

17 A. L. Kroeber, "Uto-Aztecan Languages of Mexico," *Ibero-Americana*, Vol. VIII (1934), 13–14.

an epithet often applied to the Plains Apaches, as well. The natives gave the information that Cibola was three days away and that the buffalo were four days toward the north.[18] These Querecho Indians were described as living on sheltered slopes part of the time—in winter—and in open country at other times.

> These people are enemies of the Querechos who live among the buffalo. They have droves of dogs. . . . They eat all sorts of wild reptiles, some corn, acorns, and walnuts, castile prunes, and all kinds of game. They are more friendly, loyal, and valiant than those we had met before. They possess hides from the buffalo; they do not have salt. We could not see what sort of habitations or houses they had.[19]

Traveling on down the river, the Spaniards reached the principal ruins of Casas Grandes, located near a village of the Querechos (Sumas) called, apparently, Paquime. The ruins were very impressive, with towers, patios, painted and whitewashed walls, kivas, and houses six and seven stories in height. In sharp contrast to all this were the Querechos. Obregón says that

> close by lived wild, coarse, and roaming people, who, rather than live in such large houses, preferred to dwell in straw huts like wild animals . . . they are hunters; they eat all sorts of game, wild reptiles, and acorns. The men go about naked; the women wear short skirts of tanned deerskins or cowhide.[20]

The Querechos said that the people who had lived in the ruins were living six days to the north and that they had moved because of wars with enemies from the other side of the mountains —i.e., in Sonora.[21]

Ibarra and his men were undecided about their next stop. Some of the men wished to go farther to the north, but the majority favored a return to Sinaloa. The latter course was agreed upon, and they began a tortuous journey across rugged mountains (which are largely unexplored to this day), finally reaching the lands of the Yaquis and—at last—Sinaloa. During the jour-

18 *Obregón's History,* 201–202.
19 *Ibid.,* 203.
20 *Ibid.,* 206–207.
21 *Gallegos Relation,* 253.

ney they were forced to abandon many horses which "became exhausted and others as their hoofs wore off"; still others were eaten as supplies dwindled to nothing.[22] It is conceivable that the Sumas of Casas Grandes acquired some of the horses.

The Ibarra expedition of 1565 is the only journey of exploration recorded as having gone from Nueva Vizcaya to the north in the two decades from 1560 to 1580. However, many *entradas* were made during this time for the dual purpose of punishing hostile Indians and capturing slaves to be used in the mining regions of Parral, Santa Bárbara, Indehe, and Nueva Galicia. Unfortunately, the documentation is scant and only hints at the extent of such journeys. That they were frequent, however, is apparent.

Campaigns were frequently made against the Toboso Indians and their allies living north of Indehe and east of Parral. More significant for Apache-Spanish relations, however, are the raids made for slaves along the Conchos River, as far as La Junta and the Texas border. Hernando Gallegos, as he contacted the Cabri Indians (Julimes) near La Junta in 1581, records meeting Indians who fled into the sierra for fear of the Spaniards,

> because the latter had taken and carried off many of their people during the raids of the captains who had sallied forth by orders of de Ibarra. They had caused them much harm.[23]

Thus as early as the governorship of Francisco de Ibarra, 1563–72, the Spaniards were gathering slaves and sowing seeds of hate on the border of Athapascan lands.

On another occasion Gallegos declared that

> he made, together with leaders and captains named for this purpose, many journeys into the interior beyond Santa Barbola [Santa Bárbara] in pursuit of thieving Indians.

and that a captured Indian, with tales of northern regions, helped to stimulate the Chamuscado-Rodríguez expedition of 1581.[24]

---

22 *Obregón's History*, 241, 242, 255.
23 *Gallegos Relation*, 253.
24 "Declaration of Hernando Gallegos," in Bolton, *Spanish Explorations*, 144 n.

47

In 1582 the Espejo-Beltrán expedition reached a place called "El Xacal," two leagues north of the junction of the Conchos and San Pedro rivers in Concho Indian territory, and Diego Pérez de Luxán records that

> this place is called El Xacal because Lope de Aristi, captain from Santa Bárbara, took captives there and in order that the people should not get wet he built a Xacal [jacal or hut] where they remained until they returned with them to Santa Bárbara.[25]

Upon reaching the area near La Junta, Luxán met the Otomo-aco Indians, who were also called the Patarabueys.

> This name Patarabueys was made up by the soldiers when people from this same rancheria were taken by Mateo González, chieftain of Juan de Cubia, captain from the mines of Santa Bárbara.[26]

They were to serve as laborers in the mines.

In 1581 Gaspar de Luxán, Diego Pérez de Luxán's brother, led an expedition to La Junta "by commission of Juan de la Parra, captain of Indehe, to take captives." He and "other soldiers of Juan de la Parra" erected crosses at various pueblos (possibly as a sign of taking possession of them), including those of Baij Sibiye and Casica Moyo, reached by the Espejo group in 1582. The Baij Sibiye pueblo was at La Junta, and that of Casica Moyo was two and one-half leagues away on the opposite bank of the Río Grande. Thus Gaspar de Luxán's slave raid extended into Texas.[27] It is very likely that at the La Junta pueblos these Spaniards came into contact with Jumano Apaches, close allies of the La Junta Indians.

With the dawn of the 1580's, the Europeans began to take a slightly different interest in the northern regions, in part because of the settled prosperity of the Parral-Indehe region and the availability of man power and wealth in that area, which was twenty years old. Rumors of wealth, rich mines, and many potentially exploitable Indians served to whet the appetites of ad-

[25] *Relation of Pérez de Luxán*, 52.
[26] *Ibid.*, 54–55.
[27] *Ibid.*, 54, 59, 60.

venturers such as Hernando Gallegos, who gained enough information from a slave he captured to make him want to go to
the unknown north.[28] Likewise, several Franciscan priests became interested in going to the new lands, ostensibly to convert
the heathens to Roman Catholicism, but an equally strong motive was probably a desire to discover new lands and important
provinces for His Catholic Majesty.

One of these priests was Fray Agustín Rodríguez, who obtained a commission to preach beyond Santa Bárbara. It was
reported "that along the Río Conchas were people where this
good purpose might be effected."[29] This account, of course, was
true, for the thousands of Conchos, Cholomes, Jūlimes, and other
Indians between Santa Bárbara and La Junta had never been
approached by a priest but, on the other hand, were affected by
all of the evil influences of the Hispanic frontier. Nevertheless,
Fray Rodríguez never seemed to have been interested in remaining among these unconverted tribes, for his interest merged with
that of adventurers such as Gallegos and Francisco Sánchez Chamuscado. The result of this union of interest was that on June
6, 1581 a party of three priests led by Fray Rodríguez and nine
soldiers under Chamuscado departed on an expedition to discover new lands far beyond the banks of the Conchos River.[30]

The route they followed—along which they were well received
by the natives—was down the Conchos to La Junta. The Indians
at La Junta, however, were afraid of the Spaniards, as a result
of the previous slave raids. The inhabitants said that the invaders had taken their kinsmen, wives, and children captive
and carried them away in chains.[31] The Chamuscado party reassured them, but they also acted boldly. "This fearlessness shown
by the said Spaniards towards the natives was primarily to intimidate them so that the news should spread. Many harquebuses
were fired."[32] This practice of setting off firearms to strike terror

28 "Declaration of Hernando Gallegos," in Bolton, *Spanish Explorations*, 144 n.
29 Report of the Viceroy, 1583, in Bolton, *Spanish Explorations*, 158.
30 Account of Escalante and Barrado, in Bolton, *Spanish Explorations*, 154,
and *Obregón's History*, 268–69.
31 *Ibid.*, 276.
32 *Gallegos Relation*, 253.

into the natives was a frequently practiced art of the Spaniards in the north.

The La Junta Indians' way of life was far superior to that of the natives closer to Nueva Vizcaya, for the La Juntans lived in permanent log and mud-plastered houses, practiced agriculture, and possessed many fine articles—such as buffalo-skin robes, blankets and garments, and sinew-backed bows which were stronger than and superior to those of the Nueva Vizcaya tribes. One Indian had a piece of copper around his neck, and others had bits of coral suspended from their noses.[33]

In order to impress the Indians, the Spaniards told them that the priests "were children of the sun, that they had come down from heaven, and that we were their children."[34]

From La Junta the Chamuscado-Rodríguez group traveled up the Río Grande to the Piro pueblos of New Mexico. On the way, for about eighteen days, they passed among people of similar language and customs—probably the Cholome Indians of later times, but perhaps also including some Sumas.[35]

Two days after leaving these people, and one day before reaching a swampy area—probably near present-day El Paso—the Spaniards met a new group of Indians, whom they could understand only by means of signs. These Indians—probably members of the tribe later called Mansos—presented the expedition with two bonnets made of numerous macaw feathers.[36]

Seventy leagues of travel in apparently uninhabited land (it was summer on the Jornada del Muerto) brought the suffering Spaniards from the swamps of the Mansos to the vicinity of the first Piro pueblos. Unaware of the nearness of these pueblos, they frantically pursued the first Indian they saw but lost him in a sudden shower. Shortly thereafter they came upon and captured another Indian, who guided them to a ruined pueblo. Two leagues farther on, he said, was an inhabited settlement,

[33] *Ibid.*, 252–58.

[34] *Ibid.*, 256.

[35] The Cholomes and Sumas seemingly shared the same tongue, although differing in culture to some extent. Both groups apparently spoke an Athapascan language.

[36] *Gallegos Relation*, 260.

and he offered to get corn for them. This was done, "but as he was of a different nation it seemed that he did not go to the pueblo he had mentioned."[37] In all probability, this Indian's people were Apaches.[38]

On the following day, however, the Chamuscado-Rodríguez party passed two leagues upstream and found the first Piro pueblo—abandoned. The Piroans, out of fear, had deserted their village, and the Spaniards were in need of food. In fact, Gallegos had said, many days before, that corn "was the thing we most desired."[39] Contact with the natives was made, however, and peace and corn were acquired. Thus the Piros supplied and sustained the first of many Spanish expeditions which arrived on the threshold of New Mexico empty-handed, but with the empty palm thrust forward.

The Piros claimed that they had twenty pueblos and that farther on was another nation—the Tewas—with whom they were at war. Thus they were hostile towards nations to the north and to the south—the Mansos. From the Piros the Spaniards apparently continued northeast, reaching the eastern Tewas and the Tompiros. The travelers described the Tompiros as "bellicose and feared by the other districts, especially because of their towns, for they use the houses as fortresses."[40]

Having acquired supplies from the settled Indians, the Span-

---

37 *Ibid.*, 261–62.

38 The earliest record of people living immediately south of the Piros is in the 1620's, when the Apaches del Perrillo occupied the area. There is no reason to believe that they were newcomers.

39 *Gallegos Relation*, 257–63.

40 *Obregón's History*, 292. The Spaniards apparently left the Río Grande Valley at or near Abó, for they did not meet the Tiwa Indians. Instead, they contacted the Tewas (of the eastern slopes of the Manzano Mountains) and the Tompiros. Gallegos records a small vocabulary for his "Tewa," and it is certainly closer to northern Tewa than to Tiwa. The following is a comparison of the vocabularies:

Gallegos *1581*		Tiwa of Isleta	Tewa of San Ildefonso
1. Corn	cunque	íye, hú-tú-a	ku^n
2. Water	pica	pa	po, po-qí^n (lake)
3. Turkey	dire	di-rú-de	di
4. Woman	ayu	hliú-ra-de	á-ñu^n (young girl)

Thus while the "turkey" of the Tiwa is perhaps closer to Gallegos', the words for corn and young girl definitely link his Tewa with the northern Tewa group. See *Gallegos Relation*, 266, and E. S. Curtis, *The North American Indian*, XVI, 269, XVII, 201.

iards now wished to fulfill a desire to visit the Indians of the plains who lived among the buffalo and inquired of some of the Tompiros about these *vaqueros* (literally, "cow people").

> They indicated to us that the people [of the buffalo] were not striped [these Pueblo people were]; that they live on game and eat nothing except meat of the buffalo during the winter; that during the rainy season they go in search of prickly pears and dates; that they do not have houses, only huts of buffalo-hides; that they move from place to place; that they were their enemies, but they also came to their pueblos with articles of barter, such as deerskins and buffalo-hides, for making foot wear, and with a large amount of meat in exchange for corn and blankets; that in this way, by conversing with one another, they came to understand their language.[41]

The Spaniards expressed a desire to visit these people of the buffalo, but the settled Indians said that "the Indians who followed the buffalo were very brave people, that they used many arrows, and that they would kill" the Europeans.[42] The Spaniards were not to be intimidated, however, and on September 28, 1581, they set out from the pueblo called *Mal Partida* to visit the plains.[43]

After marching east for twenty-five leagues, the Spaniards reached the Pecos River, which they followed downstream for four leagues, until reaching a Plains Apache village composed of fifty tipis and huts. Over four hundred men armed with bows and arrows came out in alarm to meet them. The Spaniards followed their customary tactics and discharged a harquebus to frighten the Apaches. The result was that "they were so terrified that not even united did they dare approach a lone horse."[44] Gallegos says of the Apaches:

41 *Gallegos Relation*, 267.

42 *Ibid.*, 267–68.

43 *Ibid.*, 334, and *Obregón's History*, 302. This pueblo has been located by some scholars in the Galisteo Valley of New Mexico. However, it may actually be a Tompiro pueblo. The "striped" pueblo people mentioned previously were certainly Tompiros, probably of the pueblo later called Jumanas. These were said to be the only striped people in New Mexico. See Forbes, "Unknown Athapaskans," *Ethnohistory*, Vol. VI, No 2 (1959).

44 *Obregón's History*, 304, 336.

These naked people wear only buffalo-hides and deerskins, with which they cover themselves . . . they have dogs which carry loads of two or three *arrobas* [about twenty-five pounds]. They provide them with leather pack saddles, poitrels and cruppers. They tie them to one another like a pack train. They put maguey ropes on them for halters. They travel three or four leagues per day.[45]

From the Apache rancheria the Spaniards evidently turned east onto the plains, becoming uncertain of whether or not they were lost. As a result, Pedro Sánchez de Fuensalida and Pedro Sánchez de Chaves armed themselves and with Fray Rodríguez returned to the Apache rancheria on the Pecos. There they seized an Indian and forced him to guide them eastward to the "Plains of San Francisco."[46] On October 19 they determined upon returning to New Mexico, but they were a little afraid of what the Apaches—now hostile—might do. Thus they freed the guide, gave him some meat as a good-will gesture, and hoped for the best; but "they took leave of these people and went on very cautiously, fearing that the natives might try to avenge the seizure of the guide."[47]

The documents do not reveal the reason, but the Chamuscado-Rodríguez party always seemed to leave hostility behind it. Now the Spaniards sought to return to the lands of the Pueblo Indians to secure food, for supplies were once again depleted. However, the Indians were openly hostile, and dissension existed among the Spaniards themselves. In September, rather than go out on the buffalo plains, Fray Juan de Santa María had separated from the others and, according to Gallegos, determined upon returning to Santa Bárbara. That a lone priest would desire to travel over hundreds of leagues of unknown land, among strange Indian tribes, is to be doubted, however. Because none of the priests survived this journey, it is impossible to learn what actually took place, for Gallegos, our sole authority, may have been involved in a factional dispute with the Fran-

45 *Gallegos Relation,* 336.
46 *Ibid.,* 336, and *Obregón's History,* 306.
47 *Ibid.,* 307.

ciscans. At any rate, one suspects that something was seriously amiss among the Spaniards, and it may have involved some of the conflicting goals of the members of the expedition: the soldiers' desires for quick wealth may have set off a dispute with the priests, for example.

According to Gallegos, the Indians were alarmed at the departure of Fray Santa María, fearing that he was going to get reinforcements. To prevent this, they are said to have followed him for several days and then to have killed him. By mid-October, the Pueblo Indians were openly hostile. At Piedra Alta the Spaniards were refused supplies and had to resort to force. At Malagon the Indians killed three horses, and the Spaniards raided the pueblo in revenge and found horse remains. The soldiers attacked the pueblo a second time to capture Indians. They actually began to burn the pueblo but determined to do something else instead. A familiar scheme was used, the object of which was to convince the Indians that the priests were their friends and protectors. The Spaniards acted as if they were going to behead some of their prisoners, and the priests melodramatically rushed up and rescued the Indians. The terrified Indians were not fooled, however, and their hostility continued.[48]

The Spaniards had succeeded in arousing widespread hostility among the Pueblo tribes, and their only course of action now was to retreat in near-flight to Nueva Vizcaya. However, for some reason difficult to understand, Fray Rodríguez and Fray Francisco López are said to have decided to remain in the Tiwa pueblo of Puaray, along with the Indian servants brought by the expedition—there were seventeen servants and two women, of whom nine belonged to the soldiers and seven, including a mestizo, had been acquired by the priests from the mines of Santa Bárbara.[49] After the departure of Chamuscado, Gallegos, and the other soldiers, the two priests were killed by the Puaray natives.

Actually, it was not Hispanic policy to leave priests among unconverted and hostile Indians without at least one armed sol-

---

[48] *Gallegos Relation,* 339–45.
[49] *Ibid.,* 356, and *Obregón's History,* 268–69.

dier to protect them. In this instance, the soldiers may have abandoned the priests to forestall any reports unfavorable to the former in Nueva Vizcaya. However, this is only a guess. The reports of the expedition mention nothing about any goods or slaves brought back from the northern regions, and yet something must have happened along these lines, for a new expedition was ready to return to New Mexico in 1582—lured by dreams of wealth as well as by the plight of the priests. We do know that eleven silver mines were supposedly located by the Chamuscado-Rodríguez expedition.[50]

The expedition of 1582, referred to as the Espejo expedition, began in a manner similar to that of the Chamuscado-Rodríguez journey—that is, with a mergence of diverse interests. Ostensibly, the *viaje* was to be made to rescue the priests left in New Mexico, but actually it was known by October, 1582, that they were dead.[51] Another ostensible reason for the trip was that Fray Pedro de Heredia received a commission from Juan de Ibarra, lieutenant governor of Nueva Vizcaya, "by which he was given authority to penetrate and explore, and subdue the Conchos Indians and other nations near them."[52] In other words, Heredia was to do what Rodríguez had failed to do in 1581.

Another view of the origin of this expedition states that Fray Bernaldino Beltrán received a commission from Captain Juan Ontiveras of Cuatro Cienagas, a settlement in present-day Coahuila.[53] However, it would hardly seem that such a commission would be valid for making a journey to New Mexico. Indeed, the real origins of the expedition are to be seen in the desires of the men who went on the trek—men such as Antonio de Espejo, a fugitive from justice and hopeful conquistador of a new province, and Gaspar de Luxán, who made a raid for slaves to La Junta in 1581.

[50] Account of Escalante and Barrado, in Bolton, *Spanish Explorations*, 157.

[51] Several Indians who stayed at Puaray with the priests returned to Nueva Vizcaya with the news of their deaths. See the Declaration of Hernando Barrado, October, 1582, in Bolton, *Spanish Explorations*, 151–52.

[52] *Obregón's History*, 316–17.

[53] Espejo's Account, in Bolton, *Spanish Explorations*, 170, hereinafter cited as Espejo's Account.

That the expedition was primarily one aimed at profit is seen clearly from the following: Fray Heredia was forced to turn back shortly after the departure, and Diego Pérez de Luxán says,

> we were ruined, because some of us had spent our estates, we entreated Fray Pedro [Heredia] not to desert or abandon us, for he could appreciate how much the expedition had cost us.[54]

In other words, the secular members of the party had invested heavily with the hope of gaining a profitable return from their enterprise.

The expedition departed from Nueva Vizcaya on November 10, 1582, and by December they were among the Indians of La Junta. These Indians were hostile because of the slave raids made upon them, and several of the Spaniards' horses were killed. Peaceable relations were restored, however, and the pueblos of the Cholomes and Julimes were visited. These Indians were called Patarabueys collectively, although divided into two different peoples—the Cholomes (called Otomoacos) and the Julimes (called Abriaches). Some of the Patarabueys' allies, the Jumano Apaches, were probably also living at La Junta, for Espejo, in his account, confuses them with the Cholome and Julime groups.[55]

From La Junta the expedition, now under the leadership of Antonio de Espejo and Fray Bernaldino Beltrán, traveled up the Río Grande for forty-five leagues among the Otomoacos (Cholomes) and for about nineteen leagues among the related Caguates (Sumas)—after three leagues reaching the Tanpachoas (Mansos) at the lagoons near El Paso. The contacts were all friendly, and at one place some Otomoacos gave the Spaniards shawls, tanned deerskins, mescal, and ornaments—such as bonnets with colored feathers. At another place an old Caguate had been guarding a horse left by Chamuscado. The Tanpachoas were also friendly and presented the Spaniards with food. Pérez de Luxán says,

> Their mode of fighting is with Turkish [sinew-backed] bows

[54] *Relation of Pérez de Luxán,* 47.
[55] See Forbes, "Unknown Athapaskans," *Ethnohistory,* Vol. VI, No. 2 (1959).

and arrows and bludgeons half a yard in length made of Tor-
nillo [mesquite] wood, which is very strong and flexible.

A Tlaxcalan gunsmith who was with the Spaniards made stocks
for their guns from the wood.[56]

From the El Paso area to the Piro pueblos, the Espejo-Beltrán
party traveled for fifty-six leagues without seeing anything except deserted rancherias and the old abandoned pueblo seen
also by Rodríguez in 1581. However, they did see smoke in a
near-by sierra.[57]

The first Piro pueblo was deserted, as in 1581, by its inhabitants, but people were found in the next pueblo. "They have a
few and poor Turkish bows and poorer arrows," remarks Luxán,
and he thought them not very bellicose. One of their weapons,
however, was a one-half-yard-long club with stones strapped on.
From the Piros the Spaniards apparently left the Río Grande
and visited the eastern Tewas or Tompiros, finding them a more
warlike and better-armed people. The expedition then returned
to the Río Grande Valley, went past Puaray—where the priests
had been killed, as the Spaniards knew—and went to the Keres
region. The Tiwas, fearing Spanish wrath, had deserted many
of their pueblos and were living in the sierra.[58]

After visiting the Keres area, Espejo led the group from Zia
to Acoma, by way of present-day Laguna. Four leagues before
reaching Laguna "we found here peaceful Indian mountaineers
who brought us tortillas even though we did not need them."
These Indians were the Navaho Apaches, called Querechos by
Espejo and Pérez de Luxán. This is the first recorded contact
between Navahos and Spaniards, and it is interesting to note
that the former were corn users—making *tortillas*—in 1582.[59]

Subsequently, the Spaniards were impressed by the strength
of the position of Acoma pueblo. Pérez de Luxán says, "Because
of the war this pueblo has with the Querecho Indians, who

[56] *Relation of Pérez de Luxán*, 64–69.

[57] Espejo's Account, 176, contradicts this and states that a rancheria of grass
huts was reached. The Indians found there guided them to the Piro settlements.
They were probably Apaches.

[58] *Relation of Pérez de Luxán*, 72–78, and *Obregón's History*, 322.

[59] *Relation of Pérez de Luxán*, 85–86.

are like the Chichimechas, it is built on a high rocky cliff."[60]
Espejo contradicts Pérez de Luxán, however, by saying:

> The mountains thereabout [around Acoma] apparently gave
> promise of mines and other riches, but we did not go to see
> them as the people from there were many and warlike. The
> mountain people come to aid those of the settlements, who
> call the mountain people Querechos. They carry on trade with
> those of the settlements, taking to them salt, game, such as deer,
> rabbits, and hares, tanned deerskins, and other things, to trade
> for cotton *mantas* and other things.[61]

Thus we are left in some doubt about relations between the
Navahos and the Keres of Acoma. However, later facts show
that Pérez de Luxán's statement was a supposition, for the Querechos are—as Espejo says—friends of the Keres.

The Spaniards continued to Zuñi, where they met the Mexican Indians who had been there since Coronado's visit. Faction-
alism broke out within this party—as it had in the Chamuscado-
Rodríguez group—between priests and soldiers. The faction led
by Espejo wished to move on to the Hopi pueblos to search for
mines, and the other faction—led by Fray Beltrán—wished to
return to Nueva Vizcaya.

The Hopis, remembering Tovar's destruction of one of their
pueblos in 1540, did not choose to welcome these Spaniards and,
instead, sent warnings not to come. Likewise, they enlisted the
aid of Navahos or other Apaches, for the Spaniards learned of
"a great gathering of wild and warlike people to fight us . . . .
[and] that the children, women, and girls were in a sierra with
their flocks."[62] Espejo, however, was able to get 150 or 180 Zuñi
warriors to help him—thus indicating that the Zuñis and the
Hopis were enemies at this time, as they were later. Espejo, nine
soldiers, the Zuñi allies, and some Concho and other Indian
slaves set out for Mohoce—the Spaniard's name for the Hopi
area—although two of the Concho slaves fled along the way.[63]

[60] *Ibid.,* 86.
[61] Espejo's Account, 183.
[62] *Ibid.,* 185; *Obregón's History,* 327; and *Relation of Pérez de Luxán,* 95.
[63] *Ibid.,* 94.

The Hopis had only been bluffing, for they did not want to lose another pueblo to the wrath of these strange men with guns. When the Spaniards halted at ruins of the pueblo destroyed in 1540, the Hopis of Awatobi—one league away—made peace. They "sent away the warriors that had been assembled in the mountains. These people are called Querechos. They go about naked and the people of this town [Awatobi] had enlisted their aid."[64] Pérez de Luxán says, "The Lord willed this, that the whole land [of Mohoce] should tremble for ten lone Spaniards, for here were over 12,000 Indians in this province with bows and arrows, and many chichimecas whom they call Corechos."[65]

Thus it appears that in the spring of 1583 the Apaches (probably Navahos), the Hopis, and the Acomas were all allies, but the Zuñis were apparently at odds with at least the Hopis.

On the last day of April, Espejo and four other Spaniards left Awatobi to visit some mines which they had heard about, located in what was later to be called the Sierra Azul—"the Blue Mountains"). After fifteen leagues of travel to the southwest, they reached the Little Colorado River. "This river flows from the south toward the north. It is settled by warlike, mountain people."[66] These people were a branch of the Western Apache, for—although Pérez de Luxán tells us little about them—Spaniards identified them for us in 1605.[67]

From the Little Colorado Espejo traveled twelve leagues to a large *ciénaga* which was two leagues in circumference (probably Mormon Lake) and surrounded by pines and cedars. "This region is inhabited by mountain people. . . . During this night some of them came to our horses and fled when they heard them as they found the sound unfamiliar."[68] The Spaniards left the *ciénaga* and journeyed seven leagues through

> broken and rough mountain with bad roads and very dangerous in an enemy country. We descended a slope so steep and dangerous that a mule . . . fell down and was dashed to pieces.

64 *Obregón's History*, 328.
65 *Relation of Pérez de Luxán*, 97.
66 *Ibid.*, 105.
67 *Ibid.*, 154–55.
68 *Ibid.*, 105.

> We went down by a ravine so bad and craggy that we descended
> with difficulty to a fine large river which runs from northwest
> to southeast.[69]

They were undoubtedly in or near the Oak Creek Canyon country west of Mormon Lake, for such a description certainly fits
the area.

The Spaniards called the river that they reached the Río de
las Parras [River of Grapevines], for it was in a warm land with
grapevines, walnut trees, parrots, natural flax, and prickly pears.
Thus the river valley was probably that of the Verde, with its
warm climate and lush vegetation along the river banks. Here
the Spaniards "found a rancheria belonging to mountain people
who fled from us as we could see by the tracks."[70]

Six leagues beyond this rancheria the Spaniards found an
abandoned pueblo near a marsh, probably to be identified with
either the ruins at Tuzigoot or Montezuma Castle National
Monument. The fleeing mountain people waited for the Spaniards near here, where they had built a hut of branches.

> Six paces from it was a large painted cross, and four small
> ones on the sides. All the men, women, and children were seated
> around with their heads low, singing of the peace they wished
> with us. They had crowns of painted sticks on their heads and
> *jicaras* [baskets] of mescal and pinon nuts and bread made
> from it.

These mountaineers

> gave us metals as a sign of peace and many of them came to
> show us the mines. In this locality we found many peaceful,
> rustic people who received us well. They had planted maize.
> We named this *ciénaga* that of San Gregorio.[71]

It seems certain that these maize-planting mountain Indians
are to be identified as a group of Western Apaches. Their use
of crowns of painted sticks immediately suggests Apache *Gaun*
("Mountain Spirit") dancers' headdresses, and their use of maize

[69] *Ibid.*, 106.
[70] *Ibid.*
[71] *Ibid.*, 107.

agrees with known facts about these Apaches. In historic times, this area of the Verde Valley near Tuzigoot and Montezuma Castle was a border area between the Western Apache and their Yavapai allies. In 1583 it was a border area between these mountain people and the Cruzado Indians, who have always been identified as the early Yavapai.[72]

From the Apache rancheria, the Spaniards marched four leagues to the mines, crossing midway "a large and copious river which flowed from north to south. We named it El Río de los Reyes." Thus they had apparently left the Verde and now returned to it, giving it a new name—although it is possible that the Río de las Parras was merely a branch of the Verde and not the main stream.[73] At the mines—in the area of present-day Jerome, Arizona—"many rustic people waited for us with crosses on their heads, even the children."[74] These were the Indians later known as the Cruzados because of their custom of wearing the cross. As mentioned above, they were undoubtedly the Yavapais—friends of the Western Apaches in the 1800's, as they seem to have been in 1583.

The mines proved to be a disappointment to Espejo, for there was no silver, only copper. As a result, he made his way back to Awatobi, meeting many peaceful mountain Apaches on the journey. By May 17 they were at Zuñi, where they met—and again disagreed with—the group led by Fray Beltrán. The latter determined upon returning to Nueva Vizcaya, whereas Espejo and eight other soldiers set off to visit the Tiwas and Maguas (eastern Tiwas or Tompiros). Pérez de Luxán says, "We took an interpreter to pacify the Tiguas, whom we had left in revolt. It is the place where the friars had been killed." The Indians evidently were anticipating the Spaniards' coming, for the invaders heard rumors that the Indians planned to kill them.[75]

On June 4 Espejo reached the area of Acoma and found the Indians in rebellion. The next day a free Concho servant, a Ton-

72 Grenville Goodwin, "Social Divisions of the Western Apache," *American Anthropologist*, Vol. XXXVII, No. 1 (1935), 56.
73 *Relation of Pérez de Luxán*, 107.
74 *Ibid.*
75 *Ibid.*, 110.

altecan Indian, and his Concho wife fled, laden with blankets and clothes (Pueblo Indian?). The Tonaltecan was found and shot by the Keres, and his wife was returned to the Spaniards. The free Concho went to the Zuñis. The Tonaltecan, before his death, confessed that Fray Beltrán had persuaded them to flee and had promised to wait for them ahead.[76]

More difficulties developed now as

> the people of Acoma and the neighboring mountaineers [Apaches] rebelled on account of this death [of the Tonaltecan, it seems] and kept shouting at us from the hills night and day. When we reached the cienaguilla of the Curechos [identified as Acomita, perhaps ten miles north of Acoma] with the camp, seeing the impudence of the Indians, we decided to give them a surprise that morning.[77]

The reasons for the hostility of the Keres and Apaches are not very clear. However, one motive may be involved—the fact that a Spaniard, Francisco Barreto, had acquired a Querecho woman at Mohoce and she had fled to her people that morning.[78] It is even possible that the Spaniards took the initiative in order to recapture the female slave.

In any case, the Spaniards mounted their horses and prepared to carry out a surprise attack upon the Indians. However, the latter became alarmed and opened fire with their arrows, wounding a horse. The Spaniards and their servants counterattacked, and "half of the men with all of the servants went to the rancheria and set fire to the huts. We destroyed also a very fine field of maize which they had." On the following day the Spaniards destroyed another maize field, in spite of Indian resistance. A woman was also captured, and on the afternoon of the following Sunday, the opposing forces agreed to an exchange. Francisco Barreto was to get his Quechero slave back in exchange for the woman recently captured.

The following day the "Corechos" tried to put over a "wicked"

76 *Ibid.*, 110–11.
77 *Ibid.*, 111–12. Obregón calls the marsh the *"Cienaguilla del Rosal"* belonging to the Querechos. *Obregón's History*, 332.
78 *Relation of Pérez de Luxán*, 112.

plan. They sent Barreto's slave home to her people and disguised a relative to look like her. When the supposed exchange was to take place, they hoped to get all the women and give the Spaniards only arrow shots. "This was planned with the help of one interpreter, who was another Indian woman belonging to Alonso de Miranda and who was trying to escape."[79] Thus we learn of one of the Spanish interests in New Mexico; acquiring Indian women as slaves. Barreto failed to get his first Indian woman back, but in a rough-and-tumble encounter, the impersonator and the woman interpreter were kept. Barreto and Pérez de Luxán risked their lives to keep these women, and both suffered wounds as a result.

Espejo determined to vacate the lands of the Apaches and Keres and decided to go through the lands of the Tiwas. The Spaniards journeyed to the Tiwa region and found that, in spite of peace offers, the Tiwa "would not bring their women to the pueblos," for all of them were in the sierra. The Spaniards then decided to punish the Indians in advance, to keep them from killing the Europeans.[80] The Indian men at Puaray and two near-by pueblos refused to give the Spaniards food, and when the latter found thirty men on the flat roofs of the pueblo, they seized them and placed them in a kiva.

> and as the pueblo was large and some had hidden themselves there we set fire to the big pueblo of Puala [Puaray] where we thought some were burned to death because of the cries they uttered. We at once took out the prisoners two at a time and lined them up against some poplars close to the pueblo of Puala and they were garroted and shot many times until they died. Sixteen were garroted, not counting those who burned to death. Some who did not seem to be of Puala were set free. This was a strange deed for so few people [the Spaniards] in the midst of so many enemies.[81]

Thus the deaths of Fray Rodríguez and Fray López were avenged, and the Indians were so intimidated that the Keres of the Río Grande Valley gave Espejo many "gifts" and supplies.

79 *Ibid.*, 112–13.
80 *Ibid.*, 115–16.
81 *Ibid.*, 116.

The Spaniards determined to return to Nueva Vizcaya by way of the buffalo plains, and thus they made their way to the Pecos area. The people of Pocos (or Pocoje) and the related pueblo of Siqui had built wooden palisades in front of their houses as a defensive measure, and they refused to aid the Spaniards. Six armed Europeans, however, were able to obtain supplies with the use of a little force. On July 5 the Espejo party left Siqui and "took two Indians by force to direct us to the buffalo."[82] They followed the Pecos River toward the south and after twenty leagues of travel reached a stream which entered the Pecos—calling it El Arroyo de las Garrochas "because we found many goad-sticks with which the Indians kill the buffalo." However, no Plains Apaches were seen, and one suspects that they were avoiding the Spaniards. Thirty-four leagues farther downstream, the party stopped at a place called *La Rancheria*.[83] This abandoned rancheria was large. It was also seen by Gaspar Castaño de Sosa in 1590 and was located one day's journey below the junction of the Río Hondo and the Pecos, on the west bank of the latter stream.

On July 30 the Spaniards reached a place where a large stream emptied into the Pecos, and, because they could see the "sierras of the Patarabueys [La Junta Indians]," they thought that the stream was one about which they knew. Five leagues farther to the south the Pecos River took its big bend towards the east, and fifteen leagues farther on the Spaniards met three Jumana (Jumano Apache) warriors who were hunting. This was probably somewhere near Toyah Lake, Texas.

By means of a Patarabuey slave owned by Pérez de Luxán, the Spaniards talked with the Jumanos and learned that the Pecos River flowed into the Río Grande far below La Junta, but the Jumanos knew a short cut and would guide the Spaniards. Two leagues farther on the Spaniards reached a stream up which they turned, and three leagues up this stream were

> many Jumana people from the rancheria of the people who
> were guiding us. They were on their way to the river to the

82 *Ibid.*, 118–20.
83 *Ibid.*, 121.

mesquite trees. We stopped on this stream where the rancheria was situated. The Indians, men and women, received us with music and rejoicing. As a sign of peace and happiness there was held a dance between the tents of the Indian men and women.[84]

The Espejo party continued up the stream (possibly a branch of Toyah Creek) for six leagues to its source. On their way they found "settled people of this nation [Jumano Apaches], who in their clothing are similar to the Patarabueys, except in their houses."[85] Thus it appears that as early as 1583 some of the Jumano Apaches were under the influence of the semisedentary La Junta culture.

The Spaniards continued for twenty-six leagues over mountains (the Davis Mountains) and through canyons and plains (the area between the Sierra Vieja and Chinati Peak) to reach the Río Grande fourteen leagues above La Junta. The Indians of the Cholome (Otomoaco) rancherias on the Río Grande gave them "quantities of ears of green corn, cooked and raw calabashes, and catfish." The same was done nine leagues down the Río Grande at the pueblo of San Bernaldino and five leagues farther on at La Junta.[86]

At La Junta, from August 22 to August 26,

> the companions all traded in blankets [from the Pueblo Indians?], of which they had many, bison skins, and Turkish bows reinforced with sinews. These are the best and strongest which there are in the land that has been discovered. They gave us calabashes, beans, and ears of green corn.[87]

Thus it is clear that the Espejo party brought back more than slaves from New Mexico.

By September 10 the Spaniards were once again at Santa Bárbara, having arrived there by a new route through the Toboso country east of the Conchos River Valley.

[84] *Ibid.*, 124.
[85] *Ibid.*, 125.
[86] *Ibid.*, 125–26.
[87] *Ibid.*, 126.

CHAPTER IV

The Lure of Wealth

🔯

The Chamuscado-Rodríguez and Espejo-Beltrán expeditions had been able to leave Nueva Vizcaya largely under the pretense of preaching to, or subduing, the Conchos Indians between Santa Bárbara and La Junta. They were "private initiative" affairs and lacked royal backing or, for that matter, approval. After 1583, however, the King, through his Viceroy, was better able to control affairs, and no new expeditions were legally allowed to go to New Mexico until 1598. Nevertheless, as shall be noted, several unauthorized groups did reach the northern regions, and Spaniards undoubtedly continued to go as far north as La Junta in search of slaves and booty.[1]

The northern frontier was far from quiet between 1583 and 1598, for the Chichimeca War was reaching a peak in the areas of Nueva Galicia and Saltillo, and a Spanish advance into present-day Coahuila precipitated warfare there. Slave-raiding bands of former Spanish soldiers were operating in the Nuevo León region, and, as mentioned before, the settlement of León was finally abandoned because of Indian hostility. The Saltillo area was continually aflame with war, and Indians robbed soldiers between that city and the Valley of Coahuila from 1582 to 1592.[2]

[1] The La Junta Indians were at war with the Spaniards in the late 1590's, in spite of peaceful relations with Espejo in 1583. Thus we are led to believe that new slave raids were made between 1584 and 1598.

[2] Arleguí, *Chrónica de la Provincia de Zacatecas*, 17.

In 1583 Luís Carabajal tried to pacify the Indians living between Nuevo León and the Gulf of Mexico, but this effort proved a failure and led only to continuous wars.[3] In 1587 the Guachichiles near Mazapil were raiding, and in 1588 all of the tribes in the Saltillo vicinity revolted.[4] The Coahuilas to the north joined the rebellion, and peace was not restored until 1595.[5]

Farther to the west the situation was the same, with the natives of Nueva Vizcaya in revolt—stealing horses and refusing to work in the mines. The governor, Rodrigo de Río de Losa, complained in 1591 that the Santa Bárbara region was suffering from a lack of Indians to work in the mines as well as from the wars of the enemy.[6] In northern Sinaloa an entire Spanish settlement was destroyed in the 1580's. These continuous wars, with mounted Indians as opponents, may have been the major factor in halting the Spanish advance between 1583 and 1598. The viceroys were forced to concentrate their efforts upon pacifying the Chichimecas of Nueva Galicia and their northern neighbors, the tribes of Nueva Vizcaya, Coahuila, and Nuevo León.[7]

Many adventurous Spaniards wished to test their mettle in New Mexico, however, and frequent petitions were presented to the royal officials. Espejo wrote an account of his expedition in 1583 with an eye toward being an *adelantado* or conquistador. Baltasar de Obregón wrote his history in 1585 for the same purpose. Other would-be conquerors were Cristóbal Martín in 1583 and Juan Bautista de Lomas in 1589.[8] The men who reached New Mexico prior to 1598 were, however, those who did not wait for royal favor but who took the initiative themselves. One such individual was Gaspar Castaño de Sosa, leader of the Spanish settlement at Almaden (now Monclova), in Coahuila.

In July, 1590 Castaño abandoned Almaden and, with all of

---

[3] *"Varias Noticias de las Misiones de las Fronteras de Nueva España," Virreinato de Méjico,"* tomo I, MN 567.

[4] Service of Francisco de Urdiñola, December 16, 1591, *Guadalajara* 28, in AGI.

[5] Report of Francisco de Urdiñola, July 7, 1595, *Guadalajara* 28, in AGI.

[6] Letter of Rodrigo de Río de Losa, October 25, 1591, *Guadalajara* 28, in AGI.

[7] The first legal expedition to New Mexico was authorized in 1595—the same year that many Chichimecos and Coahuilas made peace.

[8] *Colección de Documentos Inéditos,* XV, 63, XVI, 277.

the settlers, servants, livestock, and supplies loaded on wagons, set out to populate the supposedly rich land of New Mexico. This, of course, was an illegal enterprise, but the Spaniards probably hoped that once they had established a thriving new colony the royal officials would be pleased and give their blessings. It is also possible that they hoped to obtain booty in the new lands and return later to New Spain.

On July 28 they reached the Río de los Nadadores, where erstwhile friendly Indians stole some horses from them. September 9 saw the Spaniards on the banks of the Río Grande, perhaps near Del Rio, Texas. From that date until October 26 they struggled to cross rough and rugged lands to reach the Pecos River. Their task was made more difficult because they failed to realize that the Pecos turns west rather sharply near Sheffield, Texas, and they spent many days trying to locate the river. Finally they did succeed in getting their wagons and livestock to the river—probably near Sheffield—on October 26.[9]

This area was in the heart of the Jumano Apache country, and contact was soon made with the Indians. Soldiers had been instructed to follow any Indian sign and capture a native of the land so that the interpreters in the party could find out information on the route ahead. On October 27 Alonso Xaimez returned with a report, saying that he had followed the sign as Castaño had ordered and that

> at the end of three days he contacted a very large number of people of the Tepelguan nation [other version says "of the Depesguan nation"[10]]. He was very well received by them, and giving them to understand by means of an interpreter what their purpose was, they were very glad and gave them [the Spaniards] buffalo-skins, deer-skins, very nice shoes de su modo, much meat; and they gave them to understand that we could go by there, and that they would guide us to where there is much corn and settlements.[11]

9 Relation of Gaspar Castaño de Sosa, in *Colección de Documentos Inéditos*, IV, 284–95. Castaño de Sosa's party contained more than 170 persons.

10 *Ibid.*, XV, 207.

11 *Ibid.*, IV, 299.

68

These people were living on the Río Pecos, at a place where another stream entered it—probably near Girvin, Texas.

On October 28 the main Spanish party began moving up the Pecos, finding many Indian villages from which the natives had hastily departed. One Indian was seen, but none of the interpreters whom the Spaniards had brought from Almaden—who could speak various Uto-Aztecan and Coahuiltecan dialects—could make themselves understood.[12] On October 30 Castaño's party reached several old rancherias located near some marshes made by the river and spent the night in one of them.

These rancherias had first been reached by three Spanish soldiers who had seen

> some people traveling and they went to them and carried off [captured] four persons, because the rest fled, plunging into the marsh. These people had many loaded dogs, because it is the custom in that land, and they [the Spaniards] saw them loaded, a thing new to us, never seen [before].[13]

The prisoners—two women and two men—were interviewed by a Spanish officer, but they could not be understood, except by signs. They were then released with all the meat and corn that they could carry and "a dog loaded with two rolled-up skins; with its lariat or rope, and *taharria,* of which all were pleased to see since it was a new thing."[14] Thus these Spaniards were introduced to the Apache custom of using dogs for the transporting of goods.

These Jumano Apaches, who had received Espejo in a friendy manner in 1583, were obviously hostile to and afraid of the Spaniards in 1590. In 1583, and as late as the 1770's, these Apaches were very close friends and allies of the La Junta Indians, and their relations with the Spaniards were greatly influenced by the attitude of the Julimes and Cholomes. Thus it is very likely that their hostility in 1590 came about from more clashes between the Spaniards and the people at La Junta. Pos-

12 *Ibid.,* IV, 300.
13 *Ibid.,* IV, 300–301.
14 *Ibid.,* IV, 301.

sibly, slave raiders had even reached as far north as Jumano territory in the late 1580's.

In any case, it appears that on November 2 a small group of Spanish soldiers went ahead along the banks of the Pecos River to a site where they saw a body of Indian warriors. They talked with these warriors by means of signs for a while and then departed, leaving an Indian interpreter, Juan de Vega, alone. The Jumanos then threw Vega into the river, took his leather jacket, and gave him three arrow wounds. The next morning a large number of Indians were seen by Castaño's lieutenant, who had been out to search for lost horses. These Indians carried off a number of oxen from the Spanish herd, and the lieutenant and his men went out in pursuit. They made contact with the natives, who retreated, shooting arrows, and the Spaniards, in self-defense (as they said), killed some of the enemy and captured four Indians.[15]

As punishment for the carrying off of the oxen, one Jumano suffered death by hanging, and the other three, who were only youths, were given to three Spaniards. It was hoped that these would learn Spanish and serve as interpreters at a later time.[16]

Continuing up the Pecos River, Castaño reached, on November 5, a recently abandoned rancheria "which ought to have a great number of people, because it covered a very large area." Near by were found many pools of salt, and two days later very large sand dunes were seen.[17] The party was apparently in the vicinity of Imperial and Grandfalls, Texas. The balance of the Jumano Apache country was traversed without any further contact with the Indians, except that an Indian man and woman spent the night of November 14 near Castaño's camp, being afraid to stay with the Spaniards because of the invaders' previous killing of the Indians.

No further sign of habitation was seen by the expedition until November 23, when they reached a place where the river made a great turn to the west. Here, at a point just upstream from

15 *Ibid.*, IV, 301–302.
16 *Ibid.*, IV, 302.
17 *Ibid.*, IV, 302.

present-day Carlsbad, New Mexico, was found "a very large corral, where the Indians were in the habit of enclosing livestock."[18] Although the type of livestock involved is not indicated in the documents, one suspects that if the natives of southeastern New Mexico were able to obtain cattle or sheep, they must have had horses also. In any case, the livestock was probably some of that traded northward by the Nueva Vizcaya rebels to Quivira as early as 1574.[19]

Castaño's Spaniards were now entering the Seven Rivers Valley, well known from at least the 1650's as the home of a branch of the Faraon Apaches (now known as the Mescaleros). Documents of the 1620's indicate that *"los Siete Rios"* was probably occupied by "Vaquero Apaches," and in all likelihood it was part of Faraon *Apacheria* in 1590. Certainly the lands of the Jumano Apache lay farther to the south, for Espejo did not find the Jumanos until reaching the vicinity of Toyah Lake, Texas.

Smoke was seen in the sierra to the west—probably in the slopes of the Guadalupe Mountains—and on the following day, November 24, a large bow was found near an area of willow trees and wild grapevines. On November 26 the party crossed the river to the western side, having always traveled on the eastern bank until that time. Good grasslands were seen in this area, which was the halfway point for the Spaniards' journey up the Pecos River. This good land was apparently at the north end of present-day Lake McMillan. On November 29 the Spaniards camped in a grove of trees where they found "an *olla* and an ear of corn with the kernels recently removed."[20] This discovery pleased the party very much, for they presumed that they were nearing the lands of the corn-growing Pueblo Indians, but actually they were still some 250 miles from Pecos pueblo and in the lands of the Apache.

The next day a very large abandoned rancheria was discovered, apparently on the west bank of the Pecos River. This was *La Rancheria* found by Espejo in 1583 and probably belonged

---

[18] *Ibid.*, IV, 305.
[19] See Chapter II of this work.
[20] Relation of Castaño de Sosa, in *Colección de Documentos Inéditos*, IV, 307.

to an Apache group which had left the river valley for an autumn buffalo hunt. On the following day, December 1, the Spaniards worked their way through several miles of brush and reached the Río Hondo, which they found too deep to cross. As a result, they were forced to cross to the eastern bank of the Pecos and continue.[21]

Continuing upstream, the party found, on December 12, signs of people and very recently burned grassland. This location was apparently near Fort Sumner, for a large bend in the river was reached on the following day.[22] Finally, on December 23, advance scouts reported that from a summit in a sierra they could see Pecos pueblo. The next day they went to it and were well received, being allowed to spend the night with the Indians. However, the following day, after being given maize, the Spaniards were surprised when the Indians began shouting war cries and showering them with stones and arrows. The Spaniards retreated, with three wounded men, to a plaza and then fled to the rest of their expedition.

When Castaño's main army moved up to the pueblo, they found all of the people in arms. The pueblo had ramparts, walls, and stockades located in the places most necessary for defense.[23] The Spaniards could not quite understand why the pueblo was so well fortified until the Indians later told them that it was because they were at war with other peoples.[24] The Indians made use of their defenses against Castaño, but after a full day's battle, the Spaniards captured the pueblo. Never having seen a New Mexico Indian pueblo, the Coahuila Spaniards were very curious. The pueblo was explored, and sixteen kivas were seen. The houses were four and five stories high, there were five plazas, and the Indians had 30,000 bushels of maize.[25] Each person in the pueblo wore cotton blankets or shawls and on top of that buffalo-skin robes. Turkey feathers were used for decoration.[26]

21 *Ibid.*, IV, 307.
22 *Ibid.*, IV, 311.
23 Wooden palisades had surrounded "Pocos" in 1583. See *Relation of Pérez de Luxán*, 118–20.
24 Relation of Castaño de Sosa, in *Colección de Documentos Inéditos*, IV, 311–19.
25 *Ibid.*, IV, 329–30.
26 *Ibid.*, IV, 329–31.

On January 6, 1591 Castaño departed from Pecos, with the object of visiting the heart of New Mexico and looking for mines. Each Pecos Indian was required to contribute some supplies for the Spaniards to take on this journey.[27] While a portion of the group remained at Pecos with the wagons, the balance, led by Castaño, made their way to the Río Grande Valley, where they visited many pueblos before returning to the camp on January 27. On January 30 the entire expedition left Pecos and journeyed to the Río Grande Valley by an indirect route, visiting many new pueblos. Finally, they reached the Tiwa region and near some sierras discovered two abandoned pueblos and signs of a bloody struggle. The pueblos had evidently been attacked by enemies and destroyed.

The Spaniards then went to the Río Grande, which lay above the two abandoned pueblos, and learned that these pueblos were the ones where the priests had been killed.[28] Thus they were Tiwa villages, and in all likelihood, they had been destroyed by Espejo in 1583. The Indians living in the vicinity were afraid of the Spaniards in 1591—even those living on the other side of the river.[29] Many other abandoned pueblos were found, although Castaño was able to make peaceful contact with some.

The power of the Spanish Crown eventually caught up with Gaspar Castaño de Sosa, for Captain Juan Morlete was sent to New Mexico by the Viceroy. Castaño was arrested, and the expedition made its way back to New Spain by way of El Paso and Nueva Vizcaya.[30] Very little is known of this journey, except that the Spaniards took ten wagons with them—the ruts were seen by Oñate at El Paso in 1598. About six leagues before reaching El Paso, Captain Morlete had four Indians hung "be cause they robbed some horses from them."[31] This region was inhabited by the Manso Indians, but whether or not they were the horse thieves one cannot know. In any case, it is significant that Indians near El Paso were interested in, and capable of,

27 *Ibid.*, IV, 332.
28 *Ibid.*, IV, 350.
29 *Ibid.*, IV, 351.
30 Bolton, *Spanish Explorations*, 200.
31 "Discurso de la Jornada," in *Colección de Documentos Inéditos*, XVI, 245.

stealing horses in 1591. Coupled with the presence of a corral for livestock on the Pecos River, it indicates that by the 1590's the Indians of at least southern New Mexico and Texas were becoming horse users.

The enthusiasm of the would-be conquerors of New Mexico was in no way diminished by the passage of time, and in 1595 an application for royal approval was successfully made by Juan de Oñate, a Spaniard with the right "connections." Interestingly enough, one of this petitioner's requests was for "Indians that are to be found in this city of Mexico of the Tataragueyes nation [the La Junta Indians], for they are the nearest to that province [of New Mexico], and in particular an Indian woman [the Querecho of Pérez de Luxán's journal?] who was brought from New Mexico" to be used as interpreters.[32]

For a time it seemed that, in spite of royal approval, Oñate's plans might be frustrated as a new illegal expedition led by Captain Francisco Leyva de Bonilla penetrated to the New Mexico region. In 1593, under orders of Diego Fernandez de Velasco, Leyva left with a large party of soldiers to attack the Tobosos, Gavilanes, and other Nueva Vizcaya rebels who were raiding and stealing livestock. Instead of being content with this limited objective, Leyva and his men determined upon going on to New Mexico, undoubtedly with the hope of acquiring quick wealth. Fernandez de Velasco sent Captain Pedro de Cazorla after the group, ordering them to return or be declared traitors to the King. Leyva would not listen to Cazorla, but some of his men took the sound advice and abandoned the enterprise.[33]

Very little is known of the Leyva de Bonilla expedition, and this is unfortunate, for when one considers the type of adventurers who were involved, their aims, and the fact that they were outlaws to begin with, it is highly probable that they committed many outrages among the Pueblo and Apache Indians. It is known that they spent about a year at San Ildefonso pueblo in New Mexico and that they caused such fear to arise among the

---

32 Petition of Don Juan de Oñate, 1595, in Hackett, *Historical Documents*, I, 235.
33 Villagutierre y Sotomayor, BN 2822.

Pueblo Indians that as late as 1601 the Leyva soldiers were being blamed for Indian antagonism against the Spaniards. It was said that the invaders took some Indian women as slaves, among other things.[34]

In 1594 the Spanish adventurers left New Mexico, apparently with the aim of rediscovering Coronado's long-lost Quivira. They visited Pecos pueblo and then went out onto the plains to a great pueblo of the Vaqueros (Plains Apaches). This village of *jacales* was described as being about 150 leagues to the northeast of New Mexico, being so large that it covered 7 leagues of land.[35] Still another description refers to this village of the Vaqueros as being 9 continuous leagues in length and 2 in width, with streets and houses of *jacales* (huts). "It is situated in the midst of the multitude of buffalo."[36]

Leyva and his soldiers wandered about in the buffalo country and then turned northward to some large rivers, finally reaching a great village of grass lodges, with corn but no gold. Shortly thereafter, as a climax to bitter dissensions, a soldier named Antonio Gutiérrez de Humaña murdered Captain Leyva de Bonilla and assumed command of the expedition.[37] Several Mexican Indians who had been brought as servants now fled, and one of them named Jusepe finally made his way back to New Mexico, living among the Vaquero Apaches for about a year. The dissension probably took place along the Arkansas River among the Wichita group of Indians.[38]

The Spaniards, now led by Humaña, apparently went north as far as the Kansas River and then turned back into the lands

34 Testimony of Joan de Ortega, July 31, 1601, *México,* 26, in AGI.

35 Testimony of Jusepe Vrondate, July 28, 1601, *México* 26, in AGI.

36 Letter of Juan de Oñate, March 2, 1599, in Bolton, *Spanish Explorations,* 218–19.

37 For details see Villagutierre y Sotomayor, BN 2822; Bolton, *Spanish Explorations,* 201 n.; and Zarate Salmerón, *"Virreinato de Méjico,"* tomo I, MN 567.

38 Spanish material has been found in association with Wichita materials dating from this period. Some anthropologists have regarded this as evidence of the Coronado expedition of 1542 or the Oñate journey of 1601. However, neither of these groups are reported to have lost any equipment, while the Humaña party lost everything. Thus it seems likely that the pieces of chain armour and other items found were left in 1594 or 1595 by the Humana group. See Waldo R. Wedel, "Culture Chronology in the Central Great Plains," *American Antiquity,* Vol. XII, No. 3 (January, 1947).

of Quivira (the Wichita people). Here, according to later testimony, they were destroyed by the Quivirans. The story is that the Spaniards had found so much gold that they were worn out with the hauling of it and as they rested the Indians set fire to the grass around them. As a result, all were killed except one Spanish boy, Alonso Sánchez, and a mulatto woman who was half-burned. When the Oñate expedition reached the western part of Quivira in 1601 they found "some things of iron, some boots (or wine bags), and the bones of the horses." They also learned that the boy and the woman were still alive.[39] Thus the Wichita Indians had apparently by-passed an excellent opportunity for obtaining horses by burning them with the Spaniards.

Meanwhile, in New Spain Juan de Oñate was attempting to gather together men and supplies for his projected expedition into New Mexico. He suffered serious delays, for it seems he had many enemies. Nevertheless, men were gradually recruited; numerous inspections were held; and by 1597 the final inspections were ready to be made. Oñate was supposed to provide 200 men, and in January, 1597 he had had 205, but by the end of that year this number had decreased to 129. Likewise, he failed to provide the amounts of livestock agreed upon, but this was partly due to the impoverished condition of the frontier.[40] On May 4, 1598 the Viceroy wrote to the King of Spain that the frontier provinces were exhausted because of the long presence of Oñate's army there "and because most of the people who go on new discoveries are troublesome."[41]

If they were troublesome to their fellow Spaniards, what were they to be in New Mexico?

Early in 1598 Oñate felt ready to begin the journey to New Mexico. The main army followed the Conchos River to its junction with the San Pedro, and from there, on February 14, the

[39] Zarate Salmerón, "*Virreinato de Méjico,*" tomo I, MN 567, and Bolton, *Spanish Explorations,* 201. Another copy of Zarate Salmerón's account is printed in *Documentos para la Historia de México,* Series 3, I, 27, hereinafter cited as *Documentos—México.*

[40] George P. Hammond and Agapito Rey (eds. and trans.), *Don Juan de Oñate, Colonizer of New Mexico, 1595–1628,* I, 12, 14, 215–16, 220, 228, hereinafter cited as *Oñate Documents.*

[41] Count of Monterrey to the King, May 4, 1598, in *Oñate Documents,* I, 391.

New Mexico, 1600-1700

Sargento Mayor Vicente de Zaldívar (Oñate's nephew) was sent to discover a new, shorter route to the El Paso region. Another reason for not going by way of La Junta, however, was because the Patarabuey Indians were at war with the Spaniards.[42]

Zaldívar, with sixteen to eighteen companions, began to cut across country in order to reach the Río Grande. His guides proved useless, and the party began to suffer from thirst and hunger. By chance they struck upon an Indian village of 200 huts and two Spaniards wormed their way up to a position where they could observe the rancheria at close hand. Their report led to the adoption of the following plan: Part of the men would sneak up on the Indians, begin yelling, and send loose horses running among the habitations. Another group would discharge all the firearms, while a third party under Gaspar de Villagrá would rush into the camp and destroy all of the Indians' bows, arrows, and other arms. The plan worked to perfection, and four Indians were captured in the process.[43]

These Indians were either Conchos, Chinarras, or Sumas, but the probabilities are that they were Conchos. In any case, two of them, called Mompit (or Mompil) and Milco, were used as guides and were promised two beautiful horses when the Spaniards reached the Río Grande.[44] Subsequently, they were joined by Milco's wife Polca who came after her husband, and on February 28 they reached the Río Grande. Perhaps Milco received his horse here, but Mompil did not, for he had run away about five days before.[45] On March 7 Zaldívar returned to Oñate's camp, having pioneered the route and also aroused hostility.[46]

The army reached the Río Grande on April 20, and on the way Oñate made peace with the offended natives. After a rest, an act of possession was made on April 30, and on May 3, eight and one-half leagues farther upstream (near El Paso), the first

[42] Letter of Juan de Oñate, March 15, 1598, in Hackett, *Historical Documents,* I, 397.

[43] Villagutierre y Sotomayor, BN 2822.

[44] *Ibid.* This is another indication of the northward spread of the horse, since Zaldívar would not give horses to Indians unless they could get them on their own.

[45] *Ibid.,* and Letter of Juan de Oñate, March 15, 1598, in Hackett, *Historical Documents,* I, 397.

[46] "*Discurso de la Jornada,*" in *Colección de Documentos Inéditos,* XVI, 234.

Manso Indians were met as eight came to camp. On the following day forty Indians with "Turkish" bows, with their hair cut in such a way that it looked like a Milan cap, and with a crest made stiff with blood or some other substance, appeared. Their first words were *"manxo, manxo, micos, micos, por decir mansos y amigos"* ["for saying tame and friends"], and they held their fingers up in the sign of a cross.[47] Thus these Athapascans came to be known as the Mansos, that is, the tame; however, they were not very tame in later years.

Oñate had undoubtedly heard how the southernmost Pueblo Indians, the Piros, abandoned their pueblos and went to the sierras whenever a party of Spaniards appeared, and, as a result, Captain Pablo de Aguilar was sent ahead to reconnoiter the situation in secret. Disobeying Oñate's orders, Aguilar entered the first pueblo, thus allowing the Indians to be forewarned. Oñate was so furious that he wished to have Aguilar killed, but he was persuaded to be lenient. The Governor then gathered together fifty men to rush to the Piro pueblos before the Indians could spread the news, carry off their supplies, and abandon the pueblo.[48] Nevertheless, all of the Piro pueblos were found to be empty except one called Teipana, and here, on June 14, the Spaniards got the maize that they needed. Thus the pueblo was named Socorro, a name which a town on the same site bears today.[49]

Upon his arrival in New Mexico, Oñate had trouble with a band of forty-five men who were disappointed at not finding silver on the ground (as Oñate put it) and tried to return to New Spain. Their real intention, however, was to take slaves and clothing and commit other outrages upon the Indians. Oñate was at first going to strangle three of them, but subsequently decided not to. It is possible that this may refer to the episode of Captain Aguilar mentioned previously.[50]

Like the Piros, the Tiwas were very upset by the coming of Spaniards again, and Oñate found many pueblos empty. On

[47] *Ibid.,* XVI, 243–44.
[48] Villagutierre y Sotomayor, BN 2822.
[49] *"Discurso de la Jornada,"* in *Colección de Documentos Inéditos,* XVI, 250–51.
[50] Oñate to Viceroy, March 2, 1599, in *Oñate Documents,* I, 481.

June 27 they passed Puaray, where the priests had been killed in 1582, and in July they reached the Keres pueblo of Santo Domingo, where, on July 7, Oñate assembled representatives of some thirty-one pueblos in the vicinity and made them all subjects of the King of Spain.[51] In all likelihood, the Indians did not quite realize what was taking place, or, if they did, they put up with it only to humor the possession-taking Spaniards. However, in later years, whenever a pueblo was to seek independence, the sons of Cortés always held them to be in rebellion, for they had "willingly" rendered obedience in 1598.

Anxious to pacify all of New Mexico, the Spaniards visited in quick succession the pueblos of Picuris, Taos, San Xupal, Galisteo, Pecos, and Jemez. By September 9, Oñate was back at his headquarters, the Tewa pueblo of San Juan, where he received the submission of many more representatives from various settlements. On this date priests were assigned also. Fray Francisco de San Miguel received the area from Pecos and Galisteo south to the Tompiro region and including "all the vaqueros of that mountain-range and neighborhood as far as the Sierra Nevada [Sangre de Christo range]."[52] Even the Eastern Apaches (who had not rendered submission) were to receive the blessings of Christianity.

Fray Francisco de Zamora was to receive Picuris pueblo and "all the Apaches from the Sierra Nevada towards the north and west, and the province of the Taos with the pueblos in her·neighhood; and those of the banks of the Río Grande of that mountain-range."[53] Fray Juan de Rosas received the Keres region, and Fray Alonso de Lugo was assigned to the Jemez and "all the Apades [sic] and Cocoyes of its sierras and neighborhood."[54] Friars Andrés Corchado, Juan Claros, and Christóbal de Salazar received the balance of the area, including the lands of the Hopis, Zuñis, Keres of Acoma, Piros, and—for the latter priest —the Tewa pueblos of San Juan and San Gabriel.[55]

51 "Traslado a la posesión . . . ," in Colección do Documentos Inéditos, XVI, 102.
52 Ibid., XVI, 113.
53 Ibid., XVI, 114.
54 Ibid., XVI, 114.

In mid-September, 1598 Vicente de Zaldívar was sent to explore the buffalo plains to the east of Pecos pueblo. On September 21 he reached the Gallinas River and, according to one account, met four Vaquero Apaches there. They were regaled by the Spaniards, and one of them arose and called out, whereupon many Indians who had been hidden came and made friends with the Europeans. The Vaqueros were described as "powerful people and expert bowmen," and they gladly furnished Zaldívar with a guide.[56]

According to another account, the Spaniards reached the river and came upon

> a ridiculous figure in human form, with ears almost half a yard long, a snout horrible in the extreme, a tail that almost dragged, dressed in a very tight fitting pellico, which encircled the body and was all stained with blood; with his bow in his hand, and quiver of arrows at his shoulder.

The Spaniards caught this weird figure and took off his mask, discovering that he was a "savage Indian," but a very frightened, embarrassed, and ashamed one. The Apache asked the Spaniards to spare his life and return his mask. He said that he had worn it in jest, hoping to scare the Europeans so that they would flee and leave their baggage.[57]

Farther on, Zaldívar's party came upon an Indian who was totally white, with blueish eyes and a graceful and respectable appearance. Behind him came a fair-sized party of Indian warriors. The white Indian advanced without a word, and in an extremely dignified manner he scrutinized the fifty Spaniards. Zaldívar, wishing to instill fear and astonishment in the Apaches, had one of his men discharge a musket. This apparently intimidated the Indians, and they agreed to furnish a guide for the journey ahead. The guide was very fearful, however, and, in spite of the fact that he was closely guarded, he managed to escape.[58] The soldier who had been watching the Apache, Marcos

[55] *Ibid.*, XVI, 114–15.
[56] Bolton, *Spanish Explorations*, 224.
[57] Villagutierre y Sotomayor, BN 2822.
[58] *Ibid.*

Cortés, tried to apprehend the fleeing Indian; however, the latter was such a swift runner that it proved impossible. Cortés was fortunate, however, in that he came upon a group of twelve Indians chasing a deer. The Spaniard shot the deer and had the Apaches come with him bringing their laden dogs to Zaldívar's camp. Cortés was welcomed with great gusto by the guideless Spaniards, and he was acclaimed for his feat of capturing twelve Apaches. He, on the other hand, being quite modest, said that, if there had been one hundred Indians, he would have done the same thing.

Zaldívar then made use of all twelve of the Vaquero Apaches as guides, soon reaching the buffalo country. Here he took special pains to have his soldiers show the Indians that Marcos Cortés' shooting of the deer was no mere accident. The Spaniards demonstrated their marksmanship for the specific purpose of intimidating the Apaches. Finally, on the return journey, the Apaches were released with gifts, and other Vaqueros were also regaled.[59]

The other account of the expedition indicates that six leagues of travel after acquiring the first guides Zaldívar met three Indians. Their village was only one league away, and the *Sargento Mayor* and his interpreter (Jusepe, the Mexican Indian who had escaped from the Humaña expedition) went to visit them that night. The *Sargento Mayor's* account says:

> Most of the men go naked, but some are clothed with skins of buffalo and some with blankets. The women wear a sort of trousers made of buckskin, and shoes or leggins, after their own fashion.

Zaldívar offered them protection from their enemies and

> they asked him for aid against the Xumanas, as they call a tribe of Indians who are painted after the manner of the Chichimecos.[60]

These "Xumanas" may have been the Jumano Apaches, who

[59] *Ibid.*
[60] Bolton, *Spanish Explorations*, 225.

were sometimes hostile to other Apaches, or they may have been some other group of painted Indians.

Twenty-three leagues farther to the east Zaldívar reached the Canadian River, where he hoped to see large numbers of buffalo,

> but when he reached the river the buffalo had left, because just then many Vaquero Indians crossed it, coming from trading with the Picuries and Taos, populous pueblos of this New Mexico, where they sell meat, hides, tallow, suet, and salt in exchange for cotton, blankets, pottery, maize, and some small green stones which they use.[61]

These Plains Apaches set up a village of fifty tipis

> made of tanned hides, very bright red and white in color and bell-shaped, with flaps and openings . . . and so large that in the most ordinary ones four different mattresses and beds were easily accommodated.

Zaldívar himself bartered for a tipi and found that, in spite of its size, it weighed less than fifty pounds.

> To carry this load, the poles that they use to set it up, and a knapsack of meat and their pinole, or maize, the Indians use a medium-sized shaggy dog. . . . They drive great trains of them. . . . It is a sight to see them traveling, the ends of the poles dragging on the ground, nearly all of them snarling in their encounters.[62]

According to Zaldívar, the Apaches were numerous on the plains near the Canadian River.

> The weapons consist of flint and very large bows, after the manner of the Turks. They saw some arrows with their long thick points, although few, for the flint is better than spears to kill buffalo. They kill them at the first shot with the greatest skill, while ambushed in brush blinds made at the watering places.[63]

The *Sargento Mayor* failed to capture any buffalo, as he had

[61] *Ibid.*, 226.
[62] *Ibid.*, 227.
[63] *Ibid.*, 230.

hoped to do, and on November 8, 1598 he returned to San Juan pueblo. At San Juan he found that Juan de Oñate had left in October to explore certain unseen sections of New Mexico, and Juan de Zaldívar had been left in charge of the headquarters. Vicente now assumed command at San Juan, and Juan went on, supposedly to join Oñate in the Zuñi or Hopi country, but actually to meet death at Acoma.

A Western (White Mountain) Apache jacal or wickiup. Similar dwellings were used by the Janos, Jocomes, Mansos, and Sumas.

Courtesy Southwest Museum
J. A. Munk Collection

An Apache Camp. This one belonged to the Jicarillas, but it was probably similar to those of the Plains Apaches in general. From a photograph by W. H. Jackson in 1884.

Courtesy Southwest Museum

Two Navaho warriors, armed with lance, bow, and knife. Drawing from Lieut. A. W. Whipple, *Report of Explorations for a Railway Route . . . from the Mississippi River to the Pacific Ocean* (Washington, 1855).

Courtesy Southwest Museum

CHAPTER V

Death and Destruction

On October 6, 1598, Juan de Oñate departed from San Juan in order to visit, and receive the submissions of, the eastern Tewas, Tompiros, Keres of Acoma, Zuñis, and the Hopis. He traveled along the eastern slopes of the Sandia and Manzano Mountains to Abo and then eastward to the Tompiro pueblos called *"de los Xumanas o rayados."* The term "Jumano" in its various forms was used by the Spaniards of this period, 1598–1602, to denote Indians with a certain type of painting or marking on their faces. The evidence is not absolutely clear, but it seems likely that the marking consisted in a line drawn across the face and over the bridge of the nose.[1] Several closely associated Tompiro pueblos (now located at Gran Quivira National Monument)[2] were the only groups to make use of this style of decoration among the Pueblo Indians, and these were called "Jumanos."[3] They are to be clearly distinguished from other *indios rayados* ("striped Indians") who were also called by this name.

From the Tompiros Oñate led his party westward to Acoma,

[1] One Spaniard says, *"Un pueblo que llaman de los Jumenes que quiere decir yndios rayados porque tienen encima de la nariz una raya."* Testimony of Marcos Leandro, July 30, 1601, *México* 26, in AGI.

[2] See G. Kubler, "Gran Quivira-Humanas," *New Mexico Historical Review*, Vol. XIV, No. 4 (1939), 418–21, and France V. Scholes and H. P. Mera, "Some Aspects of the Jumano Problem," Carnegie Institution *Contributions to American Anthropology and History*, Vol. VI, Nos. 30–34 (1940).

[3] *Ibid.*, 285.

where he received a liberal "donation" of maize and fowls, going from there to Zuñi and the Hopi pueblos. At the latter place Oñate learned of supposedly rich mines located to the west, and as a result he dispatched Captain Marcos Farfan de los Godos and eight men over approximately the same route as followed by Espejo in 1583. The party crossed the Little Colorado River and angled into the highlands south of Flagstaff. There, in the same area where Espejo had met mountain people in 1583, the Spaniards met some "Jumana" Indians living in four of five rancherias. Farfan conversed with them by means of signs and reassured them. In all probability they were the same Western Apaches who inhabited the area six years later and fifteen years before.[4] After another six or eight leagues of travel, the Spaniards came upon another Indian village and beyond that another in which they met Indians called Cruzados in one of the accounts. These Indians were stained with ores, and the women and children were dressed in the skins of deer, otter, and other animals.[5]

Nine leagues farther to the west the party crossed the main fork of the Verde River and reached the mines near present-day Jerome, Arizona.

It is to be expected that the mines reached by Espejo in 1583 and Farfan in 1598 were one and the same, since the geographical descriptions and locations are so very much alike and since the mines were known to the Hopis, who probably furnished guides for both expeditions. Thus one would suspect that there was a well-used Indian trail from the Hopi pueblos to the mines, and this trail would have been followed by any Hopi guides.[6]

The Farfan account, the Espejo documents, and later journals of 1599 and 1604–1605 agree that there were two groups of people to be found southwest of the Hopis: the first group being the mountain, striped people (the Western Apache) and the second group being the Cruzados, or Yavapai. Thus the tribal situation in the Flagstaff-Jerome region was more or less the same

---

[4] Bolton, *Spanish Explorations*, 240–41.

[5] *Ibid.*, 242–43, and "*Discurso de la Jornada*," in *Colección de Documentos Inéditos*, XVI, 276.

[6] The ores, according to Farfan, were used to color the Hopi blankets. See Bolton, *Spanish Explorations*, 244.

in 1583, 1598, 1599, and 1605, as it was to be in the 1850's.[7] Farfan noted, as did Espejo, that the Indians of the Verde Valley region were growing maize, a trait carried into the historic period as well.[8]

When Farfan brought back ore specimens from the mines, Oñate remarked that "more than one hundred men in this camp, who were languishing for want of metals to smelt were reanimated."[9] It is possible that the center of Spanish interest in the north might have been transferred at this time from the Río Grande Valley to the Flagstaff-Hopi region, but for a forceful declaration of independence made by the Keres Indians of Acoma pueblo.

On October 26, 1598 Oñate and his large party had passed by Acoma, and there "the Indians furnished us liberally with maize, water, and fowls" as well as agreeing to be subjects of the King of Spain.[10] On December 1, Juan de Zaldívar and a body of soldiers reached Acoma on their way from San Juan to join Oñate, and their reception bore different fruit. The accounts differ as to just what did occur, but it seems that Zaldívar made a request (or demand) for supplies and blankets which the Indians were loath to meet—having just contributed to Oñate a month before. Several days elapsed, during which time Zaldívar and his men waited for the Acomas to gather the goods together. On December 4 eighteen Spaniards and servants entered the pueblo, leaving the balance of the men with the horses. Then, according to the "official" account set forth by Oñate and his officers, the Keres rebelled because they did not want to give

[7] The Apaches west of the Río Grande did use stripes and other markings on their faces. As late as 1886, Chiricahua warriors painted horizontal white streaks across their noses and upper cheeks. Western Apaches often used more intricate decorations as well. Southwest Museum Library Collection of Apache Photographs, Southwest Museum, Los Angeles, California.

[8] Bolton, *Spanish Explorations*, 246.

[9] *Oñate Documents*, I, 396. However, Oñate may have been fooling his followers. The mines found by Espejo were "worthless" copper deposits with no silver, and in a letter to the King, on March 31, 1605, Viceroy Montesclaros said that ores sent him by Oñate contained only one-eighth copper and no silver. France V. Scholes, "Juan Martínez de Montoya, Settler and Conquistador of New Mexico," *New Mexico Historical Review*, Vol. XIX, No. 4 (1944), 338 n.

[10] *Oñate Documents*, I, 394.

up any supplies; and fifteen men, including Zaldívar, were killed.[11] Other accounts and the testimony of certain Acomas reveal, however, that the fighting was caused by the forcible acquisition of goods by a Spaniard or Spaniards. One source indicates that the cause was "an outrage that a soldier made upon an Indian woman, taking away from her a blanket or a turkey."[12]

Another Spaniard, in a private letter, remarked that a Spaniard "took two turkeys from the Indians. And they killed him from one of the terraces. The entire pueblo then rose in arms."[13] Indian declarants mention the turkey affair, but also add that the Spaniards "asked for such large amounts" of maize and flour, that an Indian was killed or wounded by Zaldívar's men, and that this situation started the actual fighting.[14]

In 1601 several Spaniards were sent by the Viceroy to check up on Oñate, and one of these men, Marcos Leandro, was told in secret by the commissary of the missions, Fray Juan de Escalona, what had actually taken place. According to Escalona, who was Oñate's enemy, Zaldívar and his men asked for

> supplies, turkeys and blankets and began to take them by force and seeing this the Indians began to resist them and defend themselves and they [Escalona and others] have told this declarant [Leandro] that the Spaniards killed one of the Indians and with stones and rocks the said Indians killed the Spaniards.[15]

A few months later Escalona wrote to the Viceroy that Zaldívar took maize and blankets by force, "burning some houses and killing some Indians, because of which the war of Acoma erupted."[16]

Whether or not we accept the testimony of Oñate's enemies,

---

[11] *Colección de Documentos Inéditos,* XVI, 223, and *Oñate Documents,* I, 429.

[12] Testimony of Joan de Ortega, July 31, 1601, *México* 26, in AGI.

[13] Letter of Alonso Sánchez, February 28, 1599, in *Oñate Documents,* I, 426.

[14] *Oñate Documents,* I, 464–67. Captain Luís Velasco, in a letter to the Viceroy, said that the Acomas gave Zaldívar plentiful supplies of food but declined to give up any blankets. The Spaniards then began to "abuse" the Indians, who defended themselves. See Letter of Captain Velasco, March 22, 1601, in *Oñate Documents,* II, 614.

[15] Testimony of Marcos Leandro, July 30, 1601, *México* 26, in AGI.

[16] Letter of Fray Juan de Escalona, October 10, 1601, *México* 26, Ramo I, in AGI.

it is clear that the Keres of Acoma were justified in attempting to resist the excessive demands of the Spaniards. Their legitimate resistance was, however, to earn them the deep enmity of Juan de Zaldívar's brother, Vicente, and of his uncle, Juan de Oñate. The resulting atrocities perpetuated by the Spanish forces are extremely significant for an understanding of the rapid development of hostility between the Navaho Apaches and the Europeans during the next few years. The Apaches were allies of the Acomas in 1583, as noted previously, and in 1598 or early 1599 the latter asked the Athapascans for aid in the person of Bempol, an Apache war chief.[17] Therefore, it is possible that some Apaches were at Acoma in January, 1599 when the famous battle occurred.

Early in January Oñate, now at San Juan, issued the orders that were to be followed in the punishment of the Keres. Vicente de Zaldívar was to lead some seventy well-armed soldiers to Acoma; there he was to offer the Indians peace at least three times; and, if they refused, he was to attack. This peace offer, however, was nothing but a mockery, for the conditions were that the Keres had to leave their pueblo, turn themselves over to the Spaniards, and see their homes absolutely and completely destroyed. Obviously, the terms were such that the Acomas would never accept them, and this may have been Oñate's plan.

> Inasmuch as we have declared war on them without quarter, you will punish all those of fighting age as you deem best, as a warning to everyone in this kingdom. All of those you execute you will expose to public view. . . . If you should want to show lenience after they have been arrested, you should seek all possible means to make the Indians believe that you are doing so at the request of the friar with your forces. In this manner they will recognize the friars as their benefactors and protectors and come to love and esteem them, and to fear us.[18]

The poor Keres of Acoma were to be an example. They were destroyed, not merely in revenge for the death of Zaldívar, but

17 Gaspar Pérez de Villagrá, *History of New Mexico* (trans. by Gilberto Espinosa), 213.

18 Juan de Oñate, January 11, 1599, in *Oñate Documents*, I, 458–59.

to show the other Indians of New Mexico that it was suicidal to revolt against their Spanish masters.

In the massacre on the mesa of Acoma at least 800 men, women, and children were murdered in cold blood. That they were murdered is evident from the fact that such carnage was planned in advance, that no Spaniards were killed in the fighting, and that, by the Spaniard's own admission, a good part of the Keres died in the kivas of the pueblo, where they had hidden and entrenched themselves. Midway in the massacre, which lasted several days, the Indians attempted to surrender and receive mercy with a payment of blankets and other booty, but Zaldívar would not allow it. However, the booty was appropriated afterwards, anyway. Instead he began to bring up prisoners one by one to be cut to pieces and thrown off the cliff. When the Keres refused to be slaughtered helplessly and instead took refuge in their kivas, where they entrenched themselves, the Spanish commander ordered the war without quarter resumed. According to his testimony, the war of "blood and fire" was ordered to *save* the Indians who were committing mass suicide. Other sources, however, do not support this assertion, and one soldier who was there said that the Spaniards used artillery, and thus "we forced the Indians to fight."[19]

The result was that 500 men were killed, along with 300 women and children. About 500 women and children and 80 men were taken alive, thus making a total of 1,380 Keres.[20] Oñate estimated Acoma's original population at about 3,000, which, of course, is probably an overestimate. Nevertheless, some Keres probably did escape death or imprisonment and fled to the sierras, very possibly to the Navahos.

The pueblo of Acoma was, as Oñate had ordered, completely destroyed, and the 500 or 600 prisoners were marched to San Juan, where they were sentenced:

[19] Letter of Alonso Sánchez, February 28, 1599, in *Oñate Documents*, I, 427. For other accounts of the massacre, see *ibid.*, I, 460–73; Villagrá, *History of New Mexico*, 213–63; and many documents in AGI (*México* 26). See also Letter of Captain Luís Velasco, March 22, 1601, in *Oñate Documents*, II, 614.

[20] Letter of Alonso Sánchez, February 28, 1599, in *Oñate Documents*, I, 427. The author says that 500 men were killed and that a total of 800 persons died.

The males who are over twenty-five years of age I sentence to have one foot cut off and to twenty years of personal servitude.

Males between the ages of twelve and twenty-five and all women over twelve received sentences of twenty years of slavery. Girls under the age of twelve were turned over to Fray Alonso Martínez to be distributed, "in this kingdom or elsewhere"; the boys were to go to Vicente de Zaldívar.[21] From the beginning, however, the Keres fled from slavery, and gradually a community was re-established on the mesa of Acoma. By 1601 most of the slaves had escaped, and their refounded pueblo—as one might well imagine—became a center of anti-Spanish feeling.[22] It remained as such until at least 1603 or 1604, when nominally peaceful relations were established with the *Castellanos*.[23]

Very little is known of the relations of the Athapascans with the Spaniards and Pueblo Indians during the years of 1599 to 1601. Oñate wrote in 1599 of the

> Querechos, or baqueros, who live in tents of tanned hides, among the buffalo; the Apiches [Apaches], of whom we have also seen some, are infinite in number; and although I had news that they lived in rancherias; a few days ago I have ascertained [that] they live as these [Pueblo Indians] in towns, and they have one, eighteen leagues from here, of fifteen plazas; it is a people who still haven't rendered obedience to His Majesty by public instruments.[24]

It was claimed by advocates of Vicente de Zaldívar that prior to his journey to the Plains in 1598 the Vaqueros were enemies of the Pueblo Indians and that Zaldívar changed this relationship to one of peace and trade. This, however, is certainly not

21 Juan de Oñate, February 12, 1599, in *Oñate Documents*, I, 477.

22 Testimony of Marcos Leandro, July 30, 1601, *México* 26, in AGI.

23 Scholes, "Juan Martínez de Montoya," *New Mexico Historical Review*, Vol. XIX, No. 4 (1944), 339. The Viceroy wrote to the King in October, 1599, in reference to the "great cruelty perpetuated by some soldiers of Don Juan at a pueblo named Acoma." The royal *audiencia* took up the matter but decided "not to proceed against the latter [soldiers of Oñate] in order not to discourage the soldiers and the people." Letter of the Count of Monterrey, October 4, 1599, in *Oñate Documents*, I, 502–503.

24 Juan de Oñate, March 2, 1599, in *Colección de Documentos Inéditos*, XVI, 308–309.

true, for the diary of his journey shows that the Vaqueros were friends of the Taos, Picuris, and others. Late in 1599 or early in 1600 this same informant declared that he had seen a Vaquero chief and 200 warriors come to San Marcos pueblo to trade and that some buffalo meat was presented by them to the Spaniards.[25]

It is to be noted that in 1598 and 1599 the Apaches and Vaqueros are mentioned as two separate peoples. The name "Apache" is applied to the Navaho and to the ancestors of the Jicarilla living in the Taos-Pecos region. The term "Vaquero" is used for the Indians living among the buffalo to the south and east of Pecos. By 1601, however, the term Apache is extended to the latter group as well. In 1598–99 the name "Cocoye" is applied to a group of Indians living towards the north of New Mexico and also towards the northwest and west. Since they are described as agricultural and living near Jemez, they cannot have been the Utes and must have been a branch of the Navahos.[26]

In July, 1599, Vicente de Zaldívar led a party of twenty-five men on a journey to discover the *Mar del Sur,* that is, the South Sea or Pacific Ocean. Little is known of the expedition, but Zaldívar himself had this to say about it:

> During the month of July, 1599, I went . . . to explore the land toward the west . . . and traveled more than 200 leagues inland, traversing many nations of warlike people, such as the Apaches, who are very numerous and extend for more than 200 leagues, judging by what I have seen; and that I left them all at peace and friendly; and that I went up the sierra with a lone companion . . . so that they could see that we intended them no harm . . . they served as guides and gave us native blackberries.[27]

These Apaches seem to have been those living in the mountains of the Flagstaff region, and this supposition is confirmed by another declarant who said that

> they marched inland for more than 200 leagues, meeting many

25 Declaration of Leonis Tremiño de Bañuelos, July 29, 1600, in *Oñate Documents,* II, 827.

26 *Colección de Documentos Inéditos,* XVI, 308–309.

27 Declaration of Vicente de Zaldívar, July, 1600, in *Oñate Documents,* II, 814–15.

Indian nations, Apaches, Cruzados, and Tepeguanes, all able fighters. The sargento mayor left them at peace.[28]

Thus Zaldívar traveled into the lands of Western Apache and the Yavapai (Cruzados) and then went on to the "Tepeguanes," somewhere in the direction of the Gulf of California. These "Tepeguanes" were undoubtedly the Pimas of the Gila River, since the Spaniards (and modern anthropologists) often commented upon the similarity of the Pima and Tepehuan languages.[29] Zaldívar's route, then, was probably to the mines of Farfan (Jerome, Arizona) where he met the Yavapais, and from there he was perhaps guided by Apaches and Yavapais down the Verde River Valley to the Pima country.

On his way to the west the *sargento mayor* passed through the lands of the Jumano Tompiros, for it seems that the normal Spanish route from the San Gabriel area to the south or west was by way of this region east of the Manzano-Sandia Mountains. Perhaps this route was chosen because of the hostility of the Tiwas of the Río Grande Valley, or because these Indians were still avoiding the invaders by hiding in the sierras. At any rate, Zaldívar found the Tompiros somewhat hostile, for they refused his demands for food and blankets, offering stones instead.

This Acoma-like affront to Spanish authority was enough to cause Juan de Oñate himself to seek their punishment when he was on one of his frequent tours of the pueblos for tribute-gathering purposes. When he reached the Jumano pueblos he asked for blankets, but the natives gave him only twelve or fourteen, saying that they could spare no more. Oñate then retired one-half league away for the night. The following day he returned and informed the Indians by means of an interpreter that he was going to punish those who had not given supplies to Zaldívar. The Spaniards then set fire to parts of the pueblo and as the Indians retired killed five or six and wounded others with gunfire. Subsequently two native leaders were hanged, and

28 Declaration of Leonis Tremiño de Bañuelos, July 29, 1600, in *Oñate Documents*, II, 829.

29 For example, the Oñate expedition of 1604 to the Yuma area found the Ozaras—people speaking a language similar to Tepehuan—who were the Pimas or Pápagos.

the interpreter, for not translating correctly, suffered the same fate.[30]

One can well imagine that the Jumano Tompiros were rather anti-Spanish after this affair. Thus it is not surprising that in 1601, when five Spanish soldiers deserted Oñate and tried to go to Nueva Vizcaya by way of the Tompiro country, two of the soldiers and more than twenty of their horses were killed.[31] The three surviving deserters fled back to the Governor, and war was decreed against the Tompiros.

Vicente de Zaldívar, butcher of the Acomas, now led a large party of soldiers against the three Jumano Tompiro pueblos. A six-day battle was fought in which 800 or 900 men, women, and children were slaughtered, all three pueblos were burned and leveled, and 400 prisoners were taken. Each Spanish soldier received a male Indian as a slave, while the other captives were set free. By December, 1601, however, almost all of the slaves had managed to escape.[32]

The year of 1601 was a black one in the history of New Mexico: The civilization of the Pueblo Indians was undoubtedly at its lowest ebb (at least since 1540–42); the Keres of Acoma and the Jumano Tompiros were suffering the results of horrible atrocities; and the Spanish invaders were discouraged, disgruntled, and fighting among themselves. In 1599 one of the European settlers had written that the country of the Pueblo Indians

> promises excellent returns because the native Indians are excellent and intelligent farmers; they are much given to commerce, taking from one province to another the fruits of their lands.[33]

In other words, the Spaniards hoped to make good profits from

---

30 Testimony of Marcos Leandro, July 30, 1601, *México* 26, in AGI.

31 George P. Hammond, *Don Juan de Oñate and the Founding of New Mexico*, 155, hereinafter cited as Hammond, *Oñate*.

32 See Scholes and Mera, "Jumano," Carnegie Institution *Contributions to American Anthropology and History*, Vol. VI, Nos. 30–34 (1940), 279; Letter of Fray Juan de Escalona, October 10, 1601, *México* 26, Ramo I, in AGI; and Letter of Captain Luís Velasco, March 22, 1601, in *Oñate Documents*, II, 615.

33 Letter of Alonso Sánchez, February 28, 1599, in *Oñate Documents*, I, 425.

the labor of their new subjects. This, however, proved to be an illusion.

The invaders of New Mexico were, as predicted, a "troublesome" lot. They were apparently financially poor but with great expectations of gaining quick wealth from mines or from the exploitation of the Indians. No workable mines were discovered, however, and the Indians failed to provide them with an excess of wealth. Indeed, in December, 1600, the Viceroy of New Spain, the Count of Monterrey, was forced to send succor to the Spaniards in New Mexico. He also sent an "auditor general and assessor" to "help" Juan de Oñate. The latter refused to accept the auditor's commission, although gladly appropriating the supplies.[34]

The testimony of the individuals who went with this group, and who returned to New Spain in March, 1601, reveals the extremely bad situation in New Mexico at that time. The Spaniards had had only 10 or 12 cows and 4 to 6 oxen left when the aid arrived; and between the end of December and March they ate 280 of the 630 cows brought by the auditor and Captain Juan de Ortega, thus showing themselves an improvident lot. Oñate had failed to construct any *villa* (Spanish settlement), and the invaders were living in the Tewa pueblo of San Gabriel. They had simply ousted the Indians from their 400-house village and had taken over. The Indians, on the other hand, were kept in the neighborhood to do all of the labor, farming, bringing of water, and taking care of all the livestock. The Spaniards had not bothered to build any fortifications, because the Indians were naturally "tame" and made no resistance, and also because "the said soldiers are with notable disgust and doubt the persistance [of the Spaniards] in the land."[35] Thus as early as the beginning of 1601 many Europeans were ready to quit.

In a poorer condition than the Spaniards, however, were the trampled-upon Pueblo Indians. Every month Oñate's soldiers went out to the various pueblos to collect maize and other types of food, leaving very little for the Indians. Furthermore, each

[34] Testimony of Xinez de Herrera Horta, July 30, 1601, *México* 26, in AGI.
[35] Various Testimony, *México* 26, in AGI.

year every household of Indians had to contribute a cotton blanket or a tanned deerskin, even if the blanket had to be removed
forcibly from an Indian's back, as one declarant saw done to
some women. The result of all this was that the Pueblo Indians
were abandoning their towns and fleeing to the mountains. Captain Juan de Ortega noted the absence of Indians and said that
he never saw more than 400 natives together between the first
Piro pueblo of Cualacu and the Spanish camp at San Gabriel.
He learned that "many of them have fled to the mountains."
for fear of the Spaniards. As a matter of fact, many pueblos were
completely depopulated.[36] Marcos Leandro noted that whenever the Indians sighted Spaniards in the distance they got everything together that they could and fled to the sierras with men,
women, and children. Exactly the same statement was made by
Captain Luís Velasco in March of 1601.[37]

The Franciscan missionaries who had supposedly gone to New
Mexico to convert the Indians had baptized only a few children.
The priests themselves complained that the cruelty of the soldiers had alienated the Indians to such an extent that they were
hostile to the Europeans' religion. On the other hand, it seems
that of the nine clergymen who were there in 1601 three were
mozos and six were old men. Herrera Horta reported that "not
one religious [priest] knows any of the languages" of New Mexico
and that they were not really trying to reach the Indians.[38] The
six priests were distributed among only the Tewas, at San Gabriel, San Ildefonso, Santa Clara, and two at San Francisco del
Monte, four leagues from Santa Clara.[39]

As the months passed, the situation became even more desperate. Many soldiers and priests were actively planning to desert

[36] *Ibid.* Particularly the Testimony of Joan de Ortega, July 31, 1601. See also
the Letter of Captain Luís Velasco to the Viceroy, March 22, 1601, in *Oñate Documents*, II, 615.

[37] Testimony of Marcos Leandro, July 30, 1601, *México* 26, in AGI.

[38] *México* 26, in AGI. As early as 1592, the Franciscans were charged with not
bothering to learn the languages of the Indians in Nueva Vizcaya. At that time
the Governor, Rodrigo de Río de Losa, charged that a major cause of trouble was
that not a single Franciscan spoke a native language. Instead, they gave the
doctrina in Mexican, which the natives did not understand. See Rodrigo de Río
de Losa, *Guadalajara* 28, in AGI.

[39] Testimony of Jusepe Vrondate, July 28, 1601. *México* 26, in AGI.

the province, and, to make matters worse, Governor Juan de Oñate decided to take approximately 70 soldiers, 700 horses, and servants on an exploratory journey to the mythical Quivira which had caused the ruin of Coronado in the 1540's and Leyva-Humaña in the 1590's and which was almost to ruin Oñate in 1601. Doubtless, the Governor had become disgusted with the lack of wealth in New Mexico and hoped to find gold and riches in Quivira.

The departure of Oñate with most of the horses and half of the soldiers left San Gabriel in the hands of those who were determined upon abandoning the conquest.[40] The Franciscans took the leading part in attempts to get all of the settlers to return to New Spain, but a few chose to remain at San Gabriel. Among these was Fray Juan de Escalona who, although favoring the abandonment of the province, felt bound by his position as commissary to remain until Oñate returned. When Oñate did return, on November 24, only Escalona, Lieutenent Governor Francisco de Losa Peñalosa, and about twenty-five others were at San Gabriel to meet the Governor.[41]

The situation of the Pueblo Indians in the summer and fall of 1601 must have been very desperate. Fray Francisco de San Miguel, one of the leaders of the group favoring the retreat to New Spain, charged that the soldiers "leave them nothing in their houses, no wheat, nothing to eat, nothing that is alive." He had seen many pueblos entirely deserted because of fear of the soldiers who practiced cruelty when they came to rob the Indians of their food. Indian chiefs had been tortured to locate hidden maize, and thousands of natives had died of starvation. The remainder were eating tree branches, dirt, charcoal and ashes.[42] Fray Francisco Zamora declared that it was not possible to convert the Indians because of the terrible injuries inflicted upon them by the soldiers in their attempts to secure food. Fray Escalona said, "the Indians are falling dead from hunger in the

---

40 In March, 1601, there were from 150 to 200 soldiers of whom only 42 or 50 were married. Various Testimony, *México* 26, in AGI.

41 Hammond, *Oñate*, 28, 143, 148–51.

42 Declaration of Fray Francisco de San Miguel, September 7, 1601, *México* 26, Ramo I, in AGI.

places where they live and they eat dirt and carbon mixed with seeds and very little maize mixed up in order to sustain life."[43] Escalona charged also that "all the supplies that the Governor and his people carried on the journey and discovery that they went to make recently [to Quivira] were taken away from the Indians," and Escalona himself saw the great offenses done in collecting the goods. Captain Luís Velasco declared that the Spaniards entered the houses of the Pueblo Indians and took their women by force. The maize which was gathered every month was taken against the natives' will, and their blankets were seized "sometimes when it is snowing, leaving the poor Indian women stark naked." Many Pueblo Indians had died from such treatment.[44]

It should be absolutely clear, then, that the Spaniards were deadly enemies and not "protectors" of the Pueblo Indians from 1598 to 1601. During this same period there is absolutely no evidence of any hostilities carried out by the Athapascans; as a matter of fact, there is data to show that they were on good relations with the Pueblo tribes and on at least peaceful terms with the Spaniards. The Spanish headquarters at San Gabriel were located near the lands of the Navaho Apaches, and yet the Europeans felt absolutely no need for fortifications since the Indians were no danger to them.[45] Likewise, when the Spanish settlers deserted to New Spain, they were charged with treason, but this charge was dropped since there was said to be no war in New Mexico.[46]

Jusepe Vrondate and Marcelo de Espinosa, living in New Mexico from 1598 to March, 1601, both describe the trade which the Vaquero Indians of the plains carried on with the Pueblo Indians. In fact, they describe this as the only real commerce of New Mexico. The Vaqueros bring their dogs loaded with dried meat, fat (*manteca*), and tanned hides and trade them for deco-

[43] Letter of Fray Juan de Escalona, October 10, 1601, *México* 26, Ramo I, in AGI.

[44] *Ibid.*, and Letter of Captain Luís Velasco, March 22, 1601, in *Oñate Documents*, II, 609–15.

[45] Various Testimony, July 28–31, 1601, *México* 26, in AGI.

[46] "*Los Puntos de Nuevo México*," January 6, 1602. *México* 26, in AGI.

rated cotton blankets and maize, and this trading takes place not in the plazas but in particular (private) houses.[47] Marcos Leandro declared in July, 1601, that the Puebloans trade with

> a nation of Indians outside of the law [not a subject of the Crown of Spain] who are called Apaches and also are called the Vaqueros by the Spaniards since they live in the plains of Civola [Cibola] where they say there is a great number of ganado civoleno [buffalo]; these said Indians bring to the settlements hides of the buffalo which they kill, meat, and fat and they trade it with the settled people for maize.[48]

In 1601 Captain Juan de Ortega found that the Pueblo Indians' diet included

> some buffalo-meat that they get in trade from the Vaqueros in exchange for blankets and maize. The exchange is that the Vaqueros come to the pueblos from Cibola, which is some plains that are forty or fifty leagues from the real [San Gabriel], with the meat, fat, hides and tallow loaded on some dogs a little larger than water-dogs. They have them for that task and in order to carry their tents, which are mostly very white, although some [are decorated] with little black hands; and they place the tents at 300 or 400 paces from the said pueblo and there the Indians go around; and for the maize and blankets the Vaqueros named Apaches trade all the said things. On this occasion 400 or 500 came.[49]

Not only is this an excellent account of the nature of Pueblo-Athapascan relations in 1601, but it intimates that the Plains Apaches were actually coming into the Tewa region, an entire rancheria at a time, and living in the neighborhood of the pueblos during the trading period. Baltasar Martínez, in New Mexico during the same year, said that the Apaches who followed the buffalo traded tallow, fat, and hides with the Pecos, Taos, and Tewas where the Spaniards had become established.[50]

[47] Testimony of Jusepe Vrondate and Marcelo de Espinosa, July 28, 1601, *México* 26, in AGI.

[48] Testimony of Marcos Leandro, July 30, 1601, *México* 26, in AGI.

[49] Testimony of Joan de Ortega, July 31, 1601, *México* 26, in AGI.

[50] Declaration of Baltasar Martínez, April 23, 1602, in *Oñate Documents*, II, 838.

When, in June, 1601, Juan de Oñate and his seventy-man army set out on the road to Quivira, of necessity they passed through the lands of the Plains Apaches.[51] About eight days after crossing the Pecos River, the Spanish expedition reached the Canadian River, and "here some Indians of the nation called Apachi came out with signs of peace," that is, with their hands raised to the sun.[52] The Apaches

> wore a sort of buckskin jacket which reached to the knees, and some wore dressed buffalo skins like capes or blankets. All carried bows and arrows, leather shields, and war clubs with a stone at the end like a hatchet, and a strap for the wrist.[53]

The Oñate party followed the Canadian River Valley to the east for more than one hundred leagues, until they reached some sand dunes which forced them to leave the river.[54] During this time they came across camps of the Apache nation,

> who are the ones who possess these plains, and who, having no fixed place nor site of their own, go from place to place. . . . We were not disturbed by them at all, although we were in their land, nor did any Indians become impertinent.[55]

The Spaniards left the Canadian River in the area of the sand dunes and also near a great bend. In all probability, this point was near the Texas-Oklahoma state line, just west of the Antelope Hills.[56]

Upon leaving the Canadian River, the party went out onto the Great Plains and followed several small streams towards the east. Occasionally, they lost directions, and crossed a small river and a larger one before they reached any habitations.

[51] One source says that Oñate had 100 men. Perhaps this number included Indian servants and slaves. See *"Memorial sobre . . . Nuevo México,"* in *Colección de Documentos Inéditos,* XVI, 198.

[52] Bolton, *Spanish Explorations,* 252.

[53] Juan de León, April 24, 1602, in *Oñate Documents,* II, 852.

[54] Large areas of sand are to be found along the Canadian River from Hutchison County, Texas, to Ellis County, Oklahoma, the largest concentration being in Hemphill County, Texas, just west of the Oklahoma state line. See O. E. Baker, *Atlas of American Agriculture,* Plate 5, Section 6.

[55] Bolton, *Spanish Explorations,* 253.

[55] *Ibid.,* 205.

Finally, after some 60 leagues of uninhabited plains and 200 leagues of travel in all, the Spaniards came upon a large village of Indians who were called Escanxaques, because they pronounced this word when giving the sign of peace. These Indians lived in round huts made of branches and straw, most of them being covered with buffalo hides.[57] Some of their habitations were said to resemble the tipis of the Apaches. Their clothing was of hides and buckskins, but most of the men went naked because of the heat, and the women wore only small pieces of skin to cover their privy parts. Both men and women were painted or striped—the latter on their faces, breasts, and arms.[58]

The Escanxaques have sometimes been identified as a band of Eastern Apaches; however, it seems certain that they were not, as they did not speak the Apache language. In all likelihood, they were a north-roaming group of Tonkawan Indians, as their customs do not link them with any Caddoan group.

Kiowa? [handwritten annotation in margin]

There were several Apaches living with the Escanxaques, and the Spaniards were able to converse with them by means of Jusepe, the Mexican who lived for a year with the Plains Apaches. The people of the Escanxaque rancheria wished to accompany the Oñate party in order to attack some of their enemies who lived farther on. The governor wanted a guide but refused to allow all of the Indians to come with him. Oñate solved the problem, in a very poor way, by ordering his soldiers to seize an Escanxaque, place him in chains, and use him as a guide.[59]

The expedition then moved on to a large river—the Arkansas —and there contacted a Wichita people who were enemies of the Escanxaques but who made friends with the Europeans. Oñate, however, had a number of them treacherously seized and kept as hostages. This act caused the Wichitas to desert their village and failed to lead to any good, as the prisoners were released or escaped. Oñate also earned the enmity of the Escanxaques by having his men capture a number of them to use as guides and by refusing them the right to plunder more than a little corn

---

[57] Declaration of Juan Rodríguez, in *Oñate Documents,* II, 865.
[58] Declaration of Baltasar Martínez, in *Oñate Documents,* II, 841.
[59] *Ibid.,* II, 842.

from the deserted village. Finally, the army became discouraged, and a petition favoring retreat was signed by almost all of the soldiers.

Oñate agreed to the proposal, and on September 29 the Spaniards turned towards New Mexico. The Escanxaques, however, were now entrenched with their women and children in the deserted village and were hostile. The army was told not to come near them. Hostilities commenced, and the Spaniards used artillery and guns to force the Indians to give way. Finally, Oñate ordered an end to the fighting, for thirty of his men had been wounded. Some Indian women and children who had been captured were released, but one man, later called Miguel, was retained and taken to Mexico City in 1602. He claimed that he was a native of Tancoa, many days of travel from there, and that he had been captured and raised by the Escanxaques. He referred to the latter as the Aguacane.[60]

According to contemporary sources, the return journey was without incident, since no Escanxaques were seen and the Vaquero Apaches were friendly as before. An account written twenty-five years later, however, inserts some new information to the effect that an ambassador, sent by the Wichita group, caught up with Oñate and asked him for aid against the Ayxaos (Ahijados) Indians. These Indians lived near seven small hills and possessed much gold. Oñate declined to aid the ambassador's people at that time, but he did listen to some advice. The diplomat informed the Spaniards that they had come by the wrong route and that a better trail was from Taos pueblo through the lands of the Apaches of Captain Quinia. This entire conversation was supposedly carried on in the Athapascan language, which the ambassador knew very well.

Two "Quivira" Indian guides were furnished by the Indian, and they apparently guided Oñate home to New Mexico by the better route.[61] Whether or not this account is accurate, the Spaniards reached San Gabriel on November 24, 1601. Their

[60] See *Oñate Documents,* II, 842–49, 854–55, 859, 868, 872–76.
[61] Zarate Salmerón, in *Documentos—México,* Series 3, I, 28–29.

return journey had taken less than one month, although they were absent from New Mexico for about 150 days in all.

Little is known of the state of New Mexican affairs during the years of 1602 and 1603, except that a handful of Spaniards and two Franciscans continued to live at San Gabriel and poor relations with the Pueblo Indians were the rule. During this period a punitive campaign was undertaken against the Taos Indians, and possibly at this time Juan de Oñate himself carried out the murder of a young Taos chief who was hurled to his death from a roof top in the pueblo.[62] In 1602 Vicente de Zaldívar made a journey to Mexico for the dual purpose of protecting his and Oñate's interests and of taking from New Mexico "many Indian men and women whom he sold as slaves."[63] That the butcher of the Acomas and the Tompiros was interested in the slave-acquiring side of northern activities is also to be seen in the fact that prior to 1600 he claimed that he had lost "sixty of my men and women slaves worth more than 10,000 pesos," for they had run away.[64]

As far as is known, the Athapascans surrounding New Mexico remained at peace, apparently, until 1605. Pueblo Indian refugees were probably helping to prepare the way for future hostilities, however, as occasional plots were circulated against the invaders.

Late in 1603 or early in 1604 a party of Spaniards led by Captain Gerónimo Marquez visited Acoma, Zuñi, and the Hopi pueblos. From the Hopi pueblos the group made its way to the lands of the Cruzados and the mines near Jerome. There the Spaniards discovered veins of ore and brought specimens back to New Mexico. These ores turned out, however, to be of no value at all.[65]

Juan de Oñate had found wealth neither in New Mexico nor in Quivira, and now he turned his attention to following up the

62 *Oñate Documents,* II, 1110.

63 *Ibid.,* II, 1115.

64 *Ibid.,* II, 815, 822.

65 Scholes, "Juan Martinez de Montoya," *New Mexico Historical Review,* Vol. XIX, No. 4 (1944), 338.

Marquez expedition by discovering a route to the South Sea as well as to investigating rumors of a rich Mexican kingdom located somewhere to the north and west of the Colorado River region. On October 7, 1604 the party of about thirty soldiers left San Gabriel for the Hopi villages, going by way of Zuñi. At Zuñi they noted that four of the six Zuñi pueblos, although inhabited, were "almost completely in ruins."[66] This may be evidence of Athapascan or Hopi hostility, or it may indicate conflict with the Spaniards. Four of the five Hopi pueblos were also said to be half in ruins.

From the Hopi area the Spaniards traveled ten leagues to the San José River (the Little Colorado), seventeen leagues farther to the San Antonio (Oak Creek or Sycamore Canyon), and five leagues more to the Sacramento (the Verde). The latter stream flowed from northwest to southeast

> along the slopes of a high range [Mingus Mountain at Jerome, Arizona] from which the Spaniards have obtained many copper ores from some mines that had been discovered by Antonio de Espejo.

In the country of the mines were the Cruzados Indians, called thusly because of some crosses made of reeds which most of them wore on their foreheads. They were a nonagricultural people—a fact which contradicts the earlier sources—and they dressed in buckskin garments.[67] The Cruzados said that two days away was a river with little water (Bill Williams' Fork) which flowed into a larger one (the Colorado River) on which the Amacava (Mohave) Indians lived. The sea was twenty days away by way of the larger river.[68]

Oñate led his party up the Verde to its source and then overland to Bill Williams' Fork. From there they made their way down the Colorado River to the Gulf of California. After taking possession of the mouth of the river, the Spaniards turned north again, eventually reaching the lands of the Cruzados. Few of these Indians were to be seen in 1605, but those with whom

[66] Diary of Fray Francisco de Escobar, in *Oñate Documents*, II, 1013–14.
[67] *Ibid.*, II, 1015–16.
[68] Bolton, *Spanish Explorations*, 270.

contact was made confirmed the rumors of a rich kingdom and monster-like people far to the west.

> At the province of Moqui [the Hopi villages], three other Indians of this same nation of the Cruzados who were there gave us the same report, saying that they had heard it from people of their own nation who had come from the sea. Another Indian from a nation called Tacabuy, which is situated at the San Jose river [the Little Colorado], gave this report.[69]

The expeditions of Espejo in 1583 and Farfan in 1598 had made contact with Indians living between the Hopis and the Cruzados (Yavapais), and as noted previously they seem to have been the same Western Apaches who inhabited the area in later years. Then, in 1605, the Oñate expedition confirmed this thesis by locating the "Tacabuy" on the Little Colorado River.

In 1892, J. Walter Fewkes mentioned that the Hopis called the Navahos "Ta-cab-ci-nyu-mûh" or "Ta-cab people," since *ci-nyu-mûh* is Hopi for "people."[70] This might lead one to suspect that the Tacabuys were a branch of the Navahos. On the other hand, in 1775 Fray Silvestre Vélez de Escalante wrote that the province of the Hopis is bounded on the south by the Gila Apaches and on the southwest by others "whom they call here [Santa Fe] Mescaleros and in Moqui, Yochies and Tassabuess."[71] Yochies is a corruption of Yotche-eme, a Hopi name for the Apaches, and Tassabuess is undoubtedly identical with Tacabuy.[72] The term "Mescalero Apache" was applied in the 1700's to the Western Apaches by the Spaniards.[73] Thus it appears certain that the Apaches of the west were in their historic home-

69 Diary of Fray Francisco de Escobar, in *Oñate Documents*, II, 1027–28.

70 J. Walter Fewkes, "One Ceremonial Circuit Among the Village Indians of Northeastern Arizona," *Journal of American Folklore*, Vol. V, No. 16 (1892), 33 n.

71 Letter of Fray Silvestre Vélez de Escalante, October 28, 1775, in Alfred Barnaby Thomas, *Forgotten Frontiers: A Study of the Spanish Indian Policy of Don Juan Bautista de Anza, 1777–1787*, 151.

72 John R. Swanton, *The Indian Tribes of North America*, 327.

73 See, for example, the map drawn by Bernardo de Miera y Pacheco in 1776, which shows "Apaches Mescaleros" south and southwest of the Hopis. Also, Juan López' 1795 map shows "Apaches Mescaleros" in the same region and *"Coninas que hacen guerra a los Apaches o Mescaleros"* to the northwest. See *Cartografía de Ultramar: Estados Unidos.*

land and on the Little Colorado River during the period from 1583 to 1605.

On April 25 Oñate returned to San Gabriel—his little colony shrunk in size to only about eighty persons.[74] In the next few years this small group of Spaniards and Indian servants was to face a critical test as the dormant hostility of the Navaho Apaches flared into open war.

[74] Hammond, *Oñate*, 31.

CHAPTER VI

Athapascans at War

✠

In June, 1605 the Spanish settlers of New Mexico sent Fray Francisco de Escobar, their new commissary, to Mexico. The friar reported upon the new discovery of the South Sea and asked for aid from the Viceroy. It is quite significant that in his memorials he makes no mention of hostilities by the Apaches or of revolts by the Pueblo Indians. Escobar did note, however, that the Indians of New Mexico were "very affable and docile," but that their peaceful inclinations were being severely tested by an extortionately high tribute. In fact,

> many abandon their pueblos at the time when the tribute is gathered. The amount collected is now very small and a considerable obstacle to their conversion.

The Plains Apaches were, as always, trading with their Pueblo neighbors.

> In the winter they [Pueblo Indians] wear skins or hides of the buffalo which are tanned and very well dressed . . . and which are brought to these provinces to trade for corn flour and cotton blankets by the Indians who live among the buffalo.[1]

This trade must have been extremely important to all concerned, for it was reported that even the Zuñis and the Hopis used buffalo hides for winter wear.[2]

[1] Diary of Fray Francisco de Escobar, in *Oñate Documents*, II, 1012–13.
[2] *Ibid.*, II, 1014.

107

The Franciscans were not having much success at converting the Pueblo Indians; in fact, only some 400 to 600 conversions had been made since 1598, and not all of these converts were alive in 1605. The friars placed the blame for this situation on the cruelties of the Oñate regime, while the secular informants uniformly declared that the priests were not interested in learning the native languages.[3] Although the Viceroy seems to have accepted the anti-Franciscan point of view, he saw fit to meet Escobar's request; and supplies, soldiers for an escort, and two friars were to be dispatched to New Mexico.[4]

There are very good reasons for believing that the docility of the Pueblo Indians was due almost entirely to the cruel punishment which Acoma and the Tompiros had received. There is evidence to show that the conquered Indians were planning to unite and destroy all of the Spaniards when the Acoma affair took place. Their plans were dropped, however, when they saw what the Spaniards were capable of doing to a rebellious pueblo.[5]

One may be reasonably sure that the Apaches, especially the near-by Navahos, were included in any plots against the invaders; and one may also suspect that the near-annihilation of the Keres of Acoma had a tremendous impact upon them. By 1606, on the other hand, much of the fear of the Spaniards must have worn off while hostile feelings were increased by continual contact with Pueblo refugees. Likewise, Spanish strength had diminished with the desertion of most of the colony in 1601.

In 1606 Juan Martínez de Montoya was granted an *encomienda* of the Jemez Indians which entitled him to the fruits of these Indians' labor. The Jemez were in very close contact with the Navaho Apaches during this period, as always. In fact, the Tewa name for the Navaho is "Jemez Apache."[6] It is not surprising that Martínez became involved in hostilities with the Navahos. The *encomendero* is recorded as having made several

[3] Various Declarants, in *Oñate Documents*, II, 1030, 1056–57.

[4] *Ibid.*, II, 1009.

[5] *Ibid.*, II, 814, 821, 828.

[6] John P. Harrington, "The Ethnogeography of the Tewa Indians," Bureau of American Ethnology *Thirty-fifth Annual Report*, Vol. XXIX, 574.

campaigns against the Apache prior to October, 1606 and several more during the following year.[7]

The exact nature of these first hostilities is not known; however, it is probable that they involved raids by Apaches and refugee Jemez upon the livestock of Martínez. The Indians of New Mexico soon learned that one of the best ways to fight the European was to steal his horses, thus forcing him to fight on the ground and at the same time giving the natives mounts.

The Navaho Apaches soon extended their hostilities beyond the Jemez area, and sometime prior to August, 1608 they attacked San Gabriel itself. A retaliatory expedition was undertaken by Martínez and Cristóbal de Oñate.[8] The nature of the Athapascans' hostility is made clear by the Viceroy, who said in 1609 that the Apaches

> are usually a refuge and shelter for our enemies, and there they hold meetings and consultations, hatch their plots against the whole land, and set out to plunder and make war.[9]

Thus he intimates that the Pueblo Indian refugees were playing a big part in the struggle. In the same year Fray Francisco de Velasco wrote that the converted Indians (Tewas), for showing friendship to the Spaniards, had

> lost the good will of the Picuries, Taos, Pecos, Apaches, and Vaqueros, who have formed a league among themselves and with other barbarous nations to exterminate our friends.

The reason for this hostility was that

> all the hostile nations surrounding the nations among whom the Spaniards are now settled think that the Spaniards are scoundrels and people who are concerned only with their own interests. Many times these hostile natives have selfishly persuaded the peaceful Indians that the latter should throw off the heavy Spanish yoke because the hostile nations believe that

---

7 Scholes, "Juan Martínez de Montoya," *New Mexico Historical Review*, Vol. XIX, No. 4 (1944), 340.

8 *Ibid.*

9 Velasco's Instructions to Peralta, March 30, 1609, in *Oñate Documents*, II, 1089.

no benefit can come to the friendly natives from association with the Spaniards.[10]

Thus probably the basic reason for Apache hostility is revealed by a Spaniard: The Apaches and their Pueblo Indian allies thought that the European invaders were "scoundrels" and that no good was arising from their exploitation of the Indians. Were they right? The facts say that they were and that Indian resistance was justified and long overdue.

The period from 1606 to 1609 is extremely significant, not only because it sets the stage for all later Navaho-Spanish relations, but also because the first record of the acquisition of horses by these Athapascans is revealed. Late in 1607 or early in 1608 Fray Lazaro Ximénez went to Mexico City to report on New Mexico's poor situation. He said that the Spaniards and converts were ordinarily molested by the Apache Indians who were burning and destroying settlements, killing people, and "carrying off the horse-herds."[11] That this was the first acquisition of horses by the Apaches is to be doubted, however. As early as 1600–1601, the Spaniards put Pueblo Indians to work herding horses, sheep, and cattle; and, since these natives were often fleeing to the Athapascans, it is likely that the Athapascans acquired some livestock quite early.[12] Furthermore, the Spanish soldiers may have been very willing to trade horses with the Plains Apaches for buffalo hides and meat, as they did in later years. Other horses may have been strays left by Spanish expeditions, such as the Oñate trip to the plains in 1601;[13] and it must not be forgotten that the horse was rapidly spreading northward from Nueva Vizcaya and Galicia at this time, as in the 1580's and 1590's.[14]

10 Memorial of Fray Francisco de Velasco, in *Oñate's Documents*, II, 1094.

11 Viceroy to King, March 6, 1608, *Guadalajara* 28, in AGI.

12 Various Testimony, *México* 26, in AGI. See Forbes, "The Appearance of the Mounted Indian in Northern Mexico and the Southwest, to 1680," *Southwestern Journal of Anthropology*, Vol. XV, No. 2 (1959).

13 Many horses strayed on the Oñate journey. *Oñate Documents*, II, 797.

14 The Indians of northern New Spain were still hostile, and hostilities had spread farther to the north. In 1608 the Indians near Saltillo were again in revolt, and the Quamoquanes, living near the junction of the Río Sabinas and Río Grande, killed a priest. A campaign was undertaken in that area by the Spaniards. See Letter of Francisco de Urdiñola, January 22, 1608, *Guadalajara* 28, in AGI.

The situation of the invaders of New Mexico was indeed poor by 1606. Reports of the excesses and cruelties of Juan de Oñate had reached official sources, and these accounts coupled with the important fact that he had failed to contribute any wealth to the royal coffers, led to a decision by the King to remove Oñate, get him out of New Mexico, and appoint a new governor. This was on June 17, 1606. By the following year Oñate realized that his reign was at an end, and he resigned on August 24, 1607. The Viceroy, not unhappy with that action, appointed Juan Martínez de Montoya as governor in February, 1608, but the *cabildo* of San Gabriel, under Oñate's influence, refused to accept Martínez and named the former governor's son, Cristóbal de Oñate, to the governorship. The Viceroy temporarily accepted this act, but on March 30, 1609 Pedro de Peralta was officially appointed as governor, and the Oñate era came to an end.[15]

During this period of three years, the Spaniards of New Mexico continued to fight among themselves, and charges were brought against Oñate and Vicente de Zaldívar which were later to bring about their conviction and punishment. Aside from the charges of cruelty towards the Indians, Oñate was convicted of sexual immorality. Interestingly enough, such immorality was to be a characteristic of most subsequent governors of New Mexico in that century.[16]

The Apaches and their allies seem to have kept up hostilities, for in 1607 the *cabildo* of San Gabriel had reference to "the dangers we are facing from the enemy."[17] In February, 1608 Martínez was instructed by the Viceroy to protect the province but not to allow individual campaigns against the unfriendly Indians. Instead he was to have friars seek the pacification of the enemy.[18] By March, however, the Viceroy instructed Martínez to send out a patrol to halt the outrages reported by Fray Ximénez.[19] In March, 1609 Peralta was told to assemble the dispersed Pueblo Indians in settlements where they could be

15 *Oñate Documents,* II, 1038–84.
16 *Ibid.,* II, 1111.
17 *Ibid.,* II, 1040–41.
18 *Ibid.,* II, 1053.
19 *Ibid.,* II, 1059.

controlled and kept from mingling with the Apaches.[20] From that date until the 1620's, our knowledge of Apache relations is limited. Therefore, the success or failure of Peralta's new program is unknown, but the number of villages in New Mexico was probably reduced, and the activities of the Franciscans were stepped up.

With the end of the Oñate period came also a temporary end to exploration beyond New Mexico, for Martínez and Peralta were not to waste the strength of the colony on fruitless expeditions. The last expedition from New Mexico for many years was one made in 1606 to the South Sea by Vicente de Zaldívar. No details of the journey are extant.[21]

The coming of Pedro de Peralta to New Mexico brought an end to the settlers' plans to abandon the province, but no rapid improvement in the colony occurred. The soldiers were said to be interested in gold and silver or in exploitation of the Indians, and—as the viceroy himself said in 1608—"no one comes to the Indies to plow and sow, but only to eat and loaf."[22] Therefore, the exploitation of the Pueblo Indians could hardly be expected to end. However, some improvement in conditions was perhaps brought about by the presence of new supplies from New Spain and a slight lessening in the amount of tribute collected. The activity of the Franciscans seems to have increased somewhat with the addition of several new priests, and many more baptisms were reported. This latter increase was caused primarily by a new policy adopted in 1608 wherein the mass baptism of about 7,000 Pueblo Indians was carried out in order to convince the royal authorities that the Franciscans could not abandon New Mexico. The 7,000 were baptized in a two-month period, while in the ten years before only about 400 to 600 had been converted.[23]

During this period Santa Fe had been founded as a small camp

[20] *Ibid.*, II, 1089.

[21] Scholes, "Juan Martínez de Montoya," *New Mexico Historical Review*, Vol. XIX, No. 4 (1944), 340.

[22] Letter of Fray Francisco de Velasco, April 9, 1609, *México* 128, Ramo I, in AGI, and Letter of the Viceroy, December 17, 1608, in *Oñate Documents*, I, 1068.

[23] Luís de Velasco, February 27, 1608, *Guadalajara* 28, in AGI, and *Oñate Documents*, II, 1067–73.

or settlement, and in 1610 Peralta set it up as a *villa* and made it the capital. San Gabriel was abandoned by the Spaniards and was apparently never resettled by the Tewas. In all probability, the pueblo's proximity to the Navahos made it a dangerous place in which to live.

The years 1610 to 1621 are almost a complete blank in our knowledge of Apache-Spanish relations. However, one may infer that the Navahos and their allies were still usually on hostile terms with the Europeans. In 1614 some unconverted Jemez and Apache Indians killed a Keres Indian of Cochiti. Several Jemez chiefs were made prisoners, and, as a result, one of them was hanged.[24] The areas under Spanish control increased during this era to include the lands of the Keres and Tiwas of the Río Grande Valley, and in 1613 a mission was established east of the Sandia-Manzano mountains at Chilili.[25] About the year 1617 the Spaniards began to use Pecos as a gateway for trade with the Plains Apaches who seem to have always preferred peace and commerce to war—at least in New Mexico.[26] During these years all of the Athapascans in the New Mexico area must have acquired horses.

A bitter conflict between the Franciscans and the secular authorities broke out at this time, and this struggle—largely for control of the Pueblo Indians' labor—was to continue for decades. The Spaniards' hold on the province was weakened by this situation as well as by the hostility of the unconverted Pueblo and Apache Indians. In 1617 Santa Fe, with only forty-eight soldiers, was described as being in a perilous state.[27] Of the Pueblo tribes, the Hopis, Zuñis, Keres of Acoma, Piros, Tompiros, Jemez, Keres of Zia, Picuris, and Taos remained independent, although subject to the paying of tribute when and if the Spaniards could collect it.

[24] Fray Francisco Pérez Guerta, 1617, *Inquisición* 316, in AGN (Archivo General y Público de la Nación, Mexico, D. F. Mexico).

[25] Scholes and Mera, "Jumano," Carnegie Institution *Contributions to American Anthropology and History*, Vol. VI, Nos. 30–34 (1940), 279.

[26] France V. Scholes, "Church and State in New Mexico, 1610–1650," *New Mexico Historical Review*, Vol. XI, No. 1 (1936), 145.

[27] Donald E. Worcester, "The Beginnings of the Apache Menace in the Southwest," *New Mexico Historical Review*, Vol. XVI, No. 1 (1941), 6.

In 1621 the Marquis de Guadalcazar issued an *informe* on New Mexico which sheds some light on affairs in the northern province. At that time there was said to be "peace, security and quietude" among the natives in the region, but whether or not this statement means that the Navaho Apaches and the Spaniards were at peace is not known. At any rate, the Pueblo Indians were still being taken advantage of, for the Spanish settlers were forcing them to serve as human pack animals and the *encomenderos* were making excessive use of their Indians. They were ordered to pay the natives for their work and not to use them for more than harvesting and livestock-herding. The *encomenderos* were also grazing their animals in the Indians' fields, and they were told to end this practice. The priests were commanded not to interfere in the local elections of the natives, but to allow them at least this freedom.

Because of the excessive punishment which had been meted out to the Keres of Acoma, these Indians had returned to their idolatry, as the Marquis put it, and the Spaniards were forbidden to carry out such excessive punishments in the future. Tribute was not to be collected from the Zuñis and the Hopis, for they were gentiles (non-Christians) and not under Spanish rule.[28]

In 1621 a group of new priests arrived in New Mexico, and among them was Fray Gerónimo de Zarate Salmerón, our chief source of information on New Mexico for the following five years. Zarate Salmerón was assigned to the Jemez pueblos, where he established two missions—one being for Jemez Indians who were scattered about the sierras. Trouble arose, for the governor, Juan de Eulate, was at this time involved in the usual struggle with the Franciscans. It seems that he encouraged the Jemez in the practice of their own religion. Consequently, in 1623 the Indians revolted, destroyed at least one of the missions, and successfully resisted a campaign by Eulate. Zarate Salmerón seems to have then transferred his work to the Keres of Zia and Santa Ana and left the Jemez to their own devices. He also claimed that he conquered and pacified the Acomas, who were at war with the Spaniards.[29]

28 Marquis de Guadalcazar, February 5, 1621, *México* 29, in AGI.

It has been claimed by some scholars that the Navahos were raiding the Jemez during this period, but, between 1623 and 1626, the evidence indicates just the opposite.[30] Indeed the Jemez were at war with the Spaniards and the Catholic Tewas from 1623 to 1626—a situation which would seemingly make the Jemez allies of the Navaho Apaches.[31] Prior to 1623, Zarate Salmerón was able to make contact with the Navaho Apaches when he was at Jemez, and he learned that

> past the nation of the Apaches del Nabaxu Indians is a very large river, which carries its currents to this lagoon [of Copala] . . . the provinces of Quíajula, the Iutas [Utes], and farther inland to another settled nation that has stairways of stone in order to climb to their houses, and that all this is known by the Apache Indians, for they have seen all that land.[32]

The Quíajulas were also Navahos, for this word is simply a Spanish version of Kyala, the Jemez name for their Apache neighbors.[33]

In 1622 or 1623 Fray Juan de Salas attempted to convert the Tompiro Indians, and while among them he made contact with the Xumanas (probably the Jumano Apaches), who were then at war with the Tompiros. The Xumanas wanted Salas to visit them, but he was unable to do so at that time. Indeed he was not able to convert the Tompiros, for that was also postponed.[34] The Franciscans were greatly hampered in their efforts at this time by the constant struggle with the governors and by the fact that the Spaniards of New Mexico were "enemies of all classes of labor."[35]

The situation of some of the Athapascan groups during the

[29] France V. Scholes, "Notes on the Jemez Missions in the Seventeenth Century," *El Palacio*, Vol. XLIV, Nos. 7–9 (1938), 65–70.

[30] Scholes, "Church and State in New Mexico," 1610–1650," *New Mexico Historical Review*, Vol. XI, No. 1 (1936), 145–46, and Worcester, "The Beginnings of the Apache Menace in the Southwest," *New Mexico Historical Review*, Vol. XVI, No. 1 (1941), 6.

[31] Benavides, *1634*, 70.

[32] Zarate Salmerón, "*Virreinato de Méjico*," tomo I, MN 567.

[33] Curtis, *The North American Indian*, XVI, 252.

[34] Alonso de Benavides, *Memorial of 1630* (trans. by Peter P. Forrestal), 57–59, hereinafter cited as Benavides, *1630*.

[35] Zarate Salmerón, in *Documentos—México*, Series 3, I, 25.

years 1621 to 1626 is made clearer by Zarate Salmerón. To the north of Taos were the Apaches of a chieftain called Captain Quinia, and our informant indicates that these Indians were under the same chief in 1601.[36] These were probably the same Apaches of the Taos area who were referred to by Oñate in 1599 and are the ancestors of the present-day Jicarilla Apaches. From 1621 to 1626 they were in contact with the missionary at Taos pueblo, Fray Pedro de Ortega. Taos pueblo was said to be ten leagues away from Quinia's village.[37]

In the 1620's, as earlier, the Vaquero Apaches of the plains were bringing their goods to the pueblos to trade for corn flour. They reportedly did not grow crops but lived from the buffalo.[38] In the El Paso area lived the Mansos, called by Zarate Salmerón the Gorretas ("Little Caps") because of their hair style. Near by, to the west, were the related Hanos (Janos), who often visited the Gorretas to see the Spaniards passing by on their way to New Mexico or New Spain. Both the Gorretas and Hanos were apparently at peace not only with the Spaniards but also with their western neighbors—the Ópatas. Some of the Ópatas, called Cojoias by Zarate Salmerón, came in company with the Gorretas to see the Spaniards, and the priest was much interested in visiting them, for they were good agriculturists and blanket-makers. The Conchos Indians, farther to the south, were enemies of the Ópatas but were being reduced to missions at this time.[39]

In 1626 Fray Alonso de Benavides arrived in New Mexico, and his leadership gave the Franciscan missionary effort a new spurt. Priests were dispatched to the troublesome Jemez and Picuris, and Benavides himself began work among the Piros of the lower Río Grande Valley. He found that those of the pueblo of Seelocú (Sevilleta) were wandering about in the neighboring sierras because their village "had been depopulated through wars with other nations who burned it."[40] Unfortunately, it is impossible to say who the enemy was in this case, for the Apaches of the region are not accused by Benavides. It is possible that

36 *Ibid.*, I, 29.
37 Benavides, *1634*, 89.
38 Zarate Salmerón, in *Documentos—México*, Series 3, I, 26–27.
39 Zarate Salmerón, *"Virreinato de Méjico,"* tomo I, MN 567.
40 Benavides, *1630*, 16.

the Piros of Seelocú were having a controversy with other Piros, since upon the destruction of their pueblo they went to live in the mountains and not in a neighboring village. It seems unlikely that they would have found it advantageous to flee to the sierras if the mountain-loving Apaches were their enemy.

While preaching in the Piro pueblo of Senecú, Benavides met several Apaches, among whom was Sanaba, the chief of the Xila (Gila) Apaches. The Xilas' territory began fourteen leagues west of Senecú, and the two peoples—the Piroans and the Athapascans of the Gila River waterhead—were on quite friendly terms. Sanaba, it was said, "oftentimes comes to gamble" at Senecú, and in another place he was said to "frequent" the pueblo. The Gila chief was impressed by Benavides' sermons and was disposed to missionary endeavors among his people. On one occasion he presented a deerskin to the priest.

> It was very white and large; . . . in the middle of it there was a sun painted green, surmounted by a cross; and that under the sun there was a moon painted a dark gray and likewise surmounted by a cross.

To the east and southeast of the Piro area lived the Athapascans who were called the Apaches del Perrillo by Benavides —so called because they lived near a spring called Perrillo ("Little Dog"). These Apaches were said to have been on poor terms with the Piros, but, nevertheless, one of them was at the pueblo of Senecú when the friar preached. This Apache was so much impressed that later he brought one hundred of his people to be instructed with Sanaba's people. Thus it appears that even these Apaches were not the destroyers of the pueblo of Seelocú, for they were at peace with Senecú and

> although these Apaches are very warlike, they are more trustworthy than the nations mentioned above [Tobosos, Tepehuanes, Taraumaras, Sumas, and Mansos], and we need to take less precaution when traveling through their country [from the El Paso area] until we again reach the Río del Norte [below the Piros].[41]

41 *Ibid.*, 14, 43–44, and Benavides, *1634*, 82–84, 91.

The peaceful attitude of the southern Apaches continued for many years. In 1628 Fray Martín del Espíritu Santo was placed in charge of the conversion of the Gila Apaches, and he seems to have actually gone to Apache country. He had little success in the religious phase of his enterprise, although it was reported in 1630 that he had helped the Apaches to plant some crops.[42]

In 1626 Benavides sent Fray Martín de Arvide to reduce the Jemez to missions, and "while he was in that locality, I ordered him to make an expedition to the Apache Indians and to preach . . . to them. This he did."[43] The Jemez were described as very belligerent and so hostile to their eastern neighbors—the converted Tewas—that one chief wore a string of Christian ears around his neck. Their wars with the Tewas and Spaniards since 1623 had been disastrous, however, and in 1626 they were "scattered throughout the kingdom and on the point of being exterminated by famine and war." In fact, more than half of the Jemez had died, but, as Benavides put it, the King still had over 3,000 tribute-paying servants.[44] Arvide refounded the two old missions, and the Jemez seem to have settled down to a quiet acceptance of Spanish rule—at least for a few years.

The Picuris continued to resist the invaders, as they had in 1609. Benavides found that these Indians were the "most indomitable and treacherous" in New Mexico, and the priests who tried to subdue the Picuris underwent great suffering. These allies of the Plains Apaches went so far as to try to kill a friar who was among them. The first Franciscan to stay with them was Fray Ascensio de Zarate, 1629–32, and this priest also attempted to convert the Apaches of Quinia living in that vicinity.[45]

In 1627 Chief Quinia visited Benavides and asked for baptism, or so the latter said. The active friar now undertook a journey to the rancherias of these Apaches beyond Taos, where he planted the first crosses. Not all of the northern Apaches were willing to accept the religion of the Europeans, however, and it was reported that Quinia was wounded by one of his own people as

[42] *Ibid.,* 83, and Benavides, *1630,* 45.

[43] Benavides, *1634,* 79.

[44] *Ibid.,* 70, and Benavides, *1630,* 26.

[45] *Ibid.,* 27, and Benavides, *1634,* 71, 96, 281 n.

a result of his pro-Catholic attitude.[46] In 1628 Quinia went to Santa Fe to escort Fray Bartolomé Romero to the Apaches' lands, but, before leaving, one of his sons and "a famous Indian warrior whom Quinia had captured in war and whom he greatly loved" were baptized. The establishment of a mission north of Taos was regarded as an important undertaking by Governor Phelipe Sotelo Ossorio, and he, along with fifty Spanish soldiers, personally accompanied Romero to the village of Quinia. There "in one day they built a church of logs, which they hewed, and they plastered the walls on the outside." Hopes were now high for the success of the conversion, especially when Chief Manases, another Apache, became interested. But, as Benavides said, the devil perverted Captain Quinia, and the Athapascans rebelled and fled to a new rancheria. Fray Romero was forced to give up the conversion for the time being.[47]

In May 1629 Romero and Fray Francisco Muñoz were ready to try again. According to Fray Esteban de Perea, they "went to the nation of the Apaches of Quinia and Manases; as this was the first visit to that warlike nation, they were escorted by Don Francisco de Sylva, governor of those provinces, and twenty soldiers." The Apaches were friendly, but the conversion was never to be a success.[48] After all, with their Taos and Picuris neighbors always ready to revolt against the rule of the priests and soldiers, one could hardly expect the northern Apaches to submit to a life of coercion.

In 1626 the Plains Apaches to the east of New Mexico were at peace, as they had apparently always been. Fray Benavides declared that

> They trade these hides [buffalo] throughout the entire region and in this way gain their livelihood. These skins provide the dress commonly worn by both Indians and Spaniards. They use them not only for making clothing, but also for sacks, tents, cuirasses, footwear, and many other useful purposes.

46 *Ibid.*, 89–90.

47 *Ibid.*, 90, and Benavides, *1630*, 43.

48 "True Report" of Fray Esteban de Perea, in Benavides, *1634*, 212. Silva Nieto became Governor of New Mexico in 1629.

The Apaches "go out through the surrounding provinces, using these skins to trade and bargain," taking their entire villages along. The merchandise was carried on the backs of their dogs and was traded for cotton cloth and other items.[49]

Here, then, is more evidence of "continuous intercourse" between the Vaquero Apaches and the Pueblo Indians.[50] Also, the plains people were still—as in 1601—bringing entire villages into the Río Grande Valley area and trading with both Spaniards and Puebloans. The Athapascans were not only being influenced by Puebloan and Hispanic culture but also had an influence of their own. This influence of the Apache upon the settled peoples of New Mexico has never been sufficiently recognized by investigators, but it certainly should be. As early as the 1580's many of the Pueblo tribes were making use of dressed skin-clothing, which is usually considered to be an Athapascan characteristic in the Southwest.[51] As early as 1601, the Spaniards were under the Apache cultural influence for their women were wearing deerskin clothing—which surprised newcomers.[52]

In 1627 or 1628 a group of Vaquero Apaches came to Santa Fe, where they expressed interest in a statue of the Virgin and seemed interested in becoming Roman Catholics. This possibility was frustrated, however, when the demon

> had recourse to one of the wiles he is accustomed to employ in his defense, choosing as his instrument the greed of our Spanish governor [Phelipe Sotelo Ossorio]. In order to obtain slaves to sell in New Spain, the governor sent a brave Indian captain, who was an enemy of that faction [the Apaches], to bring back as many captives as he could.

The governor's warriors attacked the village of the friendly Apaches who had visited Santa Fe. The chief—who was almost a Christian—and many of his people were killed, and the rest were brought back to New Mexico as slaves. This treacherous raid became widely known, however, and such a tumult arose

49 Benavides, *1630*, 53–54.

50 Benavides, *1634*, 91.

51 In 1583 Espejo found the Piro men wearing "tanned deerskin jackets" and using tanned deerskin robes. See *Relation of Pérez de Luxán*, 72.

52 Testimony of Joan de Ortega, July 31, 1601, *México* 26, in AGI.

that the governor had to refuse to accept the captives. The slave raid "provoked a revolt throughout the entire province," and the Vaqueros declared open war on the Spaniards and their allies. By 1629 peaceful relations were being re-established.[53]

Thus after more than eighty years of provocation, the Plains Apaches were finally goaded to war against the Spaniards by a slave raid. Nevertheless, the natural inclination of these Apaches seems to have been to trade and not to wage war—at least in New Mexico. The next recorded series of hostile relations was not until 1638, when another treacherous slave raid was carried out by the Spaniards.

In slave raids the use of Indian allies by the Spaniards should be noted. The policy of the sons of Cortés was very clear on this point, and from the use of the Tlaxcalans against the Aztecs to the use of Pueblo Indians against Apaches the Spaniards tried to insure their own success by pitting one Indian tribe against another. In 1585 Baltasar de Obregón stated the policy well: "Advantage should be taken of the enemy by setting those of one district against the opponents of another."[54] This plan was initially pursued in New Mexico by forcing the Tewas to ally themselves with the invaders. Thus the Tewas lost the friendship of the Taos, Picuris, Jemez, and Athapascans and were more and more forced into a dependence upon the Europeans for protection. The same policy was to be carried out with the Keres, Tiwa, Piro, and Tompiro Indians in New Mexico. In Arizona and Sonora the Spaniards were to destroy friendship between the Sumas and the Ópatas, on the one hand, and between the Pimas-Sobaipuris and the Apaches, on the other. This policy insured the continuance of Hispanic influence among at least one portion of the tribes. Thus the Spaniards were often more interested in increasing intertribal hostilities than in establishing peace among the Indians. As one Franciscan put it in 1744, it was a good thing that the natives were fighting among themselves, for it prevented them from uniting to destroy the newcomers.[55]

[53] Benavides, *1630*, 55–56, and Benavides, *1634*, 91–92.

[54] *Obregón's History*, 238.

[55] Declaration of Fray Miguel de Menchero, 1744, in Hackett, *Historical Documents*, III, 401.

Fray Alonso de Benavides was interested in converting all Indians to the religion and culture of Spain, however, and this active preacher and church official undertook the conversion of the Jumano Tompiros in 1627. Fray Salas, operating from Isleta on the Río Grande, had worked with these Indians early in the 1620's, but conversion proved to be a slow process. Interestingly enough, upon visiting the "Xumanas" pueblo, Benavides said, "It is called Xumanas, because this nation often comes there to trade and barter."[56] In other words, by the 1620's the word "Jumano" and its various forms had lost its meaning of painted people in general and was assumed to be the proper name of one tribe—of the Jumano Apaches who came to trade with the Tompiros.

During this period the Jumano Apaches apparently came each summer to trade with the Tompiros, and in 1629 a group of fifty Jumanos went to Isleta pueblo to ask for priests to visit them.[57] Fray Juan de Salas and Fray Diego López responded to the request, and, accompanied by soldiers, they went approximately 100 to 112 leagues through Vaquero Apache territory to the lands of the Jumanos.[58] The Jumanos had been waiting in one place, but the water holes dried up. To be near the buffalo herds, they planned to take up their tipis and move, but a woman was said to have appeared to them, and they remained there. The friars stayed among the Jumanos—whom Benavides treats as a people separate from the Apaches—long enough to make contact with the Iapies (Ápés, a tribe living near Eagle Pass, Texas) and to learn of the Quiviras and Aixaos to the east.[59]

Agustín de Vetancurt, writing in the 1690's, declares that the conversion of the Jumanos failed at this time because of continuous wars and invasions being made by the Apaches of neighboring bands.[60] It seems certain, however, that Vetancurt was transposing the situation of his own day, when the Jumanos were at war with their northern neighbors, to the earlier period.

56 Benavides, *1634*, 66.
57 *Ibid.*, 94, and Agustín de Vetancurt, *Teatro Mexicano*, Cuarto IV, 96.
58 Benavides, *1634*, 92–95, and Benavides, *1630*, 56–57.
59 *Ibid.*, 59–60.
60 Vetancurt, *Teatro Mexicano*, Cuarto IV, 96.

The sources of the 1620's mention no such fighting, and, indeed, it would have been impossible for the Jumanos to have come each summer to New Mexico if the Apaches had been hostile.

In 1629 Fray Esteban de Perea and a group of new priests reached New Mexico. In the El Paso region they stayed among the Mansos for three days and were provided with refreshments of fish and other local food by the friendly natives. None of the priests remained there, however, as they were destined to go to the Piros, Tompiros, and the great Tompiro pueblo of the "Humañas." Others journeyed farther north to other pueblos.[61]

In June, Governor Silva Nieto, thirty soldiers, and several priests went to reduce the Keres of Acoma, the Zuñis, and the Hopis. Fray Juan Ramírez was placed at Acoma, where the Spaniards found not only Keres Indians but "many others, delinquents and apostates, who have sought shelter" from Spanish rule.[62] At long last Acoma, now with some 2,000 inhabitants, was "reduced to peace"—thirty years after being almost destroyed by Vicente de Zaldívar. Fray Roque de Figueredo took up his post at Zuñi, but he was not well received by these independence-loving Indians. According to Benavides, the native religious leaders ("sorcerers") were responsible for the opposition to Hispano-Catholic rule.[63]

Governor Silva Nieto declined to venture beyond Zuñi, but Fray Francisco de Porras, two lay brothers, and twelve soldiers went to Awatobi pueblo and there were received very suspiciously by the Hopis. In fact, these Indians were so upset that they passed on news of the Spaniards' arrival to their neighbors, the Apaches, with whom they were at peace. Subsequently, Fray Porras was poisoned—a unique method of Indian resistance for New Mexico.[64]

The information supplied by the reports of Fray Alonso de Benavides sheds much light upon the state of the Navaho Apaches during the years 1626–29. They were thought to be a

61 Perea's "True Report," in Benavides, *1634*, 211.
62 Benavides, *1634*, 72, and Perea's "True Report," in Benavides, *1634*, 212.
63 Benavides, *1630*, 30.
64 Perea's "True Report," in Benavides, *1634*, 216–17, and Benavides, *1634*, 75, 77.

very numerous people—reportedly assembling 200,000 warriors on one occasion—and very skillful farmers. Nevertheless, in spite of being a more sedentary people than the other Apaches, they were considered to be "the most warlike of the entire Apache nation."[65] Indeed, Benavides says the Athapascans have "proven to be the crucible of Spanish valor," and this statement probably refers primarily to the Navahos.

During much of the time Benavides spent in New Mexico, the Navaho Apaches were at war with the converted Tewa Indians, and the Tewas were reportedly suffering a great deal from attacks which their Spanish masters could not halt. Benavides believed that the Apaches were not entirely to blame for the hostilities. The Navahos' country contained mountain ranges with rock alum deposits, and the converted Indians made invasions into Athapascan territory to get the ore. In response, the Navahos fought "in defense of their country." This action led to attacks on the Tewas and Spanish retaliation against the Navahos. Thus the struggle began, according to our Franciscan authority.[66]

The Spaniards' method of dealing with the Navahos had been to enter the Indians' territory secretly and attack a village without warning at daybreak. This policy failed to accomplish much, because the Navahos were always able to assemble many warriors to meet the onslaught. Fray Benavides chose a new method of dealing with the Athapascans, preferring a peace policy to one of fire and the sword. He went to the Tewa pueblo of Santa Clara, which had suffered a great deal from Tewa-Apache hostilities, and persuaded the natives to send a peace embassy of twelve men to the Navahos. The Navahos had been preparing for a war expedition but abandoned their plans and accepted the Tewas' peace arrows. The "haughty" Apaches then came to Santa Clara, and, although the chief said that "he was deeply offended at the Christians," was willing to accept the peace offer. This armistice was apparently quite effective, and peaceful relations seemingly continued into the early 1630's, at least. The Franciscans also

65 Benavides, *1630*, 42, 44, 45, and Benavides, *1634*, 85.
66 Benavides, *1630*, 45–46.

gained an opportunity to convert the Navahos, and a priest went among them in 1629.[67]

In the late 1620's, as earlier, the El Paso region was occupied by the Mansos or Gorretas "so called because they trim their hair in such a manner that it looks as if they were wearing caps on their heads." This same hair style was in vogue among all the tribes from El Paso to La Junta and seems to have been a type of scalp lock which was allowed to grow long and then combed down over the shaved portion of the head. Benavides felt that the Mansos were a graceful, well-featured, and robust people, but one that could not be trusted—for they would cause trouble to any group of travelers which did not have a large enough escort. On the other hand, the Mansos had been greeting Spanish expeditions for almost fifty years and probably had some honest grievances against the Europeans. Certainly, they and their neighbors—the Sumas—were in contact with tribes, such as the related Cholomes and the Uto-Aztecan Conchos, who had suffered from Spanish slave raids and wars.

In 1630 Benavides proposed sending three or four friars and "only" fifteen soldiers to convert the Mansos at El Paso. This conversion would pave the way for reaching other near-by nations and

> with this protection many very rich mining camps . . . could be settled, as well as magnificent farm sites with water and tracts of very fine land.[68]

The Sumas and Janos were described by Benavides as being ferocious and indomitable peoples who waged great wars and attacked the Spaniards on the road to New Mexico. They were so hostile that they refused even to speak with the Europeans. One must, however, accept this information with some care, for Benavides says the same things of the Tepehuanes and Tarau-maras—tribes which were peaceful in the late 1620's.[69]

The geographical distribution of the Athapascan peoples in the 1620's is revealed by Benavides' information to have been

[67] *Ibid.*, 46, 48, 52.
[68] *Ibid.*, 10–12.
[69] *Ibid.*, 9.

approximately the same as in more recent times. The Sumas and Janos were living in the region south of El Paso; the Mansos occupied the area of El Paso itself and above the Río Grande for thirty leagues. At this point, on the east side of the river, began the lands of the Apaches del Perrillo, and they continued on to the Piro pueblos, bordering the latter on the east as well. To the west of these Apaches and the Piros were the Gila Apaches, whose lands commenced fourteen leagues to the west, at the pueblo of Senecú. "This nation [the Apaches] runs westward from here as far as the South Sea, a distance of more than three hundred leagues."[70] This description is, of course, an exaggeration of the size of the area inhabited by the Gila and Western Apache groups. Nevertheless, it clearly shows that the Athapascans were occupying their extensive lands west of the Río Grande at this date. As it has been demonstrated that the Western Apaches were in the Flagstaff–Little Colorado region in the 1580's, 1590's and early 1600's, it seems certain that the historic regions of the Apache in Arizona and southwestern New Mexico were occupied by them in this period.

The location of the Gila Apaches in relation to the Pueblo tribes and the Navahos is revealed by Benavides when he says:

> Leaving the province of the Xila Apaches, one continues in the same direction [towards the north] along the western edge of the settlements [Piros and Tiwas]; and advancing northward along their border for a distance of more than fifty leagues occupied by villages of the Xila province, one arrives at the province of the Navaho Apaches. Although these belong to the same Apache nation as those mentioned above, they are subject and subordinate to another chief captain, and lead a different kind of life.

Furthermore,

> all those fifty leagues from Xila up to this Navaho nation are settled with rancherias, and the territory of the latter extends for another fifty leagues of frontier.

On the east the Navahos bordered upon the Jemez and the Te-

[70] *Ibid.*, 13, 42, 43, 44, and Benavides, *1634*, 52–54, 81–83.

was, and towards the west their lands extended to the Hopis, that is, if the "Apaches" of that area spoken of by Perea were actually Navahos.[71]

The lands of the Apaches of Quinia and Manases began with a rancheria to the west of the Río Grande, where the area bordered upon the Navahos, and extended east to the area of Taos and Picuris. Somewhere in the vicinity of Pecos pueblo, the lands of the Vaquero Apaches began, and they extended along the eastern frontier of New Mexico as far as the territory of the Apaches del Perrillo.[72]

Thus New Mexico was completely surrounded by Athapascans, as Benavides repeatedly asserts. Fray Esteban de Perea essentially agrees with this idea but would insert an "almost" in the statement.[73] To the east the Vaquero Apaches were said to occupy 100 leagues of plains, and the Jumano Apaches also had extensive lands which began 100 leagues from New Mexico.[74]

In 1629–30 all of the Athapascans were at peace with the Pueblo Indians and with the Spanish invaders. Certainly this situation bade promise for the future—if it could be maintained. The situation was, however, fraught with evil potentialities, for many of the Pueblo tribes were preparing to recover their freedom, and within the next decade the Hopis, Zuñis, Jemez, and Taos were to kill their priests. The Spaniards' position in New Mexico was still primarily one of exploiting the labor of the Pueblo Indians, who were held by naked force. Santa Fe now had a population of about 250 Spaniards—or probably less—who were supported by some 700 servants and slaves of Indian and mixed blood.[75] The majority of the Spaniards consisted of 150 soldiers and their families.

> Though they [the soldiers] are few and poorly equipped, God has always enabled them to come forth victorious and has instilled into the Indians such a fear of them and of their harquebuses that at the mere mention of a Spaniard coming to their

71 Benavides, *1630*, 44–45, and Benavides, *1634*, 85.

72 *Ibid.*, 89, 91.

72 Perea's "True Report," in Benavides, *1634*, 221.

74 Benavides, *1634*, 91.

75 Benavides, *1630*, 23–24.

pueblos they run away. In order to keep them in constant fear, they deal very severely with them whenever an occasion arises for punishing a rebellious pueblo. If this were not done, the natives would have tried to murder the Spaniards.

Thus the poor Pueblo Indians were little better off than they were during the rule of Juan de Oñate. The Indians were not only oppressed by these soldiers, but they had to support them. Benavides was pleased to inform the King that no funds from his royal treasury were used to pay the soldiers; rather, as *encomenderos* of the Indian pueblos, they received a tribute from the Indians of one yard of cotton cloth and two and one-half bushels of corn each year from each house. Personal services were also rendered by the natives and tribute paid to the governor.[76]

During the 1630's the Spaniards began once again to use New Mexico as a base for reaching faraway peoples and places. In 1632 Fray Juan de Salas, Fray Diego (or Pedro) de Ortega, and some soldiers went out onto the buffalo plains to visit the Jumana (Jumano Apache) Indians on the Río de las Nueces (the Colorado River of Texas). They were received in a friendly fashion, and one of the priests stayed with the natives for six months.[77] This is the first record of the Jumano Apaches being on the Colorado River, where they were also located in the 1650's, 1680's, and 1690's. Besides being followers of the buffalo, these Athapascans were avid traders—as were the Vaquero Apaches —and frequented the area from La Junta to central Texas. In fact, their trading took them as far as the eastern Gulf Coast area of Texas.[78]

In 1632 interest also developed on the part of the Franciscans of New Mexico in the Ópatas and Pimas of Sonora and Arizona. These tribes were referred to as the Ypotlapigua and the Cipias, or Zipias. Ypotlapigua was probably a name for the Ópatas of

[76] *Ibid.*

[77] *Informe* of Fray Alonso de Posadas, in José Antonio Pichardo, "*Documentos y Noticias Históricas y Geográficas Colectadas para la Averiguación de los Limites entre las Provincias de la Louisiana y Texas,*" tomo XV, manuscript in BMAE (Biblioteca del Ministerio de Asuntos Exteriores, Madrid, Spain). Hereinafter cited as *Informe* of Posadas, in Pichardo, tomo XV, BMAE.

[78] See Forbes, "The Appearance of the Mounted Indian in Northern Mexico and the Southwest, to 1680," *Southwestern Journal of Anthropology,* Vol. XV, No. 2 (1959).

the northeast corner of Sonora and Cipias was derived from the Zuñi name for the Pimas: Tsipiakwe.[79] Two friars, Francisco Letrado and Martín de Arvide, became interested in going from Zuñi to the Zipias, and Arvide, accompanied by some Zuñis, set out on the journey. Five days later his companions killed him, and Letrado was murdered at his mission—the Zuñis had chosen this moment to cast off their chains.[80] It seems that the Apaches living southwest of Zuñi were at peace in 1632, otherwise Arvide would have never begun such a journey.

The type of retaliation taken against the Zuñis by the Spaniards is not known; however, the Indians were forced to abandon their six pueblos and unite in a defensive settlement on the rock of Caquima (K'iákima). In 1636 it was reported that they were still idolatrous and that they had come down from their rock to repopulate their former pueblos.[81]

In 1634 Captain Alonso Baca, with some soldiers and Indian servants, went 300 leagues to the east of New Mexico, reaching the Arkansas River and Quivira.[82] The reports of this journey mention no hostilities—the Plains Apaches were probably still at peace.

From 1632 to 1637 New Mexico was ruled consecutively by two governors, Francisco de la Mora y Ceballos and Francisco Martínez de Baeza, both of whom were virtually at cold war with the Franciscans. Mora was accused of allowing soldiers to set up their ranches in the Indians' fields, of abusing the natives in other ways, and of enslaving their children to sell. He also tried to sell 800 cows and 400 mares in Santa Bárbara, but the Viceroy ordered them returned to New Mexico.[83] Under Martínez, New Mexico was said to be in a miserable state.[84]

[79] Frederick Webb Hodge (ed.), *Handbook of American Indians North of Mexico,* II, 827.

[80] Another version states that both priests were killed—five days apart—at Zuñi. See Benavides, *1634,* 77, 80.

[81] Letter of Christóval de Quirós, November 28, 1636, *Provincias Internas* 35 (UTA Transcript), in AGN, and *Auto* of Francisco Martínez de Baeza, *Provincias Internas* 34 (UTA Transcript), in AGN.

[82] *Informe* of Posadas, in Pichardo, tomo XV, BMAE.

[83] Hackett, *Historical Documents,* III, 47, 130–31.

[84] Letter of Christóval de Quirós, November 28, 1636, *Provincias Internas* 35 (UTA Transcript), in AGN.

Meanwhile, other areas of New Spain had begun to expand northward once again. In 1610 the Jesuits finally succeeded in penetrating the Yaqui barrier, and by the 1620's they were working among the Pimas and Ópatas of southern Sonora. By the 1640's the Jesuits and the Franciscans were to be engaged in bitter disputes over who should control the northern Ópatas and Pimas. In Nueva Vizcaya some expansion occurred as Jesuits worked with the Taraumaras and Laguneros and as Franciscans established missions for the Conchos and Tobosos. However, the Tobosos revolted in 1612, and from 1617 to 1622 the entire province was plunged into war as the powerful Tepehuanes strove to free themselves. The Conchos, Tobosos, and Chisos— who bordered upon the Jumano Apaches—also joined this struggle and continued more or less at war for many decades thereafter.[85] The importance of these wars to the south of the Sumas, Cholomes, Julimes, and Jumano Apaches should be obvious: Hundreds of horses and other booty would reach them, and more hostile feelings would be created against the Spaniards.

The turbulent situation in Nueva Vizcaya and the hundreds of leagues of land which belonged to the hostile Conchos and Sumas and lay between Santa Bárbara and Santa Fe meant that the Spaniards in New Mexico were only very weakly under the control of royal authority. Thus the struggle between rival factions—one faction led by most of the Franciscans and the other led by the governor—were able to take an increasingly serious form. Finally, under Governor Luís de Rosas, open civil war broke out.

[85] See various documents in AGI (*Guadalajara* 28 and 143) and in BMH 971.

The Keres pueblo of Acoma as seen from the air. It was destroyed
by Spaniards under Vicente de Zaldívar in 1599. From Stanley
A. Stubbs, *Bird's-Eye View of the Pueblos* (Norman, 1950).

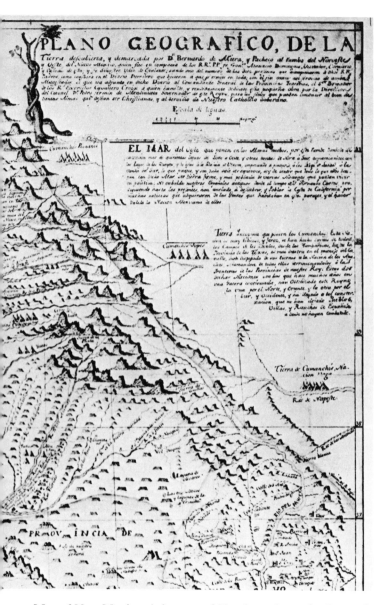

Map of New Mexico, Arizona, and Northern Areas, by Bernardo
de Miera y Pacheco, 1776.

Courtesy Servicio Geográfico del Ejército
Madrid, Spain

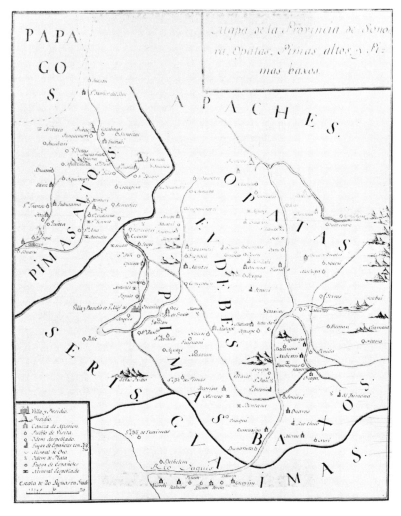

Map of the Province of Sonora (c.1760), showing locations of
Ópatas, Eudebes, Pimas Altos, Pimas Bajos, Pápagos, Apaches,
Seris, and Guaymas.

Translation of legend (from top): (1) Town and fortress; (2) Fortress; (3) Mission headquarters; (4) Inhabited town; (5) Deserted town; (6) Spanish settlement and church; (7) Gold mine; (8) Silver mine; (9) Spanish settlement; (10) Deserted mine. Scale of 20 leagues divided into single units.

Courtesy Servicio Geográfico del Ejército
Madrid, Spain

CHAPTER VII

A Land of Strife

◙

The entrance of Luís de Rosas as governor into New Mexico in 1637 was indeed a tragic event, for both Spaniards and Indians. Although Rosas cannot bear sole responsibility for the crisis which developed, he nevertheless must be held guilty of being a prime mover in the grotesque play acted out with the Franciscan fathers.

It was charged that the friars were the owners of all the wealth that there was in New Mexico and that they exercised a rule of tyranny over the Spaniards and Indians.[1] This assertion was borne out by His Majesty's Fiscal when he declared that the Franciscans had set up an *obraje* ("work factory") in a convent, using forced Indian labor, and that they refused to allow Governor Rosas to distribute *repartimientos* of natives to the settlers, insisting on doing this themselves.[2] Whether for a good or a bad end, it is clear that the friars definitely wanted to control the lives and labor of the converted Indians—a situation which naturally led to difficulties with the governors who

> come with an insatiable thirst to return rich [to New Spain], and this is not possible without notable offenses and rascalities against the Indians.[3]

[1] Francisco Gómez to the Fiscal, October 26, 1638, *Provincias Internas* 34 (UTA Transcript), in AGN.

[2] *Parecer* of Pedro Melian, the Fiscal, *Patronato* 244, Ramo VII, in AGI.

[3] Letter of Juan de Prada, January 15, 1644, *Patronato* 244, Ramo VII, in AGI.

Luís de Rosas' desire for wealth seems to have dominated him, and his methods were almost always evil. In 1638–39 he committed a series of crimes which deserve to be treated in full, for they affect the Athapascans directly. He was charged with the following:

> *Item*: that he went loaded with knives to the pueblo of Pecos to barter with a number of Apache Indians, friends of the baptized natives, pretending that he went to serve His Majesty; and as he did not find any trading he became angry and rash to such a degree with the priest [of Pecos] that he carried him captive to the *villa* [Santa Fe].

> *Item*: that in a journey that was made by order of the said governor to Quivira they [the Spaniards] killed a great number of the said friendly Apaches, and these killings were done in company with many infidel enemies of the said Apaches, an action prohibited by *cédula* of His Majesty . . . and they captured them [Apaches] in this unjust war, and they took them to sell in *tierra de paz* [in Nueva Vizcaya].

> The Christian natives of the pueblo of Pecos have made a great demonstration of feeling in regard to this, because they were living with them [the Apaches] and with them they had their commerce, by means of which they clothed themselves and paid their tributes.

> *Item*: that because of the above-mentioned war the same Apache nation remained with hatred and enmity towards the Spaniards, and on another occasion when Captain Sebastián González went as leader to trade with the Sumanas they obliged him to retire with the loss of the *alférez* Diego García, his son-in-law, whom they killed. They weren't able to resist the great gathering of Indian warriors that attacked.[4]

The term "Sumana" was applied to Athapascans living in the region southeast of El Paso. The Sumanas were apparently a branch of the Sumas, although some evidence would seem to make them a group which would link the latter with the Jumano Apaches.[5]

4 Testimony of Francisco de Salazar, July 5, 1641, *Patronato* 244, Ramo VII, in AGI.

The treacherous slave raid made by order of Rosas was said to have frightened the "always restless" Apaches and forced them to retire, according to a pro-Rosas informant.[6] On the other hand, the evidence indicates that the Plains Apaches had been at peace in 1638, prior to the raid, and that they were trading with the settled Indians, as in years gone by.[7] Certainly, the activities of Rosas helped to increase Athapascan and other Indian hostility. During these same years the Governor made an attack upon the Utacas (Utes), who had reportedly never caused any harm to either Spaniards or converted Indians. His soldiers killed many Utes and brought back more than eighty slaves, some of whom were sold—with Apaches—at Parral in Nueva Vizcaya and others placed in an *obraje* which Rosas created for himself at Santa Fe.

The Governor was charged with consenting to or permitting the Apaches—probably Navahos—who had been enemies of the Spaniards and converted Indians, to carry off the horses of the missions—apparently to damage the Franciscans' position. These Apaches took advantage of the opportunity to kill many mission Indians and acquire herds of horses and mares. In February, 1639, it was declared that the New Mexican Spaniards were unable to defend the province and castigate the enemy. Indeed, no campaigns had been made since 1628 because of the mountainous, dry, and rough lands in which the enemy lived. According to Francisco de Salazar, Rosas' enemy, the Governor did not undertake any campaigns against the Navahos. In fact, the only subsequent journeys which he authorized were the one of Captain Juan Gómez de Luna, who went to barter with the "Cavellera Larga" ("Long Hair Apaches"), and that of Captain Mathias Romero, to collect from the *encomiendas* in the Hopi area and to get slaves for Rosas' work factory and for selling in the *tierra de paz*. Gómez was responsible for arousing the hostility of the

5 See the sections on the Sumas and the Jumanos in Forbes, "Unknown Athapascans," *Ethnohistory*, Vol. VI, No. 2 (1959).

6 Francisco Gómez to the Fiscal, October 26, 1638, *Provincias Internas* 34 (UTA Transcript), in AGN.

7 Petition of Juan de Prada, September 26, 1638, in Hackett, *Historical Documents*, III, 108.

"Apaches of the Cavallera Larga" by apparently seizing some of them. Salazar declared that with this incident began all of the damages which these hitherto peaceful Athapascans were to commit on the road from Santa Fe (to New Spain?) and throughout the land as late as July, 1641. Thus the Apaches of the Gila–lower Río Grande region, who these apparently were, became active enemies of the Spaniards.[8]

Rosas was not content with making slave raids and thereby arousing the enmity of the Athapascans and Utes, however, for he began to fight actively with the Franciscans. One rupture took place when the Governor and some friars made a journey to the Ypotlapiguas (northeastern Ópatas), as a result of which the Indians fled to the sierras and Rosas continually quarreled with the priests and settlers who were with him.[9] After returning to New Mexico, the Governor apparently sought to break the hold which the Franciscans had on the Pueblo Indians by ordering the Pueblos not to obey the friars and by complaining of the priests in front of the natives—as he did at Taos. As a result, the Taos and the Jemez revolted, killing their priests and a number of other persons. Other Indians seem to have rebelled also, and large herds of livestock were stolen from the Franciscans.[10] No effort was made by Rosas to punish the rebels; on the contrary, he had his soldiers spend their time robbing the various pueblos, taking from both priests and Indians. The situation of the converted Pueblo tribes was desperate, and disease and hunger seem to have taken a large toll during these years.[11]

[8] Testimony of Francisco de Salazar, July 5, 1641, *Patronato* 244, Ramo VII, in AGI, and Letter of Mathias Romero, February 21, 1639, *Provincias Internas* 35 (UTA Transcript), in AGI.

[9] Testimony of Francisco de Salazar, July 5, 1641, *Patronato* 244, Ramo VII, in AGI.

[10] *Ibid.*; Petition of Juan de Salas, September 10, 1644, *Patronato* 244, Ramo VII, in AGI; and Testimony of Fernando Durán y Chavez, August 17, 1644, in the same *legajo*. These sources indicate clearly that the Jemez killed their priest when they rebelled. The Viceroy, however, said that "the Indians of the Hemes have had a surprise attack and assault of the Apache Indians, infidel enemies of the Christians," and during this attack the priest was killed. This leaves us in doubt about what actually occurred, but it seems wise to accept the testimony of persons in New Mexico at that time. See Scholes, "Notes on the Jemez Missions in the Seventeenth Century," *El Palacio*, Vol. XLIV, Nos. 7–9 (1938), 94.

Rosas' soldiers are said to have actually removed the priests from Nambe, San Ildefonso, and Santa Clara, and a Portuguese put on a priest's habit in front of the Piros at Socorro. Sandia, Zia, and Cuarac were also visited by the raiders.[12] The Pueblo Indians suffered the loss of most of their property, and their children were taken from them to be sold as slaves.[13] At Santa Fe Rosas expelled the authorized priest and placed in his stead Fray Juan de Vidania, an unfrocked Jesuit turned Franciscan. Vidania and Fray Pedro de Santa María sided with Rosas against the rest of their order, by which were accused of many immoralities.

Early in 1640 the Franciscans abandoned all of the pueblos and missions to unite at Santo Domingo. There they were joined by many settlers who chose the clerical side of the struggle. One of the causes of this union was the murder of one of Rosas' loyal officers by some other Spaniards, who claimed that the officer had had illicit relations with women of honor in Santa Fe. The murderers fled to the Franciscans and were protected by these priests from Rosas.[14] Of the 120 soldier-settlers in New Mexico at the time, 73 sided with the friars. The remainder, who were pro-Rosas, were said by their opponents to consist of mestizos and mulattos, and racial antagonism may have been involved.[15]

At Santo Domingo the friars and settlers fortified themselves, building defensive structures and creating a *castillo fuerte*. Then they sallied forth to raid, stealing the livestock and horses of the Governor and the loyal settlers. Reportedly, the Franciscans raised two flags at the pueblo: one of the Holy Crusade and the other of the Roman Catholic church. Obedience was to be given only to the Pope.[16]

For sixteen months this situation continued. The rival Spanish groups at Santo Domingo and Santa Fe both seem to have

11 Testimony of Nicolás de Lamar y Vargas, August 18, 1644, and of Fernando Durán y Chavez, August 17, 1644, *Patronato* 244, Ramo VII, in AGI.

12 *Ibid.*

13 Petition of Juan de Salas, September 10, 1644, *Patronato* 244, Ramo VII in AGI.

14 Letter of Bartolomé Romero, October 7, 1641, *Patronato* 244, Ramo VII, in AGI.

15 *Parecer* of Pedro Melian, the Fiscal, *Patronato* 244, Ramo VII, in AGI.

16 *Ibid.*

supported themselves by raiding the pueblos, and the Apaches are said to have taken advantage of the affair by increasing their incursions. Thus the years 1640 and 1641 must have been exceedingly harsh for the Río Grande Puebloans, although those at some distance—the Hopis, Zuñis, and Tompiros, for example —perhaps benefited from their breath of freedom.

A halt in the Spanish civil war occurred in the summer of 1641 when a successor to Rosas, Juan Flores de Sierra y Valdés, arrived in New Mexico. Flores died before he could patch up the dispute, but he did begin investigations which shed light upon the controversy. With his death the Franciscan faction seems to have acquired control of Santa Fe, and Luís de Rosas was made a prisoner. Rosas' *cabildo* was dissolved, and one favorable to the friars assumed power. The former governor was subsequently murdered in his quarters by Nicolás Ortiz, an outraged husband who found his wife committing adultery with Rosas—all of this while Rosas was still in prison. The Fiscal and the Governor of Nueva Vizcaya—who apprehended Ortiz—were of the opinion that the murder was prearranged by the priestly faction. It was charged that the faction placed Ortiz' wife with Rosas, and, when the husband discovered his spouse's absence, they took him to Rosas' rooms, where he found her. Rosas was then placed under a guard of four men, but they allowed the enraged Ortiz and some companions to murder the former governor. The rebel *cabildo* did nothing about the affair, and Ortiz went to Nueva Vizcaya, where he was apprehended.[17]

During the balance of 1641 and part of 1642 the friars' faction undertook several campaigns against the Apaches (Navahos), burning 20,000 *fanegas* of maize, taking many prisoners, killing others, and forcing the Athapascans to accept peace.[18] The peace was short-lived, however, for the subsequent governor had to continue the campaigns.

The 1639 revolt of the Taos Indians proved to be an exceedingly important event in Athapascan history. These Puebloans

17 *Ibid.*
18 Letter of Thomás Manso, January 15, 1645, *Patronato* 244, Ramo VII, in AGI.

chose to abandon their ancient community and trek out onto
the plains to live with their Apache allies. This move was probably brought about by the Taos' fear of Spanish retaliation and
a strong desire to be far, far away from the European invaders.

On the plains of western Kansas, in present-day Scott County,
the Taos established a new pueblo, called frequently El Cuartelejo by the Spaniards. Here they lived among the Athapascans
whose territory at this time included all or almost all of the High
Plains as far as the Black Hills. The Taos had some contact, it
seems, with the cultures of people farther to the east, such as the
Wichitas. The exiles lived at El Cuartelejo until twenty Spanish
soldiers and Indian auxiliaries under Juan de Archuleta brought
most of them back to their former pueblo.[19] Subsequently, in
the early 1660's, Governor Diego de Peñalosa returned the remainder of the Puebloans to New Mexico.[20]

The exact date of Archuleta's journey is not known, and only
an approximate dating in the 1650's was previously assigned.
However, Archuleta was a member of the pro-Franciscan faction
which was executed by Governor Alonso Pacheco on July 21,
1643, and therefore the journey had to take place between 1640
and 1643—probably in 1642 or early 1643.[21]

The movement of the Taos out onto the plains and Archuleta's journey must have had an effect upon the Plains Apaches
of that faraway region, and we may suppose that the Athapascans
in the El Cuartelejo area acquired the use of horses from the
Taos—if they did not already use them. Archaeologists have located village sites of these Athapascans in various places in western Kansas, western Nebraska, and eastern Colorado, and they
have also located the ruins left by the Taos at El Cuartelejo in
association with Plains Apache materials. A few pieces of "Quiviran" shell-tempered pottery shards confirm Archuleta's find-

19 Letter of Silvestre Vélez de Escalante, April 2, 1778, in Ralph Emerson
Twitchell (comp.), *The Spanish Archives of New Mexico*, II, 279–80. Also in
Documentos—México.

20 Trial of Diego de Peñalosa, 1665, in Hackett, *Historical Documents*, III,
263–64.

21 *Auto* of Alonso Pacheco, July 21, 1643, *Patronato* 244, Ramo VII, in AGI.

ing of artifacts from the Quivira villages among the Taos.[22] It is possible that some of the Plains Apaches were at peace with the Quiviras (Wichitans) during the period under consideration, both because of the pottery and because of finding Puebloan pottery of *c.* 1525–1650 among the Wichita sites. Such pottery could have come from New Mexico only by way of the Plains Apaches or the Taos and Apaches.[23]

The Athapascan sites on the High Plains reveal that their culture—referred to as the "Dismal River Culture" because of a location of a type site—included primarily a hunting way of life supplemented by the growing of maize, beans, and squash. No house ruins have been located, but pieces of turquoise, tubular incised pottery pipes, and some glass beads and iron indicate contact with Puebloans and Spaniards.[24]

Late in 1642 the rule of the insurgent *cabildo* was terminated in New Mexico by the arrival of Governor Alonso Pacheco de Heredia. Pacheco was well received by the Franciscans and their allies, and he seems to have pretended tolerance for events which had taken place. Actually, the royal officials in New Spain had, for the most part, accepted Rosas' point of view, and it would have been surprising if Pacheco had favored the rebels over those Spaniards who had remained loyal to the former governor. Pacheco evidently sought time to consolidate his position before taking action against the Franciscan faction, and he also faced serious problems with the Indians. He kept the rebel captains busy by sending them off on campaigns against the Pueblo Indians who had revolted and to castigate the Apaches. At this time Archuleta probably made his journey to El Cuartelejo.

When the land had been sufficiently pacified, Pacheco turned about-face and initiated charges of treason against eight rebel captains, and on July 21, 1643 they were executed. The Franciscan faction charged that Pacheco was backed by "a stranger and a Portuguese and mestizos and sambahigos, sons of Indian men

22 Letter of Silvestre Vélez de Escalante, April 2, 1778, in Twitchell, *The Spanish Archives of New Mexico*, II, 279–80, and Wedel, "Culture Chronology in the Central Great Plains," *American Antiquity*, Vol. XII, No. 3 (January, 1947), 151.

23 *Ibid.*, 150.

24 *Ibid.*, 151.

and Negroes, and mulattos," thus indicating that perhaps there was a racial cleavage in New Mexico, with the persons of non-Spanish ancestry supporting the secular side of the dispute. During this period there were less than 200 "citizens" in the province —including a large number of mestizos and mulattos.[25]

The Pueblo Indians experienced a period of harsh rule under Pacheco, for the Governor sought to keep the Indians under control. They were not allowed to travel from one pueblo to another without a license, and this law caused great hardship, because many of the villages were without food. In June, 1643 it was charged that Pacheco sought to levy new taxes and tributes on the poverty-stricken natives, increasing the current rate from one cotton *manta* and one *fanega* of maize per house each four or five months to the same amount collected from each individual. Some converted Indians were already fleeing to the enemy infidels—the Apaches—and, if the new tributes were levied, it was feared that they would all flee. Many Puebloans must have been taking refuge among the Apaches during this era, for five years before Fray Juan de Prada had noted that the converts would flee to the heathens at the slightest annoyance, "believing that they would enjoy greater happiness with them."[26]

The decline of the Pueblo Indians' civilization under the rule of the Spanish invaders from 1600 to 1643 is revealed in the fact that Governor Pacheco reported only 43 pueblos left in the province by 1643. At the beginning of Spanish occupation, the number of villages was said to be between 110 and 150, depending on the source of information.[27] This decline may have been due in part to the Franciscan and royal policy of congregating the Indians in fewer pueblos for the convenience of priests, soldiers, and *encomenderos*. However, the deadly nature of Spanish exploitation was chiefly to blame. The Athapascans cannot

25 Petition of Alonso Vaca, 1643, *Auto* of Alonso Pecheco, July 21, 1643, and Letter of Thomás Manso, January 30, 1648, *Patronato* 244, Ramo VII, in AGI.

26 Letter of Hernando Covarrubias, June 1, 1643, *Patronato* 244, Ramo VII, in AGI, and Petition of Juan de Prada, September 26, 1638, in Hackett, *Historical Documents*, III, 111.

27 Alonso Pacheco, August 6, 1643, *Patronato* 244, Ramo VII, in AGI, and Various Declarants, *México* 26, in AGI.

be blamed for the abandonment of any of the pueblos, with the possible exception of some belonging to the Tewas.

By August, 1643 the Franciscans and Governor Pacheco were involved in a new struggle which saw Fray Juan de Salas afraid that the Governor was going to have him taken to El Paso for either wild beasts or enemy Indians to kill.[28] Whether or not some of the Franciscans went back to their missions during this period is not completely clear, but in September, 1644 twenty-one of them were at Santo Domingo signing a protest against the rule of bad governors.[29] Certainly this affair must have helped strengthen the Pueblo Indians' preference for their own religion and to discredit Roman Catholicism. During this period there is an indication that the Zuñis and the Picuris revolted and were punished.[30]

In December, 1644, Fernando de Argüello arrived as governor, and a spirit of co-operation between secular and religious forces seems to have appeared. At the request of Pedro de Perea, "Captain Pacifier" of the Ópata region of Sonora, Fray Thomas Manso authorized the long-sought Franciscan expansion to the Ypotlapiguas in 1645. The Jesuits had been working with the Ópatas farther south, and, in spite of revolts, the priests had persevered. The Black Robes were not desirous of a Franciscan intrusion into their territory, and arguments continued for years. The friars of St. Francis established a mission "among the frontier and heathen nation of Potlapiguas, Bavispes and Baceraca," another among the Guasabas, Opotos, Techicodeguachis, and Vatepitos and still another among the Ópatas of Turicachi, Cuquiarachi, and Teras.[31] Almost all of these pueblos were on the frontiers of the Sumas, Janos, and Jocomes, and these Athapascans were soon

[28] *Relación* of Juan de Salas, September 19, 1643, *Patronato* 244, Ramo VII, in AGI.

[29] Petition of the Franciscans of New Mexico, September 10, 1644, *Patronato* 244, Ramo VII, in AGI.

[30] In BN 19258, there is a letter of December 6, 1944, signed Fernando Argüello and purporting to show that Juan Domínguez de Mendoza punished the Zuñis who were fortified on the Rock of Caquima and the "Picury." However, this letter is probably a forgery, because Argüello did not take office until after that date and would not have certified to services under another governor.

[31] Juan Mateo Manje, *Luz de Tierra Incógnita* (trans. by Harry J. Karns), 280.

objects of Franciscan interest also. First, however, the friars made a journey to the west to visit the Cipias (Pimas), but no missions were established.[32]

This area of Sonora proved to be a troublesome spot for the friars, for the Ópatas were already somewhat anti-Spanish because of battles with them in the 1540's, 1560's, and more recently in the early 1640's when Perea had conquered the Guasabas of Opotu (Opoto) by destroying their fields.[33] Nevertheless, the Franciscans worked diligently, and in five years time about 7,000 natives were baptized. Some of these may have been Athapascans, for the lands of the Jocomes and Janos extended from the Chiricahua Mountains south to the Ópata pueblos of Cuquiarachi, Turicachi, and Teras. The Sumas bordered upon the Ópata villages of Bavispe, Baceraca, and Huachinera. These Athapascan groups were probably somewhat hostile to the efforts of the Franciscans, for the Sumas farther to the east and the Conchos were continually regarded as dangerous to travelers between Nueva Vizcaya and New Mexico in this period.[34] This situation was a potentially bad one for the friars, especially since the Ópatas were restless. The fuse was soon applied to the mixture when a full-scale revolution broke out in Nueva Vizcaya among the converted Conchos, Tobosos, Cabezas, and Salineros, and among the Julimes of the La Junta region. This struggle began in 1644. It led to the death of several priests and caused the abandonment of a wide area. Furthermore, the large and powerful Taraumara nation joined the revolution in 1648, and Taraumara and Concho agitators seem to have spread the fervor to the Sumas and their allies—the Janos and Jocomes (The latter were simply called "Sumas of the north" at this time).[35]

32 See Albert H. Schroeder, "Southwestern Chronicle: The Cipias and Ypotlapiguas," *Arizona Quarterly*, Vol. XII, No. 2 (1956), 102–103.

33 Francisco Javier Alegre, *Historia de la Compañía de Jesús en Nueva-España*, II, 266.

34 Petition of Juan de Prada, September 26, 1638, in Hackett, *Historical Documents*, III, 107; Letter of Juan de Prada, March 12, 1642, *Patronato* 244, Ramo VII, in AGI; and Report of Thomás Manso, January 30, 1648, *Patronato* 244, Ramo VII, in AGI.

35 *Relación del Estado*, quoted by Carl Sauer, "The Distribution of Aboriginal Tribes and Languages in Northwest Mexico," *Ibero-Americana*, Vol. V (1934), 70.

In 1649 the revolution broke out among the Indians of north-eastern Sonora. Magicians possessed of the demon, as Juan Mateo Manje expressed it, stirred up the Ópatas and Sumas. As a result the Franciscans were hard-pressed. Spanish troops from Sinaloa came to the assistance of the friars at Turicachi, where the united Sumas had come in large numbers to attack. The Indians were repulsed—with eleven dead—but a Spanish follow-up offensive failed to accomplish anything more.[36] It appears that the Franciscans were forced to abandon their missions, for the Ópata converts were in revolt, the Sumas were unsubdued, and the Jesuits claimed the area anyway.[37] By 1651 a Jesuit priest was at Opoto, and in March he succeeded in making peace with the Sumas. Approximately one hundred men, women, and children came into Opoto to end hostilities, and the door was opened to Jesuit missionary activity among these Athapascans.

By 1653 some of the "Sumas of the east" had been baptized, and a *visita* was established for them six leagues east of Bavispe. There, 67 families, 244 persons, were congregated. The "Sumas of the north" were being reached by the Jesuits' entrance into Turicachi, where more than 30 chiefs had come in. Peaceful relations seem to have continued for years, but the number of Sumas who were actually converted was to be small.[38]

The influence of the Nueva Vizcaya rebellions, 1644–50, was to be felt in New Mexico as well as in Sonora, and in the lands of the Pueblo Indians local factors were to play a big part in the rise of the revolutionary impulse. Under Argüello's rule, 1644–47, religious control was once again established over the Río Grande pueblos, and the Governor "hanged and lashed and imprisoned more than forty Indians" for idolatry.[39] Argüello

36 *Ibid.*, 70–71, and Alegre, *Historia de la Compañía de Jesús en Nueva-España*, II, 404.

37 Manje, *Luz de Tierra Incógnita*, 281.

38 Sauer, "Distribution of Aboriginal Tribes," *Ibero-Americana*, Vol. V (1934), 70–71, and Alegre, *Historia de la Compañía de Jesús en Nueva-España*, III, 404–405.

39 Declaration of Diego López, December 22, 1681, in Charles Wilson Hackett (ed. and trans.), *The Revolt of the Pueblo Indians of New Mexico and Otermín's Attempted Reconquest, 1680–1682*, II, 299, hereinafter cited as Hackett, *Pueblo Revolt*.

also had twenty-nine Jemez Indians hanged as traitors and confederates of the Apaches. Other Jemez men were imprisoned for the same crime and for having killed a Spaniard.[40]

There is some evidence that the Apaches of the mountainous regions near Taos and Picuris—called the Apaches del Acho— made war upon those two pueblos and threatened the Pecos with an attack in April, 1646. The document which purports to show this fact is one testifying to the services of Juan Domínguez de Mendoza, with the signature of Governor Luís de Guzmán y Figueroa and a date of April 14, 1646. It appears to be a forgery, because Guzmán did not become governor until 1647 and the Apaches of the region in question were always—so far as is known—allies of the Taos and Picuris. Nevertheless, it is interesting to note that the author of the document, whoever he was, placed the Apaches del Acho in that area in the 1640's. Otherwise the name is not known until 1680.[41]

Little is known of New Mexico from 1647 to 1649, when Luís de Guzmán was governor. However, campaigns "of the Río Grande navajo y cassa fuerte" were made during his rule. Presumably, the fighting was being carried on with the Navaho Apaches since all of the above place names were within their territory—the "Río Grande" in question being the San Juan River.[42]

By 1649 news of the revolts in Sonora and Nueva Vizcaya must have reached the Apaches and Puebloans—probably stimulating a long-overdue event: a simultaneous rebellion by several of the tribes in New Mexico. Finally, after fifty years of subjection, the various pueblos began to realize that unity of action was the only way to defeat better-armed and more warlike Europeans. Unfortunately for the Indians, they had not as yet had

---

40 Declaration of Juan Domínguez de Mendoza, December 20, 1681, in Hackett, *Pueblo Revolt,* II, 266.

41 Testimony of Luís de Guzmán, April 14, 1646, in *"Servicios Personales del Maestro de Campo Don Juan Domínguez de Mendoza,"* BN 19258. Hereinafter cited as BN 19258. I am indebted to Professor France V. Scholes, of the University of New Mexico, for pointing out Domínguez de Mendoza's forgeries.

42 See Frank D. Reeve, "Early Navaho Geography," *New Mexico Historical Review,* Vol. XXXI, No. 4 (1956).

quite enough experience at warfare with the invaders for their plans to succeed entirely.

Throughout 1649 the Navaho Apaches kept the pueblo and frontier of the Jemez in continual unrest, and the Europeans had difficulty in maintaining the recently established church there.[43] Finally, in 1650, during the rule of Governor Hernando de Ugarte y la Concha, the soldiers

> discovered another plot to rebel which the sorcerers and chief men of the pueblos had arranged with the enemy Apaches, and for that purpose the Christians, under the pretext that the enemy was doing it, turned over to them in the pastures the droves of mares and horses belonging to the Spaniards, which are the principal nerve of warfare. They had already agreed with the said apostates to attack in all districts on the night of Holy Thursday, because the Spaniards would then be assembled.[44]

Captain Alonso Vaca followed a drove of mares, and the Indians were apprehended. Questioning revealed that the Tiwas of Alameda and Sandia had turned the mares over to the enemy and that these Tiwas were in league with all of the Apaches.[45] Governor Ugarte hurriedly held an investigation; the entire plan was discovered; and nine leaders from the pueblos of Isleta, Alameda, San Felipe, Cochiti, and Jemez were hanged. Many other inhabitants of these pueblos were sold as slaves for a period of ten years.[46]

Thus the first united revolt of the Tiwas, Keres, Jemez, and Apaches failed to rid New Mexico of its Spanish masters, but the seeds which were sown were to give birth eventually to the successful revolution of 1680. In 1681 a Keres of San Felipe declared that his people had been planning to rebel ever since the days of Ugarte and that they always desired it. Indeed, a few years after 1650 the Taos circulated two deerskins calling for

[43] Letter of Francisco Lucero de Godoy, February 5, 1649, *Provincias Internas* 35 (UTA Transcript), in AGN.

[44] Declaration of Diego López, December 22, 1681, in Hackett, *Pueblo Revolt,* II, 299.

[45] *Ibid.*

[46] *Ibid.*, and Declaration of Juan Domínguez de Mendoza, December 20, 1681, in Hackett, *Pueblo Revolt,* II, 266.

a new revolt, but action was postponed when the Hopis turned down the proposal.[47] The Navaho lands seem to have been a center for the dissemination of revolutionary ideas, as well as an area of refuge for the Pueblo Indians. In the early 1650's Ugarte sent a campaign against the Navahos which discovered another convocation of Christian Indians and Apaches.[48]

In 1650 a group of soldiers and Indian auxiliaries led by Captains Hernando Martín and Diego del Castillo departed from Santa Fe. They were to visit the Jumano Apaches on the Río Colorado of Texas, perhaps in the same area as that in which those Athapascans were visited by the Franciscans in 1629 and 1632. The Martín-Castillo party traveled 200 leagues to the Jumanos, probably reaching them near the junction of the Concho and the Colorado rivers. There they chose to remain for six months, for the Indians were friendly, there was sufficient food, and the rivers ýielded a number of shells containing fresh-water pearls. After their stay with the Jumanos, the Spaniards traveled toward the southeast, following the Río Colorado for 50 leagues to the limits of the Kingdom of the Texas (the Hasinai Caddo). In the intervening distance they visited the Cuitoas, Escanjaques, and Aijados, who are apparently to be equated with the Tonkawan tribes which always lay between the Athapascans of Texas and the Hasinai Caddo. Subsequently, they returned to Santa Fe by the same route—going the same distance of 250 leagues.[49]

The Viceroy of New Spain became interested in this discovery, and he instructed the Governor of New Mexico, Juan Samaniego y Jaca, to send another expedition to the region of "Las Perlas."[50] In 1654 *Sargento Mayor* Diego de Guadalajara led 30 soldiers and 200 converted Indians over the 200 leagues to the lands of the Jumanos on the Río Colorado. The Athapascans were friendly but said that their eastern neighbors—the Cuitoas —were at war with them. Captain Andrés López, 12 soldiers,

---

[47] Declaration of Pedro Naranjo, December 18, 1681, in Hackett, *Pueblo Revolt*, II, 245.
[48] Testimony of Juan de Miranda, July 27, 1671, BN 19258.
[49] *Informe* of Posadas, in Pichardo, tomo XV, BMAE.
[50] *Ibid.*

Indian allies, and many Jumanos went 30 leagues to the east to attack a rancheria of the Cuitoas. As the battle developed, different troops of Escanjaques and Aijados came to aid the Cuitoas, and the struggle endured for almost one day. Finally, the Tonkawans were defeated with considerable loss, and some 200 prisoners, many buckskins, and buffalo hides were acquired by the Spaniards. The López group returned to the main camp among the Jumanos, and the whole army made its way back to New Mexico, presumably laden with booty and slaves.[51]

The above account of the Guadalajara expedition was written by Fray Alonso de Posadas in the late 1680's, apparently after a discussion with Juan Domínguez de Mendoza, a member of the expedition and the leader of a subsequent trip to the same area in 1683.[52] Unfortunately, Domínguez de Mendoza was trying to get royal favor in the 1680's and 1690's and seemingly forged a series of documents purporting to be the letters of earlier governors of New Mexico testifying to his services. One such letter is important, as it purports to set forth certain services during the reign of Samaniego y Jaca, 1653–56. The forger, however, had forgotten the correct dates of Samaniego's rule and instead places it from 1651 to 1653. During this era Domínguez de Mendoza supposedly led a one-man war against the Apaches, as well as leading the Guadalajara expedition to the Jumanos. He was said to have made the discovery *"de las Perlas, y Reyno de Quybira, y tejas"* at his cost, and on this journey he defeated the Escanjaques and Aijados in a three-day battle. He imprisoned more than 1600 of the enemy and rescued 127 Christians from slavery, not bothering to explain how these Christians got to east central Texas. This whole story seems to have been a false account of the Guadalajara expedition and a product of the forger's imagination.[53]

In the same forged document the claim is made that Domínguez de Mendoza undertook a campaign against the Apaches of the Sierra Blanca (in the present-day Mescalero Apache reser-

51 *Ibid.*
52 *Ibid.*
53 Testimony of Juan Samaniego y Jaca, January 12, 1653, BN 19258.

vation, New Mexico) in retaliation for a raid which those Athapascans had made on the church in the Jumano Tompiros'
pueblo. Twenty-seven Tompiros who had been taken captive by
the Apaches were recovered.[54] In all probability, the forger based
this account on actual wars between Apaches and the Tompiros
which took place in the 1670 period. As late as 1663 the Apaches
of Siete Ríos (the Pecos River Valley north of Carlsbad, New
Mexico) were accustomed to bartering with the Jumano Tompiros, and these Apaches were close relatives of the Sierra Blanca
group.[55]

The forged letter also purports to show that Domínguez de
Mendoza led a campaign against the Apaches "of the mountain
ranges of Navajo, and cassa fuerte" for having carried out an
ambush in the province of the Jemez. There the Navahos were
supposed to have killed 19 and carried off 35 prisoners. The
hero of the document then undertook a superlative campaign
in which he surprised the Apaches during some dances, and the
Spaniards were able to take 211 prisoners—besides rescuing 40
Christians and a Spanish girl.[56] The trouble with this story—
aside from the fact that it is from a letter forged some thirty
years after the event—is that in another letter which purports
to be of Governor Samaniego y Jaca (but which has an impossible date—November 10, 1652) Domínguez de Mendoza is
supposed to have pacified the Jemez (and the Picuris) when
they revolted.[57] Thus in one document the Jemez, allied with
the Spaniards, are raided by the Apaches and in the other the
Jemez are revolting against the Europeans.

Still another of Domínguez de Mendoza's services during the
early 1650's, according to the forgeries, took place on a campaign which he made against the Mansos of the El Paso area.
These Indians had revolted and were threatening to kill their
priests, but the hero succeeded in pacifying them and hanging

54 *Ibid.*

55 Testimony in regards of Nicolás de Aguilar, May 11, 1663, in Hackett, *Historical Documents*, III, 143.

56 Testimony of Juan Samaniego y Jaca, January 12, 1653, BN 19258.

57 *Ibid.*

two of their leaders.[58] This document would be interesting if it could be relied upon, because this evidence would be the earliest of priests working among the Mansos.

In the 1650's New Mexico seems to have made little progress as a Spanish colony. From the early 1600's to the 1640's, the "Spanish" population seems to have numbered less than 200 persons—some of whom had Indian and Negro blood. In 1661 the province was said to have had not more than 100 citizens—including mestizos, mulattos, and all those who had any Spanish blood, "even though it is slight."[59] One suspects that by this time the only pure Spaniards were recent arrivals from Spain—governors and priests.

The slave raiding in the Rosas period and the revolt of 1650 seem to have increased the hostility of neighboring Athapascans. Nevertheless, with the exception of the Navahos, the Apaches were apparently more inclined to get along with the Spaniards than to fight back. This situation probably existed because the Plains Apaches needed peace to carry on their extensive commerce, and the Gila Apaches' trading in deerskins would likewise necessitate at least a truce with the New Mexico groups. Fray Alonso de Posadas, referring to the early 1660's when he was at Pecos pueblo, asserted that the Apaches living to the east of New Mexico

> have and always have had peace with the Spaniards, in order to sell their hides and skins and engage in commerce, promoting, on the other hand, the same Indians [of the Apache nation] who inhabit the mountains of New Mexico in all its circumference which sustain war with the Spaniards.

While Posadas was at Pecos, these Plains Apaches traded Quivira slaves with the Europeans in exchange for horses. Doubtless the need for acquiring horses also encouraged the Apaches in keeping the peace.[60] The late 1650's, 1660's, and 1670's were

[58] *Ibid.* In all probability, this is a false account of the punishing of the Mansos given by Tome Domínguez de Mendoza some years later.

[59] France V. Scholes, "Troublous Times in New Mexico, 1659–1670," *New Mexico Historical Review,* Vol. XII, Nos. 2–4 (1937), 139.

[60] *Informe* of Posadas, in Pichardo, tomo XV, BMAE.

to see a great change in this situation, however, and increasing slave raids by the Spanish governors were apparently to be the cause of this change.

Little is known of Juan Manso de Contreras' reign, 1656–59, but during this period Franciscans began to try to convert the Mansos at El Paso. Changes were made among the Piros as Governor Manso depopulated the pueblo of Sevilleta and moved the natives to El Alamillo—thanks to Fray Benito de la Natividad giving the Governor a horse and some sheep. The Franciscan probably wished to concentrate the Piros for ease of administration, but the Piros were moved back to Sevilleta after 1659 because their removal "had given free passage to the hostile Apaches."[61]

There is no doubt that Governor Manso was interested in acquiring Apache slaves to sell in New Spain. In 1659 he and his successor engaged in a controversy about who owned some Apaches recently taken in a raid carried out by some Picuris and Spaniards. Manso claimed that the eighteen captives were his, but Bernardo López de Mendizábal said that he had purchased them from the Picuris.[62] In 1665 the *Audiencia* of Guadalajara ordered that all slaves sold by Manso and López in Parral be set free. The judges must have considered that these slaves had been taken in unjust wars.[63]

During the government of Juan Manso, a campaign was carried out against the Salinero Apaches of the mountain ranges near Zuñi, and at the same time a campaign along the Río Grande was carried out. The Salinero Apaches probably lived near the saline or salt lake some eighty miles south of Zuñi. Many Apaches were killed and captured on this *campaña*.[64]

In 1658, according to certain documents, Manso received news that a powerful Apache army had attacked the Zuñi pueblo of Hawikuh (the Cibola of Coronado). Reportedly, the Athapas-

---

61 Bernardo López de Mendizábal, June 16, 1663, in Hackett, *Historical Documents*, III, 200–16.

62 Scholes, "Troublous Times in New Mexico, 1659–1670," *New Mexico Historical Review*, Vol. XII, Nos. 2–4 (1937), 382.

63 Hackett, *Historical Documents*, III, 262.

64 Testimony of Juan de Miranda, July 27, 1671, BN 19258.

cans had killed Fray Pedro de Ayala and 200 Zuñis and had taken over 1,000 prisoners. The pueblo and convent were burned and sacked, and all of the livestock was carried off. It was reported also that the Apaches were planning to return and destroy the whole province of the Zuñi with the next crescent of the moon. On October 10 a *junta de guerra* was held in Santa Fe, and it was decided to send 100 soldiers and 4,000 Indian allies to completely destroy the Apaches of Casa Fuerte and Navaho— those Indians responsible for the attack. Juan Domínguez de Mendoza was to lead the army, and no Apaches except small children were to be spared.[65]

This whole affair of 1658 seems to be pure fiction, however, as the document appears to be a forgery, and certain key facts are simply untrue. First, the pueblo of Hawikuh was not destroyed at this time—being mentioned in 1664 and later.[66] Secondly, Fray Pedro de Ayala was not killed in 1658, for he was either killed at Abó in the 1670's or at Zuñi in 1672.[67] Domínguez de Mendoza, in another of his certificates of his own service, has the Apaches killing a priest (no name given) at Hawikuh in 1673.[68] This latter date is probably more exact for the Apaches' destruction of that pueblo.

Early in the summer of 1659 Bernardo López de Mendizábal arrived in New Mexico and immediately showed his interest in the slave trade by haggling with Manso over Apache captives. He soon discovered a better way to obtain human beings to sell, for the Navaho Apaches had not come in to make assurances of peace, which was a thing they always did with new governors— or so López claimed. He sent some soldiers into Navaho territory, where they seized two Indians for questioning. An interrogation followed, and it was ostensibly revealed that the Navahos were planning extensive raids on the pueblos. In order to prevent this action, in September López sent 40 Spanish soldiers

---

[65] Letter of Juan Manso de Contreras, October 15, 1658, BN 19258.

[66] Hackett, *Historical Documents*, III, 246.

[67] Letter of Francisco de Ayeta, May 10, 1679, in Hackett, *Historical Documents*, III, 298, and Frank D. Reeve, "Seventeenth Century Navaho-Spanish Relations," *New Mexico Historical Review*, Vol. XXXII, No. 1 (1957), 49 n.

[68] Letter of Juan de Miranda, July 15, 1673, BN 19258.

and 800 allies to do as much damage as they could and to destroy all fields and crops belonging to the Apaches.[69] Several Franciscans charged that this journey was for nothing more than the acquisition of slaves and took place at a time when the rest of the province was in danger.[70]

It appears that most of the Apaches immediately bordering upon New Mexico were hostile, and little wonder, since López had sent "squadrons of men to capture the heathen Indians to send them to the *real* and mines of El Parral to sell (as he is doing at present, he having sent there more than seventy Indian men and women to be sold)."[71] In 1658 a famine had occurred, and the Apaches suffered so severely from it that they came in to the pueblos in 1659 to sell all of their slaves and their own children in exchange for food. The Franciscans purchased many of these Indians on the grounds that they could convert them. López, however, took advantage of the famine by seizing men, women, and children who had come in peace. The governor charged, however, that these seizures were made before his time and that the priests themselves had sold forty-three Indians at Parral.[72] By November, 1659 the areas of the lower Río Grande and the salines east of the Manzano Mountains were being raided severely by the enemy.[73]

In 1659 the conversion of the Mansos of El Paso and the nearby Sumanas really got under way. Fray García de San Francisco, who was also the missionary for the Piros and Tompiros, began the reduction of these Athapascans. When López passed El Paso on his way to New Mexico, he—showing his anticlerical attitude—had some arches removed which the Indians had put up for the Franciscans. López also initiated legal proceedings against the natives, and in September it was reported that they were running away. Nevertheless, a convent was established in Decem-

---

[69] Letter of Bernardo López de Mendizábal, August 30, 1659, BN 19258.

[70] Letter of Fray Juan Ramírez, September 8, 1659, in Hackett, *Historical Documents*, III, 187.

[71] *Ibid.*, III, 186.

[72] *Ibid.*, III, 191, and Trial of Mendizábal, in Hackett, *Historical Documents*, III, 216.

[73] Letter of Bernardo López de Mendizábal, November 19. 1659. BN 19258.

ber, and most of the Manso rancherias were congregated at El Paso. The Sumanas were to be included in the conversion, but, apparently, none of them had been gathered at that place. Trouble ensued, however, as the Mansos objected to being forced to dig irrigation ditches. Finally, it appears that they became stubborn, and troops had to be sent down to pacify them and rescue the priests. The Franciscans continued their efforts, but López reportedly slowed them down by refusing to allow any Piros of Senecú to assist the priests.[74]

Under the administration of López, as under most of the previous governors, there was a running conflict between the Franciscans and the secular officials. In this particular period it was intensified, because López was anticlerical and was willing to tolerate the kachina dances of the Pueblo Indians. The friars, on the other hand, sought to destroy completely the native religion and way of life.[75] The trouble reached a high point at Taos, where the Indians had preserved their independence since the 1640's. During López' rule, a priest attempted to re-establish the church at Taos, but the Governor appointed as head of the pueblo the Indian who had killed the previous priest. It was further charged by the Franciscans that the Governor ordered the Taos not to obey the friar.[76] López countered by declaring that the priest, Fray Luís Martínez, had had relations with an Indian woman and then had cut her throat, burying her body in a room of the convent. The Governor asked to have the friar removed, to forestall a new revolt.[77] By 1661 the Taos had once again destroyed the church.[78]

Not all of the Apaches were hostile during the early stages of López' government. The Apaches of Siete Ríos came to trade with the Jumano Tompiros, and Esteban Clemente, a Tompiro

[74] Trial of Mendizábal, in Hackett, *Historical Documents*, III, 203, 213; Letter of Fray Juan Ramírez, September 8, 1659, in *ibid.*; and Anne E. Hughes, "The Beginnings of Spanish Settlement in the El Paso District," University of California *Publications in History*, Vol. I (1914), 304–306.

[75] See Various Testimony, in Hackett, *Historical Documents*, III, 131–35.

[76] Trial of Mendizábal, in Hackett, *Historical Documents*, III, 206–207.

[77] *Ibid.*, III, 217–20.

[78] Testimony of Nicolás de Freitas, January 24, 1661, in Hackett, *Historical Documents*, III, 161.

chief, seems to have made frequent return visits to those Apaches. The Jumano Tompiros' largest pueblo, usually called "Humanas," was said to be a trading center "whither they gather from all sides for trade in antelope skins and corn." The friendship of the Siete Ríos Apaches was given a severe test, however, when several of their men were attacked by the Tewas of Cuarac pueblo. The Apaches had been friendly, but, as they arrived at Cuarac at night, the natives of the pueblo mistook them for enemies, killed one, and wounded another. Thereupon the Siete Ríos Indians made demonstrations, desiring to attack the pueblo to avenge the killing. Taking the initiative, Governor López sent Nicolás de Aguilar to

> wage war upon them, or pacify them before they could fall upon the pueblo of the Christians. He went, taking with him a squad of Spaniards and another of Indians; he worked hard to reduce the enemy, for they were very much determined upon war. But God willed that they should be reduced to peace, and a pact was made with them that they should not pass beyond the pueblos of Humanos and Tavira, where they come to barter; nor should the enemy of the same nation in the jurisdiction of Casa Fuerte and Navajo come, because it is from there that the whole kingdom receives hurt, for they [the Apaches] are all one people, and it is impossible to tell whether they are friends or enemies. This pact has been observed [to 1663] and the Indians of Cuarac have been ordered not to go to the pueblos of Humanos and Tavira at the times when the Apache Indians of Los Siete Ríos should come to trade, for if the nations would avoid seeing each other there would be no war.[79]

Thus it is clear that the Southern Apaches were accustomed to trade regularly with the Tompiros and that the Navaho Apaches sometimes traded with the Eastern Tewas.

During this period the Plains Apaches were coming regularly into Pecos, and some Spaniards were in the habit of going out among them. In August, 1660 López sent Diego Romero and five other men from Senecú to the buffalo plains to visit and

[79] Trial of Nicolás de Aguilar, May 11, 1663, in Hackett, *Historical Documents,* III, 143, and Scholes, "Troublous Times in New Mexico, 1659–1670," *New Mexico Historical Review,* Vol. XII, Nos. 2–4 (1937), 396.

trade with the Athapascans. Reportedly, Romero married an Indian girl, as his father had done years before, and the Apache supposedly danced the kachina as a part of the marriage ritual. After one month among the Indians, Romero and his men returned to Santa Fe by way of Galisteo.[80]

López apparently found it profitable to keep the friendship of the Plains Athapascans in order to acquire hides and skins. When it came to the Apaches who lived closer to the settlements, however, the Governor found it more advantageous to continue to deal in human lives. The *Audiencia* of Guadalajara later convicted López of treacherously attacking peaceful Apaches in order to acquire slaves. This attacking was done at Jemez, where a party of Navahos came to trade, and López had the men murdered and the women and children enslaved. The same thing was also done at Taos when Athapascans from that neighborhood were there in peace. A Spaniard later testified that he had drawn up approximately 90 decrees legalizing the seizure of Apaches. As a result of these acts, the Navahos began raiding the frontier, killing 20 converted Indians and stealing more than 300 head of livestock.[81]

Farther to the south, the same type of treachery was being perpetuated. Captain Juan Domínguez de Mendoza, in charge of the lower Río Grande region, was said to have undertaken campaigns against the Apache in time of peace and to have hanged prisoners at Isleta. Still another declarant refers to Domínguez' "butchery" of captive Athapascans.[82]

Prior to 1638, the only Apaches who were at war with the Spaniards were Navahos, but by 1661 most or all of the Athapascan groups had been goaded into some degree of hostility. Only the Plains Apaches had managed to maintain a generally peaceable attitude towards the Europeans—apparently because of

[80] Testimony of Nicolás de Freitas, January 24, 1661, and Letter of García de San Francisco, January 22, 1661, in Hackett, *Historical Documents*, III, 156.

[81] Various Testimony, in Hackett, *Historical Documents*, III, 282, and Scholes, "Troublous Times in New Mexico, 1659–1670," *New Mexico Historical Review*, Vol. XII, Nos. 2–4 (1937), 69, 74–75, 398.

[82] Testimony of Nicolás de Freitas, January 24, 1661, and Letter of García de San Francisco, January 22, 1661, in Hackett, *Historical Documents*, III, 156, 162.

their unique position as suppliers of buffalo hides. It is to be noted, however, that whereas from 1540 to perhaps 1638 these Plains Athapascans had come into New Mexico and lived among the Pueblo Indians, they were now apparently trading only at frontier pueblos such as Pecos and Humanas, and Spaniards were going out onto the plains to trade with them. Undoubtedly, the frequent slave raids and treacherous attacks of the Europeans had contributed to this avoidance of the Río Grande Valley.

To the south of the Plains Apaches, in Nueva Vizcaya and Coahuila, wars between Spaniards and Indians continued to be the rule. One exception was at La Junta, where several priests from El Paso went to preach to the Julimes and possibly to some Jumanos. According to one authority, however, the Indians became hostile and expelled the friars in 1662.[83] The Tobosos, farther to the south, were continually fighting with the miners and ranchers of Nueva Vizcaya, and in 1654 the Chisos were in league with them. Here, as in New Mexico, many slaves were taken by the Spaniards and were continually escaping to their tribesmen, spreading hatred against the Europeans. To the east, it was said that the Coahuilas and the Guachichiles were almost "consumed," but other nations had been added to the list of enemy peoples. During the 1650's and 1660's the Indians of southern Texas and northern Nuevo León–Coahuila were at war and stealing considerable numbers of horses, mares, and livestock. In 1653 and 1655 Spanish armies campaigned into southern Texas against the Cacaxtles as a result of the latter tribe's theft of Spanish herds. (In the 1690's the Cacaxtles were allies of the Jumano Apaches).[84] Needless to say, these wars contributed to the northward spread of the horse and also helped to poison the Indians' minds against Europeans. It was to be only a matter of time until the Athapascans were to be drawn directly into the affairs of this portion of the northern frontier of New Spain.

[83] Joseph Antonio de Villa-Señor y Sanchez, *Theatro Americano*, I, 424–25, and Hughes, "The Beginnings of Spanish Settlement in the El Paso District," University of California *Publications in History*, Vol. I (1914), 330.

[84] Various documents in AGI (*Guadalajara* 143); León, *Historia de Nuevo León*, 218–22; and Diary of Damian Massanet, BMH 974.

CHAPTER VIII

Prelude to Triumph

The relations of the Apaches with the Spaniards of New Mexico remained much the same under Diego de Peñalosa (1661–64) as under the previous government. The Plains Apaches maintained peace and traded at Pecos, where they received horses in return for Quiviran slaves—indicating that at least a portion of the Plains Athapascans were at war with the Wichitans.[1] The Apaches of "Jila" were reportedly asking for priests to baptize them during this period, but plans to convert them never went beyond the discussion stage.[2]

The enslavement of Athapascans continued as before; in fact, slaves became so numerous that an Apache woman could be purchased for twenty-six pesos. Governor Peñalosa declared that he had so many Apache slaves that he gave away more than 100 of them. The *Audiencia* of Guadalajara ordered that slaves whom he had sold in Sonora should be set free.[3]

Diego de Peñalosa was apparently a man with few scruples. In the early 1680's he forged a diary which purported to trace

[1] *Informe* of Posadas, in Pichardo, tomo XV, BMAE.

[2] Trial of Diego de Peñalosa, December 11, 1665, in Hackett, *Historical Documents*, III, 266.

[3] Reply of Diego de Peñalosa, October 22, 1665, and Declaration of Andrés Zambrano, February 20, 1864, in Hackett, *Historical Documents*, III, 244, 262, and Scholes, "Troublous Times in New Mexico, 1659–1670," *New Mexico Historical Review*, Vol. XII, Nos. 2–4 (1937), 38

an expedition he made in 1662 to Quivira and the Mississippi River. The diary is actually nothing but an exaggerated and fanciful account of the Oñate expedition of 1601.[4] Nevertheless, Peñalosa apparently did go out on the plains as far as El Cuartelejo, "on the frontier of La Quivira." In 1662 or thereabouts, this Governor finally punished the Taos for their revolts of *c.* 1639 and *c.* 1660 and apparently re-established their mission. Furthermore, he

> caused to be reduced . . . the Taos Indians who had been in revolt for twenty-two years, and were living as heathens among the people of El Cuartelejo, on the frontier of La Quivira. He reduced thirty-three, having caused El Cuartelejo to be laid waste for more than 200 leagues beyond New Mexico.[5]

Thus the Taos settlement among the Apaches was finally destroyed after existing from about 1640 to 1662. The destruction of the pueblo must have involved hostilities with the Apaches of El Cuartelejo, or at the very least, aroused their animosity.

The *encomenderos* of New Mexico were kept busy in 1662 with "the continuous war against infidels" and the threat of plots among the Puebloans.[6] Apaches living between the Hopis and the Zuñis were hostile, and the road from Hawikuh to Awatobi was described as the most dangerous in New Mexico. The area from Acoma to Zuñi was also subject to attack, and an ambush was reportedly prepared near Acoma by the Apaches.[7]

Governor Peñalosa made a journey in the early 1660's to the Hopi area, apparently to visit the mines in the region later known as the "Sierra Azul." This objective was not accomplished, because of wars with the Apaches and other accidents, but something was accomplished by the Spaniards: To the west of the Hopis lived the Conina or Cosnina Indians (probably the Havasupai), and Peñalosa claimed that he reduced them and the Cru-

4 *Relación* of Nicolás de Freitas, 1684, *Expediciones de 1519 a 1697*, tomo II, MN 142.

5 Trial of Diego de Peñalosa, 1665, in Hackett, *Historical Documents*, III, 263–64.

6 Letter of Diego de Peñalosa, May 7, 1662, BN 19258.

7 Various Documents, in Hackett, *Historical Documents*, III, 246, 253, 255.

zados to two pueblos in the Hopi area.[8] Whether the Governor or the Franciscans were responsible for this reduction is not clear, but a mission for the Coninas was certainly established at about this time. Fray Josef de Espeleta began the new mission fourteen leagues to the west of Oraibe, and by 1665 it was reported that thirty or forty Indians had been baptized.[9] This *conversión* of Coninas was still in existence in 1672.[10]

In 1663 the Tewa pueblo of Tajique (on the eastern slopes of the Manzano Mountains) was reportedly the object of frequent Apache raids. The Athapascans were charged with seizing Tewas and taking them off to be burned and eaten.[11] The charge of cannibalism was almost never made against the Apaches, and it is to be doubted here, especially since the declarant, Nicolás de Aguilar, was a soldier who had campaigned against the Apaches in unjust war and would therefore desire to prove that the Indians were cannibals—and consequently subject to enslavement under Spanish laws.[12]

During his final year in office, Diego de Peñalosa issued an edict which must have caused a great change in Pueblo-Athapascan relations and helped to stimulate Apache hostility to Spanish rule. The Governor decreed that enemy Indians, even though at peace, were not to be allowed to enter into the pueblos to trade. This law was ostensibly designed to keep the enemy from learning of Spanish strength, but in actuality it was probably meant to keep the Pueblo Indians from contacting the free Athapascans.[13] Perhaps it was hoped that this action would put an end to revolutionary plots and, incidentally, force the Pueblo Indians to rely upon Spanish middlemen for such things as deerskins and buffalo hides. This attitude was, however, to contribute

[8] Trial of Diego de Peñalosa, 1665, in Hackett, *Historical Documents*, III, 264. and Memorial of Juan Domínguez de Mendoza, c.1686, *Guadalajara* 138, in AGI.

[9] Declaration of Antonio Jorge, August 12, 1691, *Guadalajara* 139, in AGI.

[10] Lansing B. Bloom and Lynn B. Mitchell, "The Chapter Elections of 1672," *New Mexico Historical Review*, Vol. XIII, No 1 (1938), 117.

[11] Testimony of Nicolás de Aguilar, 1663, in Hackett, *Historical Documents*, III, 144.

[12] *Ibid.*, III, 143. He had been a soldier under López de Mendizábal.

[13] Order of Diego de Peñalosa, January, 1664, in Twitchell, *The Spanish Archives of New Mexico*, II, 2.

heavily to the effect of food shortage during the next few years and lead the Apache to undertake greatly increased hostilities.

In 1663 the governor of Nueva Vizcaya, Francisco de Gorraez Beaumont, determined upon sending a priest to the Suma Indians of the Casa Grande region of Chihuahua. As noted previously, the Jesuits and Franciscans had attempted to reach the Sumas from Sonora, but with little success. Now it was determined to send Fray Andrés Paez from the depopulated Toboso mission of San Buenaventura de Atotonilco to begin missions at Casas Grandes, at Carretas (on the Río de Carretas), and at El Torreón (to the south of Casas Grandes). Captain Andrés García, who was in charge of settling people at the Manso mission in El Paso, was ordered to pass over to Casas Grandes to start a settlement there and help Paez. García was to congregate as many Indians as he could for the new mission and receive in return the title of *Alcalde Mayor* of the region. On June 12, 1664, a letter from "San Antonio de las Casas Grandes" announced that possession had been established, the Indians had rendered obedience, and a church was under way. The letter was signed by Andrés López de Gracia (or García) and Captain Francisco Ramírez, both of whom were destined to be important actors in the future affairs of this area. By 1666 two new friars, Pedro de Aparicio and Nicolás de Hidalgo, were among the Sumas of the west.[14]

The conversion of the Mansos in the El Paso region was continuing as before, that is, there was no major revolt but always vague discontent. Fray Blas de Herrera reported in 1663 that

> it seemed to him from the actions and the things that were said to him by some of the Mansos, that Captain Andrés López de Gracia, a settler on that river [the Río Grande] was hindering the conversion of those heathen.[15]

It should be noted here that the Franciscans seldom if ever began a conversion unless accompanied by soldiers who settled on lands

[14] Founding of the Suma Missions, 1663–64, in *Documentos—México*, Series 4, III, 233, 239; Various Letters of Francisco de Gorraez Beaumont, BMH 971; and Letter of Andrés López de Gracia, etc., June 12, 1664, in Museo Nacional (Mexico), *Asuntos* 242, Folio 191.

[15] Report of Blas de Herrera, 1663, in Hackett, *Historical Documents*, III, 251.

in the area or became *encomenderos*. These Spaniards then formed a nucleus for future settlement, protected the priests from his charges, and helped to perform such tasks as retrieving runaway neophytes. The settlement of these soldiers was not in the native interest, however, for soon the best lands were in Spanish hands. Undoubtedly, this process of concentrating the Indians and allowing Europeans to settle on the "vacant" land contributed heavily to the later impoverishment and hostility of the Mansos, Sumas, and other tribes of this area.

In 1664 Fray García de San Francisco and Fray Benito de la Natividad began reducing the eastern Sumas (Sumanas) who lived twelve leagues below El Paso. In 1668 Fray Juan Alvarez was working with these Sumas, and Fray Salvador de Guerra was with the Mansos—the church of Nuestra Señora de Guadalupe de los Mansos being dedicated that year. Four hundred Mansos were present at the dedication ceremony.[16]

Fray Salvador de Guerra, the priest responsible for teaching the Mansos Catholicism, was of a questionable character, and it is little wonder that the Indians revolted—apparently against his rule. Guerra had previously been with the Hopis and it was charged that he beat one of these Indians for practicing the native religion. After the beating, he poured turpentine on the Hopi and set him aflame. The Indian began running toward Santa Fe, and the Franciscan mounted a horse and trampled him to death.[17]

From 1665 to 1668, New Mexico was ruled by Fernando de Villanueva, and, unfortunately, little is known of the first two years of his government, during which time important events occurred. First, a famine began in 1666 which was to last until at least 1671, and, secondly, Apache hostility began to assume the consistently anti-Spanish character which it was to maintain from this time on. Until *c.* 1667 no Apache groups had been "ordinarily" hostile to the Spaniards and their allies, with the exception of the Navahos, and even they were apparently more

---

[16] France V. Scholes, "Documents for the History of the New Mexican Missions in the Seventeenth Century," *New Mexico Historical Review,* Vol. V, No. 2 (1930), 56, 197–200.

[17] Testimony of Juan Domínguez de Mendoza, 1663, in Hackett, *Historical Documents,* III, 234.

peaceful than hostile during some periods, for example, from 1629 to c.1638, when no campaigns were undertaken. The Plains Apaches were consistently peaceful except when retaliating against slave raids, and the other Athapascans, although increasingly hostile after 1638 and especially after 1650, remained amenable to Spanish peace overtures. After 1667, however, the ordinary relationship between Apaches and Spaniards in New Mexico was one of almost continual war.

One of the major factors in the rise of an unremitting hatred for the Europeans was enslavement of Athapascans, which continued under Villanueva. The Governor was even charged with having sold two Christian Apache boys in Parral, and the general sale of slaves was quite common. In evidence, a German, Bernardo Gruber, was arrested by the Inquisition, and in his possession were three Apache men and women from New Mexico.[18]

Another important factor in the rise of hostility was the great famine which stalked New Mexico from 1666 to 1671. Hundreds of Pueblo Indians are known to have died of starvation, and a follow-up blow was rendered by an epidemic which killed both people and livestock. Naturally, the suffering Indians were hard-pressed to pay their tributes, and unrest was seemingly general. The neighboring Athapascans were also affected by the famine, and the Spaniards' ban on trading with the pueblos must have added to the hardships. All of these factors produced a situation which was ready to explode.

The fuse was apparently lighted not in New Mexico but in Nueva Vizcaya, where famine and epidemic also raged in 1666–67. The Tobosos and their allies, including many apostates from the missions, became exceedingly bold, attacking fairly large parties of Spaniards and even capturing a priest. The situation became so bad that on December 10, 1668, San Francisco Xavier was declared to be the patron of Nueva Vizcaya and its chief weapon against the rebels, for "the human remedies that this kingdom has are very little."[19] The Toboso war was not so easily

18 Various testimony, *Provincias Internas* 35 (UTA Transcript), in AGN, and Hackett, *Historical Documents*, III, 276, 282.

19 Various documents in BMH 971, and Alegre, *Historia de la Compañía de Jesús en Nueva-España*, II, 441, 444.

solved, for these stanch, independence-loving nomads remained almost constantly in rebellion until after 1700.

In August, 1666, it was reported that the Sumas of the Casas Grandes, Torreón, and Carretas missions were being baptized and reduced to the faith; but early in 1667 unrest developed, and open revolt occurred in the near-by Conchos region. The Conchos were subdued rather quickly, but the Sumas were still absent from their reductions as late as August, 1667. It seems that when Fray Aparicio died (of a natural death), the Indians abandoned the missions and killed a mulatto servant who had belonged to the Franciscan. (Mulattos were often used by the priests to control the natives, and the Indians were frequently goaded into revolt by the cruelty of the overseer.) This revolt did not prove to be very serious and was settled with the sending of new priests to the region, but farther north the general unrest of 1667 took a more serious tone.[20]

Early in February, Governor Villanueva received an appeal for aid from Captain Andrés de Gracia at El Paso. The Mansos had revolted and were endangering the lives of the friars there. Plans were made to send *Maestre de Campo* Tome Domínguez de Mendoza, with twenty-five soldiers, to rescue the priests, but a second letter from Gracia announced that he had executed two Manso leaders and that the aid was not needed.[21] Further concern was caused by the fact that the Mansos of Captain Chiquito and their close allies, the Apaches of El Chilmo (a chief of the Gila Apaches), had left the area of the road to New Spain, where they had been friendly and at peace. The *Alcalde Mayor* of Senecú, Juan García, was dispatched in peace to the Athapascans' rancherias in order to contact them and bring the chiefs to Villanueva, so that the Governor could discover the causes of unrest and secure the safety of the highway. García found the villages abandoned and the Indians fled to other places.

Villanueva was now very much concerned with the matter,

[20] Letter of August 8, 1666, in Museo Nacional (Mexico), *Asuntos* 242, Folio 192, and various documents in BMH 971.

[21] Letter of Fernando de Villaneuva, February 10, 1667, BN 19258.

and García was instructed to do his best to halt a renewal of the "live" war which had formerly existed between the Spaniards and the Indians of Chiquito and El Chilmo. By February 10, 1667, all of the Apaches had been forced to accept peace except those of Chiquito and El Chilmo. Villanueva dispatched Juan Domínguez de Mendoza to the El Paso region with orders to calm the two tribes without disturbing the Apaches who were already peaceful.[22]

The situation was much more serious than Governor Villanueva imagined, for many Puebloans were planning to revolt, and alliances were being made with the Athapascans. The rebellion first broke out among the hitherto peaceful Piros. A number of these Indians and their Apache allies ambushed and killed the *alcalde mayor* and four other Spaniards in the Sierra de la Magdalena. The Piros were apparently seeking to return to their old religion, but the Spaniards were able to crush the uprising, and six Indians were hung at Senecú. Others were burned as sorcerers and traitors, and still others were imprisoned and sold as slaves.[23]

The tyranny of Spanish rule and the suffering from famine were enough to keep the idea of revolution alive, and in spite of the punishments given the Piros

> another Indian governor of all the pueblos of Las Salinas [the Tompiro region], named Don Esteban Clemente, whom the whole kingdom secretly obeyed, formed another conspiracy which was general throughout the kingdom, giving orders to the Christian Indians that all the horse droves of all the jurisdictions should be driven to the sierras, in order to leave the Spaniards afoot.

A general revolt was planned for Holy Thursday, and all the invaders were to be killed, but, as in 1650, the plan was discovered, and Clemente was hanged.[24] Apaches were probably in-

22 *Ibid.*
23 Declarations of Diego López and Juan Domínguez de Mendoza, December, 1681, in Hackett, *Pueblo Revolt,* II, 299.
24 *Ibid.*

volved in the abortive rebellion, for Clemente had had close contact with the Siete Ríos groups in the late 1650's.[25]

The importance of this general unrest among the Piros, Tompiros, and Pueblo Indians should not be underestimated, because it must have had a great effect upon the neighboring Athapascans. While the Piros and Tompiros were put down by Spanish arms, the more northerly settled tribes continued their plotting into the 1670's, and the Apaches were stirred into a new type of war against the Spaniards. Heretofore, the Athapascans had largely confined their military efforts to simple raids on livestock or on weak points in the European armor—doing some harm, but not seriously endangering the hold of the invaders upon the province. In the late 1660's and 1670's, a change occurred, and an "offensive" against the Spaniards took place. No longer were the Athapascans content merely to raid Spanish-held pueblos—they now sought to destroy them.

Surprisingly, the two regions which suffered the greatest damage from the Athapascans between 1668 and 1680 were the Piro and Tompiro areas. The explanation probably lies in the fact that the Spaniards, after crushing the rebellions of these tribes, destroyed their alliances with the Apaches and used Piro and Tompiro warriors in campaigns against the Athapascans. Thus the Athapascans would have regarded their former allies as traitors and enemies to be destroyed with the Europeans. In addition to this situation, the Piros and Tompiros were exposed to easy attack, and the famines and epidemics had weakened their pueblos. For three years it was said that no crops were harvested, and many Indians perished of hunger. There were pueblos, as in Humanas, where more than 450 died in 1668, and the famine continued into 1671.[26] Even without outside interference, many pueblos might have been at least temporarily abandoned under such conditions.

By December, 1668, the province of the Tompiros was said to be a land of war, with the Apaches killing Spaniards and

[25] Scholes, "Troublous Times in New Mexico, 1659–1670," *New Mexico Historical Review*, Vol. XII, Nos. 2–4 (1937), 396.

[26] Letter of Fray Juan Bernal, April 1, 1669, in Hackett, *Historical Documents*, III, 272.

Christian Indians and robbing horse and mule herds. At this time the pueblo of Humanas had three *encomenderos* who were in charge of its defense, and on December 16, 1669, they were ordered to muster before Governor Juan de Medrano y Mesia, along with other *encomenderos*, at Isleta.[27] These soldier-exploiters bore the chief responsibility for protecting the southern regions of New Mexico, and they necessarily made use of the Indian warriors of their pueblo. These Indians had the choice either of campaigning against their neighbors, the Apaches, or of rebelling against the Spaniards. In either case they faced destruction, for the Europeans were strong enough to destroy them but too thinly spread out to defend them adequately.

The Siete Ríos Apaches led the attack on the Tompiros of Humanas pueblo, and a number of retaliatory campaigns were undertaken against them. Some of these campaigns were led by Juan Domínguez de Mendoza and one by Francisco de Madrid.[28] To the west the Navaho Apaches were apparently at war also, for a campaign was made against heathens near Acoma in January, 1669. By April, Fray Juan Bernal reported that "the whole land is at war with the widespread heathen nation of the Apache Indians."[29] Intercourse between various sections of New Mexico was limited, and the road from Santa Fe to Abó was described as being "in hostile territory" and very dangerous.[30] In May, Domínguez de Mendoza was appointed one of the *encomenderos* of Humanas—this position entitling him to the tribute of one *manta* of cotton and one *fanega* of maize from every house each year. At this time the Governor also called on all of the *encomenderos* to fulfill their obligations, because the kingdom was menaced by the Apaches.[31] By June, 1670, Domínguez de Mendoza had killed 13 Athapascans and liberated 6 Tompiro Indians taken by the enemy from Humanas. The situation continued

27 Letter of Juan de Medrano, May 1, 1669, BN 19258.

28 Report of Juan de Miranda, July 27, 1671, BN 19258, and Declaration of Pedro de Leiva, October 20, 1681, in Hackett, *Pueblo Revolt*, II, 168.

29 Various Testimony, in Hackett, *Historical Documents*, III, 272, 278.

30 Report of Francisco Gómez de la Cadena, 1669, in Hackett, *Historical Documents*, III, 276.

31 Letter of Juan de Medrano, May 1, 1669, BN 19258.

to deteriorate, and in September, 1670, the Apaches of the mountain ranges of Siete Ríos and that vicinity carried out a great attack on Humanas, killing 11 and carrying off 31 captives. The church was profaned, and sacred ornaments were broken to pieces in the attack. In retaliation, 30 soldiers and 300 Indian allies were to attack the Apaches.[32]

During 1670 and 1671, famine continued to reign in New Mexico, and in 1671 disease attacked many Indians. This situation, coupled with the Apache wars, led many Tompiros to seek new homes, and some Tompiro names began to appear in the church records of El Paso at this time.[33]

On June 24, 1671, the Apaches of the mountain ranges of "Jila" and Siete Ríos carried out a bold attack on a Spanish wagon train traveling from New Spain to New Mexico, killing four persons and carrying off the mules. Perhaps this was the Athapascan way of welcoming the new governor, Juan de Miranda, who was traveling with the train. Miranda failed to take kindly to the attack and appealed to Governor Medrano for aid.[34] Later, in July, the new governor called for campaigns against the Apaches

> because of the continuous wars that the common enemy of our Holy Catholic Faith . . . makes continually in all this kingdom and its districts and vicinity,

attacking the highways, the pueblos, and the ranches.[35] On August 1, Miranda received reports from Senecú that the Apaches of the Gila and Siete Ríos mountain ranges, led by El Chilmo and others, had attacked that pueblo in the middle of the day, brazenly hurling themselves upon the herds of livestock while being mounted on horseback. The raiding party carried off a large number of horses, and, when the Spaniards and Piros attempted pursuit, they were ambushed by a large party of

---

[32] Letters of Juan de Medrano, June 5 and September 11, 1670, BN 19258.

[33] Letter of Francisco de Ayeta, May 10, 1679, in Hackett, *Historical Documents*, III, 302, and Scholes and Mera, "Jumano," Carnegie Institution *Contributions to American Anthropology and History*, Vol. VI, Nos. 30–34 (1940), 284 n.

[34] Letter of Juan Medrano, June 27, 1671, BN 19258.

[35] *Ibid.*, and Letter of Juan de Miranda, July 27, 1671, BN 19258.

Apaches. *Alférez* Salvador Durán was wounded,.a Piro was killed, and the Spaniards were forced to retreat without regaining the livestock. This and other similar attacks were said to be filling the converted Indians with fear and making the highway to New Spain completely unsafe.[36] The style of attack used by the Apaches at Senecú continued to be the basic method of warfare" used by the Gila Apaches in Sonora during the eighteenth and nineteenth centuries.

Sometime after 1671 Governor Miranda personally led a campaign against the Apaches of Gila, but no details of the *entrada* are known.[37]

From 1672 to 1680 the Apaches carried on continuous warfare in New Mexico. Fray Francisco de Ayeta, who was in the province off and on from 1675 until 1679, wrote in the latter year that

> in the year 1672, the hostile Apaches who were then at peace rebelled and rose up, and the said province was totally sacked and robbed . . . especially of all the cattle and sheep, of which it had previously been very productive.

All but a few flocks of sheep were carried off.[38] Between 1672 and 1678 six pueblos were said to have been depopulated, primarily as a result of constant raids by the Apaches and their heathen allies. These pueblos were all in the Piro-Tompiro-Eastern Tewa region, illustrating the fact that southern Athapascans were now the Spaniards' most active or effective enemies. The allies of the Apaches have not been definitely identified, for they are spoken of merely as "the rest of the confederated nations of gentilism" or as "others of *el gentilismo*," but refugee Pueblo Indians were possibly among the Athapascans.[39]

It has been maintained that the Apaches forced the aban-

36 Letter of Juan de Miranda, August 2, 1671, BN 19258.

37 Declaration of Pedro de Leiva, October 20, 1681, in Hackett, *Pueblo Revolt*, II, 168.

38 Letter of Francisco de Ayeta, May 10, 1679, in Hackett, *Historical Documents*, III, 302.

39 *Ibid.*, III, 298, and Letter of Francisco de Ayeta, May 28, 1679, in Otto Maas (ed.), *"Documentos sobre las Misiones de Sinaloa y Nuevo Méjico," Archivo Ibero-Americano*, Vol. XX (1923), 195–96.

donment of several pueblos in 1672—specifically, of the Tom-piro pueblo of Humanas and the Zuñi pueblo of Hawikuh. Hu-manas was said to have been depopulated by March, 1678; since no priest was assigned to it in 1672, its abandonment had ap-parently occurred by that date. It should be noted, however, that no priest was assigned for Tavira in 1672, and that pueblo continued to exist until at least 1677, probably as a *visita* of Abó or Cuarac. Humanas was possibly re-established before 1680, for in 1679 Ayeta gives New Mexico forty-six pueblos—a figure so large that it must include all of the pre-1670 settlements.[40] This possibility also applies to Hawikuh, which was supposedly abandoned in 1672. According to Agustín de Vetancurt, the Apaches raided Zuñi in October, 1672, killing Fray Pedro de Avila y Ayala, and another source states that in July, 1673, a campaign was planned against the Apaches of Río Grande, Casa Fuerte, and Navaho for burning churches and pueblos, holding *juntas* and convocations, and killing the priest of Hawikuh.[41] Fray Ayeta said, however, that Fray Pedro de Avila y Ayala was killed at Abó and does not list Hawikuh as one of the pueblos depopulated from 1672 to 1678. Furthermore, Vetancurt, writ-ing in the early 1690's, mentions the pueblos involved in the revolt of 1680, and among the latter was Aguico (Hawikuh), where the church was burned but the priest escaped. Thus it appears that Hawikuh was not abandoned in 1672 but sometime after 1680. The same appears to be true of Humanas, for in 1680 Vetancurt declared that fifteen leagues to the east of Abó "there are some Xumanas," administered from Quarac.[42]

In other areas, the Spanish Empire was experiencing both advances and setbacks. The Coninas mission to the west of the Hopis was apparently discontinued between 1672 and 1678, for

[40] Letter of Francisco de Ayeta, May 10, 1679, in Hackett, *Historical Docu-ments*, III, 299, and Scholes and Mera, "Jumano," Carnegie Institution *Contribu-tions to American Anthropology and History*, Vol. VI, Nos. 30–34 (1940), 283.

[41] Reeve, "Seventeenth Century Navaho-Spanish Relations," *New Mexico His-torical Review*, Vol. XXXII, No. 1 (1957), 49 n., and Letter of Juan de Miranda, July 15, 1673, BN 19258.

[42] Letter of Francisco de Ayeta, May 10, 1679, in Hackett, *Historical Docu-ments*, III, 298–99, and Vetancurt, *Teatro Mexicano*, 320, 325.

Ayeta mentions Oraibe as the last pueblo to the west in 1678.[43]
Missionaries continued to work among the Mansos and Sumas
with no difficulties except that seemingly the Athapascans were
never enthusiastic converts. The Jesuits of Sonora were ever
hopeful of reaching the Janos and Sumas near their missions,
but little was accomplished. In 1678, the Sumas were still at
peace and coming in to trade with the Ópatas of Bavispe, Baceraca, and Huachinera. In the Turicachi region, contact was being
made with the unconverted Sumas, Janos, and Pimas, and some
Sumas were giving evidence of desires for baptism.[44]

The Nueva Vizcaya region was a land of continual war in the
early 1670's, but in Coahuila a missionary advance occurred in
1670. Even here, however, war continued, and in January, 1673,
it was reported that the Saltillo-Parras region was endangered
by the barbarous nations of the Sibolos, Colorados, Cacastles,
Tetecoras, and their bellicose allies living towards the north.
Most of these tribes were either Coahuilas or belonged to the
so-called Coahuiltecan language family (a misnomer, since the
Coahuilas evidently did not belong to that group), but the Sibolos were an Athapascan people living near the Río Grande from
La Junta to the mouth of the Pecos. The Sibolos, under the same
chief as the Jumano Apaches in the 1690's and associated with
the Lipan Apaches in the 1750's, were apparently given their
name because they were the southernmost occupants of the buffalo (*sibolo* or *sibola*) plains and traded buffalo hides to the
natives of Coahuila and Nueva Vizcaya.[45] By the end of 1673,
the Coahuilas had been reduced to peace, and this was considered
important, because they fronted upon

> the Sibola nation and other gentiles and ferocious enemies with
> whose aid they infested continually both frontiers of the king-
> doms of Galicia and Vizcaya.[46]

43 *Ibid.*, 299.

44 *"Relación de las Misiones que la Compañía de Jesús Tiene en Nueva Vizcaya,"* BMH 971.

45 Various letters in AGI (*Guadalajara* 147).

46 Report of Joseph García de Salcedo, February 1, 1674, *Guadalajara* 147, in
AGI.

Priests and soldiers combined to pacify the Coahuila tribes as far as the Río Grande, and in 1674 Fray Manuel de la Cruz advanced northward to the Sierra de Dacate on the frontier of the Jumano Apaches.[47] In 1675 a large party led by Fernando del Bosque and Fray Juan Larios went 19 leagues north of the Río Grande to the Sierra de Dacate and then 23 leagues beyond that to a place called San Pedro—about 100 miles north of Del Rio, Texas. Approximately 25 miles north of the Río Grande in buffalo country, the Spaniards reached a salty river and "the chiefs Xoman, Teroodan, Teaname, and Teimamar, with their people." These were Indians who used hides or skins to clothe themselves, and the name "Xoman" ("Choman" or "Joman") probably indicates that at least part of them were Jumano Apaches—especially since they seem to have spoken a language different from those of the previously visited tribes. In the combined village of the 4 chiefs, there were 425 warriors and 747 women and children. They were allies of the Coahuilas but enemies of the Coahuiltecan tribes farther east.[48]

The situation in Nueva Vizcaya in the 1670's was almost as serious as that of New Mexico in the same period. In 1677 the province was reportedly in danger of being lost, but in a series of campaigns the Spaniards killed many of the enemy and captured 300 to 400 Indians. The crisis had not passed, however, as the Tobosos were now being joined by the Conchos of the San Francisco de Conchos mission, the Julimes of La Junta, and the Chisos. By June the Río de Nazas area was being frequented by large squads of enemy Indians, and an alarming situation was created by the fact that Indians of the very numerous Sibolo nation were among them. In 1678 it was reported that the hostile Indians of Nueva Vizcaya had indeed called upon the nations to the north for aid.[49] Thus even the southeasternmost Athapascans had been drawn into direct hostilities with the Europeans.

[47] Francis Borgia Steck, "Forerunners of Captain de León's Expedition to Texas," *Southwestern Historical Quarterly*, Vol. XXXVI, No. 1 (1932), 10.

[48] Diary of Fernando del Bosque, in Bolton, *Spanish Explorations*, 287, 299–301, 304.

[49] Letter of Lope de Sierra Ossorio, September 26, 1678, in Hackett, *Historical Documents*, III, 211, 213, and various letters in AGI (*Guadalajara* 147, Ramo II).

In New Mexico, wars continued—apparently without halt—and in January, 1675, a campaign was planned against the "Apaches called Paraonez" and other nations joined with them. This is the first use of the name Pharaones (Faraones), or Pharoahs, in connection with the Apaches bordering New Mexico on the east from Pecos to El Paso.[50] In September a campaign was authorized against the Apaches of the mountain ranges of Navaho and Casa Fuerte and of that vicinity with the soldiers departing from Zia.[51]

A more serious and disturbing event than Apache campaigns occurred in 1675 when the long-suffering Pueblo Indians began to show their real feelings towards the Spanish conquerors. Since the abortive revolt of 1650, the Indians had been planning to throw off the European yoke, and now the situation became such that this desire for freedom expressed itself openly, not in a well-planned revolt, but in an assertion of religious and spiritual independence from the militarily enforced tyranny of the Franciscans. The actual course of events is not clear, but it appears that the Tewa, conquered since 1598, were the leaders in a movement to return to the old religion of the Pueblo Indians. According to Spanish accounts, the Indians proceeded to bewitch the Spaniards, with the result that from five to seven priests and three or four other Spaniards died. Furthermore, the priest of San Ildefonso was bewitched, and the friars of Zuñi, Taos, Acoma, and all of the Tewa district were unable to work because of "so much idolatry." Governor Juan Francisco Treviño determined to put an end to this resurgence of the old faith, and soldiers were dispatched to arrest the Indian leaders and gather up religious paraphernalia connected with the native religion. In the process, the Indian kivas were burned.

Three Tewas were hanged—one in Nambe, one in the Keres pueblo of San Felipe, and one at Jemez—and a fourth hanged himself. In addition forty-three Indians were lashed, imprisoned, and sentenced to be sold into slavery as "convicted and confessed idolaters," but, fortunately for them, this sentence was not

---

50 Letter of Juan de Miranda, January 5, 1675, BN 19258.
51 Order of Juan Francisco Treviño, September 24, 1675, BN 19258.

carried out. A large squad of Tewa warriors descended upon Santa Fe, and seventy of them actually entered the Governor's rooms in the palace, where they demanded the release of prisoners. In an act symbolizing the declining Hispanic hold upon New Mexico, Governor Treviño acquiesced to the Indians' demands, and the captives, including Popé, future leader of the revolt of 1680, were freed. Treviño, it seems, could not afford to face a rebellion of the Tewas and their allies at the same time that the Spanish soldiers were continually being kept busy by the Apaches.[52]

The Athapascan offensive had indeed made the Spaniards' position a desperate one, and another pueblo, Abó, was apparently abandoned at this time.[53] In June, 1676, a campaign was ordered against the Apaches for staying near Socorro and Senecú, killing converted Indians, and carrying off all of the sheep, cattle, and horses that they could.[54] In order to maintain the Spanish hold upon the province, Fray Francisco de Ayeta appealed to the Viceroy for aid in September, 1676, and by October the royal authorities had agreed to send succor to New Mexico "because of the invasions which the nation of the Apache Indians makes."[55] The Athapascans and their allies had, however, stepped up their attacks, and between the autumn of 1676 and that of 1677 the pueblos of Las Salinas (Tavira), Senecú, Cuarac, and Chilili were abandoned—with a priest being killed at Senecú. By 1677 the Apaches had also extended their hostilities to the El Paso region—a fact previously unknown. El Paso was described as a place of great danger and infested by the enemy, but whether this represents a southward extension of raids by the Gila or Siete Ríos groups is not known.[56] Perhaps the Mansos of Captain Chiquito were the major offenders.

Ayeta thus found the province in serious need of his aid, and

[52] Declarations of Luís de Quintana, Diego López Sambrano, and Francisco de Ayeta, December, 1681, in Hackett, *Pueblo Revolt*, II, 289, 300, 309.
[53] Letter of Francisco de Ayeta, May 10, 1679, in Hackett, *Historical Documents*, III, 298.
[54] Letter of Tome Domínguez de Mendoza, July 1, 1676, BN 19258.
[55] *Autos* relating to New Mexico, Guadalajara 138 in AGI.
[56] Letter of Francisco de Ayeta, in Hackett, *Historical Documents*, III, 297, and Undated Letter of Francisco de Ayeta, Guadalajara 138, in AGI.

between the autumn of 1677 and March, 1678, the active friar
helped resettle the pueblos of Las Salinas and Senecú, using some
of the fifty convict-soldiers which he had been given in New
Spain. Soldiers were stationed at Las Salinas, and, according to
Ayeta, the Apaches were somewhat restrained for four months.[57]
The year 1678 brought another bit of good news for the Spaniards when in July a group of Yuta (Ute) Indians came in peace
to Taos pueblo. Governor Antonio de Otermín was in hopes of
reducing them to the Catholic faith. Whether the Utes had been
at peace or war before this time is not clear, but sometime prior
to 1680 a Jemez Indian was held captive by them and taken to
the Great Salt Lake area. In 1680 Otermín reported that the
Utes had been friendly for three years, and their reduction to
the faith was hopefully anticipated. In later years, however, the
Utes asserted that they had always been enemies of the Tewas,
Picuris, Jemez, Keres, and Tanos.[58]

The years 1677 and 1678 saw the Navaho Apaches actively
raiding the Spanish-held pueblos, and campaigns were made in
turn by the Europeans. Prior to August, 1677, the Spaniards
raided the Navahos, killing 15, releasing 6 converted Indians
and a Spanish girl, capturing 35 enemies, and burning all of
their corn and supplies. In July, 1678, another *entrada* was to be
made by 50 Spaniards and 400 allies from Zia to the areas of
Casa Fuerte, Navaho, and Río Grande. The army was to return
by way of the Piedra Alumbre, where the enemy united to make
raids, and the soldiers were warned not to allow the Apaches to
stampede the horses at night and kill the allies. As a result of
this campaign, 2 captives were freed, 50 prisoners were taken,
13 horses were acquired, and the Apaches' fields and houses were
destroyed. By October, however, another *entrada* was necessary,
for the enemy had carried out an ambush at Acoma and had
committed other "atrocities" on the highways of the province.
An army of the same size as that used in the previous campaign

---

57 Letter of Francisco de Ayeta, in Hackett, *Historical Documents,* III, 297.

58 Letter of Antonio de Otermín, July 12, 1678, BN 19258; *Informe* of Posadas,
in Pichardo, tomo XV, BMAE; Letter of Antonio de Otermín, October 20, 1680,
in Hackett, *Pueblo Revolt,* I, 206; and Journal of Diego de Vargas, July 11,
1694, *Guadalajara* 140, in AGI, and *Historia* 39, in AGN.

departed from Zia—this time with orders not to kill any male prisoners without baptism. Many women and children were captured on a fortified mesa; houses were burned; and more than 2,500 *fanegas* of maize were destroyed.[59] These campaigns seem to have done much more damage to the Navahos than these Indians had done to the Spaniards, and certainly peace would have been more profitable economically for the Athapascans of that area. The European armies apparently suffered few losses, although resistance was met, for, as Otermín noted, the Apaches were able to unite very quickly by means of smoke signals.[60]

By September, 1678, Fray Ayeta was back in Mexico, begging for more aid. Plans were made to resettle Cuarac and to gather Salineros (natives of the Las Salinas region) at Galisteo to face the enemy. Thus it seems that many pueblos were still depopulated, in spite of previous succor, and, as mentioned previously, it has been asserted that seven pueblos were abandoned prior to 1680 because of Apache raids. In 1778 these pueblos were said to have been Hawikuh, Chililí, Tajique, Cuarac, Abó, Humanas, and Tavira.[61] In May, 1679, Ayeta did not include Hawikuh or Tajique in his list of abandoned pueblos, but he added Senecú. By March, 1678, both Senecú and Tavira were resettled, leaving Chililí, Cuarac, Abó, and Humanas as depopulated villages. Nevertheless, in 1679 Ayeta stated that New Mexico had forty-six pueblos from El Paso to Taos and Las Salinas (Tavira) to Oraibe. This number probably includes two settlements for the Mansos and Sumas at El Paso and the Hispanic *villa* of Santa Fe, but, even subtracting these, forty-three pueblos remain—too many for New Mexico unless the supposedly depopulated settlements were included. Either all of the pueblos had been resettled by May, 1679, or else Ayeta included even abandoned villages in his count. Vetancurt indicates that New Mexico had approximately forty-six settlements—including Santa Fe—at the

[59] Report of Juan Francisco de Treviño, August 10, 1677, Letters of Antonio de Otermín, July 12, August 23, October 28, and November 26, 1678, and *Servicios* de Juan Domínguez de Mendoza, August 19, 1694, BN 19258.

[60] Letter of Antonio de Otermín, December 11, 1691, *Guadalajara* 139, in AGI.

[61] Letter of Silvestre Vélez de Escalante, April 2, 1778, in Twitchell, *The Spanish Archives of New Mexico*, II, 269.

time of the revolt and that Abó, Cuarac, Chililí, Tajique, Humanas, Tavira, and Hawikuh were all in existence in 1680. In fact, he mentions that a priest and two Spaniards escaped from Tajique during that year. Thus it is possible that the Apache offensive of the 1670's, combined with drought and famine, forced only a temporary abandonment of certain pueblos and that permanent abandonment did not occur until 1680 and thereafter.[62]

By May, 1679, New Mexico had 17,000 Pueblo Indians with 6,000 warriors, while the Spanish-speaking population included only 170 potential fighters.[63] The Spanish enclave in the province had declined continually since 1600, especially since the newly arrived convicts were probably included in Ayeta's figure. Thus it seems that for about eighty years New Mexico had been held for the Spanish Crown by a small number of Europeans who were, of necessity, not settlers but soldier-conquerors and *encomenderos* of Indians. The province was never a colony prior to 1680, but a military outpost designed to protect the Franciscan missionaries and to control the Indians. From the 1640's to 1679, the decline in the number of pueblos was apparently arrested, for there were forty-three in 1643 and the same number in 1679 —although perhaps from four to six were not in existence in 1679, as has been noted. This stability in the number of pueblos occurs simultaneously with the increased Apache wars between 1638 and the 1670's and indicates that the earlier decline was indeed caused by Spanish policy and exploitation, because a decrease in the number of villages does not correlate with an increase in Athapascan warfare.

While Ayeta was in Mexico gathering horses and supplies to take north and asking for fifty soldiers to conquer the Apaches and make New Mexico a base for the occupation of the Californias, the Navaho Apaches were continuing their campaigns against the Spaniards. In the summer of 1679, Governor Otermín ordered a retaliatory expedition. The army was to be a

62 Letter of Francisco de Ayeta, May 10, 1679, in Hackett, *Historical Documents*, III, 298–99, and Vetancurt, *Teatro Mexicano*, 320, 325.

63 Letter of Francisco de Ayeta, May 10, 1679, in Hackett, *Historical Documents*, III, 299.

large one, divided into two sections—one proceeding westward from Taos and the other from Zia. However, neither campaigns against the Navahos nor petitions for help in New Spain could save New Mexico—for the Pueblo Indians and the Athapascans were now ready to combine in order to finish the task of driving the invaders from their lands.

CHAPTER IX

Victory for the Indians

The year 1680 was a momentous one in the history of the American Southwest. It was the high point in the Pueblo Indians' long struggle for religious and political freedom. It represented a tremendous setback for the Spanish Empire in the area of northern New Spain. It was to mark the beginning of an era worthy of this title: the period of the Great Southwestern Revolt.

For decades the Pueblo Indians had been preserving their ancient religion and beliefs in spite of harsh persecution by fanatically intolerant Spaniards. Secretly, they had passed on ancient lore from generation to generation, and during periods of temporary freedom they practiced their ceremonies in public. Gradually they had learned the method of conforming outwardly to the Roman Catholic religion while keeping faith inwardly with their old beliefs. Apparently, few Spaniards could see that conversion by naked force was a failure in New Mexico until it was too late. In 1681 one European stated rather bitterly that "most of them have never forsaken idolatry, and they appear to be Christians more by force than to be Indians who are reduced to the Holy Faith."[1] If dedicated Christians had come peacefully among the Indians of New Mexico, teaching the doctrine by means of love and high-minded examples, then many Indians

---

[1] Declaration of Luís de Quintana, December 22, 1681, in Hackett, *Pueblo Revolt*, II, 291.

might conceivably have been converted in a manner worthy of the founder of the Europeans' faith. This, unfortunately, was not the method of conversion used by the Spaniards, and it is not surprising that both the Pueblo tribes and the Athapascans continually rejected the hypocritical beliefs of their cruel task-masters.

The revolt which began in the summer of 1680 was both a political and religious phenomenon. Certainly the pueblos desired to be free of Spanish control and to have the ability to restore the old peaceful relationship with neighboring Apaches. Apaches who took part in the first stages of the revolt were likewise motivated by a political desire: the wish to see their Taos, Picuris, and Pecos friends free once again and to eliminate Spanish invasions of their own lands. On the other hand, the Pueblo Indians would possibly never have undertaken such an enterprise without a deeper motive, that is, the desire to restore a spiritual climate which meant the preservation of the people and to destroy the religion of the Europeans which was destroying the tribe and absorbing it into the Hispano-Catholic community. All testimonies agree that the primary motive for rebellion was a desire for religious freedom.[2]

The first stage of the Great Southwestern Revolt was planned very well. All of the Pueblo tribes except the unnotified Piros were involved, along with at least one Athapascan group. Plans had been in the making for years, and final decisions of the leaders were circulated by means of knotted cords, each knot representing a day of life left for the invaders. On August 9, the Spaniards first learned that trouble was at hand, thanks to some Tano Indians who turned two Tewa messengers over to the Europeans. From these prisoners they discovered that revolt was planned for several days later and that all of the Pueblo tribes and the Apaches were confederated for the undertaking.[3]

Before the governor, Antonio de Otermín, could organize his followers, the natives began to rebel in various pueblos simulta-

---

[2] Declarations of Pedro García, Pedro Nanboa, and others, September 6, 1680, in Hackett, *Pueblo Revolt,* II, 61–62.

[3] *Auto* of Antonio de Otermín, August 9, 1680, in Hackett, *Pueblo Revolt,* II, 3.

neously, killing all the Franciscans and soldiers that they could and sending squads of warriors onto the highways to halt communications. Taos and Picuris, accompanied by Apaches del Acho, liberated the northernmost regions and killed all of the Spaniards except one soldier, who was just returning from a trip to the Utes. By August 13, it was clear that all of the tribes had joined the movement, and Otermín had to content himself with making preparations to defend Santa Fe. This defense soon developed into quite a problem, for squads of Tanos, Pecos, and Keres warriors began to appear on the outskirts of the *villa,* and they were soon reinforced by Tewas, Taos, Picuris, Jemez, Apaches, and others. On August 15, Otermín arranged to speak with a Tano chief who had previously been friendly and who, with other warriors, had entered the Mexican (that is, the Nahuan) section of the town. The chief informed Otermín that the Indians carried two crosses or banners—one being red and the other white. Red symbolized the war which the Spaniards could choose, and white represented the peace which would prevail if the invaders agreed to abandon New Mexico. In connection with the latter choice, the Indians asked that

> all classes of Indians who were in our power [the Spaniards] be given up to them, both those in the service of the Spaniards and those of the Mexican nation of that suburb of Analco. He demanded also that his wife and children be given up to him, and likewise that all the Apache men and women whom the Spaniards had captured in war be turned over to them, inasmuch as some Apaches who were among them were asking for them.[4]

This request symbolizes the growth of a "Pan-Indian" spirit and also shows that the Europeans were making great use of slaves as late as 1680. As many as 700 Indian servants and captives must have been at Santa Fe when the siege began, but the Spaniards showed no inclination toward leaving New Mexico peacefully or giving up their human property.

Having chosen war, the Spaniards sought to dislodge the In-

4 Letter of Antonio de Otermín, September 8, 1680, and *Auto* of August 20, 1680, in Hackett, *Pueblo Revolt,* I, 13, 99.

dians from Analco, and many days of bitter fighting followed. Finally, on August 20, the Europeans succeeded in driving the Indians from the *villa*, killing 300 of the enemy, and executing 47 prisoners taken in the battle. Among the native dead were Pueblo Indians of all tribes and also Apaches—these Apaches contradicting Otermín's earlier belief that there were no Apaches among the attackers. Many Spanish-speaking servants had apostatized and gone over to the rebels, indicating perhaps a success for the Pan-Indian appeal.[5]

The number of Athapascans who took part in the siege has not been established; but on August 17 the rebels had reportedly summoned Apaches, and some Apaches del Acho had probably accompanied the Taos and Picuris to the attack.[6]

On August 21, 1680 Governor Otermín and his followers determined upon retreating downstream and abandoning Santa Fe. This refugee group included approximately 100 fighting men and 1,000 persons in all—the same number which had resided in the *villa* in the 1620's. Their departure led to a sacking of Santa Fe by the victorious Indians, although the *villa* was not destroyed—nor was the governor's palace, which is still standing. The retreating Spaniards found the Tiwa pueblos abandoned and the natives in revolt. They also learned that the Spanish-speaking population of the lower Río Grande area had united at Isleta but had since left for El Paso upon seeing that the Tiwas of Isleta wished to revolt. Subsequently, the Spaniards of Isleta declared that the rebels in that area had many guns taken from 120 dead men, along with large numbers of cattle, horses, and other supplies. These provisions could support the Apaches for four months in a siege, said the commander of the Isleta Spaniards, Alonso García.[7] However, one wonders where 120 armed men had come from.

García led his followers to the Piro region, where the Indians

---

[5] Hackett, *Pueblo Revolt,* I, 14, 17, 101–103; Declaration of Diego López Sambrano, December 22, 1681, in Hackett, *Pueblo Revolt,* II, 302; and Letter of Alonso García, September 4, 1680, in Hackett, *Pueblo Revolt,* I, 57.

[6] Letter of Antonio de Otermín, September 8, 1680, and *Auto* of August 21, 1680, in Hackett, *Pueblo Revolt,* I, 17, 102.

[7] Various Documents, in Hackett, *Pueblo Revolt,* I, 17, 20, 26, 69, 73.

of Sevilleta abandoned their pueblo and went with the Spaniards to Socorro. Socorro proved unsafe, however, as Apaches were in sight and the Piros were restless, having received an emissary from the rebels. García then moved to the place called Fray Cristóbal and waited for news from El Paso. There he learned" that Otermín was also retreating downriver, and later the two Spanish-led groups united still farther downstream. Fortunately for the fleeing invaders, Fray Francisco de Ayeta was at El Paso with succor from New Spain, and the refugees were thus able to remain in the El Paso region. However, many of them wished to flee to Parral and other areas, and they had to be kept near El Paso by force. The refugees were reportedly harassed by the Apaches, and this irritation probably added to their desires to bid farewell to New Mexico.[8]

Governor Otermín held muster at a place called La Salineta, a few leagues from El Paso, and reportedly there were almost 2,000 persons, of which 317 were Indians of Isleta, Sevilleta, Alamillo, Socorro, and Senecú pueblos, apparently brought against their will from their homelands. The other 1,700 persons included only 155 fighting men, from which fact one may conclude that the balance—or 1,500 persons—were women, children, and Indian servants and captives. Reportedly, 21 priests and 380 other persons had died in the revolt, but the latter figure must have been only an estimate based upon who was missing, and as it turned out many Spanish-speaking mestizos and servants had gone over to the rebels.[9]

The second stage of the Great Southwestern Revolt was now ready to commence, for the idea of revolution was being carried into the El Paso area, Nueva Vizcaya, and Sonora. Indeed, the Pueblo Indian rebels besieging Santa Fe had informed the Spaniards that the Mansos were aware of the movement and would kill any Europeans who fled to El Paso. These Athapascans apparently were not willing to attack such large numbers of refu-

8 *Auto* of Alonso García, August 24, 1680, Letter of Francisco de Ayeta, September 16, 1680, and Antonio de Otermín, October 1, 1680, in Hackett, *Pueblo Revolt*, I, 70, 74, 126, 153.

9 Antonio de Otermín, October 1 and 9, 1680, in Hackett, *Pueblo Revolt*, I, 153, 159, 194–95.

gees, however, and they bided their time.[10] The more immediate danger to El Paso lay in the operations of the Apaches of Siete Ríos and the Organ Mountains, along with those of the Mansos of Captain Chiquito. Otermín felt that the Athapascans would now begin to attack Sonora, for the Spaniards of New Mexico would no longer stand in their way. Furthermore, the Governor laid blame for the fall of New Mexico on the Apaches, with their constant warfare and attempts to get the Pueblo Indians to rebel. He felt that the same fate lay in store for Sonora unless New Mexico was subdued.[11]

The Pueblo Indians at El Paso were by no means pro-Spanish, and many of them were very restless, spreading revolutionary ideas and plotting. The *cabildo* at El Paso reported that danger had resulted from bringing the Pueblo Indians into Nueva Vizcaya and that "much damage has been done to wagons and pack trains, from which the Indians have gained great boldness, notifying the other nations" of the revolt. There were large numbers of Piros at El Paso, and many other Indians had congregated with them, living without excessive subjection to Spanish rule.[12] Rumors were current that the converted natives wished to revolt, and frequent investigations were held—as a result of which more than one Piro or Tiwa was executed. However, the presence of so many soldiers and the enmity which seems to have existed between the Piros and the Mansos prevented anything more serious than constant plotting. On the other hand, these discontented Pueblo Indians helped to spread the doctrine of revolution. As some of them made their way farther south, they gave hope to many oppressed tribes with their tales of what had happened in New Mexico.

Trouble soon began to appear, and on August 29 it was reported that the Sumas on the Río de los Janos (at the new mis-

[10] Report of the *Cabildo*, October 3, 1680, in Hackett, *Pueblo Revolt*, I, 180.

[11] Petition of Luís Granillo, October 5, 1680, and Letter of Antonio de Otermín, October 20, 1680, in Hackett, *Pueblo Revolt*, I, 183, 210, and Memorial of Francisco de Ayeta, *Guadalajara* 139, in AGI.

[12] Report of the *Cabildo*, October 16, 1680, and Letter of Antonio de Otermín, October 20, 1680, in Hackett, *Pueblo Revolt*, I, 204, 210, and Testimony of Francisco Albarel, July, 1681, in NMA (New Mexico Archives, Coronado Library University of New Mexico, Albuquerque, New Mexico), Vols. 1621–83, No. 7.

sion of La Soledad de los Janos) were beginning a rebellion. The immediate cause of the conspiracy was that a mulatto servant of the friar there had cut off a Suma's ears. However, rumors from New Mexico probably played a part in the affair. *Alcalde Mayor* Andrés López de Gracia succeeded in quieting the Indians temporarily by arresting the leaders, but plotting continued.[13]

A major cause of future trouble in the El Paso–Casas Grandes region was the fact that overnight 2,000 refugees swarmed into the area and began immediately to take over the lands of the Mansos, Sumas, and Janos. Already these Athapascans had been angered by settlers on their lands, and the encroachment had reached such a point that Ayeta was able to get 1,640 beeves from the ranches of the Casas Grandes region to aid the refugees.[14] At first, the refugees from New Mexico decided to settle on the Río Grande between the missions of Guadalupe of the Mansos (Ciudad Juárez) and San Francisco of the Sumas—also called *de la Toma* (where the irrigation ditch was tapped). However, by June, 1681, a *plaza de armas* had been set up at San Lorenzo de la Toma, and for years this place continued to be the major European settlement in the area. It was, of course, on the lands of the Indians, and the settlers also gradually appropriated the surrounding areas. Many refugees left the El Paso region and settled at Casas Grandes and on the Río de los Janos, while still others made their way to Namiquipa in Conchos territory, and others reached the Taraumara lands. Wherever they went, they encroached upon the natives and served as living evidence of the success of the New Mexico revolt.[15]

The ever-restless Indians of the Bolsón de Mapimí in eastern Nueva Vizcaya were greatly influenced by the example of their northern brothers, and their raids increased greatly in boldness after 1680. In September, Governor Bartolomé de Estrada reported that the Indians of Nueva Vizcaya and those of New Mexico were "all in communication," and he feared the conse-

13 Letter of Andrés López de Gracia, August 29, 1680, *Guadalajara* 138, in AGI.

14 Francisco de Ayeta, October 6, 1680, in Hackett, *Pueblo Revolt*, I, 193.

15 Declaration of Pedro de Leiva, and Letter of Antonio de Otermín, October 9, 1681, in Hackett, *Pueblo Revolt*, II, 30, 154.

quences. By January, 1681 the Fiscal reported that war was raging in Nueva Vizcaya and that worse things could be feared, "especially as they are now so elated and arrogant with the lamentable occurrence in New Mexico." It was also feared that the New Mexico rebels would aid others to the south and create a serious situation because "those in the kingdom of La Vizcaya are so expert and so able in the management of arms and horses."[16]

Throughout 1680 and 1681, it was repeatedly stated that the Mansos, Sumas, and Janos were ready to rebel and that they would cause a similar action by their neighbors—the Conchos. In September, 1680 it was reported from Sonora that, unless Otermín could reconquer New Mexico, the whole northern region would be lost,

> for the Janos, Yumas [Sumas], and other nations here and those who border upon them are all of the same persuasion or perhaps even worse. Seeing that they [the rebels of New Mexico] have succeeded with this, I have no doubt that they will all do the same.[17]

Governor Otermín's immediate need, however, was to hold El Paso, for if that place were abandoned, it was felt that the Mansos and Sumas would revolt and that all of the area north of Parral would be lost. In April, 1681 Juan Domínguez de Mendoza declared that the barbarian nations of the north were at the point of rebellion, and Otermín added that the Pueblo Indians there were also restless. By September Fray Ayeta expressed concern over

> the spread of the conspiracy, which now exists not only among the Indians who surround us [at El Paso] but in the provinces of Sonora as well, where many leaders of it have been punished. The said conspiracy has reached to the doors of El Parral and La Vizcaya, and these and other nations are on the point of joining it.[18]

[16] Letters of Bartolomé de Estrada, September 6, 1680, Letters of the Fiscal, January 3, 1681, and Letters of Martín de Solis Miranda, January 7, 1681, in Hackett, *Pueblo Revolt*, I, 86–87, 220, 226, 232.

[17] Francisco de Agramonte, September 16, 1680, in Hackett, *Pueblo Revolt*, I, 188–89.

Otermín maintained that only the presence of the troops and refugees at El Paso had saved Nueva Vizcaya and Sonora

> against such a large number of barbarian Indians who, discontented with our friendship and intercourse, have held so many convocations and parleys, as is apparent from the punishments inflicted in those parts.[19]

The governor's point of view was shared by the royal officials of New Spain, and several steps were taken to insure continuance of El Paso as a Spanish foothold and strong point in the north. Otermín was to be given authority over the region (formerly a part of Nueva Vizcaya), and he was to have a presidio of fifty men, armed with fresh horses and carbines instead of harquebuses. The refugees were not to be allowed to escape from their duty as future colonizers of a reconquered New Mexico. They were to remain under Otermín's authority.

The Pueblo Indians of New Mexico were not anxiously awaiting the Spaniards' return, for they had been able to take up the old way of life and to try to make an adjustment with the Apaches. To the north, northeast, and east they had nothing to worry about, for these Athapascans were normally allied with the Taos, Picuris, and Pecos. To the west, however, were the Navahos who had been the Tewas' enemies for many years. Would the Pueblo tribes be able to make peace with these Apaches now that the Europeans were gone, or would the Navahos seek to continue their raids with renewed vigor, taking advantage of the absence of Spanish arms? Needless to say, this question is important to understanding the causes of Athapascan warfare and to deciding whether the Navahos had been— from 1606 to 1680—crusaders against the European invaders or merely raiders inspired with a desire for booty—or perhaps a little of both.

The Spaniards expected and hoped that the Apaches would turn out to be raiders and that their hostilities would help to

[18] Declaration of Juan Domínguez de Mendoza, April 5, 1681, and Francisco de Ayeta, September 21, 1681, in Hackett, *Pueblo Revolt*, II, 21, 90.

[19] *Auto* of Antonio de Otermín, October 26, 1681, in Hackett, *Pueblo Revolt*, II, 183.

bring the Pueblo Indians to a willing acceptance of the protection offered by Spanish rule. As Fray Francisco de Ayeta said, it was the opinion of all of the Spaniards that the Pueblo Indians would be very anxious for return of the Europeans, because the Apaches would have raided them and reduced them to slavery. In fact, the Spaniards who journeyed to New Mexico late in 1681 with Governor Otermín expected to find the pueblos destroyed by the Apaches. "These assumptions were altered and lost force in the face of the assistance asked and received from the Apaches in the case of almost all of the Indians." Ayeta went on to assert that

> it has been experienced and seen that the Apaches have not destroyed any pueblo or even damaged one seriously. It happened that, although during the discussions of peace to which the apostates invited them, they spent some months in dances, fiestas, and entertainments, in the end the Apaches were unwilling to accept it and left, still at war, as in fact they are at present; and it is seen that this notwithstanding, they [the Pueblo tribes] have maintained themselves without the Spaniards.[20]

It appears that some hostile Apache groups did make peace with the Pueblo Indians in 1681. In April the *cabildo* at El Paso learned from three Indians who had just come from New Mexico that the forces of the rebels had been greatly increased "due to the confederation and alliance that they have with the heathen Apaches." One Indian from the north reported that he had met a Navaho Apache chief who was negotiating for peace at Santo Domingo pueblo.[21] During the same period some Piro Indians made their way from El Paso to Socorro, and on the way they were attacked twice by the southern Apaches. Later, a Tiwa chief took the Piros who had remained in their homeland northward to Isleta, perhaps because the Piros were exposed to raids by hostile Apaches and Spaniards from El Paso or because the

[20] Declaration of Francisco de Ayeta, December 23, 1681, in Hackett, *Pueblo Revolt,* II, 307–308.

[21] Report of the *Cabildo,* April 5, 1681, in Hackett, *Pueblo Revolt,* II, 27, and Reeve, "Seventeenth Century Navaho-Spanish Relations," *New Mexico Historical Review,* Vol. XXXII, No. 1 (1957), 51.

Tiwas feared that an invading Spanish army might make use of Piro warriors against them.[22]

By November, 1681 Otermín had his 50 presidial soldiers at El Paso; the settlers were largely settled at San Lorenzo; and a Piro-Tiwa plot to rebel had been crushed.[23] Otermín was then ready to attempt the reconquest of the Pueblo Indians. On November 5, an army of 146 Spaniards and 112 Indian allies—Mansos, Piros, Tiwas, and 9 Jemez—set out for the north, reaching the Piro country late in the month. In this area they found signs of mounted Apaches and discovered that all of the Piro pueblos were abandoned. Senecú, Socorro, Alamillo, and Sevilleta had been deserted by the "apostate Piros" who had gone to join the rebel Tiwas at Isleta. The Indians had burned all of the churches, and signs indicated that Apaches had later sacked one of the abandoned villages. Otermín went one step farther and had the entire pueblos burned. Indications were seen in this area that the Apaches had driven a herd of animals south from the interior pueblos.[24]

On December 6, the Spanish army reached Isleta and forced the Piros and Tiwas to surrender. The Tiwas claimed that they had taken up arms because they thought Apaches were attacking, but their real anti-Spanish feelings were revealed when it was seen that the church with all of its images had been destroyed and that cows were housed inside the ruins. The 500 Indians there were found "to be well satisfied with their liberty of conscience and not overjoyed to see the Spaniards." Otermín now adopted his policy for the reconquest: Domínguez de Mendoza was to advance to the Tiwa pueblos of Sandia, Alameda, and Puaray, force the natives to surrender their arms, burn all the kivas, and sack any houses from which the Indians fled. The same measures were also to apply to the other pueblos.[25]

Domínguez de Mendoza found the Tiwa pueblos empty, but

22 Declaration of Lucas, December 19, 1681, in Hackett, *Pueblo Revolt*, II, 243.

23 Testimony of Diego, July 9, 1681, in NMA, Vols. 1621–83, No. 7.

24 Record of the March, in Hackett, *Pueblo Revolt*, II, 183–207.

25 Record of the March, Declaration of Francisco de Ayeta, December 23, 1681, and Instructions of Otermín, December 8, 1681, in Hackett, *Pueblo Revolt*, II, 208, 216, 316.

he refrained from doing any more damage than burning some kachina masks at Sandia. He did, however, sack the three pueblos along with those of San Felipe, Santo Domingo, and Cochiti, which he reached subsequently. Meanwhile, Otermín decided to march north from Isleta, in spite of the fact that a group of Piros had deserted the pueblo after having heard that the apostates and Apaches had joined together in the sierras to destroy the invaders. All of this evidence of Pueblo Indian animosity apparently acted strongly upon the governor, and he totally sacked, burned, and destroyed Sandia, Alameda, and Puaray.

Near Cochiti, Domínguez de Mendoza met an army made up of all the Pueblo tribes except the Hopis and he was almost tricked into being destroyed. The rebels, led by a mestizo, Alonso Catiti, pretended friendship and asked for powder to fight the Apaches. The Spaniards did not succumb to this ruse, but they did allow themselves to be outflanked so that they were not in any position to use force on the Indians. Leaders of the two groups at first engaged in peace talks, but finally Catiti replied:

> What you say to me is true, but I still remember what they [the Spaniards] did in the pueblo of Los Jemez to the Apaches, killing them under promise of peace.

Thus the past sins of treachery against the Athapascans appeared to confront the Spaniards at this moment, and soon other natives began to shout that the Europeans were hypocrites and liars. Nevertheless, a battle did not develop, and it was finally agreed that the Spaniards would wait for several days at Cochiti, and then the rebels would come in for talks. For three days Domínguez de Mendoza waited, and then he decided to retreat, for the rebel army was reportedly planning to attack.[26]

Success might yet have attended the Spanish invasion but for a wise stratagem carried out by Luís Tupatu, a rebel leader from Picuris, and a squad of mounted Indians which apparently included some Apaches. This group began to harass the Spaniards at Isleta, and the Tiwas were asked to flee to them—a

[26] Declarations of Juan Domínguez de Mendoza, Diego López, and Sebastian Herrera, December 21–22, 1681, in Hackett, *Pueblo Revolt*, II, 261, 270, 271–72, 294.

policy which the Piros were already following. In order to frustrate this rear action, Otermín retreated downstream, complaining of the "confident coyotes, mestizos, and mulattos" who were with the rebels. These leaders of mixed ancestry particularly aroused Spanish animosity for they symbolized an anti-Hispanicism which the Spaniards apparently could not understand except as the work of the devil. Another thorn in their sides was the fact that the "liberated" Pueblo Indians wished to flee to the rebels, as the Tiwas and Piros were doing. Many of the Piros were reportedly now at Acoma.[27]

Otermín had failed to subdue the Pueblo Indians in a short time, as he had hoped, and in January, 1682 a retreat was made to El Paso. First, however, the pueblo of Isleta was completely destroyed, and the 385 Indians still there were carried as prisoners to the south. The Spaniards had succeeded only in destroying eight pueblos, sacking three others and bringing more unwilling settlers to El Paso.[28]

The Pueblo Indians had been found to be quite satisfied with freedom, or as Fray Ayeta said:

> They have been found to be so pleased with liberty of conscience and so attached to the belief in the worship of Satan that up to the present not a sign has been visible of their ever having been Christians.[29]

Governor Otermín had expected many of the Indians to welcome him, because he thought that they would be suffering from Ute and Apache raids and the tyranny of their leaders,

> but the damages they had received had not been very considerable, nor the tyranny of their government, as it encouraged

---

27 It seems that "many mestizos, mulattos, and people who speak Spanish have followed them, who are skillful on horseback and who can manage firearms as well as any Spaniard." Declaration of Luís Granillo, December 23, 1681, Letter of Luís Granillo, December 24, 1681, and *Autos* of Antonio de Otermín, December 24, 1681, and January 1, 1682, in Hackett, *Pueblo Revolt*, II, 322, 329, 337–39, 355.

28 *Ibid.*, and Certification of Francisco Xavier, January 1, 1682, in Hackett, *Pueblo Revolt*, II, 356–58.

29 Declaration of Francisco de Ayeta, December 23, 1681, in Hackett, *Pueblo Revolt*, II, 309.

their natural inclination toward obscenities, idolatry, and liberty.[30]

If the Apaches were not on the offensive in New Mexico, it may have been because they had shifted their interest from the north to the El Paso region, and during the month of January, 1682 they carried off 200 animals from San Lorenzo. Otermín was aware of the menace to his headquarters, and, without knowing of these raids, he determined to make a side journey to Apache country prior to returning to El Paso. On February 4, he turned to the east from Doña Ana and went about six leagues to the Organ Mountains, where he hoped to get timber and "to look about for the enemy Apaches who live in it." Nothing was found except a cave sometimes used by the Athapascans.[31]

On February 11, Governor Otermín wrote to the Viceroy that it was now impossible to subdue New Mexico, both because of the rebel's attitude and because of the Apache offensive against the El Paso region. He felt that the Pueblo Indians with him should be settled in the El Paso area as a barrier protecting Nueva Vizcaya and as an aid to reduction of the still-heathen Mansos and Sumas. This plan was accepted by royal authorities as the only solution possible, but the Fiscal was loud in his condemnation of Otermín's apparent ineptness.[32] The Crown was not willing, at this time, to put forth the money for more troops, however, and a temporary recognition of the independence of New Mexico was necessary.

The Apache offensive toward the south began to take on widening proportions by March, 1682, and the Sumas were guilty of thievery and co-operation with the raiders. At this time the Apaches of the Sierra of Gila made a raid on a ranch near Casas Grandes—an act never previously reported for them. A retaliatory expedition by Spaniards of that jurisdiction was

[30] Letter of Antonio de Otermín, February 11, 1682, in Hackett, *Pueblo Revolt*, II, 371.

[31] Letter of Nicolás Hurtado, January 30, 1682, and Record of the March, in Hackett, *Pueblo Revolt*, II, 365–67.

[32] Letter of Antonio de Otermín, February 11, 1682, and Reply of the Fiscal, June 23, 1682, in Hackett, *Pueblo Revolt*, II, 373, 375.

then made to the "ranchos" of the Apaches, and there they found Sumas holding friendly conversations with the enemy.

The Apaches had been making great raids for horses and livestock on the very frontiers of Sonora, and information on the apparent motives of the Athapascans was given by a young Jumano slave who escaped to the Spaniards. He said that

> among the Apaches who came to the said ambush were a large number of Apaches of the plains (these are from towards the east and the place of ambush is distant from their territory 200 leagues). These [Apaches] used to enter into New Mexico to trade and carry on commerce because they always were at peace, but having lacked this trade they come now to have it with the Apaches of the Sierra of Gila.

The Gila Apaches were in possession of horses which the Plains Apaches needed

> as much for war against other heathens who are their enemies, by means of which they make great massacres, as for the chase of the buffalo which is their sustenance.[33]

By the 1680's all of the Plains Athapascans were probably in possession of horses, and undoubtedly the new animal was finding a ready acceptance in the buffalo hunt, the war party, and the seasonal caravan—although apparently replacing the dog only gradually in the caravans.[34] An insight into the significance of the mounted Apache in 1682 is to be gained by reading the journals connected with a new European frontier in the west—the French frontier.

In 1673 the westward-moving French had reached the Mississippi River Valley with the expedition of Louis Joliet and the Jesuit Jacques Marquette. Serious French penetration of the area began, however, with the activities of René Robert Cavelier, Sieur de la Salle, who explored the Mississippi Valley and estab-

[33] Letter of Antonio de Otermín, March 29, 1682, *México* 53, in AGI, and in Scholes and Mera, "Jumano," Carnegie Institution *Contributions to American Anthropology and History*, Vol. VI, Nos. 30–34 (1940), 288–89.

[34] As late as the early 1700's, the Apaches northeast of Taos were still using dogs for carrying tents and other equipment.

lished a fort near the mouth of the Missouri River. There, in 1682, La Salle met a party of Missouri Indians, among whom was a Pawnee from 200 leagues to the west. From him it was learned that the Pawnees

> are neighbors and allies of the Gattacka and Manrhoat, who are to the south of their [the Pawnee's] villages, and that they sell them horses which they rob apparently from the Spanish of New Mexico.[35]

Thus by 1682 the mounted Athapascan was making an impression as far as Illinois, since "Gattacka" in its various forms was a widely used Pawnee term for the Plains Apaches.[36] That the Pawnees were allies of the Apaches, however, is to be doubted, and the impact of the Athapascans on the other Plains tribes was probably in the nature of a mounted enemy. Fray Louis Hennepin learned something of the Plains tribes from some Metontonta Indians (Otos) who visited La Salle in 1682. They had a horse's hoof and said that "the Spaniards make cruel war upon them, and that they use spears more commonly than firearms."[37] In all probability the "Spaniards" were really mounted Apaches using long lances, a trait often recorded for the Athapascans of the High Plains. Further, it is known that the Otos were often at war with the Apaches (called Padoucas at the time) and sold many Athapascan slaves to the French.[38]

It would certainly be interesting to know the exact effect of the mounted Apache upon his startled enemies, but one may surmise that the first possessor of the horse would have exercised superiority over an unmounted opponent. It is possible that the Apaches made inroads upon other plains tribes at this time, creating bitter hatreds which were to boomerang upon them after 1700 when the Comanches, Pawnees, Kansas, Otos, and others forced the Athapascan from a large part of the plains.

---

[35] Margry, *Découvertes et Établissements des Français dans l'Ouest et dans le Sud de l'Amérique Septentrionale (1614–1754)*, II, 201–202.

[36] "Gattacka," "cataka," or "kataka" was usually applied to the so-called Kiowa Apaches, but only after the other Apaches were no longer on the High Plains.

[37] Louis Hennepin, *A New Discovery of a Vast Country in America*, II, 627.

[38] About the year 1720 the Otos and Kansas carried off 250 Padouca slaves. See Nasatir, *Before Lewis and Clark*, I, 16.

On the frontier of New Spain in 1682, the phenomenon of revolution continued to plague the Spaniards as the Ópatas of Sonora became affected by freedom fever. The Indians desired to kill the Europeans and their ministers, but Lieutenant Governor Francisco Cuervo y Valdés campaigned against them successfully. Subsequently, the Ópatas of Turicachi, Cuquirachi, and Tibideguachi—pueblos on the Athapascan frontier—rebelled again, and Cuervo put them down once more. A few years later it was charged that Cuervo had ruined Sonora and by executing Ópata leaders had caused the trouble.[39] Meanwhile, in El Paso several Pueblo Indians were tried for apostasy, robbery, and co-operation with the Apaches.[40]

Apparently, the Great Southwestern Revolt was dead. The Spaniards, by strengthening their position at El Paso, at Casas Grandes, in Sonora, and in the Parral area, had seemingly halted the spread of the infection begun by the rise of the Indians of New Mexico. The Mansos and Sumas had failed to rebel; the Ópatas had been crushed; and relative quiet existed elsewhere, but the ideas inspired by the revolt of August, 1680 had not died. In 1683 the tribes of Nueva Vizcaya living near Parral rose in rebellion, inspired by the example of New Mexico. They "totally shut off communication between the provinces and kingdom of New Spain and Galicia and that of Vizcaya."[41]

The Casas Grandes region continued to be the target for frequent raids by the Apaches of Gila in 1682, and they may have been aided by the Janos and the Mansos of Captain Chiquito. In February Captain Francisco Ramírez, accompanied by some Concho and Suma Indian auxiliaries, undertook a campaign in search of the Apaches. Trouble developed, however, when Janos carried off several horses belonging to the Conchos as repayment for an earlier Concho theft of blankets. Several Spaniards pursued the Janos and murdered one of them. As a

39 Memorial of Toribio de la Huerta, in Pichardo, tomo XIX, BMAE, and Testimony of the Conde de Canalejas, January 17, 1692, *Guadalajara* 66–5–12, BLT (Bancroft Library Transcript), in AGI.

40 Trials of Juan Catiti and Juan Cucala, in NMA, Vols. 1621–83, Nos. 12–13.

41 Letter of Lope de Sierra Ossorio, in Hackett, *Historical Documents*, II, 219, and Royal *Cédula* of June 16, 1685, *Guadalajara* 147, Ramo II, in AGI.

result of this action, the natives were ready to revolt. The Spaniards at El Paso were afraid that the Mansos of Chiquito would join the convocation, because the Janos and Mansos were really one tribe; but the whole affair was smoothed over when Ramírez gave some horses and gifts to the Janos.[42] Meanwhile, a new mission, Santa Gertrudis, was established for the Sumas living near the Ojito de Samalayuca.[43]

On August 11, 1683 twelve Jumano Apache chiefs reached El Paso and sought an interview with Governor Otermín. It seems that the Spaniards of New Mexico had always been on friendly terms with these Athapascans, and throughout the years six, eight, or ten Europeans had journeyed to their lands to trade and barter. The loss of New Mexico had put a stop to these annual visits, and the Jumanos were anxious to resume commerce, as well as to ascertain just what had happened to the Spaniards. For some reason hostilities had developed between the Jumanos and their Apache neighbors, and the latter had told the Jumanos that the Spaniards were finished. The reason for this inter-Athapascan hostility is not altogether clear, but perhaps it had something to do with the fact that the Jumanos were avid traders and middlemen between the Spaniards and the Julimes of La Junta on the one hand and the Texas (Hasinai Caddo) and their allies on the other. It is known that the more northerly Athapascans were enemies of the Texas and of the Spaniards, and thus the Jumanos—in cultivating the friendship of the latter groups—must have lost that of their kinsmen.[44]

The Jumano chiefs informed Otermín that six days down the Río Grande from El Paso lived their allies the Julimes, avid farmers who had offered to donate supplies if the Spaniards came to help them against the Apaches. The Jumanos lived very near the Julimes, as well as having rancherias towards the Colorado River region, and they tried to entice Otermín into send-

42 Testimony of Francisco, etc., and *Auto* of Antonio de Otermín, March, 1683, in NMA, Vols. 1621–83, No. 16.

43 Report of Nicolás López, in Pichardo, tomo XIV, BMAE.

44 Letter of Antonio de Otermín, August 11, 1683, in Pichardo, tomo XIV, BMAE, and Declaration of Juan Sabeata, October 20, 1683, in Pichardo, tomo XIV, BMAE.

ing an expedition by telling him of the pearls in the Colorado. The Jumanos also said that the Texas were trading with white people who came to them in houses of wood which travel over the water, but this fact did not seem to worry the Governor, and the Indians finally based their case on their desire to trade in deerskins and buffalo hides.[45] The Spanish position at El Paso was not secure enough to send such an expedition, however, and Otermín's term of office was almost over. Thus the Jumanos had to wait until a new governor was installed among the Spaniards.

During this period rumors were continually circulating to the effect that the Pueblo Indians had made a "perfect union and alliance" with the Apaches and that now they sought to include all the frontier tribes of Nueva Vizcaya and Sonora in their league to destroy the Europeans.[46] A more immediate danger to the position of the new governor, Domingo Jironza Petriz de Cruzate, was the raids of the Apaches upon El Paso. Jironza reported that when he assumed office there were only a few horses left, and these had to be tied at the doors of the Spaniards' *jacales* during the night in order to save them. However, he was able to subdue the spirit of the Apaches by campaigning in their lands, killing many, and capturing twenty-two. By October 30, Jironza declared that he was disposed to reconnoiter New Mexico as far as Santa Fe and attempt the reconquest of the lost province.[47]

In October, 1683 a group of Jumanos again appeared at El Paso, led by Juan Sabeata, a principal chief who had been baptized in Parral. This important and well-traveled Indian declared that at that time he and many other Jumanos were living at La Junta, from whence he had been dispatched by six Christian chiefs (of the Julime pueblos) who were without ministers and who desired both spiritual aid and, more to the point, aid against their enemies the Apaches, "which is a ranchería very close to his." Sabeata was then asked how far it was from his home to the rest of the Jumanos, and he replied that they were six days

45 Letter of Antonio de Otermín, August 11, 1683, in Pichardo, tomo XIV, BMAE.

46 Villagutierre y Sotomayor, BN 2822.

47 Letter of Domingo Jironza, October 30, 1683, in Pichardo, tomo XIV, BMAE.

away and that the buffalo were three days from La Junta. The Colorado River was three days from the buffalo, indicating that the Jumanos were still on its banks as in the 1630's and 1650's. Sabeata then listed many nations with which the Jumanos were friendly and with which they traded. These included some Tonkawan and Coahuiltecan groups, as well as the Texas and the kingdom of Quivira. One of the tribal names, Peñunde, resembles Ypande or Ipa-nde, the source of the Lipan Apache's name.[48]

Sabeata informed the Spaniards that he was in close touch with the Texas, who lived fifteen to twenty days east of La Junta. Again he repeated the story of white men trading with the Caddos by water and declared that among the Texas was a Tewa Indian who spoke Spanish. The Caddos were in possession of horses to which they fed maize, and they were at war with the Apaches, having won a victory over a rancheria of seventy-eight tents.[49] On November 29, 1683 Governor Jironza issued instructions to Juan Domínguez de Mendoza to lead a party of soldiers and priests and reconnoiter the river of the pearls (the Colorado of Texas).[50]

Early in December the expedition traveled down the Río Grande from San Lorenzo to La Junta, passing many Suma rancherias along the way. Some of the Sumas asked aid against the Apaches, whom they claimed were interfering in their attempts at settling in pueblos. This, however, was doubtless a ruse designed to fool the Spaniards, in view of subsequent events. At the end of December the expedition reached La Junta, where the Julimes and Jumanos greeted them in a friendly manner. One of the friars, Antonio de Acevedo, remained with the La Junta Indians while the rest of the party journeyed in a northwesterly direction to the Pecos River. The Pecos was reached somewhere near present-day Fort Stockton, Texas.

Nine leagues of travel down the Pecos took the expedition to

48 Declaration of Juan Sabeata, October 20, 1683, in Pichardo, tomo XIV, BMAE, and in AGN (*Historia* 299).

49 Declaration of Juan Sabeata, October 20, 1683, in Pichardo, tomo XIV, BMAE.

50 Letter of Domingo Jironza, November 29, 1683, BN 19258.

the village of the *Jediondos* ("the Skunks," or "Stinking ones"), who met the Spaniards on horseback and with the firing, by Juan Sabeata, of a lockless harquebus barrel. The Skunks were evidently a subgroup of the Jumanos, and they lived at the foot of a great rock which served as protection against the enemy. Apaches. There Domínguez de Mendoza received news of a great attack which the Apaches were planning to make in order to carry off many horses. All the chiefs and their "governor," Juan Sabeata, appealed to the Spaniards to make war upon the enemy, and the commander of the Europeans agreed that he would. Nevertheless, the Apaches carried off a horse herd, and the Spaniards were helpless to do anything in defense of their allies.

On January 25, the expedition left the Skunks' village, and ten leagues to the east they met the "Twisted Bows," a people similar in dress and customs to the Sumas. After twenty more leagues of travel the Spaniards and Jumanos reached the middle fork of the Concho River, and in this area the Apaches stole nine horses—seven from the Jumanos and two from the Europeans. Spies reported that they had located an enemy rancheria; but this turned out to be a falsehood, and hard feelings began to develop between the erstwhile allies. Domínguez de Mendoza said that Juan Sabeata had not told him the truth about anything, and he accused the Jumano chief of trying to slow down the expedition. Finally, however, they reached the junction of the Concho and Colorado rivers, which was eight leagues farther downstream on the Colorado than the place where the Guadalajara party had come in 1654. Domínguez de Mendoza accomplished nothing by reaching central Texas, for all of the tribes which he met in the area (most of whom seem to have been Coahuiltecan groups from farther to the east and southeast) were to be disappointed in their hopes of receiving Spanish aid, if indeed that had been their hope, for this commander was hard-pressed in the defense of his own horse herd and certainly was in no position to wage offensive war. Domínguez de Mendoza determined upon returning to El Paso

> because of my not being able to sustain the great war which, from the north, the common enemies, the Apache nation, have

made upon us. They have attacked us three times by night and by day, and the last night they wounded a soldier.

The "Salineros" of Nueva Vizcaya (probably Chisos) had also made three night attacks on the camp, killing several Skunks. It should be noted, however, that by this time the Spaniards had slaughtered 4,030 buffalo—indicating that their real interest in visiting the Jumano country was to gather buffalo hides. Sabeata was also said to be curing some deerskins for the Europeans—leading one to suspect that the Jumanos were taken in, if they had had any hopes of aid against their northern neighbors.

The ill will engendered by the Spaniards was enough to cause Juan Sabeata and his Jumanos to flee from their "allies," and Domínguez de Mendoza charged that the chief had plotted "with some nations to kill us." In May, 1684 the Spaniards made their way back to the Pecos River, and there they were deserted by the Skunks, who withdrew secretly, thus showing their coolness toward the Spaniards. At La Junta the expedition found that Fray Acevedo had erected a church and baptized 1,500 Indians, but only seven nations were there instead of the eight or nine of an earlier date—thus indicating that the Jumanos had also withdrawn from this area. A more serious development, however, was that the Sumas of the Río Grande had risen in rebellion, and the party was forced to return to El Paso by way of the Conchos River and the road from present-day Chihuahua City. The revolt of the Sumas may well have had something to do with the hostility of the Jumanos, as the two peoples were in contact and ethnically related.[51]

In the years to follow, Fray Nicolás López, Fray Alonso de Posadas, and other Franciscans were to bombard royal officials with petitions for the missionary occupation of the Jumano country and the Kingdom of the Texas to the east, but this—as well as the reconquest of New Mexico—had to wait for two

[51] Diary of Juan Domínguez de Mendoza, *Provincias Internas* 37 (UTA Transcript), in AGN, *Historia* 299, in AGN, and in Bolton, *Spanish Explorations*, 320–42; Letter of Fray Nicolás López, 1686, in Hackett, *Historical Documents*, III, 361–62; Report of Juan Domínguez de Mendoza, 1684, in Pichardo, tomo XIV, BMAE; and Letter of Juan Domínguez de Mendoza, 1686, *Guadalajara* 138, in AGI.

important events. The smoldering embers of the Great Southwestern Revolt had burst into open and violent flame from the borders of Coahuila to Sonora, and all imperial expansion in the north was delayed until another event made that expansion imperative, regardless of the internal situation on the northern frontier: the French were to establish settlements in Louisiana, and La Salle was to reach Texas. All New Spain was to be threatened by the potentiality of a French alliance with the rebel and heathen tribes of the northern frontier.

CHAPTER X

The Great
Southwestern Revolt

◙

Since the 1660's, the Mansos of El Paso had been planning a revolt, and this desire was intensified by the happenings of the early 1680's. Nevertheless, certain factors made a rebellion more difficult after the Pueblo Indian success, for the Spaniards' power at El Paso was greater than before, and the Piro and Tiwa refugees were seemingly at odds with the natives at the Río Grande crossing. Still, the Indians did not give up hope, and meetings and discussions continued until, on March 14, 1684, a group of Piros and Tiwas betrayed the conspirators to Governor Jironza. Eight of the leaders, including Luís, principal chief of the Mansos and Janos, and several Apaches living among the El Paso natives, were arrested secretly. Jironza learned that the meetings had been frequent, that a revolt was tentatively planned for Easter, and that the Piros and Tiwas were to be allowed to return to New Mexico unless they aided the Spaniards, in which case they were to be killed. Jironza was inclined to strangle the eight immediately; but other counsel prevailed, and the execution was to be postponed to avoid repercussions among the natives. Nevertheless, word of this occurrence reached the Janos, Sumas, and other tribes, and new leaders arose to plan the revolt.[1]

Messengers to and from El Paso kept the Janos, Jocomes,

[1] Hughes, "The Beginnings of Spanish Settlement in the El Paso District," University of California *Publications in History*, Vol. I (1914), 338–42, and Letter of Francisco Ramírez, May 12, 1684, *Guadalajara* 147, Ramo II, in AGI.

Sumas, Chinarras, and Conchos informed of the proceedings, and one of the important messengers was Juan the Quivira, an Indian who had come to El Paso from New Mexico—apparently as an agent of the Pueblo Indians. Juan was arrested by Jironza, but managed to escape, and thereafter served in important rebel roles until he was finally captured in July while on his way with messages to New Mexico. In the meantime, he and others had performed their tasks well, and on May 6 the revolt began.[2]

The Janos and Sumas of the mission of Nuestra Señora de la Soledad (at present-day Janos, Chihuahua) were the first to rebel —not a surprising fact, since the Janos had only recently been reduced, their principal chief was the Spaniards' prisoner, and the closely related Jocomes and Mansos of Chiquito were still free and were their neighbors to the north. Fray Manuel Beltrán, Captain Antonio de Alviso, and a servant were killed at Soledad, while six females and two or three boys were carried off by the rebels. Reportedly, some Mansos of Captain Chiquito aided the Janos and Sumas. Captain Francisco Ramírez of Casas Grandes received news of the affair on May 11 and wrote immediately to the Spaniards of El Paso and Parral for aid.[3]

On the night of May 13, all of the Sumas of Casas Grandes fled from their mission, and the priest of that place feared for his life, since there was no way to escape. In one direction lay the mission of Santa Ana del Torreón of the Sumas and Chinarras, while towards Sonora lay Santa María de Carretas with more Sumas. The Sumas of these missions had intermarried and united with the Janos, and their rising was a foregone conclusion.[4] The Conchos of the area to the south of Casas Grandes revolted about the same time, and some of these Indians reportedly aided the Sumas of the Ojito de Samalayuca to rebel, destroy the new mission of Santa Gertrudis, and kill several Spaniards.[5] The Sumas of San Francisco de la Toma near El

[2] *Ibid.*, and Hughes, "The Beginnings of Spanish Settlement in the El Paso District," University of California *Publications in History,* Vol. I (1914), 343.

[3] Letter of Francisco Ramírez, May 11, 1684, *Guadalajara* 147, Ramo II, in AGI.

[4] Letter of Juan de Porraz, May 14, 1684, *Guadalajara* 147, Ramo II, in AGI.

[5] Letter of Domingo Jironza, October 7, 1684, in Pichardo, tomo XIV, BMAE, and Report of Francisco Cuervo de Valdés, June 17, 1684, *Guadalajara* 147, Ramo I, in AGI.

Paso deserted their pueblo, and the converted Mansos at Guadalupe del Paso did likewise. Governor Jironza attempted to halt
their flight; but, in spite of the fact that he held their leaders
prisoners, the natives were determined upon freedom. The governor retaliated by executing the ten captives he held.[6]

On May 25 the "General Conjuration" reached within a few
leagues of Parral; the Conchos and other tribes of that area deserted their missions, pueblos, and the ranches on which they
worked, carrying off large numbers of horses and mules. This
"retirement of the nations" was to be damaging to Nueva Vizcaya, for the large ranches and estates depended upon the labor
of such tribes as the Conchos, peaceful Tobosos, and even Julimes from La Junta. The situation was very serious and became
more so when the Julimes forced their new priests to flee and the
Tobosos raided the presidio of Cerro Gordo (the only one in
Nueva Vizcaya), wounded most of the soldiers, and carried off
all of the animals there.[7]

Governor Joseph de Neyra y Quiroga of Nueva Vizcaya and
his lieutenants, Cuervo de Valdés in Sonora and General Juan
de Retana at Parral, were faced with a serious problem, as they
did not have the troops to meet the challenge of the rebels. It
was requested that 50 new campaign soldiers and 100 paid Indian auxiliaries be supplied to wipe out the worst of the enemies,
but the Viceroy replied that he did not have the 25,000 pesos
that would be necessary to support such a group each year and
thus Nueva Vizcaya would have to depend solely upon its own
resources and the 6,000 peso annual war and peace fund. The
Viceroy was soon to learn, however, that the Great Southwestern
Revolt was going to cost Spain many more pesos than 25,000
for many, many years.[8]

The Spaniards on the northern frontier were forced to meet
the force of the "epidemic" from New Mexico, as the new revolt

[6] Letter of Domingo Jironza, October 7, 1684, in Pichardo, tomo XIV, BMAE.
[7] Letter of Juan de Retana, May 28, 1684, Guadalajara 147, Ramo II, in AGI;
Letter of Lope de Sierra Ossorio, in Hackett, Historical Documents, II, 225; and
Report of Nicolás López, Historia 299, in AGN.
[8] Conde de Paredes to the King, August 12, 1684, Guadalajara 147, Ramo II,
in AGI.

was termed, on their own, and they succeeded in doing so to a remarkable extent.[9] Cuervo de Valdés, Jironza, and Retana sent aid to Ramírez at Casas Grandes, saving that place from certain destruction. Forty former New Mexicans were sent from the Parral region; Juan Fernández de la Fuente led 30 militia troopers from Sonora; and Jironza sent 30 men from El Paso—making a total of 100 harquebus-armed Spaniards at Casas Grandes, besides the settlers of that place. They found the rebels, 2,000 of them (including women and children), occupying defensive positions on a *peñol* not far from Casas Grandes, and the Europeans were able to dislodge the Indians early in June. The Indians retreated to a new position on the Peñol del Diablo, and there they successfully resisted an assault by at least 150 Spaniards and Indian allies. The Spaniards were forced to retreat with approximately 33 wounded and several dead. The Indian losses are not known.[10]

By mid-July, the Sumas of San Francisco were forced to accept peace because of hunger, but the other Sumas continued to hold out in their mountains. Governor Jironza made a campaign against the Mansos—both converted and heathen—at the village of Captain Chiquito. These Athapascans refused to surrender, and the Spaniards burned the ranchería. In mid-August, a campaign was undertaken to kill the males of an Apache village and capture the women and children, but the Indians could not be found. Meanwhile, Cuervo de Valdés was facing the danger of the spread of revolution to Sonora, as the Sumas and their allies had raided Bavispe and the heathen had retired from the Turicachi region. The prospect of an Ópata revolt was alarming, but these Indians failed to join the rebels at this time.[11]

[9] *Junta* of July 9, 1684, *Guadalajara* 147, Ramo I, in AGI.

[10] Report of Francisco Cuervo de Valdés, June 17, 1684, *Guadalajara* 147, Ramo I, in AGI; Letter of Juan de Retana, May 28, 1684, and Report of Joseph de Neyra, November 30, 1684, *Guadalajara* 147, Ramo II, in AGI; and Hughes, "The Beginnings of Spanish Settlement in the El Paso District," University of California *Publications in History*, Vol. I (1914), 343–45.

[11] Report of Francisco Cuervo de Valdés, June 17, 1684, *Guadalajara* 147, Ramo I, in AGI; Hughes, "The Beginnings of Spanish Settlement in the El Paso District," University of California *Publications in History*, Vol. I (1914), 346–49, 359; and Hubert Howe Bancroft, *History of Arizona and New Mexico, 1530–1888*, 193.

Early in September while the militia troops were out on campaign, the Sumas, Janos, and their allies attacked Casas Grandes, where they burned the stores of corn and wheat and carried off all of the livestock. Late in the same month, a combined force of Spaniards attacked the Indians but were forced to retreat with almost thirty men wounded. By mid-October the Spanish troops, reinforced by hundreds of Indian allies from Sonora and El Paso and by Spanish settlers as well, began a new offensive which succeeded in killing many warriors and capturing all of the women, children, and booty held by the rebels.[12]

Meanwhile Fray Nicolás López journeyed from El Paso to Mexico in September, 1684 to seek aid for the north and for his pet projects—the occupation of Texas and the reoccupation of New Mexico as far as Isleta. On October 7, Governor Jironza wrote that he was ready to reconquer the lost province, but this proposal was rejected by the Fiscal, who said that it was "a fantastic discourse," for Jironza had done nothing in preparation for such an enterprise.[13]

Indeed the Governor of El Paso had failed to subdue the Mansos and Sumas of his own headquarters, although in September he had succeeded in breaking up a conference of rebels from ten nations which was held to the south of El Paso. Towards the west Cuervo de Valdés claimed to have led 300 men on a campaign 130 leagues into the interior in order to pacify the enemy; however, the exact date of the enterprise is not known. By November it was said that some of the Mansos of El Paso were anxious to make peace. Late in that same month, however, the rebels attacked a party of Spaniards on their way to Nueva Vizcaya from El Paso and seven of the travelers were killed. Jironza retaliated with severe campaigns, and Ramírez of Casas Grandes with 120 settlers and Indians forced 2,000 rebels to make peace at Ojo Caliente in December.[14]

[12] Report of Joseph de Neyra, November 30, 1684, *Guadalajara* 147, Ramo II, in AGI, and Hughes, "The Beginnings of Spanish Settlement in the El Paso District," University of California *Publications in History*, Vol. I (1914), 356–58.

[13] *Auto* of September 19, 1684, Letter of Domingo Jironza, October 7, 1684, and Reply of the Fiscal, January 22, 1685, in Pichardo, tomo XIV, BMAE.

[14] Testimony of Francisco Cuervo de Valdés, August 7, 1690, *Guadalajara*

Many of the Sumas, Conchos, and Mansos continued fighting until mid-1685, when most of them agreed to return to live under Spanish rule. The Mansos of Captain Chiquito, the Janos and Jocomes, some Sumas and Conchos, and, of course, the Apaches to the north remained free, and the Spaniards were to experience continual trouble from all of these groups for many years to come. In fact, in 1685 there was a rumor of a new revolt, and seventy-seven Suma men were clubbed to death at Casas Grandes and in Sonora.[15] Certainly Spanish brutality helped to make these Indians hate their conquerors.

The 1684 rebellion was an expensive one for New Spain. In November of that year Governor Joseph de Neyra of Nueva Vizcaya reported that the rebels had 40,000 head of livestock in their possession taken from the entire northern area. In April, 1685 it was said that Casas Grandes alone had lost 2,000 horses and mules and 2,000 head of small stock, besides many herds of cattle. The losses of the Spaniards were not to be measured in livestock alone, nor in lives, but in a serious loss of missionary control over the natives. The Jano mission of Soledad, the Suma missions of Santa Gertrudis, Torreón, and Carretas, and the settlements for the Chinarras were totally lost, never to be restored. The Julime mission was to be delayed until 1715, and the Concho and Toboso missions of San Pedro, San Francisco, Nombre de Dios, and San Gerónimo, along with the Julimes' Conchos River pueblo of San Antonio de Julimes, were temporarily destroyed.[16]

The 1684–85 phase of the Great Southwestern Revolt was never really halted, even though some of the nations involved were forced to accept peace. The Tobosos, Chisos, and their allies continued to fight on, using their dry, mountainous homeland as

66–5–12, BLT, in AGI, and Hughes, "The Beginnings of Spanish Settlement in the El Paso District," University of California *Publications in History*, Vol. I (1914), 352–54.

15 *Ibid.*, 360–61, and Sauer, "Distribution of Aboriginal Tribes," *Ibero-Americana*, Vol. V (1934), 72–73.

16 Letter of Joseph de Neyra, November 30, 1684, *Guadalajara* 147, Ramo II, in AGI; Hughes, "The Beginnings of Spanish Settlement in the El Paso District," University of California *Publications in History*, Vol. I (1914), 363–64; and Report of Nicolás López, March 26, 1686, in Pichardo, tomo XIV, BMAE.

a base for frequent raids. Likewise, the Apaches of the Gila and Siete Ríos regions, along with the Jocomes, Janos, and free Mansos and Sumas, kept up a determined war against the frontier. As a result of this flaming borderland war, the royal authorities had to take some determined action instead of merely relying upon the hard-pressed presidios of El Paso and Cerro Gordo and the militias of Sonora and Nueva Vizcaya.

In 1685 the Spanish Empire was forced to erect a series of new presidios designed to fence off the rebel tribes of eastern Nueva Vizcaya. The sons of Cortés had reached the position where they had to admit the impossibility of subduing an Indian enemy by offensive war and that the most prudent course was to erect barriers to keep the aggressive enemy out of Spanish-held territory. New presidios were authorized for Cuencamé (Pasaje), El Gallo, and San Francisco de Conchos by royal order in December, 1685. Originally, it had been planned to supply them with 25 men each, but by the time the order was issued it was necessary to give each 50 men, supplied with twenty-five new muskets. Thus by 1686 the Spanish northwestern frontier had five presidios and about 250 soldiers, besides other men at Parral, Casas Grandes, and in Sonora. In the 1700's, nineteen such presidios were to cost the Crown 283,930 pesos each year, or an average of 15,000 pesos each.[17] Certainly the cost of maintaining the northern frontier was to be great after 1685, and part of the increased expense was due to the fact that in·a few years several new presidios had to be erected to fence the Apaches off from Sonora and Casas Grandes.

At this same time, in Mexico City, friars Nicolás López and Alonso de Posadas were blindly calling for northern expansion, but their pleas, not surprisingly, went unheeded. In fact, on October 22, 1685 the King ordered that his Royal Treasury give preference to the Nueva Vizcaya war over all other matters, including the planned settlement of Baja California. The latter enterprise had to be postponed as a result.[18] Furthermore, the

[17] Various documents in AGI (*Guadalajara* 134 and 147), and *"Mapa que Comprehenda los Presidios . . . en las Provincias Internas . . . ," "Virreinato de Méjico,"* tomo I, MN 567.

[18] The King to Conde de Paredes, October 22, 1685, *Guadalajara* 134, in AGI.

Viceroy indicated that the mine owners of Nueva Vizcaya and Nueva Galicia should help pay for the northern war, since they did not pay as much tax as other areas of the empire.[19]

There are indications that Governor Domingo Jironza made a number of raids upon the Pueblo Indians of New Mexico during his first term of office, 1684–86, but he found the Indians well fortified and could not force them to submit.[20] This and later resistance by the Pueblo tribes refuted statements such as were made by the campaigning friar, Nicolás López, in Mexico. López, possibly in order to convince the royal authorities that the rebels would welcome a return of the Spaniards, had told of the coming of an ambassador from the Indians who was pro-Spanish and who told how they were suffering from Apache attacks.[21] The continued revolt of the Mansos and Sumas forced Jironza to move the presidio of El Paso to the area of the Mansos mission (Guadalupe) and the old settlement of San Lorenzo to a small Indian village two leagues below the presidio.[22]

In 1686 Jironza was replaced by Pedro Reneros de Posada, and the Great Southwestern Revolt entered into a fourth phase as the Sumas, Mansos, Janos, Jocomes, and other tribes returned to rebellion or stepped up their attacks upon the Spaniards. It seems that after the 1684 revolt the Sumas of the El Paso area had been settled at Guadalupe with the Mansos, and it was there that they rose in 1686, killed their priest, Fray Diego de Echavarria, and burned the church.[23] Reneros was unable to defeat these Sumas, and the conflagration soon spread to the west, with the result that Sonora began to be subject to frequent raids by the Indians. This fact must be regarded as the beginning of relentless warfare by the Athapascans on Sonora, although earlier in the 1680's some slight raids were apparently made on the frontiers. The year of 1686 marks the beginning of decline for

19 Conde de Paredes to the King, March 28, 1685, *Guadalajara* 147, Ramo II, in AGI.

20 Villagutierre y Sotomayor, BN 2822.

21 Report of Nicolás López, *Historia* 299, in AGN.

22 Letter of Diego de Vargas, August 14, 1691, *Guadalajara* 139, in AGI.

23 Letters of Diego de Vargas, March 30 and June 17, 1692, *Guadalajara* 139, in AGI.

Sonora as a Spanish province, for although the number of its missions was subsequently to be expanded to include many of the upper Pimas, the 200 subsequent years of Athapascan hostility never allowed the area to be more than an insecure frontier region. Indeed the wealth and population of Sonora definitely declined after 1700.[24]

Instead of focusing his attention upon the difficult task of coping with affairs in the El Paso–Sonora area, Reneros saw fit to make a raid into New Mexico which appears suspiciously like a slaving expedition. The Spaniards attacked and destroyed the Keres pueblo of Santa Ana, which was apparently the most vulnerable Pueblo Indian settlement, since all of the Tiwa and Piro towns to the south had been depopulated by previous Spanish campaigns. Reneros subsequently attacked Zia but was forced to retreat by the great numbers of Keres defenders. He managed, however, to carry off his human booty from Santa Ana and returned to El Paso.[25] During this same period Reneros attempted to acquire added wealth by discovering the famous salt lakes belonging to the Apaches and located east of El Paso (near Salt Flats, Texas), but neither he nor his successor, Jironza, could find them.[26]

By September of 1686, the Athapascan offensive in the Casas Grandes region was serious enough to cause the Viceroy to call for the construction of a presidio of fifty men there, thus further expanding the "fencing-off" policy. This presidio, though first established at Casas Grandes, was subsequently moved northward to Janos and continued in existence for the remainder of the Spanish period.[27] On the Indian side of the struggle, the major burden of the war against Sonora was quite naturally borne by the Janos, Jocomes, and Sumas, but very soon Apaches of the Gila region were drawn into the affair as allies. Nevertheless, for

24 Figures and evidence illustrating the decline are to be seen, for example, in Eusebio Guiterás (trans.), *Rudo Ensayo*.

25 Letter of Diego de Vargas, August 14, 1691, *Guadalajara* 139, in Agi, and Villagutierre y Sotomayor, BN 2822.

26 Letter of Diego de Vargas, April 7, 1692, *Guadalajara* 139, in AGI.

27 Letter of the Conde de Paredes, September 12, 1686, *Guadalajara* 147, Ramo II, in AGI.

many years the Gila Athapascans were to play a secondary role to their southern brothers.

On December 28, 1687 Governor Juan Isidro de Pardiñas of Nueva Vizcaya declared that the barbarians were convoked in order to attack the Spaniards and that in Sonora they had done very great damage and caused many deaths.[28] In the same year, however, Fray Eusebio Kino, a Jesuit, began work among the upper Pimas of Sonora, and soon the new mission of Dolores was established. Likewise, to the east, near El Paso, the new mission of Santa María Magdalena was established for the Sumas. However, it soon disappeared.[29] In March, 1688 Captain Juan Fernández de la Fuente undertook a campaign from his presidio of Casas Grandes with 40 soldiers, 30 settlers, and 200 Indian allies, but the rebels were not defeated. On May 10 the Jocomes, Janos, and Sumas, with some Apaches, attacked Corodeguachi (later to be Fronteras), in Sonora. Tebideguachi, an Ópata pueblo in the region, was attacked subsequently and burned, in spite of the fact that soldiers—part of the old garrison of Sinaloa who were serving in Sonora—were there. The horses of both pueblos were carried off and the guards left on foot.[30]

In July, 1688 the Janos and Jocomes attacked in the Casas Grandes region, killing a soldier and wounding Captain Fernández. To the west the rebels had raided Turicachi and killed or wounded all of the Sinaloa soldiers who were there. Fernández organized a large army, and on August 24 the Spaniards defeated the Janos, Jocomes, and Sumas, killing 200 and capturing the women and children; but the war was not halted as Torreón, and other settlements suffered from raids. Worst of all, the whole Pima nation revolted.[31]

The Pimas along with their northern branch, the Sobaipuris,

28 Letter of Juan Isidro de Pardiñas, December 28, 1687, *Guadalajara* 147, Ramo I, in AGI.
29 Manje, *"Breve Noticia,"* BMH 970, and Letter of Pedro Gómes, May 19, 1687, BN 19258.
30 Letter of Juan Isidro de Pardiñas, March 18, 1688, *Guadalajara* 147, Ramo I, in AGI; Description of Sonora in 1764, BMH 969; and Letter of Blas del Castillo, June 1, 1690, *Guadalajara* 152, in AGI.
31 Letters of Juan Isidro de Pardiñas, July 29 and October 11, 1688, *Guadalajara* 147, Ramo I, in AGI.

had had a long period of contact with the Spaniards but little is known of their early history except for their relations with some neighboring tribes. At one time they were at peace with the Hopis and traded with them; but hostilities developed, and commerce came to an end. In the 1630's the Pimas were reported as enemies of the Ópatas, and indeed the very name Ópata seems to be a corruption of *"Awp"* or *"Oop,"* the Pima word for enemy.[32]

Aboriginally, both the upper Pimas and the Sobaipuris were friends of the Janos, Jocomes, and Apaches until being forcibly made allies of the Spaniards and enemies of the Athapascans in the 1690's. In 1686 the Pimas were restless, and one of their chiefs was tried by the Europeans. In the interrogation it was discovered that the Sobaipuris and the Jocomes-Janos were on friendly terms and that the Sobaipuris had given the Athapascans some land to plant near Quiburi in the San Pedro River Valley of present-day Arizona.[33]

By 1688 the Pimas were undoubtedly ready to join the anti-Spanish rebellion, especially since the Jesuits were beginning to move in among them. The spark which set off the revolt was a treacherous raid upon the peaceful village of Mototicachi carried out by the Sinaloa soldiers of Nicolás de la Higuera. Some 50 Pimas were murdered, and more than 125 women and children were sent as slaves to Sinaloa. This slave raid aroused all of the nation, and many areas of Sonora were raided in retaliation. The Spaniards in turn began to attack the Pimas in Bacuachi and the Sobaipuris of the sierras of Huachuca (Arizona). In September, 1688 the largest part of the rebels was pacified as Fernández destroyed their villages and fields. Other Pimas continued to fight, however, and two subsequent campaigns by Fernández were carried out. Still, as late as March, 1690, the Pima rebels were causing much damage in Sonora.[34]

[32] See Fray Luís Velarde's Description of Sonora, May 30, 1716, BMH 970, and Schroeder, "Southwestern Chronicle: The Cipias and Ypotlapiguas," *Arizona Quarterly*, Vol. XII, No 2 (1956), 106.

[33] Sauer, "Distribution of Aboriginal Tribes," *Ibero-Americana*, Vol. V (1934), 75.

[34] Letter of Juan Isidro de Pardiñas, October 11, 1688, *Guadalajara* 147, Ramo

The successful rebellion of the Pueblo Indians and their ability to maintain their freedom was held by Governor Pardiñas of Nueva Vizcaya to be primarily responsible for rebel obstinacy on the northern frontier in 1688. In order to end the war, in December, a new Viceroy, the Conde de Galve, ordered Isidro de Pardiñas to try a more gentle approach, but the governor replied that only a vicious attack had brought the Pimas to peace and that the other rebels—the Jocomes, Janos, Sumas, Tobosos, and their allies—would not accept any other kind of an approach.[35] To complicate further the problem of frontier defense, the Chisos joined the rebellion, and tribes as far away as Coahuila and the Saltillo-Parras region were at war. Seeking still more allies, the Tobosos reportedly called upon the Terocodames and the Jumanos to join their struggle.[36]

Sixteen eighty-eight was indeed a year of great danger for the northern portions of New Spain, for at the same time that war was raging from Sonora to Coahuila, the Spaniards received the news of French penetration into Texas. Fears of a Franco-Indian alliance and the subsequent loss of the Crown-supporting mines of Galicia and Nueva Vizcaya began to haunt Spaniards from King to presidial captain.

The French under the leadership of La Salle had planted a colony, called Fort St. Louis, on the Gulf coast of Texas in January, 1685. Dissensions imperiled success of the enterprise from the first, but La Salle worked hard at the colonizing effort and attempted to win the alliance of the Indians in that area. In April, 1686 the commander led a party of Frenchmen to the northeast of St. Louis (identified as Matagorda Bay), and contact was made with Indians who had horses and a knowledge of the Spaniards. These Indians related that to the west there was a cruel and bad nation of whites that depopulated all the country

I, in AGI; Letters of Blas del Castillo, March 1 and June 1, 1690, *Guadalajara* 152, in AGI; and Manje, *"Breve Noticia,"* BMH 970.

35 Letters of Juan Isidro de Pardiñas, October 11 and December 23, 1688, *Guadalajara* 147, Ramo I, in AGI.

36 Letter of Juan Isidro de Pardiñas, October 11, 1688, *Guadalajara* 147, Ramo I, in AGI, and Herbert Eugene Bolton, "The Jumano Indians in Texas," *Texas State Historical Quarterly*, Vol. XV, No. 1 (1911), 76.

near them, and they were pleased to learn that the French were at war with the Spaniards. An alliance was made with the idea of a subsequent joint campaign against New Spain.[37]

Traveling farther to the northeast, La Salle's group reached the Cenis (Hasinai Caddo) Indians, and there they found many evidences of contact with New Spain—such as *pesos fuertes*, other types of money, silver spoons, linen, silk, clothing, religious objects, and horses. Horses were very plentiful, so much so that one could be acquired for a hatchet.[38]

The Hasinais were located more than 400 miles from the nearest Spanish settlement, and so far as is known no Europeans had penetrated to their country since De Soto's explorations. Thus all of the horses and other examples of Spanish culture had come to the Hasinais by means of Indians who either traded with or made war upon New Spain. Perhaps some of the goods had come north from the Coahuila–Nuevo León area; however, the primary source of such materials seems to have been the commercially minded Jumano Apaches with their trade route from La Junta to the Texas. Fray Anastasio Donay, in his diary of the La Salle expedition, remarked that

> they [the Cenis] have relations with the Spaniards by means of the Choumanes [Jumanos], allies of the Cenis, and they are always at war with New Spain. . . . They count it as a six days' journey to the Spaniards, of whom they gave a description so natural that no doubt of them remained to us, although the Spaniards still have not undertaken to come to their village, and only their warriors join themselves with the Choumanes in order to go make war in New Mexico.[39]

It seems then that some Hasinai braves, accompanying the Jumanos, had actually fought against the Spaniards, and this fact leads one to suspect that the Jumanos were merely pretending friendship when they visited El Paso in 1683, or perhaps they desired peaceful relations with the Spaniards of New Mexico while maintaining warfare with other portions of New Spain.

[37] Diary of Fray Anastasio Donay, in Pichardo, tomo XIII, BMAE.
[38] *Ibid.*
[39] *Ibid.*

Fray Donay actually met some ambassadors of the "Choumanes" who were among the Cenis and was pleasantly surprised when they made the sign of the cross to him. They told him of the Spanish Franciscans who were trying to convert the Indians and of large churches and gave a detailed description of the ceremony of the Holy Mass.

In January, 1687 La Salle set out on another attempt at exploration. Two accounts of the journey exist, and, unfortunately, that of Henri Joutel somewhat contradicts the information supplied by Fray Donay. The friar had stated, on the basis of information gathered during his 1686 journey, that the Cenis and the Jumanos were allied against the Spaniards. Joutel, on the other hand, indicates that these tribes were friendly toward New Spain. Just before reaching the land of the Cenis, in February, 1687, Joutel notes that the Indians

> talked of a great nation called Ayona and Canohatino, who were at war with the Spaniards, from whom they stole horses, and told us that one hundred Spaniards were to come to join the Cenis, to carry on that war, but that, having heard of our march, they went back.

A few days later the French met the Palaquechaunes, allies of the Cenis, and an Indian told them

> that their chief had been among the Choumans with the Spaniards; that the Choumans were friends to the Spaniards, from whom they got horses. . . . He also told us that the Choumans had given their chief some presents to persuade him to conduct us to them; that most of the said nation had flat heads; that they had Indian corn, which gave M de la Salle grounds to believe that these people were some of the same he had seen upon his first discovery.[40]

In March, 1687 La Salle was murdered by some of his companions, and the surviving Frenchmen in his party took up residence among the Hasinais, whom they aided in a campaign against the Canatinnos (to whom the Europeans had previously pledged friendship). Subsequently, the Frenchmen of this group

40 Isaac J. Cox (ed.), *The Journeys of La Salle*, II, 115, 117.

made their way to Canada, while the remainder who were at St. Louis were wiped out or imprisoned by Indians whom the Spaniards called Xannas, Tohos, and Caocozies (Cascosies). The Xannas were seemingly identical with the Sanas, or Chanas, supposedly a Tonkawan tribe living north of San Antonio, perhaps to be equated with the revenge-seeking Canatinnos. This group of Tonkawans was hostile to the Hasinais and thus to the Jumano Apaches. In the 1720's they were to be driven in part from their lands by the Athapascans.[41]

By 1688, word of the French colony began to reach the officials of New Spain, and in May, Captain Alonso de León of Coahuila captured a Frenchman who was living among the Yoricas and other Coahuiltecan bands on the Río Grande. In July, the Viceroy ordered León to lead a large expedition to Fort St. Louis, and this journey was made in 1689. The destroyed fort and several Frenchmen were found, but rumors of other Europeans to the north and fear of a return of the French led to the establishment of a Spanish settlement among the Texas (Hasinai) Indians in 1690.[42] Thus the position of the Jumanos as middlemen was threatened, and this was one of the factors which were eventually to lead these Athapascans into permanent opposition to the Spaniards and close association with other Apaches.

In the meantime, rumors of the French also reached La Junta, where several Franciscans were again attempting the conversion of the Julimes. At La Junta, in 1687, Fray Agustín de Colina was asked by the Sibolo and Jumano Indians to write a letter to the Spaniards who were among the Texas. Colina instructed the Athapascans to bring a letter to him instead, and in September, 1688 five Sibolos returned to La Junta, not with a letter, but with news that a harquebus-armed and helmeted "Moor" [Negro?] was living with some Indians near the Texas. This foreigner had helped the Indians wipe out half of another tribe called the Michi nation—this may refer to the attack on the Canatinnos. Afterwards, other Sibolos reached La Junta with the story that the Euro-

[41] Diary of Fray Anastasio Donay, and Report of Carlos de Siguenza y Gongora, 1691, in Pichardo, tomo XIII, BMAE.

[42] Report of Doctor Velasco, November 30, 1716, in Pichardo, tomo XVIII, BMAE, and Bolton, *Spanish Explorations*, 348.

peans among the Texas had "told the natives of that country, as well as the Jumano Sibolos, that the Spaniards of El Parral were not good people."[43] Thus a glimpse of Jumano policy can be seen, with the Athapascans telling the French of the Spanish enemy and then telling the Spaniards that the French were spreading anti-Spanish propaganda.

In November the Franciscans were forced to abandon their new missions at La Junta, because of a tumult raised by the Sumas and because the Julimes had a tendency to join with the rebel nations near them rather than to obey their ministers. Governor Isidro de Pardiñas soon learned of this situation and that the Sibolos had reported foreigners to the east. General Retana was immediately ordered to lead ninety soldiers to La Junta and there to learn of the French, as well as chastise the rebel Chisos and make peace and alliances with the neighboring nations. He was to contact especially the Sibolos who came regularly to trade at La Junta, for a Julime chief had reported that these Indians were going to bring a Spaniard with them from the Texas.[44]

Early in 1689 Retana reached the La Junta region, and, after campaigning against the Chisos, sent out scouts to learn of the Sibolos. They reported that the principal chief of the Jumanos and Sibolos, Juan Sabeata, was coming from the Texas. Retana then traveled four days to the east of La Junta, to the Pecos River, where he met Sabeata. The chief said that he was delighted to see Spaniards in his country and informed the General of the Frenchmen's deaths, showing him a drawing of a ship made by one of the Europeans. Sabeata was invited to journey to Parral, and, in April, he, with a number of other Jumanos and Julimes who were to serve as interpreters, reached that settlement.

Sabeata and several other chiefs were interviewed by the Governor, and the former chief said that he had waited for Retana late in 1688 but then had had to go to the fairs held among the

---

43 Declaration of Agustín de Colina, November 23, 1688, in Hackett, *Historical Documents*, II, 241–43.

44 Letter of Agustín de Colina, November 25, 1688, *Auto* of Juan Isidro de Pardiñas, November 2, 1688, and Declaration of Juan de Salaises, November 21, 1688, in Hackett, *Historical Documents*, II, 237, 247–51.

tribes of southern Texas and the Hasinais. He had also gone to the site of the destroyed French fort and had seen some Frenchmen among the Texas. Seven days from La Junta, on the Río Grande, Sabeata had visited one of his subchiefs, Miguel, in a rancheria where Frenchmen had supposedly come. Actually, however, the foreigners had been at a village three days farther downstream, and still later they returned to another settlement which was located one day farther. (This was probably the village of the Yoricas reached by León in May, 1688.) The French, while on the Río Grande, had asked many questions of Miguel and especially of various Indians (Julimes?) who had worked among the Spaniards near Parral. On April 12, Sabeata prepared to return to La Junta, taking with him a message ordering Retana to come back to his presidio, for his troops were needed nearer Parral.[45]

About this same time (c. 1688) Fray Alonso de Posadas was busily preparing a memorial on the New Mexico–Texas region which is of some importance, partly because it may have helped to interest the Spanish Crown in the northern regions and partly because it is a bitter attack on the Apache Indians. Posadas had not been in the north for approximately twenty years; but his interest lay in that direction, and he set out in his memorial to show the geographical extent of the Apaches' and their neighbors' lands and to prove that these Indians were enemies not only of the Spaniards but also of all the tribes which their lands bordered upon. According to the friar, the Apaches were at war with the Quiviras, Texas, Escanjaques, Cuitoas, Jumanos, Sumanas, Sumas, Mansos, Janos, Sumas of Carretas, Cipias, Coninas, and Yutas—among others—and they had forced many of these nations to retreat from their lands. The Coninas had been totally reduced to vassalage, and only the Yutas were able to fight on even terms.[46] However, Posadas let his imagination run away with him, for in 1688 the Apaches are known to have been allies of the Sumas, Mansos, Janos, and Pimas (Cipias)—at least—and

[45] Letter of Juan de Retana, March 2, 1689, and *Autos* and Testimony of Juan Sabeata and others, April, 1689, in Hackett, *Historical Documents*, II, 257–81.
[46] *Informe* of Posadas, in Pichardo, tomo XV, BMAE.

the Escanjaques and Cuitoas were tribes of the 1650's which were going by other names by 1688. As for the Coninas, they were certainly not vassals of any tribe in the 1670's, and Posadas would have had no way of knowing what had happened to them after 1680. In the 1690's and later, they were quite independent.

In 1689 the Jocomes, Janos, Sumas, and perhaps some Gila Apaches continued their warfare against Sonora. On June 11, they attacked the Ópata pueblo of Cuquiarachi, killing many defenders and burning the church—in spite of the presence, two leagues away, of fourteen Sinaloa soldiers. The soldiers were so poorly armed that only five of them could aid the Ópatas. Because of this and other attacks, the Ópatas retired to near-by Santa Rosa de Corodeguachi, where the presidio of Fronteras was soon to be established.[47] By 1689 this frontier war was costing the Royal Treasury of New Spain 90,000 pesos each year for the pay of presidial soldiers alone.[48]

At El Paso, Domingo de Jironza had returned to power as governor. He determined upon entering New Mexico in order to crush the Keres of Zia, who had resisted Reneros' raid. In 1689 Jironza led 80 soldiers and armed settlers to the north in order to carry out one of the greatest Spanish atrocities since the days of Oñate. Zia was ferociously attacked, and, in spite of a valorous defense by the Keres, more than 600 Indians were slaughtered. Still others were burned alive when they refused to surrender, and Jironza had the pueblo set aflame. About 90 inhabitants who escaped from the flames were carried as slaves to El Paso. Naturally, this barbarous raid had a tremendous impact upon the other Keres, and the pueblos of Santo Domingo, San Felipe, Cochiti, and others were abandoned in favor of more easily defended settlements in the sierras.[49]

The Pueblo Indians were in no position to take revenge upon the Spaniards; but throughout the following year of 1690 the Europeans suffered for their crimes, and the avenging angels took the form of Janos, Jocomes, Sumas, Apaches, and other rebel

47 Description of Sonora in 1764, BMH 969.

48 Report of the Conde de Galve, February 3, 1689, *Guadalajara* 147, Ramo II, in AGI.

49 Manje, *"Breve Noticia,"* BMH 970, and Villagutierre y Sotomayor, BN 2822.

nations of the northern frontier. Sonora could easily have been lost during this year if the Ópatas had rebelled instead of giving the Spaniards the aid which enabled the latter to survive. In March, 1690 Blas del Castillo, *Alcalde Mayor* of Sonora, begged for a presidio for his province, for none of the mines there could be worked. He proposed that the presidio of El Paso should be transferred to Sonora, which action, of course, would have ended any hopes of reconquering New Mexico. Castillo, however, felt that such a course of action was justifiable, since the powerful Taraumaras, Conchos, peaceful Sumas, Chinarras, and certain other tribes were holding *tlatoles* ("meetings" or "talks") and a terrible new phase of the Great Southwestern Revolt was threatening.[50] During March and April, the Jocomes and their allies raided Turicachi and Teras, while the helpless Sinaloa soldiers could do nothing. The rebels, in fact, were continually looking for the Spaniards in order to fight them.[51]

In April, the Taraumaras and the Conchos joined the northern revolt, and the forces of Ramírez at Casas Grandes were no longer in a position to give aid to Sonora. During the same month, the Jocomes took sixty pack mules from the Sinaloa soldiers and killed six of these soldiers, along with the Ópata chief of Huachinera. Turicachi's horse herd was carried off, but the Ópatas managed to recover it. The Spaniards were not so fortunate, however, for one of the last herds of the mines of Bacanuchi was driven off by the Pimas. These Indians were again in open rebellion, especially towards Ostimuri (the Yaqui country), where Jesuits and other Europeans had already been killed. The pueblos of Sahuaripa and Arivechi were threatened, and haciendas near Tacupeto had already been destroyed.[52] During the month of May, no ranch or pueblo of Sonora between the Casas Grandes region and Bacanuchi—a distance of 110 leagues—was spared from rebel attack.[53]

In June, Blas del Castillo charged that the Janos and Sumas had formerly lived in the Casas Grandes region, but, because of

[50] Report of Blas del Castillo, March 1, 1690, *Guadalajara* 152, in AGI.
[51] Report of Blas del Castillo, June 1, 1690, *Guadalajara* 152, in AGI.
[52] *Ibid.*
[53] *Ibid.*

the great strength of Spanish arms in the area, the rebels and their allies had retired to the frontier of Sonora, where they had allied themselves with the Pimas, Sobas, and Sobaipuris. The rebels left their women and children with their new allies for safety while the warriors raided the province. Furthermore, Castillo said that Captain Fernández' thirty troopers (stationed at Janos) were not numerous enough to halt the ruin of Sonora by the Sumas, Jocomes, Janos, Apaches, Pimas, and their allies. Governor Isidro de Pardiñas seconded this assertion with the information that most of the soldiers had always to remain in the presidio in order to save it from the continuous threat of the Apaches joined with the Jocomes and Janos. These Athapascans were arriving by day to steal the troops' horses, and the Governor ordered Ramírez at Casas Grandes to aid Fernández on a campaign.[54]

At this time (August, 1690) Governor Jironza of El Paso, instead of aiding his fellows, was planning a new *entrada* into New Mexico. Isidro de Pardiñas wrote to him, requesting that he postpone his journey until a more opportune time, but Jironza's plans were changed only by a more effective means. The Governor of El Paso—as he was called by his neighbors—learned from a Piro Indian that the Janos, Sumas of the Río Grande, Conchos, and some Apaches were united at La Junta (or near by) and were planning to destroy El Paso absolutely when Jironza left for New Mexico. The Governor led his New Mexico-bound army southward to break up this union, but a spy whom he had captured escaped and warned the Indians. Most of the natives fled, and the remainder were fortified on a *peñol*. Subsequently, Jironza admitted some of the Sumas to peace, as his successor Diego de Vargas charged, without subduing them properly. He allowed them to settle in the ruined mission of Guadalupe and elsewhere without proper subjection to Spanish rule. As a result, the Sumas were in fact independent, and soon they were secretly aiding the other tribes in the Janos region. Jironza likewise gave peace to the Apaches without defeating them, and

<hr/>

54 *Ibid.*, and Letter of Juan Isidro de Pardiñas, August 8, 1690, *Guadalajara* 152, in AGI.

Vargas charged that this enabled the Athapascans to scout out the best places to attack in the El Paso area.[55]

On January 9, 1691, all of the soldiers and officials of Sonora petitioned for a presidio of 65 men to be made up primarily from the old Sinaloa presidio. They charged that the province was in a serious condition from the raids of the Jocomes, Janos, Sumas, Apaches, Seris, Conchos, Jovas, Sobaipuris, and some Pimas and added that "each day the rebels are making new conversions and many nations that were at peace before are now declared as enemies."[56] The fact that the Jovas, close relatives of the Ópatas, had joined the revolt was indeed serious, and the news regarding the Seris was an evil portent for the future. The Seris had a new mission called Nuestra Señora del Pópulo, and, although they had not revolted completely, they were accused of thievery, and their heathen relatives—the Tepocas, Tecomaques, and Salineros—were at war with them and with the Spaniards.[57] From his Pima mission of Dolores, Fray Eusebio Kino denied that the Pimas were raiding and asserted that the activities of the Janos, Jocomes, and Sumas were blamed upon his charges. Nevertheless, the evidence shows clearly that some of the Pimas and Sobaipuris were following the warpath at this time.[58] To the south the Taraumara revolt was raging, and General Retana was forced to use approximately 500 Indian allies on several campaigns. Among the allies were recently pacified Chisos, as well as Julimes, Sibolos, Conchos (called Tapacolmes and living at La Junta), and the usually loyal Tepehuanes.[59]

To the east, in Texas, the Spaniards were to discover that their years of making enemies on the northern frontier were to cause the failure of their first attempt at settlement. In 1686–87 the French had discovered that almost all tribes of that region—including the Jumanos and the Hasinais—were anti-Spanish,

[55] *Ibid.*, and Letters of Diego de Vargas, April 29, 1691, and June 17, 1692, *Guadalajara* 139, in AGI.

[56] "*Ynforme sobre el Estado de Sonora,*" *Guadalajara* 152, in AGI.

[57] *Ibid.*

[58] Eusebio Kino, *Kino's Historical Memoir of Pimería Alta* (ed. and trans. by Herbert E. Bolton), I, 121, hereinafter cited as Kino, *Historical Memoir.*

[59] Relation of Joseph de Berroteran, 1748, *Guadalajara* 136, in AGI.

and the fact that the Hasinais allowed a strong force of soldiers to establish missions did not alter their basic animosity. Nevertheless, the priests, guarded by a group of unprincipled soldiers —one of whom had attempted to rape the wife of the Texas' chief—held on to their new conversion. In September, 1690, Chief Juan Sabeata of the Jumanos was among the Texas, and Fray Miguel Font Cuberta gave him a letter to deliver to the Governor of Nueva Vizcaya. At that time the Franciscans' only job was learning the Hasinai language, and little progress had been made otherwise.[60]

In May, 1691 a new expedition left Coahuila under the leadership of Domingo Terán de los Ríos—its object being to aid the priests and explore the Caddo region northeast of the Hasinais. On June 18, the Spaniards reached the Guadalupe River where it crosses the series of hills north of San Antonio, and there they met the chiefs of the Choma, Cibola, Cantona, Cholome, Catquesa, and Caynaya nations who came to receive the Spaniards in peace. The Choma nation (or Chomanes) was the Jumanos; the Cholomes were from La Junta; and the Cantonas and Catquesas were central Texas tribes. All of the chiefs had very small saddles on their horses, which they said had been taken from the Apaches.[61]

On the same day, a procession was held with Juan Sabeata and his Jumanos leading the way. The chief of the Catquesas proved to be a well-traveled Indian who spoke Spanish and Mexican and who had lived in Parras and New Mexico but who had returned to his people to live in "liberty of conscience." Fray Damian Massanet learned also of the territories of the several tribes:

> The referred to Choma, Cibola and Caynaya Indian nations are Indians that live upon—and it is their land—the banks of the Río Grande; they border upon the Salinero Indians, who live along the banks of the Pecos River, which joins itself with the Río Grande; also they border upon the Apache Indians,

---

[60] Letter of Fray Miguel Font Cuberta, September 4, 1690, in Hackett, *Historical Documents*, II, 283.

[61] Diary of Fray Damian Massanet, 1691, BMH 974.

and have wars with them. The Apaches are a cordon running from west to east, and they have war with all; only with the Salineros do they have peace; . . . in the end they dominate all the nations, and the other nations say that they are not valiant, because they fight with armed horses, and they have defensive and offensive arms; they are very able and warlike Indians.[62]

The Jumanos reportedly came each year to the Guadalupe River, and from there some would go on to the Texas. In the Guadalupe River region they killed buffalo, taking the skins with them afterwards. Sabeata informed Massanet that many of his people had been baptized in Parral and El Paso, and the priest wished to know where they would found a pueblo and settle down with instruction. Sabeata replied that his nation had to travel about to follow the buffalo and to trade skins.

In this area, the Spaniards lost horses, and the Jumanos were commissioned to look for them. In July, the Indians turned fourteen steeds over to the Spaniards, who in the meantime had been exploring and had acquired two French captives from the Caucozis. After the Jumanos had turned over the horses, the Spaniards learned that the Athapascans intended to attack and kill them all. The Europeans maintained a heavy guard, and no attack occurred. On the following day, Terán de los Ríos gave the Jumanos gifts—including a gun and powder for Sabeata—in order to show the Indians that they were not afraid.

In all probability, the Jumanos were in league with the Hasinais, who were very anxious to be rid of their unwelcome guests. Thousands of Caddoans had died of disease introduced by the Spaniards, and their women were continually molested by the undisciplined soldiers. By the middle of 1691, the Hasinais were killing the invaders' horses and were ready to rebel.[63]

In August, 1691 one of the Franciscans made a summary of the relations of the Hasinais with other tribes. Their friends included the Chumans, Cantouahonas (Cantonas), Caquizas (Catquesas), and the Xanas (Sanas). Their enemies included the

[62] Ibid.
[63] Ibid., and Testimony of Alonzo de Rivera, March 18, 1691, BMH 974.

Tanquaays (Tonkawas), Canabatinus (Canatinnos?), Sadamos, Apaches, and Caucozis. The Sadamos were described as a large nation with houses covered with buffalo hides, many horses, mules, and instruments of iron. They were not painted, and most of them wore clothing. In 1805, José Pichardo equated the Sadamos with the Apaches; however, in the 1691 summary the groups are mentioned as separate.[64]

In July, 1692, Chief Juan Sabeata of the Jumanos delivered the Franciscan's letter (of September, 1690) to Governor Isidro de Pardiñas in Parral. He would not have been there so soon, he said, except that he had learned that some of the Chisos were attacking his people for not joining them against the Spaniards. As a result, Sabeata had come south to San Antonio de Julimes in order to find the principal chief of the Julime tribe. He hoped that this chief would go to La Junta and give him 400 or more of his warriors to help the Jumanos defeat the Chisos. Sabeata may have also hoped for Spanish aid, for he stressed the point that the Chisos were infesting Nueva Vizcaya.[65] Thus it is clear that, although the Jumanos may have been willing to fight the Spaniards in Texas—to keep the Hasinais' friendship—they were anxious to maintain an alliance with the Europeans of Nueva Vizcaya. By the middle of 1693, General Retana was at La Junta, and with Julime and Sibolo aid he defeated some of the Chisos, forcing several groups to split from the main body.[66]

In Texas, conditions continued to deteriorate for the Spaniards, as the Hasinais allied themselves with the coastal tribes to kill the mission livestock. Finally, in October, 1693, the Franciscans learned of a Franco-Indian plot for rebellion, and the new conversion in the Kingdom of the Texas was abandoned. Henceforth, the Franciscans were to concentrate their efforts on developing northern Coahuila as a buffer area.[67]

[64] Report of Fray Francisco de Jesús María, August 15, 1691, in Pichardo, tomo XVII, BMAE.

[65] *Auto* of Juan Isidro de Pardiñas, July 7, 1692, in Hackett, *Historical Documents*, II, 285–87.

[66] *Auto* of Juan de Retana, July, 1693, in Hackett, *Historical Documents*, II, 329–30.

[67] Report of Doctor Velasco, in Pichardo, tomo XVIII, BMAE.

The loss of the Hasinai region in 1693 was largely offset by a Spanish advance in another direction: By 1693, Diego de Vargas had been governor at El Paso for two years, and he was in the process of forcing the Pueblo Indians and their allies to accept a reassertion of Spanish rule in New Mexico.

CHAPTER XI

The Spanish
Counteroffensive

In 1691 the Spanish Crown saw fit to appoint a governor of New
Mexico who had the ability and ambition to reconquer the lost
province. Diego de Vargas Zapata y Luján was from an influential family and his replacement of men such as Reneros and
Jironza—who were little more than frontier captains in rank
and authority—indicated that Spain was interested in establishing another buffer against the threat of rapidly expanding New
France.

Vargas soon discovered, however, that an immediate reconquest of New Mexico was impossible, for he had only the presidial complement of fifty soldiers and the Great Southwestern
Revolt was still raging. The new *adelantado* was faced with the
task of either helping to crush the rebels first or giving priority
to the subjection of New Mexico. Choosing the latter course, he
had to engage in an extended controversy with all of the other
Spanish officials on the northern frontier. Vargas had to aid his
fellows to some extent, but his influence was eventually able to
persuade the royal bureaucracy of the correctness of his position.

Conditions in El Paso were in a very poor state in 1691, for
the Apaches and their allies had succeeded in taking away most
of the settlement's livestock. Vargas found that the 50 soldiers
and 100 settlers had only 200 horses and mules and that they
were without leather jackets and swords. There were approxi-

mately 1,000 Indian warriors and men in five settlements and missions, but this number included heathens reduced to peace. Nevertheless, the enterprising Vargas was able to improve the situation by obtaining peace with the El Paso Mansos, who had been free since 1684, and in April they were settled at the new mission of San Francisco de los Mansos. Likewise, the Governor reduced some of the Río Grande Sumas to peace.[1]

In Sonora, peace had been arranged with the Seris, Sobas, and some of the Pimas, but the Janos, Jocomes, and Sumas were still battering the Ópata pueblos and the Spanish mining camps. Early in February, Fray Marcos de Loyola of Chinapa wrote a letter to Vargas requesting aid in the form of several Mansos from El Paso, including Captain Chiquito, whom Loyola had baptized years before. The priest indicated that the Mansos had authority with the Janos and Jocomes and spoke the languages of these tribes, while there were no natives in his area who could communicate with the rebels. Loyola hoped to persuade the Athapascans to accept peace under the influence of the recently pacified Mansos.[2] His plea was seconded by serious raids made by the rebels and their Pima allies upon Bacanuchi and Chinapa in March. At Bacanuchi, sixteen persons were killed and eleven carried off, and much of the village was burned.[3]

On March 20 Vargas sent six Mansos toward Chinapa, but they never reached the Jesuit; their mission was a failure by the time they arrived at Janos presidio. Captain Fernández was skeptical of the success of any peace plan, for Apaches had recently come into Janos under signs of peace to sell deerskins and afterwards they had stolen horses and departed. Fernández maintained that the Janos and Jocomes were holding *tlatoles* with Captain Chiquito's Mansos and that the Sumas of the Ojito de Samalayuca, Guadalupe, and other places were in league with them. Thus the Athapascans were strengthening their forces and

[1] Letter of Diego de Vargas, April 19, 1691, *Guadalajara* 139, in AGI, and of August 14, 1691, *Historia* 37, in AGN.

[2] Letter of Juan María de Salvatierra, February 8, 1691, and Letter of Marcos de Loyola, February 6, 1691, *Guadalajara* 139, in AGI.

[3] Letter of Juan Fernández de la Fuente, April 16, 1691, *Guadalajara* 139, in AGI.

not inclined towards peace. This fact was borne out by the discovery of a well-made cross left by the Apaches—on which were signs which led the leader of the Manso emissaries to declare that it was fruitless to ask for peace. Furthermore, these Mansos claimed that they were not familiar with the country of the rebels, and Fernández was not willing to aid them on any peace embassy. The Captain of Janos wanted instead to carry out a joint campaign with Vargas against the Apaches of the Sierra of Gila, who were confederated with the Janos, Jocomes, Sumas, Pimas, and Sobaipuris. Fernández expressed his philosophy when he recited, *"la guerra dura haze la paz segura"* ["cruel war makes peace secure"].[4]

At the same time, Blas del Castillo reported from Sonora that

> it is declared that in some rancherias of Quiburi [on the San Pedro River] that the Suma, Jacome, Xano, Apache, Manso and Pima [Sobaipuri]nations are united with the determination of coming to assault the pueblos of Theuriache, Bacuachi and Valley of Bacanuchi, and the mines of San Antonio and Nacosari.

The portion of the Sinaloa presidio stationed in Sonora had been strengthened to about twenty men under General Diego de Quirós, and a campaign was planned. However, in order to make it successful, Fernández was asked to send twenty-five soldiers. When he did not, the enterprise was attempted with the aid of thirty settlers. In spite of a series of journeys along the Nacosari-Teras frontier, nothing was accomplished except that the enemy ran off some horses from Cuchuta.[5]

On April 29, Vargas replied to Fernández' proposal of a joint campaign by stating that he would go when the opportunity arose and not according to a fixed plan. The condition of his forces and the great distance involved in reaching the Gila Apaches—forty leagues toward New Mexico and then thirty to the west—precluded any such enterprise. However, he would aid Fernández against the combined Sumas and Apaches. As for Fernández' assertion that some of the Sumas of the El Paso

4 *Auto* of Diego de Vargas, March 20, 1691, and Letter of Juan Fernández de la Fuente, April 16, 1691, *Guadalajara* 139, in AGI.
5 Letters of Blas del Castillo, April 14 and 30, 1691, *Guadalajara* 152, in AGI.

region were raiding near Janos, Vargas would see to their punishment and blamed their disloyalty on Jironza's easy peace.[6]

Diego de Vargas was anxiously awaiting an opportunity to
invade New Mexico, and even the Viceroy was interested in
the project. On May 27, the Conde de Galve wrote to Vargas
requesting information about the mines near Moqui, and the
Governor soon began to collect information about the Sierra
Azul. The condition of the Indian frontier, however, precluded
any early action, and the Spaniards were indeed in a poor posi-
sition. In order to enter New Mexico, the settlers would have to
face the danger of attack by six or more Apache groups, including the Faraones, the Plains Apaches, the Apaches of Siete Ríos,
the Salineros (east of El Paso), the Apaches of El Chilmo (the
Gilas), and the Apaches of the Pecos River Valley.[7] Furthermore, the situation at El Paso was made rather dangerous by
the newly reduced Mansos having intimate relations with the
Apaches of Gila, the Sumas, and the Mansos of Chiquito. In
fact, the Apaches would come two, four, or six at a time to
communicate with the Mansos. The two groups, along with the
rebel Mansos and the Sumas, had intermarried.[8]

In Sonora, war raged on as the rebels raided and completely
burned Turicachi in June. *Commandante general* Quirós was
helpless to halt the attacks, and his soldiers turned back when
they found signs of the passing of approximately 1,000 enemies.
In July, the Viceroy apparently gave permission for a joint campaign by the forces of El Paso, Janos, and Sinaloa, but by that
time Fernández was of the opinion that even this effort could
not handle the problem. He declared that the enemy remained
victorious and without punishment. Late in June, a large group
of Conchos had come to aid the Spaniards at Janos, but at the
same time the rebels carried off horses. Three of the thieves were
killed—others being captured—and their scalps were taken by
the Spaniards. From the prisoners it was learned that there had
been a large meeting of Apaches and other groups near by, but

[6] Letter of Diego de Vargas, April 29, 1691, in *Guadalajara* 139, in AGI.

[7] Letter of the Conde de Galve, May 27, 1691, and Letter of Diego de Vargas,
April 17, 1691, *Guadalajara* 139, in AGI.

[8] Letter of Diego de Vargas, August 14, 1691, *Historia* 37, in AGN.

by then a very large rancheria of Sobaipuris had departed for their own country. A rancheria of Sumas was reportedly twenty leagues away in rough territory, and Fernández hoped to attack them with the aid of some Conchos.[9]

During June, the rebels attacked Casas Grandes, and Ramírez made use of some Concho allies in driving them off. Thus it appears that the Spaniards were now beginning to settle loyal Conchos in the former homeland of the Sumas and Janos in order to have available a ready supply of Indian auxiliaries.[10]

In July, 1691 steps were finally taken by the Viceroy to halt the ruin of Sonora, but at the expense of Nueva Vizcaya. The conde de Galve authorized the formation of a *compañia volante* ("a flying company") of thirty men to be made up from the Sinaloa soldiers in Sonora and ten men obtained from the presidios of the north. This company was to be in continual movement on the Sonora frontier to keep the enemy from finding an opportunity to attack. At first, this action simply meant that the province received ten more soldiers and an able officer to command them—Captain Francisco Ramírez of Casas Grandes. In August, the Viceroy supplemented this move by ordering Vargas and Fernández to undertake a joint campaign.[11]

Governor Isidro de Pardiñas of Nueva Vizcaya hated to take even ten soldiers from his overworked presidios, which were attacked, as he said, by the Tobosos, Chisos, and the Athapascan Cholomes. Governor Vargas was likewise unhappy at the viceregal order, and on August 14 he sent a letter to Mexico complaining that his soldiers were needed at El Paso. He had divided his men into three squads—one to guard the horse herd, one for his headquarters, and one to sally forth against the Apaches and others who appeared on the opposite bank of the Río Grande. He could spare no aid for Fernández, in spite of the latter's plight under attack by the Pimas, Janos, Jocomes, Gila Apaches, Sumas, and Mansos of Chiquito living in the Sierra Florida.

[9] Report of Juan de Escalante, June 19, 1691, Letter of the Conde de Galve, June 22, 1691, and Letter of Juan Fernández de la Fuente, June 29, 1691, *Guadalajara* 152, in AGI.

[10] *Ibid.*

[11] Conde de Galve, July 18 and August 20, 1691, *Guadalajara* 152, in AGI.

Vargas then gave his primary reason for putting the reconquest of New Mexico before the pacification of the frontier: If the Pueblo Indians were gentiles such as the Apaches and Sumas, it would be possible to postpone the reconquest, but since they were apostates, they had to be brought back into the faith in order to save their souls and those of their unbaptized children. However, Vargas forgot that many of the frontier rebels were also apostates.[12]

The will of the Viceroy prevailed in 1691, and on September 9 Vargas wrote to Fernández that he would campaign against the Gila Apaches on October 10. Both he and the Captain of Janos agreed that it was best to attack the most important and powerful group of enemies—the Athapascans living in the Sierra of Gila—"since the rest of the enemies are some rancherias of little foundation." Nevertheless, Vargas still insisted that it was more important to subdue New Mexico, "the origin of all of the rest of the revolutions," for the longer those apostates remained, the bolder the other rebels would be.[13]

The combined forces of Vargas and Fernández journeyed northward from Janos into Apache country, but nothing was accomplished there. They then determined to cross over to the lands of the Pimas and Sobaipuris, because the other rebel nations were with them; however, no crossing with sufficient water could be found. As a result, they went south to Turicachi for supplies and guides, turning north from there to enemy country. The route followed has not been clearly established, but the Spaniards reached a westward flowing, powerful river—the Gila —which they presumed could be followed to the lands of the Pimas and Sobaipuris.

> On its banks we came upon rancherias of Apaches, for they have their settlements on both edges [of the river], and although they were spying we tried to give a surprise attack at dawn, dividing our people, [but] because of the forests and the rough

[12] Letter of Juan Isidro de Pardiñas, August 2, 1691, *Guadalajara* 152, in AGI, and Letter of Diego de Vargas, August 14, 1691, *Guadalajara* 139, in AGI, and *Historia* 37, in AGN.

[13] Letters of Diego de Vargas, September 9 and October 4, 1691, *Guadalajara* 152, in AGI.

land nothing could be accomplished but the capture of twenty-three women and children with two warriors which they captured alive. They afterwards brawled and as many as sixteen persons died.

Soon thereafter a snow storm began, and the Spaniards, 100 leagues from the frontier, determined to return to their own posts.[14] Fernández was disappointed with the joint campaign, for it failed to hurt the Gila Apaches. Concerning the effort and its results, he later said:

> The entrada that we made in company with the said captain general and governor of New Mexico who led the force was not made against the Indians that infest the neighborhood of El Parral but to the Apaches who used to make war in the Kingdom of New Mexico when the Spaniards were settled in it, and after it was abandoned they made and are making a very raw war of fire and blood on the frontiers of El Paso del Río del Norte, of this presidio and province of Sonora . . . and after the retiring of the forces from their lands [October, 1691], and having arrived at this presidio . . . the said Apaches made a formidable union of all the people of their nation and of that of the Janos, Jocomes and Sumas.

The rebels followed the Spaniards' trail to Janos and began securing revenge for the campaign. In December, a Jumano captive fled from the Apaches and informed the Spaniards that the rebels were killing all of their captives and forming a great union to destroy El Paso, Janos, and Sonora.[15]

January, 1692 saw the frontier war still raging, but Fernández and Vargas were both able to bring some improvement to the affair. In February a battle took place near Janos, and the rebels asked for peace. It was granted, and, subsequently, gifts of clothing and supplies were used to gain the Athapascans' good will. Twenty days passed in which no Indians came to Janos, and on March 24, Fernández prepared for an attack, for he feared that

14 Letter of Juan Fernández de la Fuente, December 12, 1691, *Guadalajara* 139, in AGI.

15 *Ibid.*, and Report of Juan Fernández de la Fuente, April 29, 1692, *Guadalajara* 139, in AGI.

the Apaches would try to get vengeance for the deaths inflicted in the October campaign. Nevertheless, it was found that the rebels were still peaceful, and a number of them came to Janos on March 28—including a group of Apaches of the sierra. This visit was merely a ruse, however, for the Athapascans fell upon the Spaniards, killing several and wounding others. Then they retired to their own lands, apparently satisfied for the moment with their revenge.[16]

Early in 1692 Vargas began to have trouble with the Sumas of Samalayuca, Guadalupe, and the Sierra Florida (New Mexico). He received a letter from Fernández, informing him that the Sumas had aided the Janos and Chinaras in a raid on Casas Grandes, and he also discovered that the Sumas of Guadalupe had risen from their village and were stealing horses from the Piros and Tiwas. The Governor prepared for a campaign, but the Sumas were persuaded by Fray Antonio Guerra to reduce themselves to a pueblo seven leagues below El Paso, to be called San Diego de los Sumas. Three hundred converted and heathen Indians were settled there, although some of them had had to fight with their old allies—the Apaches—in order to do it. Vargas also led a successful campaign against Captain Barbón's Sumas in the Sierra Florida, capturing and killing the Indians.[17]

A very important item on the northern frontier was salt, and there was a shortage of this precious preservative at El Paso, for a small saline along the Río Grande was no longer usable and the big salines between El Paso and Janos were used for Parral. To the east, however, were the salines of the Apaches for which Jironza and Reneros had searched in the 1680's. In September, 1691 Vargas had captured an Apache who was from the region of the saline, and an expedition was planned with a dual purpose: to locate the Athapascans' habitation sites and to find the valuable salt deposit. With the Apache captive as a guide, the Spaniards left Socorro pueblo—a Piro village below El Paso—on March 8, soon reaching the Hueco Mountains—a retreat of the enemy. No Athapascans were seen, and the Spaniards traveled

16 *Ibid.*
17 Letter of Diego de Vargas, March 30, 1692, *Guadalajara* 139, in AGI.

due east to the salt lake lying midway between El Paso and the Pecos River. They discovered a range of mountains—called the Sierra Negra (Guadalupe Peak range)—east of the saline, and Apaches were said to inhabit it as well as the Pecos River. Vargas led his men into the sierra; but no Athapascans could be located, and the party returned to El Paso. Later, in a letter to the Viceroy, he made much of this find and mentioned that the salt could be used in mining operations in the Sierra Azul.[18]

During the spring of 1692, the controversy between Vargas and the other Spanish leaders of the frontier reached a new peak. Fernández wrote that the reconquest of New Mexico was impossible with only 100 soldiers—Vargas was busy trying to get 50 more men at this time—and in any case it would not profit the crown. Governor Juan Isidro de Pardiñas of Nueva Vizcaya was likewise in opposition to any such plan. However, the Governor of New Mexico's influence was such that in March he received permission to refuse to join in any joint campaigns, and in May Isidro de Pardiñas was ordered to supply 50 of his presidial soldiers to Vargas. This action at a time when Nueva Vizcaya was so short of soldiers that Sonora had almost no protection. Naturally, Isidro de Pardiñas and all of his captains sent long memorials to Mexico, but to no avail. The reconquest of New Mexico was to come before the pacification of the frontier.[19]

An embarrassing event occurred in May, 1692, when the Franciscans at El Paso discovered that no acts of possession existed for the pueblos and missions of that area. This fact did not mean, however, that the land had to be restored to its aboriginal owners, for the matter was simply solved when Vargas took possession of the various places. Among the pueblos so treated were the new conversions of San Francisco de los Mansos, San Diego de los Sumas, and five belonging to the Piros, Tiwas, and Spaniards.[20]

The month of June saw the raids of the Apaches and their allies continue in Sonora, Nacosari being the chief victim. In

18 Letter of Diego de Vargas, April 7, 1692, *Guadalajara* 139, in AGI.
19 Letter of Juan Fernández de la Fuente, April 29, 1692, and *Parecer* of Juan Isidro de Pardiñas, May 19, 1692, *Guadalajara* 139, in AGI, and Letters of the Conde de Galve, March 29 and May 28, 1692, *Guadalajara* 152, in AGI.
20 *Auto* of Diego de Vargas, May 21, 1692, *Guadalajara* 139, in AGI.

July, the Athapascans concentrated their efforts on the Ópata pueblos of Bavispe, Baceraca, and Huachinera—killing 11 Indians (among whom were several chiefs), forcing others to flee wounded, and bottling up the Spanish forces. Then the rebels headed for the old Suma village at Carretas, and Fernández prepared for trouble fourteen leagues away at Janos. A campaign using Concho Indian auxiliaries and settlers from Casas Grandes was planned for August, but news that an Apache meeting was taking place only eight leagues from the presidio forced the soldiers into immediate action. On July 26 they sallied forth to attack the Indians at the *aguaje* of Palotada but were forced to retreat before a force of 200 Indians fighting on foot and another large group on horseback. The Spaniards' mules were stampeded, and several were wounded.

Fernández immediately led a stronger force to the *aguaje* and discovered the entire enemy village three leagues beyond. Athapascan spies had sighted the Spaniards in the meantime, and the Indians sent their women and children to the highest *picachos* while the warriors formed a half-moon with different squads. In the first encounter, many Indians were killed, although the Spaniards had only one soldier and many horses wounded. Fernández was unable to follow up his advantage, but the rebels were seemingly worried enough to desire peace talks. *Tlatoles* continued on the next day, and the two groups exchanged stolen goods. The Indians with whom Fernández was talking were Janos, Jocomes, Mansos, Sumas, and some Apaches and Pimas, and they numbered 300. However, there were many other rebels living in their villages on the frontier of Sonora. Two Indians' of each nation accompanied the Spaniards to Janos, and there they were regaled with tobacco, clothing, and other gifts. They agreed to retire their nations, each to its own land. Fernández regarded this as the only solution to the problem, for the united rebel force was so large that it could not support itself without warfare. The captain was forgetting, however, that much of the lands belonging to the Janos and Sumas were now in the hands of Spaniards and their allies.[21]

[21] Reports of Juan Fernández de la Fuente, July 26 and 31, 1692, *Guadalajara* 152, in AGI.

From July 28 to August 10, squads of rebels continually came to Janos to affirm their accord with the peace plans. The principal Jano chief and El Tabovo of the Jocomes wished to see Fernández in person in their villages. The Indians wished assurances from the Captain, for many of them were very much afraid of the Spaniards and their allies—there were 100 Ópatas and Conchos at Janos. On August 11, Fernández went to the Jocomes' village, and talks and dances were held. It was agreed that the Sumas and Mansos would return to their lands on the Río Grande, while the Jocomes would retire north and the Janos would settle near the presidio—since that was their land. The Janos would support themselves on mescal·and seeds until it would be time to plant their crops. All together, there were approximately 1,000 Indians, and Fernández requested financial support in order to regale them properly and thereby preserve the peace. He considered the expense to be much less than that incurred because of the rising of these four nations, which had in turn started the nation of the Apaches and those of the Pimas and Sobaipuris on the warpath. He asserted further that peace was necessary because each day the numbers of the rebels had been increasing as Christians and malcontents went over to the enemy.[22]

During July and early August, Diego de Vargas completed preparations at El Paso for a preliminary expedition into New Mexico. He had already gathered as much information as he could about the lost province, particularly as it related to the Sierra Azul mines—called *los cerros colorados* by Vargas. From the testimonies of former settlers and soldiers in New Mexico, as well as from an *informe* of former Governor Antonio de Otermín, it was learned that the direct route from old Socorro, or Isleta, to Moqui and the mines was very dangerous, because it was entirely occupied by groups of Apaches. Antonio Jorge, who had been born at Santa Fe about 1651 and who had lived with his father at Oraibe and Halona during the 1660's and 1670's, declared that

[22] Report of Juan Fernández de la Fuente, August 14, 1692, *Guadalajara* 152, in AGI.

235

the said land [of Moqui] for one part and another is all surrounded by Apaches and likewise from where one leaves this said place [of El Paso] are the Apaches of the Sierra de los Organos [and of] the Sierra de Jila which is extensive because it begins at the Peñol of Acoma . . . and comes to an end at the Sierra Florida [in southern New Mexico] and runs towards the provinces of Sonora; and [that region] is populated by Apachería in different parts and that he thinks that 150 soldiers are necessary

to make the journey from El Paso to the mines near Moqui.[23] Other informants concurred on the dangerous nature of the direct route to Moqui, and likewise they all agreed that there were many tribes in the Hopi region which would be a threat to mining operations. They could not, however, agree about just which tribes these were—some saying Apaches; others Apaches, Cruzados, and Coninas; and still others confusing the Apaches and Coninas.[24] The testimony was enough to lead Vargas to write the Viceroy that the best plan was to reduce New Mexico first, then to subdue the Hopis and the Coninas and gain entrance to the region of the mines.[25]

Early in August, Governor Vargas and most of the presidio soldiers left El Paso for Santa Fe: The reconquest of the lost province had begun. Captain Juan Fernández de la Fuente of Janos presidio had said that there was no reason to attack the Pueblo Indians, "who for twelve years had made no damages, robberies or killings . . . but had been in their pueblos," and, furthermore, royal money should not be spent to conquer a region that would contribute nothing to the Royal Treasury.[26] Other motives were responsible for the royal backing received by Vargas, however, for the French menace was considered very real; and the desire to exploit the Sierra Azul mines, the ache to get revenge for the 1680 defeat, the feeling that continued freedom of the Pueblo Indians gave hope to other rebels, and

[23] Declaration of Antonio Jorge, August 12, 1691, *Guadalajara* 139, in AGI.
[24] Various Testimony, August 9, 1691, and Letter of Antonio de Otermín, December 11, 1691, *Guadalajara* 139, in AGI.
[25] Letter of Diego de Vargas, August 26, 1691, *Guadalajara* 139, in AGI.
[26] Letter of Juan Fernández de la Fuente, July 26, 1692, *Guadalajara* 152, in AGI.

the wish to save the souls of apostates and their pagan children all worked together to promote the enterprise. The most important factor was Diego de Vargas himself, who had come to El Paso to reconquer New Mexico and was not going to let anything stop him.

The invading Spaniards realized that their task was not an easy one, for they knew that the Tewas and Tanos had fortified Santa Fe, and Vargas suspected that the Apaches would aid the Pueblo tribes.[27] Contact was made with only deserted pueblos until the army reached Santa Fe, and there the Indians were found to be entrenched and willing to fight. In 1692 Vargas' plan was apparently to pacify the pueblos by peaceful means if possible, and considerable discussion took place between the Governor and the rebel leaders. As a result, a truce was arranged between opposing forces, and the chief of the Tanos at Santa Fe sent for the principal chief of all of the Tewas, Tanos, and Picuris—Luís Tupatu. At that time the chief was visiting the Navaho Apaches.[28]

The situation of New Mexico in 1692 was opportune for Vargas because the Pueblo tribes were no longer united but had divided into several factions. The surrounding Athapascans were likewise disunited and were allied with, or members of, the various Pueblo divisions. One group, and the first to be contacted by the Spaniards, was led by Luís Tupatu and consisted in his own people—the Picuris—and the neighboring Tanos and Tewas. This faction occupied twelve pueblos—Tesuque, Nambe, Cuiamunque, Pujuaque, Jacona, Santa Clara, San Ildefonso, San Juan, San Cristóbal, San Lazaro, Santa Fe, and Picuris—and maintained some degree of friendship with the Navaho Apaches. A second faction consisted of the pueblos of Pecos and Taos and the Apaches of the east—the Achos, Faraones, and others. The third group was composed of the Keres of Cochiti, San Marcos, San Felipe (united for defensive purposes in a new pueblo called La Cieneguilla), and Santo Domingo and the Keres remnants of

27 Letters of Diego de Vargas, October 4, 1691, and July 13, 1692, *Guadalajara* 139, in AGI.
28 Diary of Diego de Vargas, 1692, *Guadalajara* 139, in AGI.

Zia and Santa Ana (united at a pueblo called Cerrillo Colorado).

The second and third groups were at war with the division led by Luís Tupatu, as was another faction consisting of the Jemez, the Keres of Acoma, the Hopis, most of the Navahos, the Gilas and Western Apaches, the Coninas, and the Utes living near the Hopis. All of the anti-Tupatu groups seem to have been on good terms with each other. The Zuñis were apparently not in any alliance except with their close friends the Salinero Apaches. Wars with the Navahos and other groups had forced the Zuñis to abandon their outlying pueblos and concentrate at the *peñol* of Caquima.

As regards the Athapascans specifically, it seems that the Plains Apaches east of Pecos (called Faraones by Vargas) were as always extremely close allies of the Pecos. Likewise, the Apaches north and east of Taos were as always united with the Taos, and all of the above were on friendly terms with each other as well. Whether or not they actively took part in any fighting with the followers of Tupatu is not clear, but it seems unlikely, as they continued to trade at Picuris.

The Navaho Apaches were allies of the Hopis and the Keres of Acoma and Jemez and were friendly with the western Utes, the Coninas, and the other Apaches—with the possible exception of the Salinero group, which was allied with the Zuñis. Some of the Navahos, however, were at least friendly with the Tupatu faction, perhaps for trading purposes.

So far as is known, the Gila and Western Apaches were friendly with the Hopis, Navahos, and Keres of Acoma. The Keres of Cochiti, San Marcos, and San Felipe had suffered from Apache attacks but from which tribes in particular is not clear. The Jemez, while being close allies of the Navahos, had had some wars with other Apaches, perhaps Navahos friendly with the Tewas, Tanos, and Picuris.[29]

The above discussion indicates clearly that those scholars who try to create the picture of the Athapascan and the Pueblo Indians continually at war are mistaken, for the truth is that in 1692 most of the Athapascans and most of the Pueblos were

[29] *Ibid.*

friendly with each other. Furthermore, those Pueblo groups which had suffered attacks by enemies—such as the Keres of La Cieneguilla and the Jemez—always listed the Tewas and Tanos as their principal foes, not the Apaches. The Puebloans were occupying the defensive positions because of the raids made by Reneros and Jironza.[30]

At Santa Fe, Luís Tupatu and his brother Lorenzo met with Vargas in mid-September and apparently attempted to fool the Spanish leader into believing that they were glad to see him. They asserted that they desired his aid against their enemies—the Pecos, Faraon Apaches, Taos, Jemez, and Keres of San Felipe, Santo Domingo, and Cochiti. Vargas was suspicious, but he determined to take advantage of the division among the rebels to crush the Pecos and Keres. Late in September, the Spaniards and their allies hurried to surprise the Pecos, but their plan was partially thwarted when several Apache scouts saw them and warned the pueblo. Thus the invaders found the pueblo deserted, and little was accomplished besides the theft of maize and capture of a few persons. The Pecos said that they did not want the Spaniards' peace or friendship and that they would flee to the Taos and Apaches.[31]

The balance of September and early October was spent in receiving the submission of the various Tewa and Tano pueblos. On October 7 Vargas went from Picuris to Taos, where the Indians were in the sierra. Possession was taken of their pueblo, and contact was made with the rebels, although nothing more was accomplished than the making of peace between the Taos and the Tupatu faction, and some bad news was received. Two Taos men had just returned from Zuñi, and on the way back they had seen a great *junta* of chiefs of the Hopis, Zuñis, Jemez, Keres, Pecos, Apaches, and Coninas which lasted three days and nights and during which a defense against the invaders was planned.[32]

On October 15 Vargas returned to Santa Fe and on the fol-

30 *Ibid.*
31 *Ibid.*
32 *Ibid.*

lowing day reported to the Viceroy, noting that "it would be easier to defer the Jews from the Inquisition" than to reduce the apostates of New Mexico who have taken to the sierras.[33] Even the supposedly friendly Tewas were living away from their their villages. During mid-October, the Spaniards visited the Keres groups living in their defensive pueblos, and peace was agreed upon. The Jemez proved to be more hostile, and a large party of them and their Apache allies threatened the Spaniards with demonstrations of war. Nonetheless, Vargas continued his policy of a peaceful approach, and talks were held. The Jemez continued to be haughty, and the Governor was reminded of rumored plans to destroy the invaders. After eating his dinner, Vargas was surprised to meet twelve Apache warriors with their weapons in their hands just outside the entrance to the house in which he had dined. They said that they had come in peace and desired to be Christians. Vargas' replied that he would return the following year and that, if they did not reduce themselves to Christianity and live in settlements as men of reason, he would not want their friendship. Thus the Governor made it clear that there was no possibility of peace between equals; the Indians must conform to the Spaniards' dictums in regard to religion and culture.[34]

Evidence of the close alliance existing between the Jemez and the Apaches was to be seen in the fact that the Jemez were housing the Athapascans within their own homes, and Vargas suspected that there were Apaches hidden in every dwelling. The Spaniards left Jemez without accomplishing anything, and on November 4 they reached Acoma, having followed a roundabout route via Isleta—doubtless to avoid the lands of the Navahos. The Keres of Acoma were very hostile, and Vargas had to be content with talking to only a few Indians, for the others were on their rock. He learned that the Navaho Apaches were their friends and that two Mansos and other Apaches had visited the Acomas and told them

that when the Governor of the Spanish tells them that he comes

[33] Letter of Diego de Vargas, October 16, 1692, *Guadalajara* 139, in AGI.
[34] Diary of Diego de Vargas, 1692, *Guadalajara* 139, in AGI.

to see them and speak of peace do not believe him, because under the sign and security [of peace] he had demanded to cut off the heads and hang all and carry off their women and children to the district of El Paso del Río del Norte as they had done it with those that they had taken from the pueblos of Isleta, Zia and Santa Ana.[35]

Vargas attempted to make the Keres believe that the Mansos were liars, but in this he failed. Finally, he departed out of fear that the Acomas were talking merely to give the Apaches time to arrive.

The Zuñis received the Spaniards in a friendly manner at Caquima, but, on the night of November 10, the Navahos (called Faraones by Vargas) succeeded in stealing sixteen horses from the invaders. On November 13, a Salinero Apache chief with eight to ten warriors arrived at Zuñi and informed Vargas that his people had always been friends of the Zuñi and that they desired friendship with the Spaniards. At first, the Governor responded politely but soon insulted the Apache with an intimation that his people had stolen the missing horses. The conversation ended on a better note, however, as Vargas offered the Athapascans the chance to reduce themselves to Christianity.[36]

On November 17, the Spaniards approached Awatobi with caution, for they had learned from a Hopi that the Navahos had warned the Indians of the invading army. Almost 1,000 Hopi warriors met the army. Approximately 300 of them were on horseback and armed with leather jackets, lances, swords, and guns. The infantrymen had bows and arrows, clubs, and other arms. The governor was able to convince the Hopis that they had nothing to fear from his visit, and, after a lengthy series of discussions, the Spaniards were allowed to visit the several villages. At Walpi, Vargas saw a great number of warriors, some of whom did not appear to be natives, and, upon asking one of the Hopi chiefs, he was told that "some were of the Ute nation, and the others of Apaches, Coninas, their allies and neighbors who surround them." Vargas confused the Western Apaches and

35 *Ibid.*, and Villagutierre y Sotomayor, BN 2823.
36 Diary of Diego de Vargas, 1692, *Guadalajara* 139, in AGI.

the Havasupais and in other reports refers to the "Conina Apaches" as one group, although in places they seem to be treated as two separate peoples.[37] This confusion was natural, since he had not actually visited either of the groups and Spanish informants at El Paso had failed to differentiate adequately between them.

Upon returning to Awatobi, Vargas made enquiries about the mines of *zerro colorado,* where the Hopis were said to get *almagre,* or vermillion. He learned that some ten leagues away to the west was the place where Fray Joseph de Espeleta held his *conversión* of the Coninas and beyond that was a water hole where a group of Coninas lived. Still farther was a canyon which was too deep for men on horses to cross (the Little Colorado perhaps), but by going on foot it was possible to go beyond to the *zerro colorado.* This hill was pine-covered and was apparently only one day beyond the canyon, thus it was not the same mineral deposit as was seen by the earlier Spaniards but was probably only a high butte or peak from which reddish ore was extracted.[38] In any case, Vargas was unable to visit either the mines or the pueblo of Oraibe, for his horses were in poor condition and he feared being stranded among enemies.

On November 22, the Spaniards left Awatobi for Zuñi, traveling always with caution, for new rumors of a large *junta* of Apaches had reached their ears, and some Athapascans had run off nine horses from the Zuñis. These animals were returned to the Zuñis by the Salinero Apaches, who again appeared on the scene to aid their allies.[39]

At this point, the Governor of New Mexico determined to forsake a return to the central Río Grande Valley and to go instead by a direct route from Zuñi to the ruins of Senecú and thence to El Paso, although the entire area between was the land of hostile Apaches. On the journey from Zuñi to El Morro, Apache signs were seen—the night of December 1 being spent under guard at El Morro. On December 2, they

[37] *Ibid.*

[38] *Ibid.* It was probably Red Butte, north of Williams, Arizona, and about 112 miles west of Awatobi.

[39] Letter of Diego de Vargas, May 16, 1693, *Guadalajara* 139, in AGI.

took the road that looks to the south and later after one league from a rise discovered different mountain ranges of which the one was called the Black Mountains and much to one side was another called the large rock and in this he [the guide] said a rancheria of the Apaches Colorados live and that they raise maize.[40]

Vargas' party was able to reach the deserted pueblo of Socorro without incident, no Apaches being contacted. It is to be assumed that much new geographical knowledge was added which would prove useful, and the "discovery" of the high peaks of the Gila Mountains was made. In the *jornada del muerto* between Fray Cristóbal and El Paso, contact was made with a band of Apaches. A party of Spanish soldiers took out in pursuit of the Indians, and a short battle resulted. The Spaniards suffered the loss of Lieutenant General Martín de Alday, who died from four wounds, and Juan Paez Hurtado was wounded in the leg. The Apaches lost one man and had a warrior captured. The Apache prisoner was asked if he had ever raided El Paso, and, as his reply was affirmative, Vargas ordered him shot to death after he was hurriedly instructed in the Roman Catholic faith and baptized. This was the first example of the Governor's subsequent policy in New Mexico: All prisoners were to be shot immediately unless the whole nation was submitting to Spanish authority.[41]

On December 20, the Spanish army arrived at El Paso, and Vargas was informed of the only important events which had occurred in his absence: In September, fifty soldiers had arrived from Nueva Vizcaya, and the Apaches had raided twice, carrying off twenty horses. On January 12, 1693 the Governor made a report to the Viceroy in which he outlined his plans for the reconquest of New Mexico. These plans included the recruiting of settlers and the reestablishment of the Piros at Socorro and the Tiwas at Isleta. Shortly thereafter, Vargas journeyed to the south to gather *pobladores* in the Zacatecas region.[42]

By January, 1693 warfare had resumed on the Sonora frontier,

40 Diary of Diego de Vargas, 1692, *Guadalajara* 139, in AGI.
41 *Ibid.*, and Villagutierre y Sotomayor, BN 2823.
42 Letter of Diego de Vargas, January 12, 1693, *Guadalajara* 139, in AGI.

as the peace of August, 1692 was short-lived. Trouble broke out when a Concho Indian auxiliary informed a woman—who was a daughter of a Concho man and a Jocome woman, but who had been with the rebels—that the Conchos and Ópatas were planning to cut the throats of the various rebel chiefs living at the time with Captain Fernández and that the Spanish peace was not good. This information led many of the rebels to flee during a Mass; but Fernández executed the Concho, and calm was partially reestablished. By September 22, Janos had stolen horses in Sonora, and the other rebels—although desiring peace—were very restless. In December, Fernández protested the removal of fifteen of his men for service in Sonora on the grounds that his presidio was on the frontier of the very numerous and astute nations of the Apaches, Janos, Sumas, Jocomes, and their other allies "who ordinarily enter to infest these frontiers."[43] A report from Sonora dated early in 1693, declared that the peace of the previous August endured only fifteen or twenty days and that the rebels then gathered on the Sonora frontier and

> began to convoke the nations of Sobaguipuru [the Sobaipuris], a great part of the Pimas, and others, and all together, in the month of November, they carried away from the frontiers of Bacanuche, San Antonio de la Natividad, mining towns, and the pueblo of Chinapa, all the horses and mules that there were.[44]

Captain Francisco Ramírez had been placed in charge of the body of soldiers who were supposed to defend Sonora, and one of his most important acts was to attempt a destruction of the alliance and friendship existing between the Pimas and Sobaipuris on the one hand and the Apaches, Jocomes, and Janos on the other. Doubtlessly spurred on by these tribes' combined raids in November, 1692, Ramírez entered the very heart of Sobaipuri country in an effort to break the alliance. He traveled up the San Pedro River to a point twenty-three leagues past Quiburi and eleven leagues before reaching Arivaipa, achiev-

[43] Letters of Juan Fernández de la Fuente, September 22 and December 30, 1692, *Guadalajara* 152, in AGI.
[44] Letter of February 6, 1693, in Hackett, *Historical Documents*, II, 295.

ing at least some success in his aims. Actually it is not possible to say just what Ramírez did, and all that we know was summed up by Fray Luís Velarde more than twenty years later:

> In former years, before there were priests here [in Pimería Alta], when the Indians were all gentiles, the Sobaipuris had the last communication with the Apaches of the Sierra of Chiguicagui [Chiricahua Mountains], but since Captain Ramírez, with great diplomacy and tact and without shedding blood, separated them, the Sobaipuris are implacable enemies of the Apaches.[45]

This separation was good for the province of Sonora. Certainly the Spanish policy of pitting tribe against tribe was to prove advantageous, and for many years the Pimas and Sobaipuris were to form the major defense for western Sonora. The Indians did not benefit from this alliance, however, for their Spanish masters were eventually to fail them and the Sobaipuri lost the San Pedro Valley to the Apaches in 1763. That the alliance bloomed forth in its full vigor as a result of Ramírez' expedition late in 1692 is to be doubted, for subsequent co-operation between Sobaipuris and Athapascans did occur prior to 1697.

Early in 1693 Ramírez personally journeyed to appeal to the Viceroy for aid, and he was given permission to have a force of fifty men. However, he died before he could return north. While he was absent, the rebels raided Opoto, closed the mines of Nacosari, carried off everything from the Baceraca–Huachinera region, and killed the Ópata governors there. On February 6, many citizens of Sonora appealed to the higher authorities to send the new soldiers quickly and to name a new commander for the *compañía volante*, for the province "is being depopulated." The enemy was said to be very numerous, and hitherto peaceful groups were joining them. Even converted Indians had revolted, for the Eudeves (close relatives of the Ópatas) were in the sierras

45 Letter of February 6, 1693, in Hackett, *Historical Documents*, II, 291; *Relación* of Fray Luís Velarde, 1716, translated by Harry J. Karns and published in Manje, *Luz de Tierra Incógnita*, 247; Luís Velarde, "*Relación* of Pimería Alta, 1716" (trans. by Rufus Kay Wyllys), *New Mexico Historical Review*, Vol. VI, No. 2 (1931), 114; and Manje, "*Breve Noticia*," BMH 970.

and refused to come back to the priests. On February 5, the rebels had raided Nacosari and carried off all the mules. At the same time, others had attacked Turicachi and carried off everything, but the most dangerous aspect of this attack was that the rebels had talked for a long time with a Christian prisoner and then had set him free—an act of the rebels never before observed. From these occurrences the Spaniards inferred that a general rebellion was in the making.[46]

Sonora's affairs had certainly taken a turn for the worse in 1693, with the Sumas, Janos, Jocomes, and Apaches raiding as usual and the Eudeves, Conchos, and Jovas in rebellion for the first time. On February 28, Domingo de Jironza, the former governor of New Mexico, was named commander of Sonora's *compañía volante,* and, on March 2, he was appointed *alcalde mayor* —thus giving him military and civil control under the Governor of Nueva Vizcaya. Jironza immediately went out on campaign against the northern rebels and also against the Jovas and Conchos who had raided Nacosari.[47] On April 1, 1693 Governor Isidro de Pardiñas reported that the Pimas had been reduced to peace (apparently by Ramírez) but that the Janos, Jocomes, and Sumas were still at war. He would have liked to have gone to Sonora in person, but the frontier war with the Tobosos and their allies was raging, as usual. Instead, he planned to transfer the whole presidio of Sinaloa to the northern province, in spite of the protests of the officials on the Río Yaqui.[48] By May, a new governor was in power in Nueva Vizcaya and this official, Gabriel del Castillo, was concerned to discover that the Viceroy had granted a fifty-man *compañía volante* to Jironza, the members of which were to be drawn from Castillo's presidios. His counterproposal was to return the fifty men taken from Nueva Vizcaya for Vargas' use in New Mexico and put them to use in the Parral area.[49] This plan, however, was mere wishful thinking, for the influential Don Diego was not going to allow his chances

---

[46] Letter of February 6, 1693, in Hackett, *Historical Documents,* II, 293–95.
[47] Manje, *"Breve Noticia,"* BMH 970.
[48] Letter of Juan Isidro de Pardiñas, April 1, 1693, *Guadalajara* 152, in AGI.
[49] Letter of Gabriel del Castillo, May 2, 1693, in Hackett, *Historical Documents,* II, 307.

of reconquering New Mexico to be lost. In fact, at that very time Vargas was in Nueva Galicia recruiting settlers, and, on May 16, he informed the Viceroy that he had already reconquered New Mexico—possibly in an effort to prove that he had gone too far with the enterprise to stop.[50]

In their northern wars, the Spaniards always made great use of Indian auxiliaries, and the student of Indian history might wonder if they were actually able to get these forced or paid allies to fight against their neighbors. In 1693 Gabriel del Castillo declared that "the friendly Indians that are enlisted are not fighting, nor have they ever been used for this." They were said to serve only as guides and spies.[51] On the other hand, it seems probable that where previous enmity existed between the Spaniards' allies and the enemy tribes, the auxiliaries might well partake in the fighting.

Early in 1694, Lieutenant Antonio Solis of the Sonora forces became suspicious that the Sobaipuris and Pimas of the north were raiding again. In order to ascertain the truth, he led a party of soldiers up the San Pedro and then west across the Sierra del Comedio to the Pimas of San Xavier del Bac, finding no sign of stolen horses. In the San Xavier del Bac region, however, he came upon some Pimas who were eating meat and who fled out of fear. Assuming that they were eating stolen horseflesh, he pursued the Indians and killed three of them, although he found out subsequently that the meat was venison. Solis then returned to his presidio—newly founded Fronteras—but he did not reestablish harmony with the Pimas. Instead, he told them that, if they wished to prove their friendship for the Spaniards, they would have to help in a campaign against the Athapascans.[52] He thus presented the Pimas with the choice of either helping the Spaniards or facing the consequences of being under suspicion.

Meanwhile, the *compañia volante* went out on campaign in April against the Jocomes, Janos, and Apaches. This *entrada* lasted until June; but only 13 Athapascans were killed, and 7

---

50 Letter of Diego de Vargas, May 16, 1693, *Guadalajara* 139, in AGI.

51 Letter of Gabriel del Castillo, May 2, 1693, in Hackett, *Historical Documents,* II, 307.

52 Manje, *"Breve Noticia,"* BMH 970.

were captured. In September, the Pimas decided to aid the Spaniards and 300 warriors came to the new presidio of Fronteras for a campaign which netted 3 women captives. Upon returning to the presidio, it was learned that the enemy was raiding Cuchuta, and the Spanish-Pima force quickly went to that place, where they engaged in combat with approximately 600 Athapascans. Apparently, the auxiliaries took no part in the fighting at first, but, when it looked as if the Spaniards were going down to defeat (with four casualties), the Pimas and some Ópatas jumped into the struggle. As a result, 24 of the enemy were killed, and 86 were wounded. All of the wounded supposedly died, for the Pimas, along with other Sonoran tribes, poisoned their arrows.[53] In November, a joint campaign was planned with the forces of Janos presidio, and 200 Pimas were called upon to join in the enterprise. The Sonoran forces reconnoitered the sierras near Piticachi, Batepito, and the area to the north—killing one Athapascan but allowing another to get away and warn his fellows. With two days still to elapse before their union with Fernández' men, the 36 Sonora soldiers and the 200 Pimas advanced into narrow, rocky canyons where they

> combated more than 700 Jocome Apaches and Janos enemies killing on our side a valiant soldier with five wounded, and ten Pimas, although we killed a few more of them, striking out blindly with harquebus and swords; but without the loosening of sixty horses that we had in a *remuda* we might have perished at their hands. We arrived that night at the arroyo of Guadalupe where General Xironza had remained with soldiers guarding the rest of the horses and baggage.

Two days later, Fernández arrived, and the combined forces returned to the scene of battle to collect their dead. They could find no enemies, for the Apaches had, during two days and nights, retreated fifty leagues to the region beyond the Río Gila.

Thus, in spite of the presence of approximately 100 soldiers and 200 Pimas, the Athapascans could not be defeated—rather clear evidence of the increasing astuteness of the Apaches as fight-

53 *Ibid.*

ers against the Europeans. One important result of the campaign, according to one informant, was that "from then the Pima nation remained a more declared and sworn enemy of Apaches, Jocomes, and Janos, and fond friends of the Spaniards."[54]

The end of 1694 saw the Sonora frontier war continuing in spite of the use of additional troops, and farther to the north, in New Mexico, Diego de Vargas and his invading army were likewise experiencing the effect of growing Indian capabilities to resist European aggression.

[54] *Ibid.*

CHAPTER XII

The End
of an Era

◙

In September, 1693 Diego de Vargas gathered his groups of settlers and soldiers together at El Paso in preparation for invasion
of New Mexico. Early in October, departure was made, the army
traveling in two groups—one of soldiers and the other of soldiers,
settlers, and supplies. A few leagues beyond Fray Cristóbal, signs
of an Apache ambush were found, but otherwise nothing event-
ful occurred until the advance group led by Vargas made camp
between the deserted pueblos of Sandia and Puaray and contact
was made with some Pueblo Indians.

During 1693 the Pueblo tribes had set to work, uniting themselves to resist the return of the Spaniards. Their plans were only
partially realized, however, for the Pecos and some of the Keres
decided upon a policy of appeasing the invaders. Nevertheless,
the Tewas, Tanos, Picuris, Taos, Jemez, Keres of Cochiti and
Santo Domingo, Acomas, Zuñis, Hopis, and all of the Apache
groups except the Faraones—who were allies of the Pecos—were
friendly to each other and committed to expelling the aggres-
sors. The rest of the Keres seem to have been haunted by what
had happened to Zia and Santa Ana only a few years before, and
they were apparently loath to resist the Spaniards.[1]

For several months after the setting up of his camp near present-day Bernalillo, Vargas was to receive a great number of con-

[1] Diary of Diego de Vargas, 1693, *Guadalajara* 140, in AGI.

flicting and confusing reports from ambassadors of the Indians, for many of the pueblos sought to beguile the invaders into a false sense of security. Still others endeavored at all costs to prove their pueblos' friendship for the Spaniards. On November 12, a number of Keres leaders visited Vargas and told of the plans of the Jemez, Tanos, and Tewas to attack the Keres of Santa Ana and Zia because of their disagreement on how to receive the Europeans. Apaches had notified the Jemez of the coming of the Spanish army, and the Jemez had sent messengers to the other tribes. The Pecos and some of the Keres had turned down the call for resistance.[2] In spite of such rumors and others to the effect that the Tewas, Tanos, Picuris, Taos, Navaho Apaches, and Apaches of the Río Colorado (the Red River north of Taos) had attempted to persuade the Keres of La Cieneguilla to join them in ambushing the invaders, the four principal leaders of the Tewas, Tanos, and Picuris came to see Vargas and pretended friendship. Luís Tupatu apologized for not having come sooner by saying that he had been trading for deerskins with the Apaches and that his brother Lorenzo had been on the buffalo plains.[3]

On November 19, the Spanish forces were united, and Vargas took forty soldiers on a visit to the Keres of La Cieneguilla. There he found the people of Cochiti and San Marcos living together, although each preserved their separate tribal government. They asserted that the Apaches who lived in the mountains fronting on old Socorro were their enemies, and Vargas promised to aid them in the future. From La Cieneguilla Vargas marched to Santa Ana, Zia, and Jemez, being troubled only by news brought by the Indian Governor of Pecos to the effect that the Keres of Cochiti had left Cieneguilla and had united with the Apaches of the Río Colorado and the Navahos to attack the Spaniards. Later, the same Indian informed Vargas that all of the rebels and the Apaches mentioned above were uniting for an ambush at a place near Santo Domingo called Dos Cerrillos. This information, however, was offset by the opinion of a Keres leader who thought that the Tewas and their allies "now are good."[4]

2 *Ibid.*   3 *Ibid.*
4 *Ibid.*, and Villagutierre y Sotomayor, BN 2823.

On December 16, the Spanish forces entered Santa Fe, or at least that part of the settlement not occupied as a pueblo by the Tanos and Tewas. On December 17, Vargas received word from the Pecos that the Tewas, Tanos, Picuris, and many Apaches were preparing for hostilities at the mesa of San Juan pueblo. On the same day, in a *junta general,* the Spaniards ordered the Indians to abandon their section of Santa Fe, and, when the Indians began making preparations for defense, the invaders stormed the settlement and took it from the natives bit by bit. Most of the warriors escaped, but the women and children were captured and divided among the Spaniards.

With the *villa* under control, Vargas was in a position to carry out his policy of conquest which was to be successful in spite of determined resistance of the Indians. His methods were to raid the pueblos individually if possible, capture the women and children, sack the pueblos of all useful items such as maize and blankets, burn them if necessary, keep the Indians from growing any crops by constant harassment, and thus force the warriors to submit to Spanish rule. On their part, the Indians were forced to wage a defensive war, hitting the horse and cattle herds of the invaders. They also attempted to force the traitors among them into fighting the Spaniards, but in this they were unsuccessful. From the very first, many Tewas and Tanos fled to the Apaches in order to be safe from the Spaniards' raiding. Governor Vargas followed a strict policy of killing all male rebels regardless of whether they surrendered or were captured in battle. The only exception to this rule was when a whole pueblo was willing to submit. The Spanish policy was ruthless but effective.[5]

On December 31, the war chief of Zia reported that the Jemez and Navahos were going to unite with the Keres of Cochiti and attack the Europeans' horse herds. News of the following day revealed that the Tewas were abandoning their villages out of fear, and some were going to the Taos and others to the Apaches. The main body, however, congregated in a strong defensive posi-

[5] The following account of the war in New Mexico during 1694 and 1695 is taken from the Diary of Diego de Vargas, 1694–95, *Guadalajara* 140, in AGI, except where cited otherwise.

tion at the *peñol* of San Ildefonso. On January 4, a Faraon Apache came to Santa Fe from Pecos and reported to his friend the Indian Governor of Pecos that a large *junta* of Tanos, Tewas, Picuris, Apaches, and Taos was two leagues from his pueblo. Thirty soldiers were dispatched from Santa Fe, but nothing occurred. On January 8, Vargas formally declared the Tewas and Tanos to be rebels and traitors, following up this statement with a campaign against San Ildefonso. The near-by pueblos were partially sacked, but the Indians refused to submit. For the next few months, groups of soldiers visited the various deserted pueblos continually, gathering up all of the booty which could be stolen. One group of raiding soldiers was at Tesuque when they heard riders coming from the direction of Santa Fe. They mounted quickly and rode out to meet what proved to be a group of Apaches who had stolen fourteen horses from the *villa*. One of the Athapascans was killed and another captured. The Apache prisoner and two Tewas seized at Tesuque were taken to Santa Fe, where they were questioned. The Apache said that he was of the Río Colorado and that he had come to the "point of the sierra" and was going to make peace when several other Apaches from the *río abajo* (where they had eleven tents of people) had persuaded him to help them raid the Spanish horse herd. This was the first time that he had come, but he and the two Tewas who had simply been getting supplies at Tesuque were shot to death as "traitors."

On February 25, Governor Vargas reported that a new *junta* of Keres, Acomas, Zuñis, Hopis, *"Apaches Coninas y los de Navajo y las rancherias de las dilitadas de los de el Chilmo"* had been discovered. Thus it seems that the Gila Apaches led by Chilmo were being drawn upon for support by the hostile Indians. Likewise, the Keres rebels were attempting to get their brothers to fight for independence, but the latter still chose to aid the invaders. The following day, Vargas led an army of 100 soldiers in a campaign to force the Tewas and Tanos of San Ildefonso to surrender. The Indians showed great fighting ability in defense of their freedom, and, in spite of repeated charges by the Spaniards and a siege lasting until March 20, the *peñol* remained in Indian hands. The invading army had to return to Santa Fe with many men suffering from wounds. Subsequently, both the Tewas and Spaniards visited the deserted pueblos—one group gathering and the other stealing supplies. During the same period, some Tanos who had been in La Cañada de San Juan joined the Tewas and other Tanos at San Ildefonso.

In mid-March, a group of Plains Apaches arrived at Pecos, and upon hearing that the Spaniards had returned to Santa Fe they sent three of their number with the Governor of Pecos, Juan de Ye, to visit Vargas. The group reached the *villa* on March 27 and was received with friendship by the governor. It was arranged that trading could take place, and a body of Spaniards accompanied them to Pecos for that purpose. The Apaches declared that at the end of the wet season they would return for more trading.

The Europeans were much impressed with these Plains Apaches and remarked that they had a better behavior, a greater perseverance of friendship, and a finer interchange with the Spaniards than did the converted but apostate Indians of the pueblos. Of course, the Spaniards failed to note that the Plains Apaches' lands were not being occupied by force.

The Pueblo Indians and their Apache allies continued their raids upon Spanish livestock, and early in April it was learned that a league had been formed by the Tewas, Tanos, Jemez, "Apaches Colorados," and Navahos to destroy the Keres who were aiding the invaders. As a result, Vargas issued a notice of war on April 2 and undertook to punish the Keres of Cochiti and the Jemez. While in Keres country, he met a small party of Zuñis coming from Jemez. This excited his suspicion, but the Zuñis claimed that they had only been trading with other Indians to obtain buffalo hides. They further declared that the people of their nation were content and very secure and

> that they have defense from the Apaches *de el mechon* [of the large hair lock] they being their enemies and also they were [their enemies] the Moquinos, Yutas and Conina Apaches and that these last three nations gave a large ambush from which

they were able to defend themselves and resist because their pueblo and rancheria was on the mesa of the *peñol* of Jaquima.

Vargas seemingly believed the Zuñis, and, subsequently, he directed a letter to them, acknowledging that the Hopis, Utes, and "Cononinas Apaches" had attacked them. He offered the Zuñis the chance to settle on the lower Río Grande, where they could live near Santa Fe and also trade for buffalo skins with the friendly Apaches of the plains.

On April 17, the Keres of Cieneguilla were attacked by the Spaniards, and, in spite of hard fighting and defensive stockades, the pueblo was taken and sacked. Three hundred and forty-two women and children were captured along with thirteen men. The men were shot immediately.

On May 2, Governor Ye of the Pecos and one of the principal chiefs of the Plains Apaches (Faraones), accompanied by eight warriors, arrived at Santa Fe. The Athapascan chief brought three very beautifully decorated buffalo skins and a fine tipi as a gift for Vargas, who was extremely pleased with them. The Apaches sought permission to hold another fair during the *"tiempo de elote"* ("when the corn begins to ripen"). The Governor of New Mexico took advantage of the opportunity to ply his visitor with questions about lands to the east. He learned that it was ten days to the buffalo and fourteen days to the chief's villages and that there was a small hill near by. The first settlements of the Kingdom of Texas were said to be seven days away from the chief's village, and the land in that area contained many buffalo. In reply to the question of whether or not there were any Spaniards in the Texas area, the chief declared that there had been some in past years but he did not know of any there now.[6] The chief said that it was twenty-five or thirty days from his village to the first settlements of Quivira and that his people knew the distance well because they made wars there in order to capture children to sell for horses. The Apache chief spent two days in Santa Fe, and then he and Ye departed, be-

6 The Spaniards had retreated from Texas in 1693, but some individuals remained in the region and reportedly fought against the Apaches until as late as 1700.

cause they each had to attend to the sowing of their fields, thus indicating that these particular Apaches were at least semiagricultural. Upon their departure, Vargas wrote that he was much impressed with the Athapascan leader, *"aunque gentil, y atheista sin Dios, sin Ley, y sin Rey, mostraba ser hombre de bien, de realidad, de ynteligenzia, y de razon."*

During the latter part of June, a campaign was planned against the Jemez, but because the Río Grande was high the enterprise was diverted to the north. On July 3 the Spaniards reached the vicinity of Taos pueblo and met a large number of Plains Apaches who had come to trade with the Taos, "as was their custom." The Athapascans were known by Ye of Pecos, who was with the Spaniards, and they guided the Europeans to a place where they could communicate with the Taos—who were in the sierra. Ye chose to remain overnight with the rebels in order to talk with them. When he did not return the next day, Vargas became concerned. The Taos spokesmen informed him that Ye had gone to recruit his people against the Spaniards and that they would attack with the help of Apache allies. Other Apaches were said to be gathering from the Río Colorado.

Vargas gave up hope of subduing the Taos at that time, and July 5 and 6 were spent in sacking the deserted pueblo. On July 7, the army departed for the north to establish commercial relations with the Utes and to hunt buffalo on the headwaters of the Río Chama. As Vargas said, he wished to get some meat to supplement the toasted maize diet of his followers. Seven or eight leagues beyond Taos, the Spaniards spied signs of the passing of a squad of warriors, and a portion of the troops made contact with a party of eighty Taos sent out to attack them. Several Indians were killed and others captured and shot. That night the army camped on the banks of the Río Colorado (Red River), and Vargas wrote:

> They gave me notice that the sierras which border upon the Río Colorado are peopled by the Apaches who are called del Acho and that the said Yuta nation that I am looking for does not allow them in their territory, for which reason I should

flee . . . from this said country which is towards the farthest where the rebel Taos come in search of the buffalo even though they place sentinels and guards around.

The Spaniards went on to the Culebra River and then followed it to the Río Grande, working their way back toward the south to the region of San Antonio Mountain where they found some 500 head of buffalo. On July 11, a party of Utes appeared and attacked the Spanish camp. As a result, six soldiers were wounded and eight attackers killed. The Utes then signaled a desire for peace, declaring that they had mistaken the Spaniards for their enemies the Tewas, Tanos, Picuris, Jemez, and Keres who since 1680 had often come north dressed like Spaniards to hunt buffalo. Vargas accepted their explanation, and the buffalo hunting was continued. On July 17, the army returned to Santa Fe by way of the Río Chama.

On the same day, a group of Pecos arrived with goods to sell to the Spaniards. They informed Vargas that Ye was still at Taos, thus contradicting the rebels' information. Soon thereafter, the Spanish army took the field again, going this time to attack the Jemez. News had been received that a large party of Jemez, Tewas, Keres of Cochiti, and Navaho Apaches had attacked Zia —killing four persons and retreating when a chief was killed by the defenders. On July 24, the Spaniards and their Keres allies attacked the *peñol* of the Jemez, which was defended by Apaches as well as its natives. Finally, the pueblo was gained by the invaders after killing approximately seventy defenders, but other Indians held out in individual buildings. Many of these were burned alive, and the pueblo was completely sacked and destroyed. Three hundred and sixty-one women and children were captured, and one Jemez and one Apache warrior. The two warriors were executed.

Vargas remained in the vicinity for several days, hoping to inflict a final defeat upon the free warriors, but they did not return. On July 26, he said that

the few [families] of this pueblo that have escaped have scattered; that thirteen families have gone to Taos and others have set out to join with the Keres of Cochiti and a few others with their friends the Apaches of Navajo.

Many Jemez refugees were to remain with the Navahos until as late as 1705.[7] On August 26, a group of Jemez men came into Santa Fe and asked for their families. They were told that they would have to aid the Spaniards in an attack on the Tewas and Tanos first, and they reluctantly agreed to this. The campaign was immediately planned, but it was suspended when the Pecos announced that the Plains Apaches had arrived and wished to hold their fair. Many persons then went from the *villa* to trade with the Athapascans at Pecos.

On September 4, a large army of soldiers and Indian auxiliaries departed from Santa Fe to attack the fortified *peñol* of San Ildefonso. Their task had already been partially accomplished by the destruction of the Indians' sources of food, and, although the Tanos and Tewas resisted to their utmost, they were forced to send out peace feelers on September 8. On the following day, the Indians agreed to return to their pueblos within fifteen days, and, on September 11, the Jemez were allowed to return to their village with their women and children. By the end of the month, priests and Spanish officials were being placed at San Felipe, Pecos, Zia, and Jemez, and the Keres of Cochiti and Santo Domingo agreed to submit. As of January, 1695 priests had been placed at most of the Río Grande Valley pueblos, with the exception of Taos, Picuris, San Lazaro, and three of the Tewa villages. Thus the reconquest of New Mexico was well under way, although the Keres of Acoma, the Zuñis, the Hopis, many refugees, and all of the Athapascans were still free and independent.[8]

---

[7] *"Gobierno de Don Francisco Cuervo de Valdés,"* in *Documentos—México,* Series 3, I, 191–92.

[8] In his *"Apuntamientos,"* Juan Amando Niel wrote, in 1753, that the Navaho Apaches were accustomed to raiding the Pawnees and Wichitas (Jumanes) every February and that in July they sold children of these tribes to the Spaniards of New Mexico. When the Spaniards did not buy them, as happened in 1694, the Navahos would kill the slaves on the spot. Certain scholars have accepted this information at face value—for example, Alfred Barnaby Thomas, in his *After Coronado: Spanish Exploration Northeast of New Mexico, 1696–1727,* 13–14. How-

Little is known of affairs in the El Paso region during this period, and one must infer that the Athapascans were not as menacing as before 1692. However, Vargas wrote in May, 1694 that the presidio there could not be eliminated, as it was necessary for the maintenance of peace with the Mansos and Suminas (Sumas) for without it they would certainly combine with the Apaches of near-by rancherias. This would seem to indicate that the Mansos and Sumas groups were at peace at that time.[9]

Warfare on the Sonora frontier continued unabated into 1695, and in March of that year the Janos, Jocomes, and Apaches raided Tonibavi—killing eighteen persons. In the same month, the converted Pimas revolted from Tubutama to Caborca, the spark being the cruelty practiced by the Jesuits and their servants at Tubutama mission. One of the priests was killed before soldiers could take the field. A campaign was undertaken by Antonio de Solis to Tubutama, and the rebels were forced to surrender, being promised peace if they would come unarmed to the Spanish camp. The rebels came, but, when Solis attempted to bind the leaders, trouble occurred, and fifty Pimas were massacred in cold blood. This treacherous act brought the revolt to life again, and it was not suppressed until August, 1695.[10] The Sobaipuris of the Upper San Pedro River remained on friendly terms with the Spaniards, and thus the Pimas' rebellion had little if

ever, an examination of Niel's work reveals it to be completely unreliable, and the above information is contrary to all facts known about the Navahos. For one thing, Niel called the Plains Apaches "Apaches del Navajo," and thus his statements refer to the eastern Apaches and not to the Navahos. He simply did not know anything of the ethnography of New Mexico—a fact borne out by some of his other assertions. For example, he said that the other people of the buffalo plains were the Utes—and not the Comanches—that the northernmost nation of New Mexico was that of the Tompiros, that Picuris was northwest of Santa Cruz, and that San Felipe and Cochiti were *visitas* of that pueblo. In a copy of Niel's work at the Southwest Museum, Los Angeles, California, Charles F. Lummis wrote in the margin, "a most stupidly ignorant and mendacious cuss as to New Mexico," and in another place he called Niel "a fine able-bodied liar." Lummis was certainly correct, and the information supplied by Niel cannot be accepted at anything approaching face value. See Juan Amando Niel, *"Apuntamientos,"* in *Documentos—México,* Series 3, I, 56–108.

9 Letter of Diego de Vargas, May 20, 1694, *Guadalajara* 140, in AGI.

10 Diary of Juan Mateo Manje, 1699, BN 3165; Kino, *Historical Memoir,* I, 162 n.; and Hubert Howe Bancroft, *History of Texas and the North Mexican States,* I, 261–63.

any effect on Athapascan-Piman relations, except that the north-ern Sobaipuris may have once again resumed friendly relations with the Jocomes (although it is possible that they had never become hostile).

Meanwhile, a large army had been organized in Chihuahua to aid Sonora against the Pimas, and, in order to reach the Pimas' lands, the force passed through the country of the Janos and Jocomes,

> and in those lands, in the cerro of Chiguicagui, they found al-most all of the spoils of the many robberies which, during all these years, had been committed in this province of Sonora and on its frontiers, including many harquebuses, swords, daggers, spurs, saddle-bags, saddles, boots etc.

The bugle belonging to General Quirós bugler was also found.

> Among these Hocomes were found the spoils of the soldier Juan de Ochoa, whom, a few weeks before, they had captured alive, killing his three companions, on the road between Guachinera and Guasavas.[11]

Another campaign was carried out in September by a large force under Jironza, Fernández, and Domingo Terán de los Ríos, with the result that sixty Apaches, Janos, and Jocomes were killed. Those males who were captured alive were hanged, and approxi-mately seventy women and children were divided up among the three groups of soldiers. Thus the campaign took the form of a slave-raiding expedition, although being in retaliation for Atha-pascan attacks.[12]

In 1696 the Apaches destroyed the church at Cocóspera, and reportedly the number of Christians they had killed in two years rose to thirty-two.[13] In March the Jocome Apaches and Janos raided the *estancia* of Tonibavi, where they carried off 200 horses. One hundred of the animals were recovered by the Spaniards, the Athapascans having eaten or killed the rest. At about the same time, the Jocomes killed Captain Cristóbal de León and

11 Kino, *Historical Memoir*, I, 145–46.
12 Manje. *Luz de Tierra Incógnita*, 67.
13 Juan Mateo Manje, *"Estado Presente de Sonora,"* BN 3165.

nine others near Opoto, and the Spaniards retaliated by killing three Indians and recovering some mules, harnesses, and silver near Batepito. Subsequently, the soldiers of Jironza and Fernández combined with Pimas to pursue the Apaches to the Sierra Florida and Gila River region, killing thirty-two men and capturing fifty women and children.[14]

From these accounts it should be clear that warfare on the Sonora frontier was no longer profitable for the Athapascans, at least in terms of human lives lost, although one must allow for the possible exaggeration in Spanish sources. According to Juan Mateo Manje, the Athapascans had 680 persons killed, most of whom were warriors, between 1694 and 1700, and hundreds of women and children were placed in slavery by the Spaniards.[15] That the Apaches continued to fight under these circumstances is indeed evidence of their stubborn love of independence and hatred for the Europeans. It is difficult to believe that the Athapascans' warfare was motivated entirely or largely by the desire for horses and booty in this period—as some writers maintain—since the cost in lives was far too great to make such raiding worthwhile. The conclusion is that the Indians were fighting for independence and in revenge for past wrongs.

In 1696 the Spaniards' hold on Sonora was seriously threatened by a rebellion of many of the Ópatas instigated by the Chief of Baceraca, Pablo Quihue (or Guigue). The revolt broke out prematurely in the Turicachi region, where the people fled to the mountains; otherwise, it might have been a success for many other Ópatas, southern Pimas, and the Taraumaras were also anxious to strike for freedom. The Turicachi Ópatas were put down by December, although Quihue and his followers fought on until the middle of 1697. The revolt had also spread to the Taraumaras, but there it was likewise crushed. Quihue based his revolt on the fact that the Spaniards had taken the Indian lands, had often made virtual slaves of the Indians, and had brought no benefits. He claimed that the Europeans had murdered more Ópatas and Pimas than the Apaches had or ever

---

14 Manje, *"Breve Noticia,"* BMH 970, and Kino, *Historical Memoir*, I, 161–62.
15 Manje, *Luz de Tierra Incógnita*, 173.

could have killed.[16] The revolt was, however, poorly timed, for it should have occurred simultaneously with the Pima attempt of 1695.

Apparently, the Sumas of El Paso were still at peace in 1696, for a list of priests needed for the New Mexico region includes one for the Piros and Sumas of Socorro.[17]

The year 1695 was relatively uneventful in New Mexico, for those Pueblo Indians who had been defeated returned to their pueblos and concentrated upon replenishing their food supplies. The Spaniards did not attempt to subdue Acoma, Zuñi, or Hopi villages, and the Athapascans seemingly caused little trouble. Vargas spent his time consolidating his gains and establishing two new settlements, at Bernalillo and at Santa Cruz in the north. The number of settlers that he had was fewer than he had requested, and many had already fled to New Spain. Of those remaining, many were Mexicans, that is, Nahuans. In March, Vargas wrote that he was concerned over the defense of the San Juan region, for it was a gateway for Apache and Ute raids, but whether or not any hostilities were occurring is not clear. During 1695 an epidemic swept through the province, and more than 50 fighting men were lost to the Spaniards. Nevertheless, the number of soldiers was maintained at 100.[18]

On May 9, Vargas reported to the Viceroy that a few days before the news had arrived that

> some rancherias of Apaches who live to the east and are called the Chipaines have arrived and they gave information in the pueblo where they entered which is that of the Pecuries nation, how some white and blonde men have consumed a very large nation of the Apaches Conejeros which resides very far towards the interior from that of theirs [the Chipaines] and that they have returned.

The Chipaines said that they would return to New Mexico in September, and Vargas had to postpone any close questioning

[16] Bancroft, *History of Texas and the North Mexican States,* I, 273–74, and Manje, *Luz de Tierra Incógnita,* 70.

[17] Priests needed in New Mexico, November 1696, *Guadalajara* 141, in AGI.

[18] Report of Diego de Vargas, March, 1696, *Guadalajara* 140, in AGI, and Letter of Diego de Vargas, July 30, 1696, *Guadalajara* 141, in AGI.

until then.[19] Some scholars have supposed that this account had reference to a French attack upon the Apaches; however, it is very unlikely that any Frenchmen were in a position to aid the Athapascans' eastern enemies in the 1690's. On the other hand, a party of Spanish soldiers and Texas Indians had twice attacked the eastern Apaches in 1692. In the first encounter, the Athapascans had defeated their enemies, but later they suffered a reverse, with the loss of 136 persons. From 1693 to 1700, at least one Spaniard remained among the anti-Apache tribes of Texas and fought against the Athapascans on occasion.[20]

The Pueblo Indians of New Mexico had apparently accepted peace only to gain time to heal their wounds and then later, if possible, catch the invaders off guard. After being free for fourteen years, the Pueblos were not willing to live once again under Spanish tyranny. As early as December, 1695, Indians were going among the pueblos agitating and spreading anti-Spanish propaganda. Rumors of revolt soon reached the Spaniards' ears, and Vargas had to rise from his sickbed to show the Indians that he was ready for any trouble. In February, 1696 the priest at Picuris overheard natives say that they wanted to kill him, and Fray Joseph Díaz at Tesuque was told by the traitorous governor of that pueblo that all of the nations planned to rebel. In particular, it was said that the Pecos were to rise, kill their priest, and retire to their former pueblo of Piedra Blanca. Vargas investigated and found things satisfactory, or at least quiet.[21] He was, however, troubled by the Utes, who were stealing horses from Taos and San Juan—necessitating the placing of thirty soldiers in the north. The activities of the Navaho Apaches during this period are not known in detail, but it seems that they were "exciting" and aiding the Pueblo Indian rebels in their plans for a resumption of hostilities.[22]

[19] Letter of Diego de Vargas, May 9, 1695, *Guadalajara* 140, in AGI.

[20] William Edward Dunn, "Apache Relations in Texas, 1718–1750," *Texas State Historical Quarterly*, Vol. XIV, No. 3 (1911), 204, and Letter of the Marqués de Aguayo, November 2, 1715, in Pichardo, tomo XIX, BMAE.

[21] Letter of Francisco de Vargas, March 7, 1696, and Letter of Diego de Vargas, March 8, 1696, *Guadalajara* 141, in AGI.

[22] *Ibid.*, and Juan Paez Hurtado, December 23, 1704, in NMA, Vols. 1704–1707, No. 104.

On March 7, 1696 the leader of the Franciscans in New Mexico, Fray Francisco de Vargas, addressed a letter to Governor Vargas in which he said that all of the priests were convinced that a new Indian revolt would take place, because of the hostile demonstrations of the Indians and because the natives now had plenty of food and arms—while the Spaniards did not. Evidently, the priests had no soldiers to back up their authority, and the Indians had already profaned the new churches and taken over the missionaries' herds of livestock. Fray Vargas declared that the Pueblo Indians would not accept the Roman Catholic faith after their years of rebellion.[23] On March 8, Governor Vargas answered by saying that he had only 100 men and that they had to be used as escorts from Santa Fe to El Paso, as well as to protect the province from invasion. The Governor cited the fact that a report had come in to the effect that there was a *junta* of the Keres on the *peñol* of Acoma and "of the Apaches, Chilmos, and Pharaones, Janos, and Manzos" and that they were waiting for the Hopis and the Zuñis in order to destroy the Spaniards.[24]

On March 13, the Franciscans petitioned Governor Vargas for escorts for most of the pueblos—their total request adding up to perhaps 50 soldiers. There is evidence for believing that their demands were purposely placed impossibly high to force the Governor into action against the Indians. Don Diego replied that his 100 men were used in the following manner: two squads of 30 men each to guard the horses, 10 to guard the gate at Santa Fe, 26 for the escort to El Paso, and 4 officers of the upper ranks. Nevertheless, the Governor decided to supply escorts for San Juan, Taos, Picuris, and Jemez—or a total of 20 men. The Franciscans refused to accept this offer (with two exceptions), and they deserted their pueblos to unite at Santa Fe. On March 22, they issued impossible petitions: Some priests who had asked for no or small escorts now asked for large ones, and others refused under any circumstances to return to their posts. The truth was that they were dissatisfied with Vargas and de-

23 Letter of Francisco de Vargas, March 7, 1696, *Guadalajara* 141, in AGI.
24 Letter of Diego de Vargas, March 8, 1696, *Guadalajara* 141, in AGI.

clared that the Indians had not been sufficiently subdued and that the settlers lacked arms and horses. An example of the priests' demands can be seen in that of Fray Alonzo Ximénez de Cisneros of Cochiti, who on March 13 had needed no escort but on March 22 asked for 24 soldiers. Other friars followed this pattern.[25]

The friar from Pecos declared that a rancheria of Faraones was living in the pueblo of Pecos and that another rancheria was near by on the Pecos River. The pueblo's inhabitants were said to be behaving in a strange manner, and the priest had heard that his life was in danger. Another friar declared that the Tanos were in the sierra and were not actually at peace. The basic complaint, however, was that the Indians would not give up their religion and that the priests had no troops to force the natives' adherence to Roman Catholicism. The governor attempted to meet the Franciscans' demands for escorts as best he could while ignoring their other complaints. It appears that all or most of the friars returned to their conversions, having gained at least one point.[26] Governor Vargas kept a close watch on the pueblos, and in May he dispatched soldiers to watch out for the Utes and Apaches near Taos.[27]

On June 3, 1696 the Keres of Cochiti abandoned their pueblo, and the other Indians soon followed suit. Several priests and a number of Spaniards were killed in the process, and at San Ildefonso the Navaho Apaches combined with the Tewas in their revolt. The Pecos were split on the question of whether or not to rebel, but at this time they decided to aid the Spaniards, sending warriors for that purpose. Some of the Keres remained loyal, and the Tesuque chief with some of his men did not revolt.[28]

From several Jemez prisoners, Vargas learned that the Hopis, Zuñis, Keres of Acoma, and Apaches were sending warriors to Jemez in order to attack Santa Fe. The Tewas and Tanos had united for defense at the hill of Chimayo, and the Apaches had

25 *Auto* of Diego de Vargas, March 14, 1696, and Petition of Francisco de Vargas, March 22, 1696, *Guadalajara* 141, in AGI.
26 *Ibid.*, and *Auto* of Diego de Vargas, March 22, 1696, *Guadalajara* 141, in AGI.
27 Villagutierre y Sotomayor, BN 2823.
28 Various Documents, June, 1696, *Guadalajara* 141, in AGI.

retired to their own country to dance; but their aid was expected for the future. It seems that the Apaches were going to decide what course of action to take, although the opinion of a Tewa prisoner of the Spaniards was that during the month

> all of the Apachería will unite with the other nations in order to fight and that the Zuñis and Moquinos, Acomas [and] Apaches who live and are neighbors of the Zuñis and Moquinos and the Yuttas and another nation that this declarant does not know, they say as a thing certain and fixed that when the ears of corn form or when the maize is smaller all these nations will unite, and that which the Apaches have discussed is that they should attack the horse herds first and that the reason that they did not do it on the night after the disgrace [the revolt] was because the river crest came and some of the Apaches did not know how to swim.

Already, some of the Pueblo Indians had decided that it was useless to try to expel the invaders and that the only way to live in freedom was to go to the Apaches or other independent peoples. Thus it was said that the Tanos of San Cristóbal had already gone to the Navahos and thence to the Zuñis.[29] On June 13, a Piro Indian who had turned down a chance to go with the Tanos informed Vargas that the Faraon Apaches and all of the Keres were united in the Sandia Mountains in order to attack Bernalillo. This rumor, however, was probably false, for many of the Keres had decided not to rebel. One lone Spaniard managed to escape from the Taos-Picuris region, and on June 14 he reported that he had seen rancherias of Apaches in the mountains between Picuris and Tesuque.[30]

On June 30, the "Españoles Mexicanos" of Santa Cruz expressed a desire to abandon that settlement because the Apaches were near by and had killed several persons. Vargas campaigned without success against the rebels in that region, while the Spaniards of Bernalillo carried out an operation from Zia against the Jemez and their allies. One of the Indians captured in the latter

[29] Report of Diego de Vargas, and Testimony of Diego Jenome, June 12, 1696, *Guadalajara* 141, in AGI.

[30] Testimony of Francisco Tempano, June 13, 1696, and Report of Diego de Vargas, June 14, 1696, *Guadalajara* 141, in AGI.

campaign was from Acoma, and under questioning he declared
that Zuñis, Hopis, and "many Apaches de Nabajo and forty-five
Indians of the *peñol* of Acoma of his nation and of those of
Cochiti and Xemes, that all these nations had united and came
to fight at the pueblo of Zia and take away the horses and kill
the priests," after which they planned to do the same at Santa
Ana. To further questions, he replied that the Acomas' friends
were the Zuñis, Hopis, Navahos, Apaches of the mountains near
Acoma, and the Tanos and twenty Pecos who had fled to them.
The Tanos were now living at Zuñi. Their enemies were the
Tewas, Picuris, Taos, and the rest of the Tanos. All of the Keres
of Acoma were living on the *peñol,* and, because little maize had
been planted, none were living at Laguna. The Indian prisoner
was then confessed and shot to death, for Vargas' policy was still
death to all prisoners.[31]

As mentioned above, some Pecos Indians had chosen to flee
to the rebels, and it is clear that only the influence of a pro-
Spanish chief kept the whole pueblo from rising. In fact, the
Indian governor had to execute five of his own people in order
to stave off the rebellion, which action had serious results when
the relatives of the deceased persons attempted to foment an
anti-Spanish rising in 1700. This attempted rising was put down,
but many Pecos fled to the Apaches of the valley of La Jicarilla
at that time. In July, 1696 it was decided to withdraw the priest
from Pecos, for the Indians, although still loyal, were acting
strangely "and more with the friendship that they have with
the Apaches Faraones with whom they can retire and rise to the
Piedra Blanca and knowing that the said pueblo [of Pecos] is
divided in factions as is notorious." Many of the Keres Indians
were fleeing to Acoma at this time, and in mid-July Vargas pursued some of them without success. Those of Cieneguilla, Santo
Domingo, and Cochiti actually took up residence at Acoma, and
later, in 1697, they founded a permanent pueblo at Laguna, a
place used only seasonally by the Keres prior to that time.[32]

31 Report of Diego de Vargas, June 30, 1696, and Testimony of an Acoma Indian, July 3, 1696, *Guadalajara* 141, in AGI.
32 Petition of Francisco de Vargas, July 6, 1696, *Guadalajara* 141, in AGI, and
"*Sesto Cuaderno,*" in *Documentos—México,* Series 3, I, 177, 180.

On July 20, 1696 the leading settlers of New Mexico petitioned for aid, for they were starving because of lack of rains
and the fact that after retirement of the Indians they could get
no maize. They were apparently willing to abandon the province
unless some change occurred. Their protest seems to have been
the first public evidence of an undercurrent of opposition to
Vargas which was to cause his imprisonment in little more than
a year's time. On July 30, Vargas made a report to the Viceroy
in which he stated that the rebels had killed twenty-six persons,
burned one church and now were retiring to the lands of the
"Apaches de Nabajo Cassa Fuerte y Quartelejo," where there
were good places to live. Retirement of the Indians meant that
the war would be long and costly, for the forces at Santa Fe
were insufficient for such an enterprise and the allies could not
leave their pueblos and could be used only as spies. Furthermore,
thirty or forty soldiers had to be used as escorts from El Paso
to the capital, since the southern Apaches were always dangerous. Finally, Vargas declared that the province would be lost
because of hunger unless supplies were sent immediately.[33]

Early in August, the Spaniards began a campaign against the
Keres of Acoma, and a Zuñi prisoner was questioned about the
peoples he had seen on the road from his pueblo to Santa Fe:

> He said that he met two Jemez warriors on the road and no
> others and that in the Sierra of Acoma coming from her they
> met four Apaches, and that far from here he met some Apaches
> in their fields on the road from Zuñi in front of the Ojo Cali-
> ente.[34]

On August 14, a Spanish army reached Laguna, and several Indians were surprised and captured. One of them, a Keres of
Cochiti, declared that there were eighty of his fellows at Acoma,
all planting crops, and that there were also twenty-five Keres of
Santo Domingo and five Jemez families, but no Tewas and
Tanos, as these two tribes had gone to Zuñi. He said that during the coming month a *junta* of the Zuñis, Aloqueños, Coninas,

[33] Petition of the Settlers of New Mexico, July 20, 1696, and Letter of Diego
de Vargas, July 30, 1696, *Guadalajara* 141, in AGI.

[34] Testimony of Antonio, August 1, 1696, *Guadalajara* 141, in AGI.

Utes, and the Apaches of Gila and Chilmos was to be held in order to plan an attack upon Zia. Finally, he declared that there were several Spanish captives at Acoma and that one woman had been given to the Navaho Apaches. Another Keres (of San Marcos) said that there were Tewas and Tanos at Acoma and that the Hopis, Zuñis, Utes, and Apaches were coming to attack Zia and Bernalillo in October.[35] After the questioning was over, the two Keres were hanged.

On the same day, Vargas remarked that the near-by rancherias of the Apaches were accustomed to trading at Acoma. He was afraid that they would surprise him from the rear.[36]

On August 15, Vargas advanced to the base of the *peñol* of Acoma, where he succeeded in capturing 9 horses, 1 mule, and 400 head of small stock, as well as twelve persons. The Governor was afraid to attack the pueblo, although he had fifty soldiers and Indian allies. Instead, he attempted to force the Keres into giving up their refugee allies by threatening to burn and destroy their fields. The Keres refused to give in to his demand, and Vargas damaged the crops as best he could and in anger killed two of his prisoners. Then the Spaniards retreated out of fear that the Apaches would come. This campaign affords a striking contrast with a similar one made by Vicente de Zaldívar in 1599, almost 100 years before. The relative strength of the Spaniards and the Indians had certainly changed during those years, in spite of the fact that the arms available to Vargas were superior to those of Oñate's day.[37]

On August 27, a Tewa of San Juan was questioned by Vargas at Santa Fe, and the Indian revealed that both the Picuris and the Taos were contemplating fleeing to the Apaches, although there were some among them who wished to make peace and remain in their pueblos. Concerning the "Apaches of the North," he declared that they had visited the Tewas twice—once with many people and clothing to trade but with no slaves to sell. The second time they brought many Ute women and children

35 Testimony of Juan and Cristóbal, August 14, 1696, *Guadalajara* 141, in AGI.
36 Diary of Diego de Vargas, August 14, 1696, *Guadalajara* 141, in AGI.
37 Diary of Diego de Vargas, August 15–17, 1696, *Guadalajara* 141, in AGI.

to sell and said that they wanted to see the Spaniards. The Picuris and the Taos told the Apaches that the soldiers would kill them, so the Athapascans did not come. Vargas learned also that all of the Tanos had gone to the Hopis, that all of the Tewas of Santa Clara had gone to the Hopis, and the Navahos, and that only the Taos, Picuris, and Tewas of San Juan remained in their entirety in the north. The other tribes, including one-half of the Jemez and Keres of Cochiti, had gone to the Hopis or the Navahos.[38]

From the above information, one gains insight into Ute–Northern Apache relations in the 1690's and also realizes the background for the post-1700 Ute-Comanche alliance and offensive against the Athapascans. Of at least equal significance is the knowledge of the large numbers of Pueblo Indians who chose to live with the Navahos during this period. These refugees, along with earlier ones, were to have a great impact upon the Navaho way of life and religion, and many of them were to be absorbed into the Athapascan ethnic group by intermarriage. Archaeologists have discovered many "pueblo" structures in Navaho country, associated with defensive towers and Navaho houses and dating from post-1700 to as late as c.1770. Undoubtedly, many of the refugees returned eventually to their former pueblos after 1698, but it is clear that others chose to live with the Navaho Apaches for years, preferring life with the Athapascans to Spanish dictation.[39]

On September 20, Diego de Vargas led an army northward to Picuris and Taos, which were found to be entirely abandoned, with all of the crops harvested and the food gone. At El Embudo, they found the Taos fortified with some Tanos, Tewas, and Picuris, and a long series of small encounters began. Finally, on October 3, talks were held with the Taos chief, and a large part of the Tewas agreed to submit, since their women and children were dying of cold and hunger in the sierras. On October 10, Vargas passed on to Picuris, where Indians greeted

[38] Testimony of Miguel, August 27, 1696, *Guadalajara* 141, in AGI.

[39] Dorothy L. Keur, "A Chapter in Navaho-Pueblo Relations," *American Antiquity*, Vol. X, No. 1 (1944), 75–84.

him with news that one of their chiefs had gone with many people to receive the Apaches who had come to trade, "because the Theguas and Thanos might find them and relate to them some lie or plot that they might turn around and they might go with them to the Apaches del Río Grande and that for that reason Don Antonio has gone to receive them."[40] The governor returned to Santa Fe, and there, on October 13, he was notified by Antonio, a Picuris chief, that the Apaches had brought much clothing and other articles of trade and that some had passed on to the new *villa* of Santa Cruz in order to barter. These Apaches had declared that their only friends were the Taos, Picuris, Pecos, and the Spaniards. On October 18, Vargas received word from Santa Cruz that all of the Tewas of Santa Clara who had horses and all of the Picuris were going to live with these Apaches of the Plains and that the Puebloans had taken all of their belongings with them. Two days later, Vargas and his soldiers—under Captain Antonio Valverde y Cossio—were in pursuit of the Indians. Determined as they were not to allow the Indians to abandon their pueblos and live in freedom, the Spaniards tried until October 28 to apprehend the refugees, attacking these Indians' Apache friends in the process. About eighty Indians were captured, along with a number of horses, clothing and provisions, but the main group of Picuris escaped with the Apaches to El Cuartelejo in western Kansas, where they were to live until 1706.[41]

In 1699 charges were brought against Valverde y Cossio to the effect that on this expedition in pursuit of the Picuris slaves were gathered and sold in Nueva Vizcaya. There is no doubt that the captured Pueblo Indians were divided up among the soldiers, but Valverde was also charged with selling two Christian boys in the south. Roque de Madrid declared that

> it is true that in the last campaign which was made to the plains, among the Apache children that he took to sell in Vizcaya the said Antonio Balverde carried two little Christian In-

40 Diary of Diego de Vargas, 1696, *Guadalajara* 141, in AGI.

41 Letter of Roque de Madrid, October 18, 1690, and Diary of Diego de Vargas, 1696, *Guadalajara* 141, in AGI.

dians and he sold them as slaves as [he did] with the rest that he carried.[42]

No charge was made against Valverde for selling Apaches as slaves in Nueva Vizcaya. In fact, this part of the affair was treated as a quite acceptable thing. From this and other charges, it is to be inferred that Athapascan slavery was as much a part of the Vargas regime as it had been in the earlier days. It is regrettable that so little is known of this phase of Spanish activity, for it may have had a great deal to do with the continued hostility of the Apaches and other Indians.

Upon his return to Santa Fe in November, Vargas discovered that many of the Tewas were disposed to accept peace and that the Acomas and other Keres were in a similar mood. On November 11, however, Roque de Madrid reported that he had visited San Ildefonso and had found only seventeen men with their families. The rest had gone to the Hopis and the Navaho Apaches. The Tewas of Jacona were in the sierra but were coming back. In spite of this situation, Vargas was able to write to the Viceroy on November 24 that San Ildefonso and most of the other Tewa pueblos were reduced and that only the Tewas of Pujuaque, Cuyamunque, and Santa Clara, along with the major part of the Keres and the Jemez, were still free. By November 28, the Governor asserted that the nations still not reduced were the Jemez, Tanos, Tewas of Santa Clara, Picuris, and many Keres. The Tewas of Santa Clara had fled to several places— some to the Hopis and Zuñis, some to the Acomas, "others to the next nations [from their pueblo] and surrounding neighbors of the Apaches of Navajo, Embudo, and Sierra de los Pedernales." Vargas described the *peñol* of Acoma as a great stronghold and declared that the Keres

> are very good friends of the rancherias of the Apaches, Pharones and Salineros, and of those of the Sierra of Jila of El Chilmo who commands all of the Apachería of the said sierra and in the aforementioned *peñol* are the *juntas* both of the apostate rebels and of the gentiles.[43]

[42] Testimony of Roque de Madrid, February 20, 1699, *Guadalajara* 142, in AGI.

272

Diego de Vargas had originally been granted a term of office of five years as Governor of New Mexico, but by using his influence he was able to get an extension of the position for another five years. Unfortunately for Don Diego, the information concerning this extension did not reach New Spain in time to prevent the appointment of Pedro Rodríguez Cubero as governor in 1697, and Vargas was forced to give up his office to Rodríguez on July 2 of that year. Almost nothing is known of the internal affairs of New Mexico from November, 1696 to July 1697, but it seems clear that the Indians remained in rebellion and were not subdued by Vargas. According to pro-Rodríguez testimony, fourteen pueblos of the Río Grande Valley, along with Acoma, Zuñi, and the Hopi villages, were in revolt when the new governor assumed office. The province was likewise in a bad state with a shortage of food and arms, and Vargas had made many enemies. On October 2, 1697 he was arrested by Rodríguez and a puppet *cabildo,* and as of March, 1698 he was still in prison. Many charges were brought against Don Diego and especially against Captain Antonio Valverde y Cossio. The latter was charged with adultery and sexual immorality, as well as with selling many Pueblo Indians as slaves in Nueva Vizcaya. Valverde did not suffer imprisonment, however, as he made his way to Spain in order to plead for Vargas' interests. Vargas, meanwhile, had all of his property and slaves sold by the *cabildo—* action which confirms the suspicion that the Governor did acquire slaves during his term of office. The balance of the struggle between Vargas and his enemies, which lasted until Vargas' death in 1704, had the unfortunate effect of filling the archives with charges and countercharges to the exclusion of information on Indian affairs. Thus almost nothing is known of occurrences under Rodríguez.[44]

43 Report of Roque de Madrid, November 11, 1696, and Letters of Diego de Vargas, November 24 and 28, 1696, *Guadalajara* 141, in AGI.

44 Petition of Diego de Vargas, no date. Charges of the *Cabildo* of Santa Fe, February 20, 1699–May 21, 1702, and *Informe* of the *Cabildo,* December 28, 1698, *Guadalajara* 142, in AGI. According to Juan Amando Niel (1753), the Navahos attacked the Pawnees, Jumanes (Wichitas), and French in 1697, but the latter surprised the Athapascans and killed almost 4,000 of them. As a result, the Navahos

By December, 1698 the new governor is said to have reduced the rebels of New Mexico to peace and to have reestablished ordinary relations with Acoma and Zuñi. Even the Apaches were at peace and anxious for baptism, if one may believe the information supplied by the pro-Rodríguez *cabildo*.[45] Thus by the end of 1698 the Great Southwestern Revolt was brought to an end in New Mexico, and the Spaniards were solidly in control of the upper Río Grande Valley. The Hopis were never reconquered, and thus the limits of Spanish control established in 1698–99 were to remain more or less the same for the following 120 years.

To the south, important events were occurring during 1697 and 1698. In retaliation for raiding by the Apaches, Jocomes, Janos, and Sumas—the latter had apparently joined the rebels once again in 1697—Fray Kino called upon the Pimas for a campaign in March of 1697. In September, a battle took place between the Sobaipuris of both the Río San Pedro and San Xavier del Bac and the Jocomes and Janos. Four Jocomes and Janos were killed, and two children were made slaves. On October 26, the Sobaipuris of Captain Coro of Quiburi defeated sixteen Athapascans—killing thirteen.[46] The most important event which occurred in 1697 on the Sonora frontier was a Spanish expedition made in November. This *entrada* was to further cement the Hispano-Sobaipuri alliance and likewise heal a split among the Sobaipuris.

On November 9, a group of soldiers under Lieutenant Cristóbal Martín Bernal met a smaller group led by Juan Mateo Manje and Fray Kino at Quiburi on the San Pedro River. Captain Coro made them very welcome and they were entertained by a dance around the thirteen Athapascan scalps taken in October—the thirteen were variously described as Apaches, Jocomes, and Jocomes and Sumas. Bernal discovered that the Sobaipuris of

---

did not visit New Mexico in 1698 to sell slaves. This, of course, is another of Niel's confused tales—or pure inventions. See Chapter XII, footnote 8, of this book.

[45] *"Sesto Cuaderno,"* in *Documentos—México*, Series 3, I, 177, and *Informe* of the *Cabildo*, December 28, 1698, Guadalajara 142, in AGI.

[46] Kino, *Historical Memoir*, I, 166; Eusebio Kino, *"Breve Relación,"* May 3, 1698, BMH 969; and Horacio Polici, *"Relación del Estado de la Primería,"* BMH 969.

Coro and those of the principal chief Jumari, living to the north, were hostile to each other. In fact, the northerners had recently killed a messenger sent by Coro. It was suspected that the northern Sobaipuris were friendly with the Jocomes, and in all likelihood the Pimans had divided on the question of whether to be allies of the Spaniards or the Athapascans.

Ten leagues to the north of Quiburi, the Spaniards reached Los Alamos, and special precautions were taken, as they were, according to Manje, now on the Apache frontier. On November 13, they reached Jiaspi after sixteen leagues of travel. Here they met Jumari and discovered that these Pimans were now enemies of the Athapascans; in fact, they had six Apache scalps to prove it. Arivaipa was reached after six leagues of travel to the north, and here Bernal learned that there had been a settlement of Jocomes fourteen leagues to the east but that the Athapascans had now retired. Nine leagues to the north, the Spaniards reached a Sobaipuri village called Victoria de Ojito. This was the northernmost village and was also the residence of Chief Jumari. Six or eight leagues farther to the north was the junction of the San Pedro and the Gila.

While at Victoria, the soldiers met some Piman chiefs with their followers and families whom Manje described as coming from two settlements on a stream running from the east into the San Pedro. These Sobaipuris were neighbors and sworn enemies of the "Apache Jocomes, y Janos." Bernal's diary contains more details about this meeting as he says:

> A captain arrived who lives towards the east in another valley called Babitcoida, bringing with him to give me obedience sixty-one warriors, without arms, and twenty women, and some children; and asking him what news he could give me of the Jocomes he said that he had lived with them some time on occasion of having made entrance to their land, and that the Spaniards having surprised the Jocomes at dawn, imprisoning their women and children, five Jocomes escaped and they came to contact their rancheria, and after a few days the Governor of the Jocomes died of a natural death and after he died they retired, the others do not know to where.

It appears that the northern Sobaipuris were friendly with the Jocomes until the following occurrence:

> Also they gave me the news of how in days past they surprised some Jocomes who had established themselves near their rancheria, and the Sobaipuris of the west had called upon them for that action, and that they killed four Jocomes and they captured two pieces [of chusma, i.e., slaves] whom they say the Sobaipuris of the west have, and that the Apache enemy camps in their lands, and that they have wars, having deaths on one side and the other.[47]

Thus it seems that the Sobaipuris of San Xavier del Bac had persuaded the northern Sobaipuris to attack their neighbors, the Jocomes.

On November 16, the Bernal-Manje party reached the Gila River and proceeded to follow it to the Casa Grande region. Care had to be exercised, for the route down the Gila was on the Apache frontier, and both Manje and Bernal refer to the necessity of being on watch as far as the Casa Grande area. On November 24, the party reached San Xavier del Bac (called de Bacoida), and there they found the two Jocome prisoners mentioned by the Sobaipuris of the Victoria region. The captives were, according to Bernal, "a girl of twelve years, and a boy of almost ten. I purchased the girl, and the *alférez* Francisco Acuña the boy; I paid their owners very well and they remained very content."[48] This Spanish practice of purchasing slaves from friendly tribes tended to encourage intertribal wars. New Mexico provided a market for the Plains Apaches and later for the Comanches, while Sonora bought slaves of the Pimas, Sobaipuris and Maricopas, causing a great deal of harm to the Yavapais and the Apaches. Needless to say, the whole phenomenon illustrates the Spanish desire for slave labor and helps to further the belief that many punitive campaigns made by the Europeans were as much for profit as for punishment.

[47] Diary of Cristóbal Martín Bernal, November, 1697, BMH 969; Manje, *"Breve Noticia,"* BMH 970; and Kino, *"Breve Relación,"* BMH 969.

[48] Diary of Cristóbal Martín Bernal, November, 1697, BMH 969, and Manje, *"Breve Noticia,"* BMH 970.

Early in 1698 the Jocome Apaches, Janos, and Manso Sumas attacked at Cocóspera and elsewhere. They were pursued by soldiers and Pimas to the Chiricahua Mountains, and the Pimas killed 30 Athapascans—taking 16 prisoners. On March 30, a force of 500 or 600 Athapascans—including Apaches, Jocomes, Janos, Mansos, and Sumas—is said to have attacked a Sobaipuri pueblo in the vicinity of Quiburi. According to Spanish sources, the Athapascans killed 3 Pimans, burned the houses, sacked the village, and forced the defenders to take refuge in an adobe structure (many of the Sobaipuris' houses were of adobe). The Athapascans had a harquebus, and one of them got on the roof of the house, from which vantage point he shot a defender. Then, according to one account, the attackers settled down to relax and eat, feeling quite secure.[49]

Several facts are strange about the above story, the first being that the Athapascans would wish to attack a pueblo which was very close to Quiburi (less than two leagues away, says Kino) and secondly that the raiders would have had their women and children along, which they did. The truth, of course, will never he known, but it is possible that the Athapascans had originally come in peace. This is really the only way that the presence of their women can be explained.

In any case, 500 Sobaipuri warriors from Quiburi fell upon the Athapascans, and, according to Manje, a fierce battle raged from the morning until midafternoon. News of the affair reached the Spaniards, and 22 soldiers helped pursue the enemy for seven leagues. They counted 60 dead Athapascans. Kino's account is somewhat different, as he describes a preliminary combat between 11 Sobaipuris and 11 Apaches, Jocomes, and Janos —the result of a challenge issued by the Jocome leader El Capotcari. In this affair, the Pimans were uniformly victorious, and a general battle followed in which more than 300 Athapascans died, either directly or as a result of the Piman's poisoned arrows. On April 23, Kino personally inspected the bodies of the dead enemies and found that there were 54—31 men and 23

49 *Ibid.*; Eusebio Kino, *Las Misiones de Sonora y Arizona*, 61–62; and Kino, *Historical Memoir*, I, 178–81.

women. According to Manje, the total number of Athapascans who died was 168.[50]

Whether one accepts the account of Kino or Manje, it is clear that the battle of March 30, 1698 was a severe defeat for the allied Athapascan groups, and especially for the Jocomes and Janos, who seemed to have suffered more than their allies. Certainly this affair ended for all time any tendencies which the rebels might have had to make peace with the Sobaipuris, and eventually it was to react adversely on this tribe.

According to both Manje and Kino, a very important result of this defeat was that the Janos and Sumas decided to make peace at Janos and El Paso. The Jocomes attempted some three different assaults upon Piman rancherias but in each case were repulsed with losses, and they, too, asked for peace. By October, Kino learned that negotiations were under way at Janos presidio, and the Athapascans were reportedly making public their fear of the Pimans and asking for aid against them.[51] From the records of Fernández at Janos, it is learned that the united Janos and Jocomes, along with some Sumas, came to make peace. It was reported that "otherwise they have relations only with two other rancherias of Apaches, who also desire to make peace." A decorated deerskin was presented by a Jocome as a sign of peace from "the chief of his nation and those of the Jano, Suma, Manso, Apache," and others. On the deerskin were symbols representing various objects, including

> six large circles that come on another part [and] are six tents of Indians of Apaches nation that likewise come to give obedience to His Majesty and that they are the same that offered to give it [for] those of their nation and that 120 signs that come painted in the form of jacales of their usage in four divisions are four rancherias of Janos, Jocomes, Mansos, and Sumas Indians with their families that come to give the said obedience to His Majesty.[52]

[50] Kino, "Breve Relación," BMH 969; Manje, "Breve Noticia," BMH 970; and Kino, Historical Memoir, I, 178-81.

[51] Informe of Eusebio Kino, in Fernando Ocaranza, Parva Crónica de la Sierra Madre y las Primerías, 53-55; Manje, "Breve Noticia," BMH 970; and Kino, Historical Memoir, I, 181.

It seems likely that 120 families were involved in the peace talks, and thus it is probable that other Athapascans remained in revolt. The evidence indicates that the latter were few, however.

With the end of 1698 also comes the end of an era, for the Great Southwestern Revolt had now run through the last of its several phases. It also marks the beginning of a new period, with the Spaniards in control of both Sonora and New Mexico, and with the old rebel tribes of Nueva Vizcaya largely destroyed, though still fighting. Warfare had been continuous on the Sonora-Janos frontier since 1682–84, and the Indians of New Mexico had been independent or fighting since 1680. The Great Southwestern Revolt in its many phases had endured for almost twenty years, but, in the end, the Spanish Empire had recovered much of the ground it had previously lost. The Hopis were never to be subdued; the Zuñis were to prove stubborn; and the Sonoran frontier war was soon to be renewed; but the Europeans had managed to recover from a number of serious blows; and they were now to hold on to what they possessed.

Many changes occurred between 1680 and 1698, and, in spite of the fact that outwardly the situation of New Mexico and vicinity appeared to be the same or much the same at the end as at the beginning of the period, certain factors made things very different: Pueblo Indian refugees were now living with several groups of Apaches, and they were to have a great effect on Athapascan culture, as well as upon relations with other peoples. The close connections existing between the Apaches and the subdued Pueblo tribes were almost to develop a new general revolt in 1704–1705. Likewise, the French were advancing closer on the east, but as yet they were only affecting the Plains Apaches indirectly by being allies of the Osages, Missouris, and Kansas and enemies of the Apaches' enemies, the Pawnees and Wichitas.

In some ways, the Spaniards were in a better position in 1698 than in 1680. The Ópatas were now firm allies, and they were to serve, along with the Pimas, as the chief barrier against the Apaches in the 1700's. The Pimas were certainly enemies of the

52 Sauer, "Distribution of Aboriginal Tribes," *Ibero-America,* Vol. V (1934), 75–76.

Apaches, although not too loyal allies of the Spaniards, since they were to rebel several times. The Athapascans, on the other hand, were more experienced at warfare in 1698 than in 1680, and this advantage was to offset the large numbers of warriors which they had lost. Eventually, they were to become easily the equals of the Hispano-Mexican soldiers. From 1700 to 1848, neither the Spaniards nor the Mexicans were to make any real gains against the Apaches, while the latter were to move south—under Comanche pressure—and occupy large sections in Coahuila, Nueva Vizcaya, and Sonora-Arizona. The "Apache problem" was to absorb the interest of all of the viceroys of New Spain and was certainly to play a big part in keeping the treasury of New Spain in poor condition for most of the eighteenth century.

The relations of the Apaches with the Europeans and with the Mexicans after 1700 were in large part determined by the development of Hispano-Athapascan hostility from 1540 to 1698.

CHAPTER XIII

Apache,
Navaho,
and Spaniard

⋈

The anthropologist Frederick Webb Hodge once declared: "For nearly two hundred years after the coming of Oñate the history of the Pueblo tribes is one of Apache rapine."[1] This view has often been reiterated by other writers and has become a commonly accepted idea, frequently being expressed in secondary sources and popular articles. According to this point of view, the Athapascans of the Southwest were essentially predatory Indians who were at war with the settled peoples of the region prior to the coming of the Spaniards. The Europeans thus inherited the Athapascans as enemies when they became the "protectors" of the Pueblo tribes and attempted to introduce "civilization" into New Mexico. From Oñate's time to the days of Gerónimo, the Apaches were nothing more than savage bandits raiding the industrious and peacefully inclined Spaniards (or Mexicans) and their Pueblo Indian subjects. Coupled with this view is the thesis that the Athapascans were invaders or newcomers in the Southwest, only appearing themselves a few years or decades before the Spaniards.

The foregoing reconstruction of the history of the Southern Athapascans from 1540 to 1698 should expose the above point of view as a spurious one based upon false preconceptions and

[1] Frederick Webb Hodge, "The Early Navajo and Apache," *American Anthropologist*, Old Series, Vol. VIII, No. 3 (1895), 236.

the inherited anti-Apache bias of Hispano- and Anglo-Southwesterners. The documents clearly reveal that the essential relationship existing between the Athapascans and the Pueblo Indians prior to Spanish interference was one of peace and commerce. This is not to say that warfare was completely absent; however, when hostile relations did occur, they were apparently initiated as often by Pueblo groups as by Athapascans. The documentary evidence indicates that the Pueblo tribes were as often at war with each other as with Apaches, and individual Athapascan groups were sometimes on hostile terms with other Apache bands. There is no basis, then, for the thesis that the Athapascans and the settled peoples of the Southwest were basically enemies. This is clearly seen in the events of 1680–92, when the Spaniards were absent from New Mexico. The Pueblo tribes divided themselves into several factions, with different Apache groups associated with each faction. Fighting which took place was carried on primarily by the Pueblo Indians.

Documentary evidence reveals many instances in which Apache groups were living in a close, almost symbiotic, relationship with pueblos—for example, the Pecos-Faraon Apache, Taos-Jicarilla Apache, Picuris-Plains Apache, Zuñi-Salinero Apache, and Jemez-Navaho friendships. Furthermore, evidence also suggests that strong bonds existed, prior to Spanish interference, between the Hopis and some Athapascans, the Piros and the Gila Apaches, the Jumano Tompiros and Plains Athapascans, the Tewas and Plains Apaches, and the Navahos and the Keres of Acoma.

Archaeological evidence indicates that Pueblo Indian culture was experiencing a renaissance from c.1300 to c.1600 and that this cultural climax was brought to an abrupt conclusion by events of the seventeenth century.[2] That archaeology should reveal a decline in indigenous Southwestern culture after 1600 is certainly not surprising in view of the reign of terror and exploitation introduced by Oñate and maintained by Rosas, Mendizábal, and subsequent Spanish governors. Heretofore this decline has been blamed to a large extent upon Athapascan raiders,

[2] Martin, *Indians Before Columbus,* 160.

CANADA

Lake Superior

Lake Michigan

Snake River

(Kiowa Apaches)

Missouri

Platte River

(Comanches)

Pawnees River Otos

Kansas River

Colorado River

Utes

Apaches Carlanes

Kansas River Osages

Cuartelejo Apaches Wichitas

Ohio River

Hopis Navaho Apaches

Coninas

Yavapais Mescalero Apaches

Salinero Apaches Gila

Gila River Apaches

Jocomes

Sobaipuris

Pimas Janos

Opatas Sumas

Pimas Chinarras

Conchos Chisos

Cholomes

Tobosos

MEXICO

Apaches de la Jicarilla

Apaches del Acho

Faraones

(Natajes)

Pueblo Tribes

Northeastern Apaches

Padoucas

Arkansas River

Canadian River

Lipan Apaches

Red River

Tonkawan Bands

Colorado River

Jumanos (Pelones)

Sibolos

Rio

Coahuiltecan Tribes

Brazos River

Mississippi River

Tennessee River

Grande

Gulf of California

Gulf of Mexico

(...) Groups which appeared after 1700

0   100   200   300   400   500

Scale in Miles

Modern names of rivers are supplied; boundaries are approximate

Southern Athapascans, c. 1600–1700

but the foregoing study should clearly indicate that the enemy of native civilization in New Mexico was primarily the Spaniard and not the Apache.

It seems clear that the entrance of the Spaniards into the Southwest resulted in the breaking up of many peaceful relationships between tribes and led to an increase in warfare. This situation is to be seen in the development of Athapascan-Puebloan hostilities and also in Piman-Athapascan relations. The evidence clearly indicates that, prior to 1693–97, the Pimas and Sobaipuris were friends and allies of the Apaches. This friendly relationship was purposely destroyed as a part of the Hispanic policy of "divide and conquer." Evidence also suggests that, prior to the 1680's, the Ópatas were friendly with Athapascans, but this relationship was also altered by the Spaniards.

The historical evidence of the sixteenth and seventeenth centuries reveals the great importance of the Athapascans in Southwestern history. Their significance in warfare stands out immediately, and they clearly served as a barrier to the northward expansion of the Spanish Empire. They served as a refuge for the Pueblo Indians and other enemies of the Europeans, and they helped to stimulate rebellions on numerous occasions. The weak position of the Spanish Empire in New Mexico, Sonora, Nueva Vizcaya, Coahuila, and Texas was due in great part to the activities of the Apaches and the post-1769 weakness of Alta California was due in large part to the Spaniards' preoccupation elsewhere with Athapascan warfare.

The Southern Athapascans àre of great import for other than military reasons. Documentation reveals clearly the tremendous importance of the Plains Apaches as traders and suppliers of buffalo hides, antelope skins, dried meat, and tallow to the settled people of New Mexico. Before Spanish interference, the Plains Apaches and the various pueblos apparently existed in a close reciprocal commercial-cultural relationship, with the Athapascans acquiring maize, cotton blankets, and other goods in return for the products of the buffalo and other game. The Southern and Western Athapascans were also commercially active, and the importance of the Jumano Apaches in the La

Junta–East Texas trade should be noted. Certainly the Plains and Jumano Apaches must be ranked with the Hopis and Mohaves as the outstanding examples of commercially minded Indians in the Southwest.

Unfortunately the entrance of the Spaniard into the Southwest was a disturbing factor. In this connection, a study of Southern Athapascan history reveals the weaknesses of the northern frontier policy of the Spanish Empire. In theory, of course, Hispanic policy toward the indigene was relatively enlightened, but, in fact, it was in many ways harmful and a failure. The northern frontier was far away from Madrid and Mexico City, and the officers and governors in the frontier provinces were usually men of low morality, poor talent, and corrupt tendencies. The settlers and soldiers were also of a poor caliber and were anxious to exploit the Indian. The priests were unable to offset the bad tendencies of the civil authorities and the failings of certain of their own group. Any good which might have arisen from conversions was offset by the high death rate in the missions, by the excessively rapid suppression of native culture and by the slave-raiding exploitation practiced by the secular authorities. Thus the Spanish Empire failed to introduce an era of progress and civilization in the Southwest prior to 1698 and instead introduced an epoch of warfare, population decline, and cultural decay. As a part of this process, the Spaniards won the enmity of the Athapascans and created a northern barrier which was to outlast the Spanish Empire in the Southwest.

Bibliography

ARCHIVAL COLLECTIONS

Archivo General de Indias, Seville, Spain.
  Legajos: Guadalajara 28, 134, 136, 138–43, 147, 152.
          Indiferente 1384.
          México 26, 29, 53, 128.
          Patronato 244.

Archivo General y Público de la Nación, Mexico, D. F., Mexico.
(Unless specified otherwise, materials of these archives were seen as microfilm or photocopies in the Bancroft Library of the University of California, Berkeley, California, and in the Coronado Library of the University of New Mexico, Albuquerque, New Mexico.)

  Legajos: Historia, 37, 39, 299.
          Inquisición, 316.
          Provincia Internas 34, 35. Transcripts in the University
             of Texas Archives, Austin, Texas.
          Provincias Internas 34, 35, 37.

Biblioteca del Ministerio de Asuntos Exteriores, Madrid, Spain.
  Pichardo, José Antonio. *"Documentos y Noticias Históricas y Geográficas Colectadas para la Averiguación de los Limites entre las Provincias de la Louisiana y Texas."* Bound manuscript.

Biblioteca del Ministerio de Hacienda, Madrid, Spain.
  969 *"Materiales Para la Historia de Sonora,"* tomo XVI. Bound
         manuscript.

970 *"Continuación de los Materiales Para la Historia de Sonora,"* tomo XVII. Bound manuscript.

971 *"Documentos Para la Historia de la Nueva Vizcaya,"* tomo XIX, libro 1. Bound manuscript.

974 *"Documentos Para la Historia Eclesiástica y Civil de la Provincia de Texas,"* tomo XXVII, libro 1. Bound manuscript.

Biblioteca del Museo Naval, Madrid, Spain.

142 *"Expediciones de 1519 a 1697,"* tomo II. Bound manuscript.

567 *"Virreinato de Méjico,"* tomo I. Bound manuscript.

Biblioteca Nacional de Madrid, Madrid, Spain.

2822–23 Villagutierre y Sotomayor, Juan de. *"Historia de la Conquista, Perdida, y Restaurazión de el Reino y Provincias de la Nueva México en la América Septentrional."* Bound manuscript.

3064 *"Descripción de la Villa de Nombre de Dios"* and *"Relación de Nuestra Señora de Zacatecas."* Manuscripts.

3165 *"Relación ytineraria del Nuevo Descubrimiento que hizieron los Reverendos Padres Eusevio Francisco Kino y Adamo Gil y el Capitán Juan Mateo Manje"* and *"Estado Presente de Sonora."* Bound manuscripts.

19258 *"Servicios Personales del Maestro de Campo Don Juan Domínguez de Mendoza."* Bound collection of manuscripts.

Museo Nacional, Mexico, D. F., Mexico.

Asuntos 242. Bound copy in the Coronado Library of the University of New Mexico. Albuquerque, New Mexico.

New Mexico Archives, Coronado Library, University of New Mexico, Albuquerque, New Mexico.

Volumes: 1621–83, 1704–1707.

PUBLISHED DOCUMENTS

Adams, Eleanor B. (ed.) "Bishop Tamarón's Visitation of New Mexico, 1760," *New Mexico Historical Review*, Vol. XXVIII, No. 3 (1953).

Alegre, Francisco Javier. *Historia de la Compañia de Jesús en Nueva-España.* 3 vols. Mexico: J. M. Lara, 1841–42.

Arleguí, Joseph. *Chrónica de la Provincia de N. S. P. S. Francisco de Zacatecas.* Mexico: J. B. de Hogal, 1737.

Arregui, Domingo Lázaro de. *Descripción de la Nueva Galicia*. Seville: Escuela de Estudios Hispano-Americanos, 1946.

Bandelier, Fanny (trans.). *The Journey of Alvar Núñez Cabeza de Vaca and His Companions from Florida to the Pacific, 1528-1536*. New York: A. S. Barnes and Company, 1905.

Benavides, Alonso de. *Memorial of 1630*. Trans. by Peter P. Forrestal. Washington: Academy of American Franciscan History, 1954.

———. *Fray Alonso de Benavides' Revised Memorial of 1634*. Trans. and ed. by Frederick Webb Hodge, George P. Hammond, and Agapito Rey. Albuquerque: University of New Mexico Press, 1945.

Bloom, Lansing B., and Lynn B. Mitchell. "The Chapter Elections of 1672," *New Mexico Historical Review*, Vol. XIII, No. 1 (1938).

Bolton, Herbert Eugene (ed. and trans.). *Athanase de Mézières and the Louisiana-Texas Frontier, 1768-80*. 2 vols. Cleveland: Arthur H. Clark Company, 1914.

——— (ed.). *Spanish Exploration in the Southwest, 1542-1706*. New York: Charles Scribner's Sons, 1916.

Cartografía de Ultramar: Estados Unidos. Madrid: Imprenta del Servicio Geográfico del Ejército, 1955.

Cox, Isaac J. (ed.). *The Journeys of La Salle*. 2 vols. New York: Allerton Book Company, 1906.

Davenport, Harbert (ed.). "The Expedition of Pánfilo de Narváez," *Southwestern Historical Quarterly*, Vol. XXVII, Nos. 2-4 (1923-24), Vol. XXVIII, No. 1 (1924).

Documentos para la Historia de México. Series 3. 21 vols. Mexico: Vicente García Torres, 1857.

Guiterás, Eusebio (trans.). *Rudo Ensayo*. Tucson: Arizona Silhouettes, 1951.

Hackett, Charles Wilson (ed. and trans.). *Historical Documents Relating to New Mexico, Nueva Vizcaya and Approaches Thereto, to 1773*. 3 vols. Washington: Carnegie Institution, 1923-37.

———. *The Revolt of the Pueblo Indians of New Mexico and Otermín's Attempted Reconquest, 1680-1682*. 2 vols. Albuquerque: University of New Mexico Press, 1942.

Hammond, George P., and Agapito Rey (eds. and trans.). *Don Juan de Oñate, Colonizer of New Mexico, 1595-1628*. 2 vols. Albuquerque: University of New Mexico Press, 1953.

———. *Expedition into New Mexico Made by Antonio de Espejo, 1582-1583, as Revealed in the Journal of Diego Pérez de Luxán*. Los Angeles: Quivira Society, 1929.

————. *The Gallegos Relation of the Rodríguez Expedition to New Mexico.* Santa Fe: El Palacio Press, 1927.

————. *Narratives of the Coronado Expedition, 1540–1542.* Albuquerque: University of New Mexico Press, 1940.

————. *Obregón's History of 16th Century Explorations in Western America.* Los Angeles: Wetzel Publishing Company, 1928.

Hennepin, Louis. *A New Discovery of a Vast Country in America.* 2 vols. Chicago: A. C. McClurg and Company, 1903.

Kino, Eusebio. *Kino's Historical Memoir of Pimería Alta.* Ed. and trans. by Herbert E. Bolton. 2 vols. Cleveland: Arthur H. Clark Company, 1919.

————. *Las Misiones de Sonora y Arizona.* Mexico: Editorial "Cultura," 1913–22.

León, Alonso de. *Historia de Nuevo León.* Mexico: Bouret, 1909.

Maas, Otto (ed.). *"Documentos sobre las Misiones de Sinaloa y Nuevo Méjico," Archivo Ibero-Americano,* Vol. XX (1923), Vol. XXI (1924), Vol. XXXII (1929), Vol. XXXIII (1930).

Manje, Juan Mateo. *Luz de Tierra Incógnita.* Trans. by Harry J. Karns. Tucson: Arizona Silhouettes, 1954.

Margry, Pierre. *Découvertes et Établissements des Français dans l'Ouest et dans le Sud de l'Amérique Septentrionale (1614–1754).* 6 vols. Paris: D. Jouaust, 1876–86.

Nasatir, A. P. *Before Lewis and Clark.* 2 vols. St. Louis: St. Louis Historical Documents Foundation, 1952.

Ocaranza, Fernando. *Parva Crónica de la Sierra Madre y las Pimerías.* Mexico: Editorial Style, 1942.

Pacheco, Joaquín F., and Francisco de Cárdenas (eds.). *Colección de Documentos Inéditos.* 20 vols. Madrid: Manuel B. de Quirós, 1865.

Pérez de Ribas, Andrés. *Historia de los Triunphos de Nuestra Santa Fee entre Gentes las más Bárbaras y Fieras del Nuevo Orbe.* Madrid: A. de Paredes, 1645.

Scholes, France V. "Documents for the History of the New Mexican Missions in the Seventeenth Century," *New Mexico Historical Review,* Vol. V, No. 2 (1930).

Schroeder, Albert H. "Southwestern Chronicle: The Cipias and Ypotlapiguas," *Arizona Quarterly,* Vol. XII, No. 2 (1956).

Suárez de Peralta, Juan. *"Noticia Inédita sobre los Caballos en Nueva España," Revista de Indias,* Año V, No. 15 (Enero–Marzo, 1944).

Thomas, Alfred Barnaby. *After Coronado: Spanish Exploration*

Northeast of New Mexico, 1696–1727. Norman: University of Oklahoma Press, 1935.

———. *Forgotten Frontiers: A Study of the Spanish Indian Policy of Don Juan Bautista de Anza, 1777–1787.* Norman: University of Oklahoma Press, 1932.

Velarde, Luís. *"Relación* of Pimería Alta, 1716" (trans. by Rufus Kay Wyllys), *New Mexico Historical Review,* Vol. VI, No. 2 (1931).

Vetancurt, Agustín de. *Teatro Mexicano.* Mexico: María de Benavides, 1697.

Villagrá, Gaspar Pérez de. *History of New Mexico.* Trans. by Gilberto Espinosa. Los Angeles: Quivira Society, 1933.

Villa–Señor y Sanchez, Joseph Antonio de. *Theatro Americano.* 2 vols. Mexico: J. B. de Hogal, 1746–48.

SECONDARY SOURCES—BOOKS

Baker, O. E. *Atlas of American Agriculture.* Washington: Government Printing Office, 1936.

Bancroft, Hubert Howe. *History of Arizona and New Mexico, 1530–1888.* San Francisco: The History Company, 1889.

———. *History of California.* 7 vols. San Francisco: The History Company, 1890.

———. *History of Texas and the North Mexican States.* 2 vols. San Francisco. The History Company, 1890.

Curtis, E. S. *The North American Indian.* 20 vols. Cambridge: Harvard University Press, 1907–30.

Goodwin, Grenville. *The Social Organization of the Western Apache.* Chicago: University of Chicago Press, 1942.

Hallenbeck, Cleve. *Alvar Núñez Cabeza de Vaca.* Glendale: Arthur H. Clark Company, 1940.

Hammond, George P. *Don Juan de Oñate and the Founding of New Mexico.* Santa Fe: El Palacio Press, 1927.

Hodge, Frederick Webb (ed.). *Handbook of American Indians North of Mexico.* Bureau of American Ethnology *Bulletin No. 30.* 2 vols. Washington: Government Printing Office, 1912.

Martin, Paul S., George I. Quimby, and Donald Collier. *Indians Before Columbus.* Chicago: University of Chicago Press, 1947.

Mecham, John Lloyd. *Francisco de Ibarra and Nueva Vizcaya.* Durham: Duke University Press, 1927.

Powell, Philip Wayne. *Soldiers, Indians and Silver.* Berkeley: University of California Press, 1952.

Bibliography

Swanton, John R. *The Indian Tribes of North America.* Washington: Government Printing Office, 1953.

Tudela de la Ordén, José. *Los Manuscritos de América en las Bibliotecas de España.* Madrid: Ediciones Cultura Hispánica, 1954.

Twitchell, Ralph Emerson (comp.). *The Spanish Archives of New Mexico.* 2 vols. Cedar Rapids: The Torch Press, 1914.

SECONDARY SOURCES—ARTICLES

Bloom, Lansing B. "The Governors of New Mexico," *New Mexico Historical Review,* Vol. X, No. 2 (1935).

———. "Who Discovered New Mexico?" *New Mexico Historical Review,* Vol. XV, No. 2 (1940).

Bolton, Herbert Eugene. "The Jumano Indians in Texas," *Texas State Historical Quarterly,* Vol. XV, No. 1 (1911).

Brant, Charles S. "Kiowa Apache Culture History: Some Further Observations," *Southwestern Journal of Anthropology,* Vol. IX, No. 2 (1953).

Donoghue, David. "The Route of the Coronado Expedition in Texas," *New Mexico Historical Review,* Vol. IV, No. 1 (1929).

———. "The Route of the Coronado Expedition in Texas," *Southwestern Historical Quarterly,* Vol. XXXII, No. 3 (1929).

Dunn, William Edward. "Apache Relations in Texas, 1718–1750," *Texas State Historical Quarterly,* Vol. XIV, No. 3 (1911).

Fewkes, J. Walter. "One Ceremonial Circuit Among the Village Indians of Northeastern Arizona," *Journal of American Folklore,* Vol. V, No. 16 (1892).

Forbes, Jack D. "The Appearance of the Mounted Indian in Northern Mexico and the Southwest, to 1680," *Southwestern Journal of Anthropology,* Vol. XV, No. 2 (1959).

———. "Unknown Athapaskans: The Identification of the Jano, Jocome, Suma, Manso and other Indian Tribes of the Southwest," *Ethnohistory,* Vol. VI, No. 2 (1959).

Goodwin, Grenville. "Social Divisions of the Western Apache," *American Anthropologist,* Vol. XXXVII, No. 1 (1935).

———. "The Southern Athapaskans," *Kiva,* Vol. IV, No. 2 (1938).

Grinnell, George Bird. "Who Were the Padouca?" *American Anthropologist,* Vol. XXII, No. 4 (1920).

Gunnerson, James H. "Plains-Promontory Relationships," *American Antiquity,* Vol. XXII, No. 1 (1956).

Hall, Jr., Edward Twitchell. "Recent Clues to Athapascan Prehistory in the Southwest," *American Anthropologist,* Vol. XLVI, No. 1 (1944).

Harrington, John P. "The Ethnogeography of the Tewa Indians," Bureau of American Ethnology *Thirty-fifth Annual Report,* Vol. XXIX. Washington: Government Printing Office, 1916.

———. "Southern Peripheral Athapaskawan Origins, Divisions and Migrations," *Smithsonian Miscellanous Collections,* Vol. C (1940).

Hodge, Frederick Webb. "The Early Navajo and Apache," *American Anthropologist,* Old Series, Vol. VIII, No. 3 (1895).

Hoijer, Harry. "Athapaskan Kinship Systems," *American Anthropologist,* Vol. LVIII, No. 2 (1956).

———. "The Southern Athapaskan Languages," *American Anthropologist,* Vol. XL, No. 1 (1938).

Hughes, Anne E. "The Beginnings of Spanish Settlement in the El Paso District," University of California *Publications in History,* Vol. I (1914).

Kelley, J. Charles. "Juan Sabeata and Diffusion in Texas," *American Anthropologist,* Vol. LVII, No. 5 (1955).

Keur, Dorothy L. "A Chapter in Navaho-Pueblo Relations," *American Antiquity,* Vol. X, No. 1 (1944).

Kroeber, A. L. "Uto-Aztecan Languages of Mexico," *Ibero-Americana,* Vol. VIII (1934).

Kubler, G. "Gran Quivira-Humanas," *New Mexico Historical Review,* Vol. XIV, No. 4 (1939).

Linton, Ralph. "Nomad Raids and Fortified Pueblos," *American Antiquity,* Vol. X, No. 1 (1944).

Malouf, Carling. "Thoughts on Utah Archaeology," *American Antiquity,* Vol. IX, No. 3 (1944).

Reeve, Frank D. "Early Navaho Geography," *New Mexico Historical Review,* Vol. XXXI, No. 4 (1956).

———. "Seventeenth Century Navaho-Spanish Relations," *New Mexico Historical Review,* Vol. XXXII, No. 1 (1957).

Sauer, Carl O. "The Credibility of the Fray Marcos Account," *New Mexico Historical Review,* Vol. XVI, No. 3 (1941).

———. "The Discovery of New Mexico Re-considered," *New Mexico Historical Review,* Vol. XII, No. 3 (1937).

———. "The Distribution of Aboriginal Tribes and Languages in Northwest Mexico," *Ibero-Americana,* Vol. V (1934).

Scholes, France V. "Church and State in New Mexico, 1610–1650," *New Mexico Historical Review,* Vol. XI, No. 1 (1936).

————. "Juan Martínez de Montoya, Settler and Conquistador of New Mexico," *New Mexico Historical Review,* Vol. XIX, No. 4 (1944).

————. "Notes on the Jemez Missions in the Seventeenth Century," *El Palacio,* Vol. XLIV, Nos. 7–9 (1938).

————. "Troublous Times in New Mexico," 1659–1670," *New Mexico Historical Review,* Vol. XII, Nos. 2–4 (1937).

Scholes, France V., and H. P. Mera. "Some Aspects of the Jumano Problem," Carnegie Institution *Contribution to American Anthropology and History,* Vol. VI, Nos. 30–34 (1940).

Secoy, Frank R. "The Identity of the Padouca: An Ethnohistorical Analysis," *American Anthropologist,* Vol. LIII, No. 4 (1951), Pt. 1.

Sjoberg, Andrée F. "Lipan Apache Culture in Historical Perspective," *Southwestern Journal of Anthropology,* Vol. IX, No. 1 (1953).

Steck, Francis Borgia. "Forerunners of Captain De León's Expedition to Texas," *Southwestern Historical Quarterly,* Vol. XXXVI, No. 1 (1932).

Wedel, Waldo R. "Culture Chronology in the Central Great Plains," *American Antiquity,* Vol. XII, No. 3 (January, 1947).

Worcester, Donald E. "The Beginnings of the Apache Menace in the Southwest," *New Mexico Historical Review,* Vol. XVI, No. 1 (1941).

Index

Index

Apaches del Río Colorado, New Mexico: 251, 253, 256
Apaches del Río Grande: 271
Apaches of Chiricahua Mountains, Arizona: 245
Apaches of Quinia: 102, 116, 118–19, 127
Apaches of the North: 269–70
Apaches of the Organ Mountains: 182, 190, 236
Apache-Tewa relations: 99, 158
Apache-Tonkawan relations: 101
Apache-Ute relations: 256–57, 269–70
Apache-Yavapai relations: 61, 105
Aparicio, Pedro de: 159, 162
Ápé Indians (Iapies): 122
Arenal, New Mexico: 14
Argüello, Fernando de: 140, 140 n., 142
Aristi, Lope de: 48
Archuleta, Juan de: 137
Arivaipa, Arizona: 244
Arivechi, Sonora: 218
Arkansas River: 18–19, 21, 75, 101, 129
Arvide, Martín de: 118, 129
Athapascan language family: xi, xii, xiv; original home, xx; kinship terms, xxi n.
Atsina Indians: xxi
Avila y Ayala, Pedro de: 150, 168
Awatobí, Arizona: 59, 61, 123, 157, 241–42
Axa: 14
Ayeta, Francisco de: 167, 172–75, 181, 184, 186
Ayona Indians: 213
Aztecs: 121

Babitcoida, Arizona: 275
Baca, Alonso: 129, 144
Bacanuchi, Sonora: 226–37, 244
Baceraca, Sonora: 140–41, 169, 234, 245, 261
Bacuachi, Sonora: 210, 227
Baja California, occupation delay: 206
Barbón (Suma chief): 232
Barreto, Francisco: 62–63
Bavispe, Sonora: 140–42, 169, 203, 234
Beltrán, Bernaldino: 55–56, 58, 61–62
Beltrán, Manuel: 201
Benavides, Alonso de: xviii, 116–17, 122–23
Bernal, Cristóbal Martín: 274–75
Bernal, Juan: 165

Bernalillo, New Mexico: 266, 269; founded, 262
Bigotes (a chief of Pecos): 11–12, 14
Bill Williams' Fork, Arizona: 104
Blackfoot Indians: xxi
Black Hills, South Dakota: xvi, xxii
Bosque, Fernando del: 170
Brant, Charles S.: xvi

Cabeza de Vaca, Alvar Núñez: 3, 4, 5, 7, 8, 16, 45
Cabeza Indians: 33, 141
Caborca, Sonora: 259
Cabri Indians: 47
Cacaxtle Indians (Cacastles): 155, 169
Caddo Indians: 20, 221
Caddoan Indians: 27, 101
Caguate Indians: 56
Cahita Indians: 3
California: 175
Campo, Andrés del: 22
Canadian River: 83, 100
Canatinno Indians (Canohatinos, Canabatinus): 213–14, 223
Cantona Indians (Cantouahonas): 221–22
Caocozie Indians (Cascosies, Caucozis): 214, 222–23
Caquima (Jaquima, Kiakima), New Mexico: 129, 140 n., 238, 241, 255
Carabajal, Luís: 67
Caravajal, Francisco: 42
Carretas, Río de: 159
Casa Fuerte: 143, 147, 150, 153, 168, 171, 173, 268
Casa Grande, Arizona: xvii, 27, 276
Casas Grandes, Chihuahua: 5, 44–46, 159, 161, 183, 190, 193, 201, 204–209, 218–19, 229, 232, 234; presidio at, 206
Castaño de Sosa, Gaspar: 36, 64–73
Castillo, Blas del: 218, 227
Castillo, Diego del: 145
Castillo, Gabriel del: 246–47
Catiti, Alonso: 188
Catquesa Indians (Caquizas): 221–22
Caynaya Indians: 221
Cazorla, Pedro de: 74
Cenis Indians: see Hasinai Caddo
Cerrillo Colorado, New Mexico: 238
Cerro Colorado, Arizona: 235, 242
Cerro Gordo presidio, Chihuahua: 202, 206

Index

Eastern Apaches: 80, 101
Echavarria, Diego de: 207
El Capotcari (Jocome leader): 277
El Chilmo (Gila Apache chief): 162–63, 166, 253
El Cuartelejo, Kansas: 137–38, 157, 271
El Embudo, New Mexico: 270, 272
El Gallo presidio, Chihuahua: 206
El Morro, New Mexico: 242
El Paso, Chihuahua: 4–5, 21, 50, 56, 73, 78, 116–17, 125–26, 132, 147, 149, 151, 152, 155, 160, 163, 166, 172, 174, 180, 187, 189, 193, 195, 202–204, 206–208, 217–20, 224–26, 228–29, 243, 250, 259, 278
El Tabovo (Jocome chief): 235
Escalona, Juan de: 88, 97–98
Escanxaque Indians: 101–102, 145–46, 216–17
Escobar, Francisco de: 107
"Españoles Mexicanos" in New Mexico: 266
Espejo, Antonio de: 55–63, 67, 73, 104–105
Espejo-Beltrán expedition: 48–65, 73
Espeleta, Josef de: 158, 242
Espinosa, Marcelo de: 98
Espíritu Santo, Martín del: 118
Esteban (Negro slave): 3–7
Estrada, Bartolomé de: 183
Epidemics: in New Mexico, 161, 164, 262; in Nueva Vizcaya, 161; in Texas, 222
Eudeve Indians: 245–46
Eulate, Juan de: 114
Eurafricans: 76, 135, 139, 148, 162, 183, 189, 189 n.
Eurindians: 135, 138, 148, 188, 189, 189 n.

Famine: in New Mexico, 160–61, 164; in Nueva Vizcaya, 161
Faraon Apaches: 71, 171, 228, 237–39, 241, 250, 253, 264–67, 272; live at Pecos, 265
Farfan de los Godos, Marcos: 86–87
Fernández de la Fuente, Juan: 203, 209–10, 226–36, 244, 260–61, 278
Fernández de Velasco, Diego: 74
Fewkes, J. Walter: 105
Figueredo, Roque de: 123
Flores de Sierra y Valdés, Juan: 136
Font Cuberta, Miguel: 221

Fort St. Louis, Texas: 211, 214
Franciscans (Order of St. Francis): 39, 49, 96–97, 116, 121, 128, 141, 149, 158–59, 171, 179, 213–15, 221–23, 233; fail to learn Indian language, 96, 96 n.; favor abandonment of New Mexico, 97, 103, 108, 112; conflict with secular officials, 113–15, 129, 131–36, 138–40, 152; purchase slaves, 151; conflict with Jesuits, 130, 142; murder Indian, 160; struggle with Vargas, 264–65
Fray Cristóbal, New Mexico: 181
French expansion: 191–92, 199, 225, 236, 279; to Texas, 211–14; said to have attacked Apaches, 262–63
Fronteras, Presidio of, Sonora: 209, 217, 247–48

Galisteo, New Mexico: 80, 154, 174
Gallegos, Hernando: 47, 49, 51, 51 n., 53–54
Gallego, Juan: 23
Gallinas River, New Mexico: 81
Galve, Conde de: 211, 228–29
García, Alonso: 180, 181
García, Diego: 132
García, Juan: 162–63
Gattacka Indians: 192, 192 n.
Gavilan Indians: 74
Gila Apaches: 26, 105, 117–18, 126, 134, 148, 162–63, 166–67, 172, 190–91, 193, 206, 208, 217, 227, 231, 236, 238, 253, 261, 269, 272; ask for priests, 156
Gila River: 93, 230, 248, 261, 275–76
Gómez de Luna, Juan: 133
González, Mateo: 48
González, Sebastian: 132
Gorreaz Beaumont, Francisco de: 158
Gorretas Indians: 116, 125
Governador, New Mexico: 11
Grinnell, George B.: xxii
Gruber, Bernardo: 161
Guachichile Indians: 30, 32, 35, 67, 155
Guadalajara, Bishop of: 39
Guadalajara, Diego de: 145
Guadalupe River, Texas: 221–22
Guadalcazar, Marquis de: 114
Guamare Indians: 30
Guaraspi, Sonora: 43–44
Guasabas, Sonora: 140–41
Guerra, Antonio: 232
Guerra, Salvador de: 160

297

Index

Index

Index

227, 229–30, 235, 244–47, 259–60, 274–78, 284
Soberanes, Diego de: 42
Socorro (El Paso region): 232, 262
Socorro, New Mexico: 79, 135, 172, 181, 186–87, 235, 243
Solís, Antonio: 247, 259
Sonora, beginning of Athapascan offensive against: 207
Sonora Indians: 8, 23, 26; *see also under individual tribes*
Sopete: 14, 17–18
Sotelo Ossorio, Phelipe: 119–20
Southern Athapascans: *xi;* population, *xii;* migrations, *xiv–xvii;* culture, *xv–xvi;* antiquity in Southwest, *xvii*
Suárez de Peralta, Juan: 35
Suma Indians: *xvii, xxi,* 5, 45–47, 50, 56, 78, 117, 121, 125–26, 130, 132, 140–42, 159–61, 169, 174, 182–84, 190–93, 96–211, 215–20, 226–35, 244, 246, 259, 262, 274, 278
Sumana Indians (Suminas): 132, 151–52, 160, 216, 250
Suya, Indians of: 8
Sycamore Creek Canyon, Arizona: 104
Sylva Nieto, Francisco de: 119, 123

Tacabuy Indians: 105
Ta-cab-ci-nyu-mûh: 105
Tacupeto, Sonora: 218
Tajique, New Mexico: 158, 174–75
Tancoa: 102
Tano Indians: 173, 178–79, 237–39, 250–54, 258, 265–69, 272
Tanpachoa Indians: 56
Taos, New Mexico: 80, 83, 92, 99, 102–103, 109, 113, 116, 118–21, 127, 134–37 143–44, 152, 157, 171–74, 176–80, 185, 237–39, 250–58, 263–70
Tapacolme Indians: 220
Tarascan Indians: 22
Taramara Indins: 117, 125, 130, 141, 183, 218, 220, 261
Tassabuess Indians: 105
Tatarrax: 14, 19
Tavira, New Mexico: 153, 168, 172, 174–75; *see also* Las Salinas
Tawakoni Indians: 19 n., 20
Tawehash Indians: 19 n., 20; *see also* Wichita
Teaname: 170
Techicodeguachi, Sonora: 140

Tecomaque Indians: 220
Teimamar: 170
Teipana, New Mexico: 79
Tenamaxtle: 29
Tepehuan Indians: 32, 35, 37, 39, 93 n., 117, 125, 130, 220
Tepelguan Indians: 68
Tepoca Indians: 220
Terán de los Rios, Domingo: 221–22, 260
Teras, Sonora: 140–41, 218, 227
Terocodame Indians: 211
Teroodan: 170
Tesuque, New Mexico: 237, 253, 263, 265–66
Tetecora Indians: 169
Teucarea (Taraque, Touacara): 19, 19 n.; *see also* Quivira
Tewa Indians: 51, 51 n., 57, 80, 95–96, 99, 108–109, 113–15, 118, 121, 124, 127, 140, 153, 158, 171–73, 178–79, 185, 196, 237–40, 250–54, 258, 265–72; flee to Apaches 272
Texas Indians: *see* Hasinai Caddo
Teyas Indians: 5, 15–18, 20, 24–25
Tibideguachi, Sonora: 193, 209
Tiguex, New Mexico: 10–14, 21–25
Tiwa Indians: 51 n., 54, 57, 61, 63, 73, 79, 93, 113, 121, 126, 144, 180, 182, 186–89, 200, 208, 232–33, 243
Tlaxcalan Indians: 34, 39, 57, 121
Toboso Indians: 33, 36, 39 n., 40, 65, 74, 117, 141, 155, 159, 161, 170, 202, 205, 211, 229, 246.
Toho Indians: 214
Tompiro Indians: 51–52, 52 n., 57, 61, 80, 85, 93–94, 108, 113, 115, 121–23, 136, 147, 151–53, 163–68
Tonaltecan Indians: 62
Tonibaví Sonora: 259–60
Tonkawan Indians: *xvii,* 101, 145–46, 196, 214, 223; Tancoa, 102
Tonto Basin, Arizona: *xviii*
Tovar, Pedro de: 10
Toyah Creek, Texas: 65
Treviño, Juan Francisco: 171–72
Tsipiakwe, Zuñi name for the Pimas: 129
Tubutama, Sonora: 259
Tupato, Lorenzo: 239
Tupatu, Luís: 188, 237–39, 251
Turicachi, Sonora: 140–42, 169, 193, 203, 209, 218, 227–29, 246, 261

303